Ius Gentium: Comparative Perspectives on Law and Justice

Volume 91

Ius Gentium is a book series which discusses the central questions of law and justice from a comparative perspective. The books in this series collect the contrasting and overlapping perspectives of lawyers, judges, philosophers and scholars of law from the world's many different jurisdictions for the purposes of comparison, harmonisation, and the progressive development of law and legal institutions. Each volume makes a new comparative study of an important area of law. This book series continues the work of the well-known journal of the same name and provides the basis for a better understanding of all areas of legal science.

The *Ius Gentium* series provides a valuable resource for lawyers, judges, legislators, scholars, and both graduate students and researchers in globalisation, comparative law, legal theory and legal practice. The series has a special focus on the development of international legal standards and transnational legal cooperation.

More information about this series at https://link.springer.com/bookseries/7888

Masahisa Deguchi
Editor

Effective Enforcement of Creditors' Rights

Springer

Editor
Masahisa Deguchi
Faculty of Law
Ritsumeikan University
Kyoto, Japan

ISSN 1534-6781 ISSN 2214-9902 (electronic)
Ius Gentium: Comparative Perspectives on Law and Justice
ISBN 978-981-16-5608-8 ISBN 978-981-16-5609-5 (eBook)
https://doi.org/10.1007/978-981-16-5609-5

This Springer imprint is published by the registered company Springer Nature Singapore Pte Ltd.
The registered company address is: 152 Beach Road, #21-01/04 Gateway East, Singapore 189721, Singapore

Dedicated to my two academic mentors, the late Professor Dr. Dr. h.c. Peter Arens in Germany and the late Professor Dr. Dr. h.c. mult. Akira Ishikawa in Japan

Masahisa Deguchi

Preface

This book explores the commonalities and divergences in enforcement proceedings of the following countries: Germany, Japan, Korea, France, UK, Switzerland, Austria, Spain, Poland, Russia, The Netherlands, North America, Taiwan, Brazil, Argentina, and the EU. The problem of enforcing a money judgment exists in every legal system in the world, but the methods and orientation vary significantly. Effective enforcement proceedings are crucial to ensure full access to justice for creditors. Complete and full knowledge of the debtor's assets is crucial to choose the appropriate enforcement measure. But each legal system must balance the creditors' right to an efficient enforcement with the debtors' rights. The wide differences between enforcement proceedings mirror the way each society tries to find a balance between confronting rights and interests.

This book explores and compares how different legal systems approach these issues with a focus on the discovery of debtor's assets, which is a common problem to enforcement and execution proceedings in almost every jurisdiction.

The editor organized the international symposium "Effective Enforcement of Creditor's Right in Civil Execution through Effective Discovery of Debtor's Assets" from 6th through 8th November 2019, at Ritsumeikan University in Kyoto/Japan. This book is based on this symposium, and it is the first book to compare enforcement proceedings around the world and presents a variety of articles and country reports from leading experts from four continents. It represents the joint work of professors and legal authorities.

I would like to thank my dear colleagues who have contributed to my academic adventure. They were contributing as reporters, moderators, commentators, and discussants to the three days of this academic and cultural event. I am very glad and honored that I could realize a really fruitful and exciting academic activity with my dear distinguished colleagues.

This book was supported financially by JSPS KAKENHI, Grant Number JP20K01407, the Shihokyokai, Nihon Hosei Gakkai, Shakaikagaku Kokusaikoryu Egusa Kikin, Zenkoku Ginkou Gakujyutsukenkyuu Shinkouzaidan, Kokusai-bunkakoryuujigyoudan, Jinbun Research Office of Ritsumeikan University. I also thank Prof. Dr. James Maxeiner and Prof. Dr. Mortimer Sellers who have accepted this book as part of their book Series *Ius Gentium: Comparative Perspectives on Law and Justice* of Springer Science + Business Media. I would like to thank all of them sincerely.

Lastly, I must also thank my academic assistant Mr. Tha-Phuong VO from Freiburg/Germany and my colleagues, staff, and students at Ritsumeikan University, who have supported my international academic adventure.

Kyoto, Japan
July 2020

Prof. Dr. Masahisa Deguchi
Honorary Vice President of International Association of Procedural Law (IAPL)

Contents

Editor and Contributors

About the Editor

Masahisa Deguchi Professor of Civil Procedural Law at Faculty of Law, Ritsumeikan University, Kyoto/Japan. He studied at Chuo University and Freiburg University (Germany) and got Master of law (Keio University 1988) and Doctor of law (University of Freiburg 1991) through DAAD-Scholarship. Fellow of Alexander von Humboldt Foundation in Freiburg (1994–1995, 2007), Regensburg (2015) and Colon (2015). JaDe-Preis [Die Stiftung zur Förderung japanisch-deutscher Wissenschafts- und Kulturbeziehungen in Köln] (2002). Verdienstkreuz am Bande des Verdienstordens der Bundesrepublik Deutschland (2006). Board Member of Notarial Law in Japan (since 2005). Vice President of International Association of Procedural Law (2007–2015) and Honorary Vice President of International Association of Procedural Law (since 2015). Member of Judicial State Examination in Japan (2012). Vice President of DAAD-Tomonokai, Presidium Member of Freiburg Alumni and Board Member of Alumni Freiburg e.V. (since 2016).

Contributors

Samuel P. Baumgartner University of Zurich, Zurich, Switzerland

Antonio Cabral University of Rio de Janeiro State, Rio de Janeiro, Brazil

Loïc Cadiet Sorbonne Law School (Paris 1 University), Paris, France

Anastasiya Chekmareva Department of Civil Procedure, Saratov State Law Academy, Saratov, Russia

Masahisa Deguchi Ritsumeikan University, Kyoto, Japan

Ian Forrester General Court of the European Union (Luxembourg), Kirchberg, Luxembourg

Fernando Gascón-Inchausti Complutense University, Madrid, Spain

Peter Gottwald Faculty of Law, Regensburg University, Regensburg, Germany

Omi Hatashin Osaka Jogakuin (Wilmina) University, Osaka, Japan

Martin Heisch Attorney at Law, Zurich, Switzerland

Burkhard Hess Max Planck Institute Luxembourg, Luxembourg, Luxembourg

Moon-hyuck Ho Seoul National University School of Law, Seoul, Republic of Korea

Shigehide Koyanagi Yokohama Minato Law Office, Yokohama, Japan

Bart Krans Leiden University, Leiden, the Netherlands

Wolfgang Lüke Leipzig University, Leipzig, Germany

Maiko Miyashita Faculty of Law, Surugadai University, Hanno, Japan

Richard Marcus University of California, Hastings College of the Law, San Francisco, USA

Hans-Peter Marutschke Doshisha Law School, Kyoto, Japan

Hiroko Namura Osaka, Japan

Guillermo Ormazabal University of Girona, Girona, Spain

Eduardo Oteiza National University of La Plata, La Plata, Argentina

Álvaro Pérez Ragone Instituto de Estudios Sociales, Políticos y Culturales de la Universidad de San Pablo-Tucumán, Tucumán, Argentina;
Univeresidad Católica del Norte, Antofagasta, Chile

Walter H. Rechberger University of Vienna, Vienna, Austria

Pauline Ribbers Leiden University, Leiden, the Netherlands

Piotr Rylski Faculty of Law and Administration, University of Warsaw, Warsaw, Poland

Kuan-Ling Shen National Taiwan University, Taipei, Taiwan

Hiroshi Tega Tokyo Metropolitan University, Hachioji, Japan

Karol Weitz Faculty of Law and Administration, University of Warsaw, Warsaw, Poland

Enforcement Against Movable Property in Germany

Peter Gottwald

1 The Search for Assets Before the Reform 2013

A creditor being not familiar with the financial circumstances of his debtor who wanted to enforce his title by way of general execution was until 2013 confronted with practical difficulties. Without knowledge about concrete bank accounts or real property, he could just file an application with a bailiff for attaching movable property. The German legislator of the 19th century assumed that a civil debtor had a well equipped home with many assets, subject to execution, which would find a buyer in a compulsory auction.[1] Such times are gone for a long time. In just about 1 ‰ of such applications, the bailiff can attach movable property and sell it by auction.[2] Attachment of bank accounts or garnishment of wages are by far more successful. Yet, a creditor had first to try to attach movables and only if this failed he could request the debtor to give an affidavit as to his assets, his place of work and his bank account. It seems however justified to assume that a debtor who did not pay his debt voluntarily, at least by way of instalment, would try to hide attachable assets from any act of attachment. This awkward situation was claimed for many decades.[3]

According to the 1931 draft for a code of civil procedure the competence for all measures of enforcement should be concentrated with the courts enforcement division. Having received an application for enforcement, these courts should investigate the financial conditions of the debtor, order him to discover his property and confirm

[1] Cf. BT-Drucks. 16/10069 vom 30.7.2008, S. 20.

[2] F.-M. Goebel, *Die Reform der Sachaufklärung*, 2012, Section 1 Rn. 2.

[3] Stein/Jonas/Würdinger, *ZPO*, 23rd ed. 2017, Vor Section 802a N 3.

P. Gottwald (✉)
Faculty of Law, Regensburg University, Regensburg, Germany
e-mail: gottwald-p@t-online.de

M. Deguchi (ed.), *Effective Enforcement of Creditors' Rights*,
Ius Gentium: Comparative Perspectives on Law and Justice 91,
https://doi.org/10.1007/978-981-16-5609-5_1

it by declaration on oath in a court hearing.[4] This draft and the concentration of all kind of enforcement with the court were nether realised.

To avoid such declaration on oath, in 1991 the German legislator gave the bailiff the power, to ask the debtor (or in his absence another person of his household) about his employer or other claims against third persons (e.g. bank accounts) (Section 806a CCP). As these persons were not obliged to give any information, it is likely that the bailiffs not always did try to use this possibility.[5]

In 1997 the German legislator gave the bailiff the authority to work towards an amicable settlement in any position of the enforcement proceeding. If the bailiff could not find any attachable property, but the debtor made plausible that he could settle his debt within 6 months, the bailiff should stay the enforcement procedure provisionally and collect the instalments, provided that the creditor did not object (Section 806b CCP former version). If the bailiff could attach movables, he could postpone the compulsory auction, if the debtor was willing to pay the debt within one year. If the creditor objected, the enforcement court could grant the same postponement (Sections 813a, 813b CCP former version). Already since that time, the predominant portion of all payments recovered by bailiffs consisted in such instalments by the debtors.

Nevertheless, many scholars insisted on a reform of the law by improving the possibilities of a creditor to gain information about the financial situation of his debtor by introducing a duty to make an affidavit as to assets already at the beginning of enforcement procedures.[6]

In May 2008 the "Bundesrat" (The Upper House of the German Parliament), passed a bill for the reform of inquiry into financial condition of debtors and presented it to the German Bundestag (The Lower House) in July 2008.[7] The law was finally passed in July 2009.[8] To enable bailiffs and court administration to adapt all technical facilities the law became operative not before January 2013.

2 Principles of the Reform 2013

1. The new law adheres to the scheme that the bailiff has competence to attach movables, but not claims. There have been demands to broaden their competence

---

[4] Cf. *Entwurf einer Zivilprozessordnung* (published by Reichsjustizministerium), 1931, Sections 774 ff u. Reasoning, S. 408ff; dazu J. Schnigula, *Das Offenbarungsverfahren – Darstellung und Reform der Sachaufklärung in der Zwangsvollstreckung*, 2001, S. 173ff.

[5] Goebel (N 2), Section 1 Rn. 4.

[6] Gaul, *Neukonzipierung der Sachaufklärung der Zwangsvollstreckung*, ZZP 108 (1995), 3, 30 ff; Hess/G. Vollkommer, *Die Reform der Sachaufklärung in der deutschen Zwangsvollstreckung*, Festgabe M. Vollkommer, 2007, S. 349, 351, 353; Schilken, *Reform der Sachaufklärung in der Geldvollstreckung*, Festschrift Yessiou-Faltsi, 2007, S. 589, 595ff.

[7] BT-Drucksache 16/10069.

[8] Bundesgesetzblatt I 2009, 22850.

in favour of a more effective enforcement,[9] but the legislator did not take up this idea, in particular because at that time the bailiffs themselves objected to more paperwork. Today, they favour an overall competence, provided if they get a better professional training.[10]

2. According to the new law, the bailiff has the unchanged duty to ensure the recovery of monetary claims promptly, fully and in a cost-efficient manner (Section 802a I CCP).[11] The most relevant amendment is that on application of the creditor, the bailiff may obtain information from the debtor on his financial circumstances and the assets he owns at the very beginning of the enforcement procedure, and if this information is insufficient, he may obtain information from third parties on the debtor's financial circumstances and the assets he owns. The creditor can decide whether the bailiff requests first just this information (together with a declaration in lieu of an oath) or whether he pursues the attachment and realisation of physical objects at the same time (Section 802a II CCP).
3. The leitmotif of the bailiff's work of today and its practical emphasis lies in his endeavour of amicable termination of the matter (Section 802b I CCP).[12] The bailiff may now grant a period within payment to be made, or allow payment by instalments if the debtor demonstrates plausibly that he can redeem his debt within 12 months (Section 802b II 1, 3 CCP). He will make a payment plan according to the income of the debtor, insurance benefits or regular grants by relatives.[13] When this payment plan is determined, the enforcement shall be deferred (Section 802b II 2 CCP), unless the creditor opposes without undue delay, or the debtor is in arears for more than two weeks with a payment determined (Section 802b III 2, 3 CCP). While the payment plan is valid, the debtor is not obliged to give information on his assets.[14]
4. The most important point of reform is without doubt to advance the obligation of the debtor to give information on his assets to the beginning of the enforcement procedure, irrespective of an unsuccessful attempt to enforce (Sections 802a

---

[9] Cf. M. App, *Überlegungen zur Zweckmäßigkeit der Übertragung der Forderungspfändung auf den Gerichtsvollzieher*, DGVZ 2006, 53; Seip, DGVZ 2006, 1, 8; Gietmann, *Die neuen Reformgesetze in der Zwangsvollstreckung*, DGVZ 2009, 157, 158f; Hergenröder DGVZ 2010, 201, 208; Goebel (N 2), Section 4 Rn. 2; Hess, *Rechtspolitische Perspektiven der Zwangsvollstreckung*, JZ 2009, 662, 665 und DGVZ 2010, 7, 9f; finally Walker, *Zur Übertragbarkeit der Forderungspfändung auf den Gerichtsvollzieher*, DGVZ 2019, 89.

[10] Cf. Graf-Schlicker, *Schrittweise Reformen ins Auge fassen*, DGVZ 2017, 161, 162.

[11] Goebel (N 2), Section 7 Rn. 5; Stein/Jonas/Würdinger Section 802a N 2.

[12] Cf. Becker-Eberhard, Abschied von der Zwangsvollstreckung – Gütliche Erledigung (jetzt auch) der „Königsweg" im Vollstreckungsverfahren?, DGVZ 2016, 163; Hergenröder, Gütliche Erledigung der Zwangsvollstreckung als Leitprinzip, DGVZ 2012, 105 and 129; Stein/Jonas/Würdinger Section 802b N 1.

[13] M. Wilhelm, *Die erweiterte Sachaufklärung in der Zwangsvollstreckung*, in Seibel/Grothe u.a., Zwangsvollstreckung aktuell, 2nd ed. 2013, Section 1 Rn. 10f.

[14] Münchener Kommentar/*Wagner*, ZPO, 5th ed. 2016, Section 802b Rn. 24; Hk-ZV/*Sternal*, 2nd ed. 2013, Section 802b Rn. 12.

II No. 2, 802c CCP).[15] As before the reform (on application of the creditor) the debtor is to record a statutory declaration in lieu of an oath stating that he made correct und full statements (Section 802e III CCP). This reform was welcomed euphorically as a paradigm shift and a big step forward from 19th to 21st century.[16]

3 The Reform in detail

Before assessing the reform, I would like to explain its details.

1. The application for enforcement

Whether and what kind of enforcement takes place is subject to the disposal of the creditor. According to the former law, he however had no big choice. If he did not knew the employer or a bank account of the debtor, he could only mandate a bailiff to attach movable property (Section 753 I, 803 CCP former version). If this attempt remained insufficient, the bailiff could ask the debtor about active debts. If he informed the bailiff on a voluntary basis the bailiff could transfer this information to the creditor (Section 806a I CCP) who could then apply for a garnishee order (Sections 829, 835 CCP). If the debtor remained silent he had to make an affidavit as to his assets (Section 807 CCP former version).

(a) The new law provides the creditor with more options. According to Section 802a II CCP he can mandate the bailiff,

(1) To make efforts at amicable terminating the matter,
(2) To obtain information from the debtor on his financial circumstances and the assets he owns, and
(3) To obtain information as to financial situation and the assets of the debtor from third parties.

The creditor has to make concrete orders in his application (Section 802a II 2 CCP);[17] he may restrict his mandate to one of these measures or apply for all measures at once.[18]

---

[15] Schilken, *Zur Reform der Sachaufklärung in der Zwangsvollstreckung*, Rpfleger 2006, 629, 634; Prütting/Gehrlein/Meller-Hannich, *ZPO*, 10th ed. 2018, Section 802a N1; Stein/Jonas/Würdinger Section 802c N 1 ff; crit. Seip, DGVZ 2006, 1, 5 (Feared, that this would increase the number of arrest warrants) u. DGVZ 2008, 38, 40.

[16] Würdinger, *Die Sachaufklärung in der Einzelzwangsvollstreckung*, JZ 2011, 177, 183; Stein/Jonas/Würdinger Vor Section 802a N 1; zust. G. Vollkommer, *Die Reform der Sachaufklärung in der Zwangsvollstreckung*, NJW 2012, 3681; Hess JZ 2009, 662, 664.

[17] Nober, in Baumbach/Lauterbach/Hartmann/Anders/Gehle (BLHAG), *ZPO*, 78th ed. 2020, Section 802a N 14, 17; Thomas/Putzo/Seiler, *ZPO*, 41st ed. 2020, Section 80a N 2.

[18] Zöller/Seibel, *ZPO*, 33rd ed. 2020, Section 802a N3; Harnacke/Bungardt, Das neue Recht – Probleme über Probleme, DGVZ 2013, 1ff; Goebel (N 2), Section 8 Rn. 8ff; G. Vollkommer NJW 2012, 3681, 3682.

(b) The creditor may place a combined order for attachment, obtaining information as to assets, compulsory auction, auction via internet and, if the place of residence of the debtor is unknown, to find out his place of abode (Sections 754, 755 CCP).

(c) In practice (and according to the application form) the amicable termination by the bailiff is most important. In his application, the creditor can give concrete instructions. He can restrict his application to the amicable termination (Section 802a II CCP). He can fix terms of payment, fix a monthly minimum rate, may agree with payment by up to 12 instalments and with an extension of the time according to the discretion of the bailiff.[19] He can however rule out any payment agreement, binding for bailiff and court.[20] The creditor has to use an official application form[21] where he can mark his wishes. The more wishes the more difficult and time consuming is the work for the bailiff. As each partial order triggers a special fee for the bailiff, payable in advance by the creditor, most of them restrict their order to the first two steps.[22] Isolated orders just for trying an amicable settlement are rare.[23]

2. Determining the debtor's place of abode

If the debtor's address is unknown, the bailiff may request the registration authority to find out the actual address of the debtor, provided the creditor has made an application for enforcement and has given him an enforceable execution copy of the title (Section 755 I 1 CCP).[24] In case of companies, the bailiff may determine the principal place of business and the statutory seat in addition to the current address by inspecting the commercial register or by requesting the trade supervisory authority. As this request triggers a separate fee the creditor must make an express order for it[25] and can do it cheaper by an own inquiry with the registration office.

If the registration authority cannot find the actual address, the bailiff may inquire of the Central Register of Foreigners, the statutory pension insurance funds and the Federal Motor Transport Authority for the actual place of abode resp. the data of the

---

[19] Goebel (N 2), Section 8 Rn. 20ff, 29f.

[20] Schwörer/Heßler ZVI 2007, 589, 595; krit. Seip DGVZ 2006, 1, 5; Gietmann DGVZ 2009, 157, 158; Hergenröder DGVZ 2010, 201, 206f (Putting pressure on relatives).

[21] Salten, *Das neue Gerichtsvollzieherauftragsformular*, MDR 2016, 125. The form was amended as to 1.12.2016, vgl. Salten, *Das Reparaturgesetz zur Reform der Sachaufklärung in der Zwangsvollstreckung*, MDR 2017, 61.

[22] In 2018: 2.933.800 orders (All figures for 2018 are for Germany without Bavaria).

[23] In 2018 just 226.455 orders.

[24] In 2018, the German bailiffs found the address by contacting the registration authority in 227 681 cases.

[25] *Münchner Kommentar*/Heßler, Section 755 N 2; Zöller/Seibel Section 755 N 2; Mroß DGVZ 2010, 169, 181; Harnacke/Bungarth DGVZ 2013, 1, 2; Ulrici, *Verschlimmbesserung der Adressermittlung durch den Gerichtsvollzieher*, DGVZ 2017, 137; cf. BT-Drucks. 16/10069, S. 23.

vehicle keeper (Section 755 II CCP).[26] Again, the creditor specifics the extent of all this inquiries and, he has to pay a special fee to the bailiff and to the requested office for each step.[27]

3. The amicable termination of the matter

Under the new law a creditor may apply to the bailiff to start enforcement together with the request to the debtor to provide information on his financial circumstances and his assets (Sections 802 II no. 2, 802c CCP). If the creditor, however, did not exclude an amicable termination, the bailiff has first to try this possibility (Section 802b I CCP). This termination can be made in every situation of the procedure. In most cases, such a termination is reached after a first visit of the bailiff in the apartment of the debtor or of the debtor in the office of the bailiff after a concrete discussion of realistic possibilities. The bailiff then makes a payment plan, the enforcement is deferred until the end of schedule (Section 802b II 2 CCP).[28] This is however not automatically linked with granting an extension in civil law or a freeze of interest.[29] Such effects must be stipulated separately.[30] In any case, so long as the payment schedule is valid, the debtor is not obliged to give information as to its assets (affirmed by declaration in lieu of an oath).

The bailiff has to inform the creditor about the payment schedule. Unless he did expressly to a payment plan in his application, he can object to it without undue delay; then, the payment plan shall be rendered invalid (Section 802b III 2 CCP).[31] The same occurs if the debtor is in arrears for more than two weeks with a payment determined (completely or partly, even without his fault) (Section 802b III 3 CCP).[32] It is however possible to make a new (more realistic) settlement.

4. The information from the debtor on his assets

Regularly, debtor is obliged to self-disclosure of his financial circumstances and all of his assets at the beginning of the enforcement procedure,[33] but already this duty is deferred, if the matter is terminated amicably. In 2018, German bailiffs received

---

[26] In 2018, there were 14 488 cases.

[27] Cf. Volpert, *Neuerungen im Kostenrecht* …, in Seibel/Grothe (N 13), Section 2 Rn. 13ff.

[28] In 2018, bailiffs could transfer payments of 1.072.975.208 € to the creditors. Most of this amount is based on payments on payments plan; there were only 1259 compulsory auctions in 2018.

[29] Zöller/Seibel, *ZPO*, 33rd ed. 2020, Section 802b Rn. 13; Thomas/Putzo/Seiler, Section 802b N 5; Musielak/Voit/Voit, *ZPO*, 15th ed. 2018, Section 802b N 11; Prütting/Gehrlein/Meller-Hannich, Section 802b N 5.

[30] Schwörer DGVZ 2011, 77, 85; Stein/Jonas/Würdinger, Section 802b N 11.

[31] Nober, in BLHAG Section 802b N 20; Zöller/Seibel Section 802b N 15; Moß, *Grundzüge der Reform der Sachaufklärung*, DGVZ 2010, 181, 182; crit. U. Gottwald/Mock, *Zwangsvollstreckung*, 6th ed. 2012, Section 802b Rn. 6.

[32] Nober, in BLHAG Section 802b N 24; Musielak/Voit/Voit Section 802c N 17 f; Prütting/Gehrlein/Meller-Hannich Section 802c N 6..

[33] This was the goal of the reform, cf. BT-Drucks. 16/10069, S. 25; Schwörer/Heßler, *Vom Offenbarungseid zur nachprüfbaren Schuldnerauskunft*, ZVI 2007, 589, 591; Stein/Jonas/Würdinger Section 802c N 1 ff; crit. U. Gottwald/Mock (N 31), Section 802b Rn. 6.

2.933.800 applications for providing full information from the debtor on his financial circumstances, but only 616.730 cases were executed.[34]

(a) Even if there is no payment plan, the debtor is still not obliged to provide information immediately. On the contrary, the bailiff shall first set a deadline of two weeks, within which the debtor is to settle the claim.[35] For the (highly probable) case that the claim is not settled in time the bailiff shall arrange a meeting for a date shortly after expiry of the deadline on which the debtor has to provide full information (Section 802f I 1, 2 CCP). This summons together with the deadlines must be served formally to the debtor in person (Section 802f IV CCP).[36] Even if the place of abode of the debtor is known, there are four weeks between the issue of the enforcement application and the self-disclosure of the debtor. With regard to this practical time, the "immediate" duty to provide information cannot be regarded as a disproportionate duty.[37]

(b) Where the creditor has applied for an immediate attachment of assets of the debtor and for a self-disclosure of the debtor, but the debtor refused to consent to the search by the bailiff or the efforts to attach assets have a result insufficient for full satisfaction of the creditor, the bailiff may take the information on the debtor's financial information and assets immediately (Section 807 I 1 CCP). Yet, the debtor may oppose to the immediate taking of information and then the bailiff has to arrange a meeting in his office shortly after that on which the debtor has to provide the information (Section 807 II CCP).[38] According to Sec. 185f Business Instruction for Bailiffs this meeting shall take place after two days at the earliest, at the latest after four weeks.

(c) In general the bailiff shall summon the debtor to his office and request him to bring along all documents required to provide the full information (Section 802f I 2, 3 CCP). In many cases, this procedure is not useful: the debtor might be handicapped or it is likely that he will not bring along all necessary documents (like savings bank books, account statements, vehicle registration documents, rental agreements). In such cases the bailiff may determine that the debtor has

---

[34] Cf. „*Übersicht über die Geschäftstätigkeit ... der Gerichtsvollzieher im Jahre 2018*", DGVZ 2019, 268.

[35] Zöller/Seibel Section 802f N 2; Stein/Jonas/Würdinger Section 802f N3; Nober, in BLHAG Section 802f N 6; Thomas/Putzo/Seiler Section 802f N 4; Musielak/Voit/Voit Section 802f N 3; Prütting/Gehrlein/Meller-Hannich Section 802f N 3; Hergenröder, *Verfahrensfragen der Vermögensauskunft*, DGVZ 2019, 1, 2; against such a deadline *Gaul/Schilken/Becker-Eberhard*, Zwangsvollstreckungsrecht, 12th ed., Section 60 Rn. 61.

[36] Nober, in BLHAG Section 802f N21; Stein/Jonas/Würdinger Section 802f N 21; Zöller/Seibel Section 802f N 6; Hergenröder DGVZ 2019, 1, 3.

[37] Cf. Schwoerer/Heßler ZVI 2007, 589, 591; Mroß DGVZ 2010, 181, 184; G. Vollkommer NJW 2012, 3681, 3685.

[38] Zöller/Seibel Section 802f N 5; Stein/Jonas/Würdinger Section 807 N 15; Musielak/Voit/Voit Section 807 N 11; Weber, in BLHAG Section 807 N 11 f; Mroß DGVZ 2010, 181, 181; Goebel (N 2), Section 8 Rn. 184.

to provide the self-information in his own residence (Section 802f III 1 CCP).[39] If the debtor opposes to this determination within one week, the bailiff has to summon him to his office (Section 802f I 2, II 2 CCP).[40]

(d) If the debtor comes to the office of the bailiff without necessary documents and is therefore unable to inform completely about his financial circumstances and his assets, some are of the opinion that the debtor has failed to comply with his obligation to inform about his circumstances. This would have the consequence that he is entered in the public list of debtors (Sections 802f III 2, 882c I no. 1 CCP), may be personally arrested on application of the creditor (Section 802g CCP) and information by third parties may be obtained (Sections 802f III 2, 802l CCP).[41] Even if the law does not provide for a remedial procedure, it seems more appropriate to give the unable or clumsy debtor the possibility to improve his information and to adjourn the meeting.[42] In addition, the creditor, whom the list of assets is sent, may put concrete questions and request an improvement of the list, if it is apparently incomplete, inaccurate or contradictory (Section 185o I Business Instruction for Bailiffs). The request for such improvement is not an application for a new information which could be requested after two years only (Section 802d CCP).[43] Once the list of assets is complete, the debtor is not obliged to provide a new information about his financial situation within two years (cf. Section 802d I 1 CCP).[44]

(e) With regard to its content, the new duty of information does not distinguish from the former affidavit as to the assets. The debtor has to inform about his person and all his assets in Germany or abroad (except items being apparently non-attachable) (Section 802c II 4 CCP).[45] He has also to inform about uncertain assets, future claims, assets subject to an exchange attachment, and about debit accounts.[46] He has also to answer additional questions of the creditor.[47] Assets must be listed in a way that they can be identified for being attached.[48] The debtor has also to inform about contestable asset transfers within the last

[39] Stein/Jonas/Würdinger Section 802f N 16; Thomas/Putzo/Seiler Section 802f N 6; Schilken (Rpfleger 2006, 629, 635f) was in favour of a visit at home as a rule. Gietmann (DGVZ 2009, 157, 158) thought that enforcement on site is more successful.

[40] Cf. Nober, in BLHAG Section 802f N 17 ff; Stein/Jonas/Würdinger Section 802f N 18; Hergenröder DGVZ 2019, 1, 5.

[41] So Sturm, *Das Verfahren zur Abnahme der Vermögensauskunft*, JurBüro 2013, 63, 64.

[42] So *Hk-ZV*/Sternal, Section 802 f Rn 27; Sturm JurBüro 2013, 63, 64; Nober, in BLHAG Section 882c N 4; Thomas/Putzo/Seiler Section 802c N 25; Prütting/Gehrlein/Meller-Hannich Section 802c N 28.

[43] Zöller/Seibel Section 802d N 17 ff; Musielak/Voit/Voit Section 802d N 13; Stein/Jonas/Würdinger Section 802d N 2 ff; Hergenröder DGVZ 2019, 1, 9.

[44] Goebel (Fn. 2), Section 8 Rn. 156ff; Zöller/Seibel Section 802d Rn. 2; cf. Mroß DGVZ 2010, 181, 184.

[45] Stein/Jonas/Würdinger Section 802c N 12 ff, 20 f.

[46] Goebel (Fn. 2), Section 8 Rn. 65ff; U. Gottwald/Mock (N 31), Section 802c Rn. 22ff.

[47] Cf. Hergenröder DGVZ 2019, 1, 4.

[48] Nober, in BLHAG Section 802c N 14 f; Thomas/Putzo/Seiler Section 802c N 17.

years, in particular about transfers without consideration and transfers to related persons (Section 802c II 3 CCP).[49] On application the debtor has to affirm in lieu of an oath that his information is correct and complete (Section 802c III CCP).

(f) The bailiff has to prepare the formal list of assets according to the oral statements of the debtor as an electronic document (Section 802f V 1 CCP) and has to draw up a protocol about this act (Sections 762, 159 ff CCP).[50] By this way it can easily be sent to the central enforcement court where it can be viewed and queried via internet (Section 802k I 2 CCP) by other bailiffs, enforcement authorities, enforcement courts, insolvency courts and prosecuting authorities (Section 802k II CCP). To enable the debtor to provide diligent information it seems appropriate to hand him over with the summons not only the instruction sheet about his rights and duties in this situation (Section 802f III CCP), but also the printed form of the list of assets[51] to enable him to fill it in informally at rest.[52] Summons and instructions must be served formally to the debtor in person, even if he is represented by a counsel (Section 802f IV 1 CCP).[53]

(g) To given the creditor a fair hearing (Art. 103 I Basic Law), the date for providing the information shall be communicated to him (Section 802f IV 2 CCP). He could then attend the meeting and ask the debtor questions.[54] In practice, only a few creditors are using this possibility.

(h) When the schedule of assets is drawn up and approved by the debtor (cf. Section 802f V CCP), the bailiff shall lodge it with the central enforcement court and shall forward a hard-copy printout to the creditor (Section 802f VI CCP).

Every German state has a central enforcement court (in Bavaria the local court of Hof), where the schedules are maintained for inspection via internet (Section 802k I CCP), until they were deleted ex officio after two years or after the entry of a new schedule (Section 802k I 3 CCP).[55] This possibility becomes relevant when the debtor relocates or resides and another bailiff is competent for a new enforcement. As already stated, only enforcement authorities are entitled to inspect the schedule

---

[49] Cf. Nober, in BLHAG Section 802c N 36 ff; Stein/Jonas/Würdinger Section 802c N 28 ff, 38 ff; Prütting/Gehrlein/Meller-Hannich Section 802c N 22; Sturm JurBüro 2013, 63, 64.

[50] Hergenröder DGVZ 2019, 1, 7; Stein/Jonas/Würdinger Section 802f N 29 f; Musielak/Voit/Voit Section 802f N 8.

[51] For a sample of the form, cf. Vermögensverzeichnisverordnung of 26.7.2012, BGBl 2012 I, 1663.

[52] Rightly so Wilhelm (N 13), Section 1 Rn. 74.

[53] Zöller/Seibel Section 802f N 6; Thomas/Putzo/Seiler Section 802f N 8.

[54] Goebel (N 2), Section 8 Rn. 142; Harnacke/Bungardt DGVZ 2013, 1, 7; Stein/Jonas/Würdinger Section 802 f N 27.

[55] Nober, in BLHAG Section 802k N 3; Thomas/Putzo/Seiler Section 802k N 3; Hergenröder DVGZ 2019, 1, 11.

of assets, not private creditors (Section 802k II CCP).[56] This kind of electronic inspection seems to work well as nationwide.

5. New information on assets

Having provided information on his financial situation, the debtor is not obliged to once again provide such information within two years, until the creditor can make plausible that there is a significant change in the financial situation or the assets of the debtor (Section 802d I 1 CCP). Indication for such a change may be a move, a succession, a change of place of work, a change of car, closing or opening a bank account,[57] maybe an expensive vacation trip.[58] As long as there are no indications for a change, the bailiff shall forward to the new creditor a hard-copy printout of the last schedule of assets (Section 802d I 2 CCP).[59] In this way, the new creditor is rather quickly informed about the (mostly bad) financial situation of the debtor. Again, the debtor has to be instructed that he may be (again) entered in the public list of debtors if he does not pay his debt within four weeks (Sections 802d I 4, 882c I no. 3 CCP).[60]

6. Obtaining information from third parties

(a) In general, the creditor can just demand a self-discovery by the creditor. Only subsidiarily, the creditor may instruct the bailiff to obtain additional, information from third parties.[61] This is the case, if the debtor refuses to comply with his obligation to provide information about his assets or if it is foreseeable that the enforcement against the know assets will not achieve full satisfaction of the creditor, from (1) the statutory pension insurance funds,[62] (2) the Federal Central Tax Office,[63] and (3) the Federal Motor Transport Authority[64] to identify further assets (Section 802l (1) 2 CCP).[65] This is the first possibility for a

[56] Zöller/Seibel Section 802k N 3; Schwörer/Heßler ZVI 2007, 589, 595; G. Vollkommer NJW 2012, 3681, 3681; Schuschke/Walker, *Vollstreckung und vorläufiger Rechtsschutz*, 5th ed. 2011, Section 802k Rn. 9; crit. Goebel (N 2), Section 8 Rn. 217, 223.

[57] Zöller/Seibel Section 802d N 7 ff; Seip, *Zum Entwurf eines Gesetzes zur Reform der Sachaufklärung…*, DGVZ 2006, 1, 3; crit. Stein/Jonas/Würdinger Section 802d N 15; Prütting/Gehrlein/Meller-Hannich Section 802d N 3.

[58] Cf. Goebel (N 2), Section 12 Rn. 90; opposite opinion Thomas/Putzo/Seiler Section 802d N 6.

[59] Cf. Thomas/Putzo/Seiler Section 802d N 3; Salten MDR 2017, 61, 62; Seip, *Zur Pflicht des Gerichtsvollziehers, dem Drittgläubiger gemäß Section 802d Abs. 1 S. 2 ZPO einen Abdruck des Vermögensverzeichnisses zuzuleiten*, DGVZ 2016, 23.

[60] Zöller/Seibel Section 802d N 13; Harnacke/Bungardt DGVZ 2013, 1, 4f.

[61] Zöller/Seibel Section 802l N 3; Thomas/Putzo/Seiler Section 802l N 1, 2; Prütting/Gehrlein/Meller-Hannich Section 802l N 1, 4.

[62] In 2018: 319.412 inquiries. Information according to "*Übersicht über die Geschäftstätigkeit der Gerichtsvollzieher.. im Jahr 2018*", DGVZ 2019, 268.

[63] In 2018: 495.259 inquiries.

[64] In 2018: 44.554 inquiries.

[65] The originally prescribed minimum amount of 500 € for the claim to be enforced was deleted by law of 21.11.2016 (BGBl I 2591); cf. Salten, MDR 2017, 61.

creditor to check the self-discovery of the debtor.[66] His application is always permissible; the creditor has not to make creditable that there are some irregularities in the list of assets. Any bailiff, even the one, who has just passed a schedule of assets to a further creditor, may obtain this kind of information.[67]

The statutory pension insurance fund may inform about the employer of the debtor, so that a garnishment of wages can take place.[68] The Federal Central Tax Office may inform of bank accounts (not the account balance), to enable an account attachment.[69] The inquiry with the Federal Motor Transport Authority may reveal that the debtor is keeper (owner?) of a vehicle subject to execution.[70]

(b) These possibilities are well considered. Since the bailiffs are connected to the electronic facilities of the courts electronic queries are easily possible and obtaining information from third parties is quickly available. In 2018, such information was obtained in about 29 % of all cases, where the creditor applied for information by the debtor.

(c) A further creditor whom an old schedule of asset is forwarded may nevertheless mandate the bailiff to obtain information from third parties so far this has not been made and the other requirements are met.[71] The right to obtain such information does not contradict with the power of the bailiff to interview the debtor or in his absence adult persons of his household about monetary claims against third parties or the debtor's employer and to inform the creditor about insights he has gained on this occasion (Section 806a CCP).[72]

7. Entering in the list of debtors

(a) As the debtor is now obliged to give full information on his financial situation and his assets at the beginning of a compulsory execution procedure, one cannot conclude from this that he is insolvent and not credit-worthy. It may well turn out that he is just unwilling to pay or that he has substantial assets, which are not easy to be sold. Therefore, providing information on his financial

---

[66] Schwörer/Heßler ZVI 2007, 589, 590; Sturm JurBüro 2013, 63, 68f.

[67] Goebel (N 2), Section 8 Rn. 241. In Belgium, bailiffs obtain information from third parties immediately after having received the enforcement application; cf. Hesterberg/Schmitz, *Effektivität und Erfolge in der Zwangsvollstreckung*, DGVZ 2006, 84, 86.

[68] Prütting/Gehrlein/Meller-Hannich Section 802l N 11; Thomas/Putzo/Seiler Section 802l N 7; Moß DGVZ 2010, 181, 185; Goebel (N 2), Section 8 Rn. 249.

[69] Prütting/Gehrlein/Meller-Hannich Section 802l N 13; Moß DGVZ 2010, 181, 185; Goebel (N 2), Section 8 Rn. 259. This does not help to disclose bank accounts abroad; therefore, crit. Holzapfl, *Sachaufklärung und Zwangsvollstreckung in Europa*, 2009, S. 224, 231ff.

[70] Moß DGVZ 2010, 181, 185; crit. Goebel (Fn. 2), Section 8 Rn. 264 (debtor may use a leased car).

[71] Musielak/Voit/Voit Section 802l N 2; Nober, in BLHAG Section 802l N 16; Harnacke/Bungardt DGVZ 2013, 1, 7.

[72] Differing opinion Schilken, *Zur Reform der Sachaufklärung in der Zwangsvollstreckung*, Rechtspfleger 2006, 629, 637.

circumstances cannot automatically lead to the entry in the list of debtors, the so-called "black list".[73]

(b) If the debtor has provided information on his financial circumstances or his schedule of assets has been forwarded to another creditor, the debtor has one month to satisfy the respective creditor.[74] Only when this period is expired without success, the bailiff ex officio orders the debtor to be entered into the list of debtors (Section 882c I no. 3 CCP). As already explained, this does not happen if bailiff and debtor have concluded a payment plan so long as it is valid.[75]

(c) The debtor is entered in the list of debtors earlier, when he refuses to provide the information on his financial circumstances, though he may be rich.[76] The immediate entry is also made, if a compulsory enforcement in disclosed assets would obviously be insufficient to satisfy the creditor (Section 882c I no. 1, 2 CCP). If the debtor provides the information on his financial circumstances and according to it he is not obviously insolvent, he has one month time to find money (from relatives or friends) to satisfy the creditor.[77] Even within this month a payment plan can be made with the effect that the debtor is not entered into the list of debtors (Section 882c I no. 3 S. 2 CCP).[78]

(d) The reasoning for the instruction to have the debtor entered in the list of debtors is to be served on the debtor, unless he has been informed orally and the grounds have been included in the record (Section 882c II CCP). Against the order to enter the debtor in this list he can lodge an objection within two weeks with the enforcement court (Section 882 d I 1 CCP), against the decision of the enforcement court he can lodge an "immediate complaint" (Section 793 CCP).[79] The objection of the debtor does not prevent the entering from being carried out; on application of the debtor the enforcement court may instruct that the entry be temporarily stayed (Section 882d II 1 CCP).[80] In this case,

---

[73] Schilken Rpfleger 2006, 629, 638; Schilken, *Die Eintragung in das Schuldnerverzeichnis….*, Festschrift für Alangoya, 2007, S. 485, 490; Schwörer/Heßler ZVI 2007, 589, 592; Prütting/Gehrlein/Lugani Section 882c N 1; Gaul/Schilken/Becker-Eberhard (N 35), Section 60 Rn. 70.

[74] Seip DGVZ 2006, 1, 4f; Prütting/Gehrlein/Lugani Section 882c N 5; Nober, in BLHAG Section 882c N 8; Stein/Jonas/Bartels, *ZPO*, 23rd. ed 2017, Section 882c N 13 ff.

[75] Nober, in BLHAG Section 882a N 4, 11; Thomas/Putzo/Seiler Section 882c N 1, 4; Musielak/Voit/Voit Section 882c N 2.

[76] Zöller/Seibel Section 882c N 3; Thomas/Putzo/Seiler Section 882c N 2; *Hk-ZV*/Sternal, Section 882c Rn. 5 (justified sanction); crit. Schilken Rpfleger 2006, 629, 638; Schilken, Festschrift für Alangoya, S. 485, 492f.

[77] BT-Drucks. 16/10069, S. 37f; Sturm JurBüro 2013, 63, 65; Goebel (N 2), Section 8 Rn. 48; für eine Frist von 2-3 Monaten Schilken Rpfleger 2006, 629, 639; Schilken, Festschrift für Alangoya, S. 485, 492f.

[78] Zöller/Seibel Section 882c N 5; Thomas/Putzo/Seiler Section 882c N 4; Prütting/Gehrlein/Lugani Section 882c N 4; Seip, *Die Eintragung im Schuldnerverzeichnis …*, DGVZ 2017, 65.

[79] Zöller/Seibel Section 882d N 6; Stein/Jonas/Bartels Section 882d N 2 ff, 11 ff; Thomas/Putzo/Seiler Section 882d N 2, 7; G. Vollkommer NJW 2012, 3681, 3682.

[80] Nober, in BLHAG Section 882d N 16 ff; Stein/Jonas/Bartels Section 882d N 15.

the central enforcement court is to refrain from entering the debtor in the list of debtors or delete an entering, which has been already carried out.[81]

During the time for lodging an objection, the debtor has once again the opportunity to satisfy the creditor or to make a payment agreement with the bailiff, and thereby averting the entry in the list of debtors.[82]

(e) If the debtor is unable to pay and his formal objections are not successful, he will finally be entered in the list of debtors (after about 7 weeks).[83] This list is kept with the central enforcement courts of the German states. To enable an internet query, every registration is forwarded to the central enforcement court in Hagen (in North Rhine-Westphalia).

For reasons of data protection, the entry is not completely public. After registration, access is permitted to everyone who has a legitimate interest in it. This may be the case for the purpose of enforcement, to check the economic reliability of a loan applicant, to check the requirements for granting of social benefits, for averting economic disadvantages in the event of non-performance by the debtor liable to pay, or for purpose of criminal prosecution (Section 882f I CCP). Upon request, professional self-governing bodies, private protective associations, banking institutions, trade supervision offices, credit inquiry agencies and tax offices receive copies from the list of debtors for ongoing reference (Section 882g II CCP).[84] They must keep the information confidential, but may inform their members about the content (Section 882g III, IV CCP).

(f) In principle, the debtor remains registered in the list of debtors for three years (Section 882e I CCP). At the order of an enforcement court, the entry is deleted prematurely, if the debtor has paid his enforcement creditor in full (Section 882e III no. 1 CCP). The entry is also deleted if it is known that the entry was made for no reason or if the registration order is set aside or suspended by a court (Section 882e III no. 2, IV CCP).[85]

(g) When another creditor tries to enforce with insufficient result, the debtor will be again entered in the list of insolvent debtors after one month. This has the consequence that the time of entry is prolonged until the last enforcement creditor is paid in full or up to three years after the last entry.[86] A premature deletion will only take place if the satisfaction of all creditors has been proven.

8. Custody to enforce obtaining information from the debtor

---

[81] Thomas/Putzo/Seiler Section 882d N 4; *Hk-ZV*/Sternal, Section 882 d Rn 5.

[82] *Hk-ZV*/Sternal, Section 882d Rn 3.

[83] Mroß DGVZ 2010, 181, 185.

[84] Details are regulated in „Verordnung über den Bezug von Abdrucken aus dem Schuldnerverzeichnis“ of 26.07.2012 (BGBl I 1658) and in „Verordnung über die Führung des Schuldnerverzeichnisses“ of 26.07.2012 (BGBl I 1654).

[85] Thomas/Putzo/Seiler Section 882e N 6 ff; Musielak/Voit/Voit Section 882e N 3 ff.

[86] Zöller/Seibel Section 882e N 2; Thomas/Putzo/Seiler Section 882e N 5; Schwörer/Heßler DGVZ 2007, 589, 594.

If the debtor was entered in the list of insolvent debtors because he did not give information about his financial situation and his assets, the enforcement procedure is not finished. On the contrary, the creditor may (explicitly) apply for issuing a warrant of arrest against the debtor to enforce the information about the financial situation (Section 802g I 1 CCP).[87] The warrant of arrest is never issued ex officio.[88] The warrant is rendered by the judge of the enforcement court and is valid for two years (Section 802h I CCP). Requirements and content of the custody are practically unchanged. It takes approximately three months from the application for enforcement until the arrest by the bailiff, which still happens in a remarkable number of cases.

The duration of custody is limited to six months (Section 802j I CCP); in practice custody is mostly very short. After two or three days the latest, even the most stubborn debtor provides the requested information. Immediately afterwards, the debtor is released from custody (Section 802i II CCP).

4 Assessment of the Reform

1. As before the reform, the new law proceeds from the assumption that a debtor has assets, but is unwilling to pay its debts. In reality, this is the great exception. Entrepreneurs as well as consumers are mostly willing to pay throughout, but are simply unable to do it in most cases.[89] The reasons for that are unemployment, divorce, and death of the spouse, disability as consequence of accident or similar blows. A consumer does not pay, because he has neither attachable earnings nor property. Only self-employed persons have a certain probability that they have attachable assets. Moving the information on financial circumstances and assets to the beginning of the enforcement procedure only leads to the fact that the creditor gets clarity more quickly about the bad economic situation of the debtor. The result is quite the same. If there are no attachable assets, the quicker information does not lead to a better grade of satisfaction. Only the fee for the attachment attempt is saved. The greater pressure, which derives from the earlier duty to provide information about the financial situation and the impending danger of entry in the list of insolvent debtors, may lead the debtor to pay his debts only, if finally he has the necessary means or is able to raise them.[90]

2. According to the new law, the debtor provides the information on his financial circumstances normally not immediately after the bailiff has been mandated with the enforcement, but two to three weeks later in the bailiff's office. Therefore, the

---

[87] Cf. Zöller/Seibel Section 802g N 2 ff; Nober, in BLHAG Section 802g N 6; Stein/Jonas/Würdinger Section 802g N 3 ff.

[88] Crit. Schilken Rpfleger 2006, 629, 636.

[89] C. W. Hergenröder, *Vom Forderungseinzug zum Forderungsmanagement – Zwangsvollstreckung im 21. Jahrhundert und soziale Wirklichkeit*, DGVZ 2010, 201, 203, 205.

[90] C. Holzapfl (N 69), S. 241.

timely difference to the former law is not too big. Only the hope to find something attachable dies a little earlier.

There are still no statistical figures available whether the new discovery duty of the debtor has led to better enforcement results in favour of the creditors. Practitioners doubt that. It is also unlikely that the German Justice System now enjoys a better esteem by foreign lawyers.

The bailiff is faced with more paper work, more service of documents, notices in writing, setting of deadlines.[91] Moreover, the creditor has to pay more fees in advance.

3. As before the reform, the focus of the bailiff's work lies in concluding instalment agreements with the debtor, and to transfer the partial payments made to the creditor. The legislator has placed this task at the top of the powers of the bailiff. The time for such payment agreement has been prolonged to twelve months. It is however not entirely satisfactorily that the creditor can refuse to agree even with a realistic payment plan and thereby force the debtor to be entered in the register of insolvent debtors. In general, the refusal of the creditor cannot be regarded as a measure that due to the very special circumstances is immoral. The enforcement court therefore may stay enforcement proceedings according to Section 765a CCP only in very exceptional cases.[92]

4. If the debtor cannot pay the claim of two creditors, he is insolvent and can file for bankruptcy himself and the creditors can do the same (Section 13 I 2 InsO).

If insolvency proceedings are opened, the instalment payment of the last month is ineffective (Section 89 I InsO) Previous payments according to a payment agreement concluded within enforcement proceedings may be contested as incongruent coverage (Section 131 InsO)[93] or even as intentional creditor's disadvantage (Section 133 InsO).[94] It is certainly okay that a creditor has to repay payments on the instalment plan, which he received within the last three months before filing for bankruptcy. It was problematic, however, that he had to repay payments within the last ten years before filing for bankruptcy as the Federal Supreme Court held that a creditor who concludes an instalment agreement with the debtor who cannot pay the debt acts with conditional intent to harm other creditors.[95] This case law was certainly in line with the principles of insolvency rescission, but it led the system of amicable settlement of enforcement procedures to absurdity.[96]

---

[91] The legislator estimated a 21 % increase in the burden of bailiffs (BT-Drucks. 16/10069, S. 22).

[92] Cf. Mroß DGVZ 2010, 181, 182; U. Gottwald/Mock (N 31), Section 802b Rn. 21.

[93] So BGH ZIP 2010, 191 = NZI 2010, 184. H.G. Ganter, *Weiterentwicklung der Rechtsprechung zu Section 133 InsO*, WM 2014, 49, explains nothing else. For restriction of Insolvency rescission Marotzke, *Vertrauensschutz contra Gesamtgläubigerinteresse*, ZInsO 2014, 417.

[94] Vgl. BGH ZIP 2010, 191 = NZI 2010, 184; BGH NZI 2013, 133; Ganter, NZI 2014, 185, 196; zu Recht crit. U. Gottwald/Mock (N 31), Section 802b Rn. 17ff.

[95] BGH NZI 2003, 597.

[96] In favour of an exclusion of payment agreement in the enforcement application Gottwald/Haas/Huber, *Insolvenzrechts-Handbuch*, 6th ed. 2020, Section 48 Rn. 10.

By 5 April 2017, the German legislator passed a reform of the law of insolvency rescission.[97] The time for repayment of satisfactions was reduced to four years (Section 133 II InsO as amended). Payments in instalment according to a payment agreement within enforcement procedure are still classified as incongruent coverage. In addition, it is now presumed according to Section 133 III 2 InsO (as amended), that a creditor had no knowledge about the insolvency when the debtor made the payments. This is however just a presumption, and the insolvency administrator can try to show that there were more intensive business relations between creditor and debtor and offer evidence that the creditor therefore had detailed knowledge about the real situation of the debtor. If he can prove it, the creditor will still have to repay the instalments of the last four years.[98]

5. Taken as a whole, result of the reform is disillusioning. Creditors do not receive more satisfaction than before the reform; they just learn more quickly that enforcement will be unsuccessful. The risk of repayment instalments in case of later insolvency proceedings is now reduced, but still exists.

Peter Gottwald Professor Emeritus of Civil Law, Procedural Law and Conflicts of Law at Faculty of Law, Regensburg University. He is Honorary President of the International Association of Procedural Law and Co-Editor-in-Chief of the Journal of Family Law (FamRZ). He is among others the author of *Rosenberg/Schwab/Gottwald, Zivilprozessrecht*, C. H. Beck 2018, and of *Nagel/Gottwald, Internationales Zivilprozessrecht*, Otto Schmidt 2020, as well as Co-Editor of *Gottwald/Haas, Insolvenzrechts-Handbuch*, C. H. Beck 2020.

[97] By law of 29.3.2017, BGBl I, S. 654.

[98] Cf. Kindler/Bitzer, *Die Reform der Insolvenzanfechtung*, NZI 2017, 369, 375.

Clarification of Facts in Austrian Enforcement Law

Walter H. Rechberger

In Austria—as everywhere—the vast majority of enforcement proceedings are **pecuniary execution** (*Exekution wegen Geldforderungen*), i.e. proceedings for the compulsory enforcement of payment claims of the creditor (in the terminology of the Austrian Law on the enforcement of judgments [*Exekutionsordnung*—EO] the "enforcing creditor"). The second Chapter of the first Part of the Austrian Enforcement Law provides for executive access to the assets listed therein for such claims; the creditor is free to carry out the impounding procedures on the immovable (Sec. 88 to Sec. 247 EO) and on the movable assets (Sec. 249 to Sec. 345 EO), called real estate or movables execution. In case of pecuniary execution in general it is essential that the application for execution shall include the designation of the objects to be seized, as it is part of the necessary content of this petition (Sec. 54 Para. 2 No. 3 EO).

If the creditor wants to seize access of a **registered property**, not only the name of the cadastral municipality and the deposit number of the land register in which the property is registered are necessary for the application, but usually also the description of its topographical location, if such a description can be considered according to local municipality, street and house number. Knowledge of a concrete property

Keynote Speech on the occasion of the International Colloquium in Kyoto "Effective Enforcement of Creditor's Right in Civil Execution through Effective Discovery of Debtor's Assets" on 6 November 2019. The presentation was based on my article entitled "Zur Effizienz der Sachaufklärung in der Zwangsvollstreckung" in: Meller-Hannich/Haertlein/Gaul/Becker-Eberhard (ed.), Rechtslage—Rechtserkenntnis—Rechtsdurchsetzung, Festschrift für Eberhard Schilken zum 70. Geburtstag, München 2015, 763. The text has been edited slightly, in order to incorporate changes resulting from the recent amendment of the Austrian Enforcement Law in 2021, which left the fact-finding-regime largely unchanged but renumbered several legal provisions.

W. H. Rechberger (✉)
University of Vienna, Vienna, Austria
e-mail: walter.rechberger@univie.ac.at

M. Deguchi (ed.), *Effective Enforcement of Creditors' Rights*,
Ius Gentium: Comparative Perspectives on Law and Justice 91,
https://doi.org/10.1007/978-981-16-5609-5_2

of the debtor (in the terminology of the EO: the "obligor") is therefore unavoidable for the creditor's enforcement. The possibility of inspecting and consulting the land register as a public register is therefore of particular importance with regard to the fact-finding concerning immovable property. Pursuant to Sec. 6 Para. 1 of the Austrian Land Register Computerization Act (*Grundbuchsumstellungsgesetz*—GUG), everyone is authorized—subject to the technical and staff possibilities—to query the land register, the collection of documents and the auxiliary directories from the land register, the property database and the database of documents by means of automated data processing. However, the list of persons is explicitly excluded from this general land register query: apart from the land registry courts themselves, only notaries and lawyers are authorized to query this list—in addition to the offices of the Federal Government, the federal provinces and the municipalities as well as the social insurance institutions and their umbrella association—under certain conditions, e.g. in order to determine the registered rights of the creditor as the representative of the debtor of an enforceable pecuniary claim (Sec. 6 Para. 2 GUG).

If the obligor does not own immovable property, the enforcing creditor only has the right to enforce his claim by execution of the **movable property**. Within movable execution, the execution of claims (in particular salary execution) and the levy of execution play by far the most important role. In the application for execution directed towards the **execution of claims**, the receivable to be seized must in principle be individualized, which is typically done by designating the third-party creditor and the legal basis of the claim. The requirement to designate the object of execution (Sec. 54 Para. 2 No. 3 EO) is met in the execution of claims according to the judicature if both the third-party debtor and the obligor can recognise which claim is being enforced. From the perspective of the factual clarification under enforcement law, the problem may now arise that the enforcing creditor assumes that the obligor will continue to receive remuneration within the meaning of Sec. 289 Para. 3 EO (recurring payments, especially remuneration for work), but he/she cannot determine which third-party debtor (in particular which employer) these claims are against. Therefore, Sec. 295 EO contains provisions on the initiation of execution on income as defined by Sec. 290a EO in the case of an unknown third-party debtor.

The special feature is that, in deviation from the basic rule, the enforcing creditor does not have to designate either the third-party debtor or the legal basis of the claim. In the application for execution, he/she only has to state the date of birth of the obligor, which he/she can inquire at the registration office. The court of execution shall then grant the execution and shall subsequently request the umbrella association of the social insurance system ex officio to disclose whether the obligor, according to the stored data, has a legal relationship from which he/she may be entitled to claims within the meaning of Sec. 289 Para. 3 EO and, if so, with whom. If the aforementioned umbrella association announces one or more third-party debtors, the court of execution has to seize the existing claims according to Sec. 294 EO. Once the payment prohibition has been delivered to the specific third-party debtor, the execution according to Sec. 295 EO leads to a normal execution of the claim according to Sec. 294 EO. If the information provided by the umbrella association is negative, a procedure for the submission of a list of assets will generally be initiated.

The execution on movable tangible things (**levy of execution**) is the most frequently used type of execution. The reason is that for some groups of debtors, salary execution is ruled out from the outset (legal entities, self-employed persons, housewives/husbands, &c.). The hope for the existence of realizable assets is a reason for the creditor to file an application for a levy of execution. However, this kind of execution is not exclusively aimed at the seizure and executive sale of these objects; rather, it is primarily intended to induce the obligor to pay voluntarily under the pressure of the (forthcoming) impounding execution.

In the case of an application for a levy execution, a general description of the execution objects is considered admissible in such a way that the execution is requested to bring in the claim "*by seizure and sale of movable tangible property of all kinds in the custody of the obligor*" (form for the execution petition). Such a petition is thus directed at the impounding execution of the entire movable, tangible property of the debtor and not against specifically listed objects. The reason is that when the application for execution is filed, the creditor will normally have very little information about which execution objects are available at the debtor's premises. After the issuance of the execution permit, the execution court must hand over the execution deed to the bailiff for execution. If the levy of execution is unsuccessful, the obligor must submit a list of assets (Sec. 47 Para. 1 No. 1 EO).

A **list of assets** according to Sec. 47 EO can only be demanded from the obligor within the framework of the execution in order to obtain a pecuniary claim if the levy of execution or the salary execution according to Sec. 294a EO has been unsuccessful. If, on the other hand, another execution is unsuccessful, the enforcing creditor does not have the instrument of the register of assets at his disposal in order to investigate other assets of the obligor. The central criterion for carrying out the procedure pursuant to Sec. 47 Para. 2 EO is the unsuccessful pertinent execution.

A levy of execution has been unsuccessful within the meaning of the law if only objects were found in the debtor's possession which are not seizable, the inadequacy of which is clear in view of their low value or the liens already established in favour of other creditors or which are claimed by third parties. The seizable objects found must provide full cover for the satisfaction of the claim, whereby this assessment is to be based on the estimated realizable proceeds of these objects determined by the bailiff. The failure of an enforcement attempt cannot be qualified as an unsuccessful levy of execution yet. The salary execution according to Sec. 295 EO is to be qualified as unsuccessful if either the umbrella association of the social insurance system has not answered the request of the court positively, or if the proceeds of this execution will presumably not be sufficient to repay the enforceable claim including ancillary fees in the course of one year. If the enforcing creditor has combined a levy of execution and salary execution in his/her application, the procedure for handing over the list of assets may only be initiated if both the enforcement of the claim and the *subsequent* levy of execution have failed.

It follows from the above-mentioned criterion of the unsuccessful pertinent execution that the EO considers the inclusion of a list of assets to be merely a subsidiary means of investigating the assets of the obligor. The request to the obligor to declare his/her assets constitutes a **last resort**; it may only be used as a means of information if the most important means of execution provided for in the EO to satisfy the claim have been exhausted to no avail. Notwithstanding the latest reforms in 2021, the Austrian EO thus continues to follow the original concept of the affidavit of means procedure of the German Code of Civil Procedure and has not understood the paradigm shift in German enforcement law by the reform of fact-finding in 2013.

The list of assets pursuant to Sec. 47 EO is intended to provide the enforcing creditor with an overview of those assets of the obligor which may be considered as further objects of execution in the pending enforcement procedure. It is—as already mentioned—excluded to use this means of information independently of a concrete impounding execution. Just like the procedure for the affidavit of means of the original version of the EO, today's procedure for submittal of the list of assets is not conceived as a "primary investigation procedure", which the creditor could already use before the execution to obtain information about the location of objects or about the debtor's financial situation. For the time being, the creditor is rather dependent on his/her own efforts in order to be able to locate and name the execution objects.

Since the amendment of 1991, the initiation of the procedure for the submission of a list of assets is no longer dependent on an application by the enforcing creditor, but takes place **ex officio**. The official inclusion of the list of assets shall only be waived if either the enforcing creditor has waived its collection (Sec. 47 Para. 1 No. 1 EO) or if no more than one year has elapsed since the last list of assets was submitted or the detention pending trial was carried out (Sec. 49 Para. 1 last sentence EO). With the exception of the imposition of coercive detention, the inclusion of the list of assets does fall within the functional competence of the judicial officer (Sec. 17 Para. 2 Subpara. 3 of the Judicial Officers Act [*Rechtspflegergesetz*]), but the request to the obligor to state his/her assets must be made by the bailiff at the place of execution when the execution of the levy of execution has been (unsuccessfully) carried out, provided that the obligor is present. If the obligor was not present at the execution and the bailiff is unable to find the obligor despite several attempts, he/she shall be summoned by the court to draw up the list of assets there. If the obligor does not comply with this summons, the submission of the list of assets will be enforced, i.e. the obligor will be compulsorily presented and, in the event of refusal to submit the list of assets, coercive detention will be imposed on him/her. In order to protect the fundamental right to personal freedom (Art. 5 Para. 4 European Convention on Human Rights—ECHR), the court of execution must clarify the existence of the relevant preconditions in oral evidence proceedings prior to the imposition of imprisonment. Since the detention in this case does not constitute a penalty but a means of coercive measure, the detention ends as soon as the obligor hands over the list of assets, but in any case after a total period of six months (Sec. 48 Para. 2 EO). The decision on detention itself shall cease to be effective if it is not executed within one year (Sec. 48 Para. 3 EO).

Whoever submits a false or incomplete list of assets in the course of enforcement or insolvency proceedings before a court or before an enforcement body and thereby endangers the satisfaction of a creditor is to be punished according to Sec. 292a of the Criminal Code (*Strafgesetzbuch*) with imprisonment for up to six months or with a fine of up to 360 daily rates.

The electronic compilation of the list of assets and its central availability via a database is today—as in Germany—state of the art in Austria. The judicial officer or bailiff fills in the list of assets according to the information provided by the obligor directly on the screen. The list can then be accessed by the courts throughout Austria by court automation support. This makes it easier for the courts, especially in later insolvency proceedings, to check whether cost-covering assets are available.

Within a vesting period of one year, the debtor is obligated to submit a new list of assets if it is shown credibly that he/she later acquired assets (Sec. 49 Para. 1 EO).

Ultimately, it must be pointed out that there are significant differences between the Austrian regulation of fact-finding in enforcement proceedings and the German legal situation: Even after the mentioned reform in Germany, the priority collection of the debtor's information on his/her financial status is dependent on the creditor not only applying for it but also expressly excluding the amicable settlement in the enforcement order. In addition, the use of the most effective coercive measure, namely coercive detention, also depends on a petition to that effect. In the Austrian EO, all these measures are subject to official procedures; a petition by the enforcing creditor is not required. In Austria's view, this does better justice to the interests in the context of money execution because the enforcing creditor primarily wishes to have his/her claim satisfied promptly; the question of the concrete (possible) procedural steps tends to play a subordinate role for him/her.

Walter H. Rechberger (born in 1945), Professor emeritus at the Vienna University Faculty of Law. He held the position of Dean and of Head of the Department of Civil Procedure Law (Institut für Zivilverfahrensrecht) at this faculty. For many years he was member of the Council of the International Association of Procedural Law (IAPL) and of several boards, such as of the Vienna International Arbitral Center (VIAC) and the Institute for Danube Region and Central Europe (IDM). He received his J.D. from Vienna University and holds degrees of an honorary doctor of the University of Pècs, Hungary and of the University of Athens, Greece. In 1989, he acted as a visiting professor at the Kansas University School of Law, Lawrence, US. Publications of Prof. Rechberger comprise of more than 300 legal works, seven books of which represent standard literature on Austrian Civil Procedural Law. He gave almost 100 lectures abroad (in most European countries and worldwide, e.g., China, Cuba, Iran, Israel, Japan, Mongolia, Singapore, South Africa, and the US).

Comments on the Paper of Professor Dr. *Walter H. Rechberger;* Clarification of Facts in Austrian Enforcement Law

Maiko Miyashita

1 Fact Finding System in Austria

The paper of Professor Dr. Walter H. Rechberger sets out, inter alia, the special features extant in Austrian law to facilitate the operation of an effective enforcement system. In Austria, as in other jurisdictions, before commencing an execution procedure, a creditor needs to know the details of the assets of a debtor. A creditor is able to access the database of the land registry to ascertain detail regarding immovable properties.

When it comes to movable property, such as the salary of a debtor or tangible assets, a creditor may have to work somewhat harder to obtain the information about the assets of the debtor in order to be able to carry out the appropriate form of execution. However, Austrian law provides a simple measure to start the execution process if it is the apparently problematic case that the creditor does not know the identity of a third party debtor. A creditor merely needs to state the date of birth of the debtor for execution to be granted. Subsequently, details of any contract under which the debtor is entitled to a money claim can be made known by an Office of the national social insurance system. Professor Dr. Rechberger points out that Austrian execution law is only able to require the disclosure of a full list of the assets of a debtor if the main methods of execution have been attempted but have not been successful and he explains that Austrian law thus adheres the affidavit of means of procedure, which was formerly enshrined within German legal procedure.

M. Miyashita (✉)
Faculty of Law, Surugadai University, Hanno, Japan
e-mail: buona-fortuna@suou.waseda.jp

M. Deguchi (ed.), *Effective Enforcement of Creditors' Rights*,
Ius Gentium: Comparative Perspectives on Law and Justice 91,
https://doi.org/10.1007/978-981-16-5609-5_3

2 New Japanese System

The Japanese civil law system has for a long time faced criticism for lacking effectiveness and reliability. The weakest point is said to be its enforcement system. It may transpire that, although a party obtains a favourable judgment, often at great cost, the successful litigant will struggle to enforce the decision if a debtor does not pay willingly. An enforcing creditor has had to determine and seize the assets of a debtor personally with inadequate support from the Court system. Creditors have waited a long time for an effective enforcement system that is expected in Japanese society.

In 2003, the civil enforcement law was amended, and a property disclosure system was introduced. Under this system, a court summons a debtor and orders the disclosure of a list of his assets. However, the numbers of applications applying this new system have remained at a modest level.

Consequently, a new amendment law came into force in 2020. A revision of the Civil Execution Act was implemented in Japan on the 10th of May 2019 and became law in 2020. Japan thus fell into step with other national jurisdictions, such as Germany, the U.K., France, and the US, which have a court-led system to disclose the list of the assets of a debtor further to an application submitted by a creditor.

The reform targets three main points. One of them is the disclosure of the assets of debtors; a new asset disclosure procedure has been introduced in order to make it more straightforward to determine the extent of the property of the debtor. Under the new law, a creditor can obtain information about a debtor from third parties. Under the current law, in order to access savings and salary, a creditor has to specify the exact home address of the debtor or that of his/her workplace. Under the new system, a creditor can request a District Court to order a third party such as banks and municipalities to provide financial information about the debtor further to a final and binding Court judgment. A municipality can seek out such information by obtaining details of income tax returns from them. This new system is expected to improve the Japanese enforcement procedures markedly.

3 Comparative Perspective

3.1 France

In France, there is no similar system of disclosure of the assets of a debtor. The amended law of execution in 1991 introduced a property enquiry system and under the new law, debt execution has been largely promoted. Thus, French law needed to prepare a system by which a creditor could obtain the information more readily. A creditor does not need to operate the disclosure process alone. A bailiff is delegated by a creditor to apply for the disclosure, and by that application a prosecutor requests the state or a financial institution to provide the details of the assets of the debtor.

This system is only possible in France as they have a particular system in which a prosecutor is involved even within civil litigation and the jurisdiction has the power to seek data from financial institutions.

3.2 Germany

In Germany, a new law was enacted in 2009. According to the new law, a creditor first brings an action against a debtor to disclose a list of his/her assets and then implements a procedure to obtain asset information from a third party that is carried out by a bailiff. The steps a bailiff can take is limited under German law; they can obtain the employment details of a debtor, details from an insurer of legal annuity insurance, account information from financial institutions and information from the Federal Central Tax Office. They can determine from the Federal Automobile Agency whether or not the debtor owns a car.

Prior to the amendment of the law, an unsuccessful levy of execution had to have taken place, before the application for the disclosure of a list of the assets of the debtor could be made. However, under the new law, a creditor is allowed to apply for the disclosure of assets at the time of applying for execution and a debtor has to reveal their assets at the commencement of execution procedure. However, for a bailiff to exercise his authority to obtain information about the debtor, the following requirements need to have been met; ① a debtor has not fulfilled the obligation to provide a list of his assets. ② Although a debtor reveals his assets, it is clear that the debt execution applied to those assets would not fully extinguish the debt of a creditor.

3.3 The United States

In the U.S., there are two main systems to obtain asset information about debtors at the stage of execution; supplementary proceedings and post judgment discovery. Post judgment discovery is the means to share necessary information between parties. A creditor can send interrogatories directly to a debtor and there is no need to obtain permission from the Court. A debtor is expected to answer the interrogatory within 30 days. Further, a creditor can request the production of and right to inspect documents, and copies of documents that a debtor possesses, with the aim of obtaining information which is necessary to start a money execution. If a debtor declines to comply, a creditor can apply to the Court for an order compelling compliance. A debtor who does not obey the order can be punished by a fine for being in contempt of Court. Supplementary proceedings are more powerful ways to reveal information about assets. A creditor can apply for an order of examination to permit cross-examination in Court or before an arbitrator. If a debtor does not attend the Court, they may be punished by a fine for being contempt of Court, imprisoned further to an arrest warrant, or ordered to meet the burden of the costs of the creditor in relation to the supplementary proceedings.

Maiko Miyashita currently works at Faculty of Law, Surugadai University (Japan) as Assistant Professor. My research fields are Civil Procedure, ADR, Civil Enforcement Law and Comparative Law. Especially, English arbitration system and execution system of child support in the USA are my recent research themes. I hold Master degree at Waseda University (Japan) and LL.M. at University College London (U.K.). I was a visiting scholar at Columbia University and Cornell University, as a member of Japan Internship for the Development of the Young Leaders (IDYL), which is supported by U.S. Department of State and Ministry of Foreign Affairs of Japan.

The Effective Disclosure of the Debtor's Assets in Enforcement Proceedings

Burkhard Hess

Abstract Every efficient enforcement system needs to provide for sufficient transparency of the financial situation of the debtor, especially as concerns information about the location of the debtor's assets. This article assesses latest developments in Germany and in European Union law, especially Regulation (EU) 655/2021 on the European Account Preservation Order.

[1] In some instances, the need also arises to locate the debtor's place of residence. German procedural law addresses this issue in Section 755 ZPO:

(1) "Where the debtor's place of residence or his usual place of abode is not known, the court-appointed enforcement officer is permitted to determine the debtor's place of abode, based on the enforcement instructions and due to his having been physically handed over the enforceable execution copy, by obtaining the current addresses along with information on the debtor's main residence and secondary residence from the registration authority.

(2) Should it not be possible to determine the debtor's place of abode pursuant to subsection (1), the court-appointed enforcement officer is permitted to take the following actions:

1. To initially obtain from the Central Register of Foreigners information on the foreigners authority keeping the files on the debtor, along with information on the debtor's having moved to or from a location, and subsequently to obtain the debtor's place of abode from the foreigners authority keeping the files on the debtor identified by the inquiry made with the Central Register of Foreigners.
2. To obtain from the statutory pension insurance funds the address of the debtor as currently filed there, as well as his current or future place of abode.
3. To obtain from the Federal Motor Transport Authority (Kraftfahrt-Bundesamt) the vehicle keeper information pursuant to Section 33 (1), first sentence, no. 2 of the Road Traffic Act (Strassenverkehrsgesetz, StVG)".

B. Hess (✉)
Max Planck Institute Luxembourg, Luxembourg, Luxembourg
e-mail: burkhard.hess@mpi.lu

M. Deguchi (ed.), *Effective Enforcement of Creditors' Rights*,
Ius Gentium: Comparative Perspectives on Law and Justice 91,
https://doi.org/10.1007/978-981-16-5609-5_4

1 Introduction

1.1 Information Inequalities in Enforcement Procedures

Every efficient enforcement system needs to provide for sufficient transparency of the financial situation of the debtor, especially as concerns information about the location of the debtor's assets.[1] However, a considerable imbalance may be detected among the different creditors regarding the necessary information about the financial situation of the debtor. Usually, commercial creditors are to some extent in a favourable position since they acquire some information in the course of the commercial relationship, especially about the debtor's bank account where they made prior payments. Furthermore, businesses are registered and creditors may access the commercial registers in order locate the debtor's business address and acquire some information about the bank accounts. Public authorities dispose of additional information: Some of them establish entire dossiers of the debtor's financial situation, especially tax administrations and social security authorities (with regard to the debtor's employer). Finally, the debtor's car may be registered with the Federal Motor Transport Authority. This information can be used in order to find the whereabouts of the debtor's assets when enforcement proceedings are instituted.

However, pertinent information is not equally available to all creditors. The case may even be that some creditors lack any information about the financial situation of the debtor. This is the case, typically, with respect to maintenance claims (where debtors often try to disguise their financial situation). Similar situations arise in disputes between the landowner and (former) tenants after the termination of the lease contract (when the former tenant does not communicate his or her new address to the proprietor); or in disputes arising out of unpaid invoices for the delivery of goods or services. In these circumstances, debtors do not necessarily act in bad faith, although there are debtors who deliberately hide their assets from the creditor knowing that enforcement (or even bankruptcy) is imminent. In these cases, creditors face difficulties when they depend on proper and timely payment—again, the most pertinent case relates to the recovery of maintenance.

1.2 Information Deficits and Enforcement Structures

This unequal situation of the creditors conflicts with two fundamental cornerstones of the German law of enforcement: the principle of priority and the decentralized organization of the enforcement organs.[2] The latter implies that the creditor must access the competent enforcement organ according to the different asset to be seized. Designating the competent organ means that the application for enforcement must be filed with the bailiff in case the creditor seeks to seize movables (Section 753 et seq.

[2] *Hess*, Rechtspolitische Perspektiven der Zwangsvollstreckung, Juristenzeitung 2009, 662, 664.

ZPO); it goes to the court officer (Rechtspfleger) in case the creditor seeks to seize bank accounts and intangible assets (like salaries), Sections 828, 857 ZPO. Finally, the creditor must apply to the land registry if he wants to seize immovable property (Section 864 ZPO). If the creditor does not know the whereabouts of the debtor's assets, he equally does not know where to apply. Eventually, he might waste time and money when he contacts an enforcement organ that cannot localize and seize the targeted asset.[3]

The unequal status of creditors regarding the information of the financial situation of the debtor is even more problematic with regard to the priority principle. This principle addresses the competition among several creditors targeting and seizing, at the same time, the assets of the debtor.[4] According to the priority principle, the creditor who comes first and seizes an asset can fully recover his claim. Concurring creditors who seize later can only recover the rest of the asset. The priority principle is all about time. Better-informed creditors have better chances to recover (fully) their debts whereas creditors without the pertinent information might eventually see a (partial) fall out of their enforceable title.[5]

Against this background, powerful creditors, especially banks, established private mechanisms for gathering information. In Germany, the most important organization in this regard is the so-called Schufa AG. This abbreviation stands for "Schutzgemeinschaft für allgemeine Kreditsicherung". The General Credit Protection Agency was founded in 1927.[6] As Germany's leading credit bureau, Schufa operates as a source of information for corporate and private customers, holding credit rating information about 67.7 million persons and 6 million companies. The operational modus is as follows: Every time a customer opens a bank account, enters into a credit contract or into a mobile phone contract, he or she must give consent via a standard clause to relevant data being transferred and stored by Schufa. According to the clause, the other party is entitled (under data protection law) to access Schufa in order to get information about the financial situation of the customer. Generally, Schufa collects positive data (repayment of loans) but also negative data (defaults, payment orders, enforcement proceedings). As getting information from the Schufa AG is expensive, only powerful creditors usually use this (private) source of information.[7]

---

[3] Recent reforms of the German enforcement law tried to overcome this situation by reinforcing the role of the bailiff in the enforcement proceedings, see infra at B I..

[4] The principle is stated in Section 804 (1) and (3) ZPO which read as follows: "(1) By the attachment, the creditor acquires a security right to the object so attached. (3) Any security right established by an earlier attachment shall take precedence before a security right established by a subsequent attachment".

[5] In this regard, it must be added here that public creditors in Germany have additional advantages in enforcement proceedings: They dispose over the most comprehensive information about the financial situation of the debtor and they are even authorized to establish enforceable titles via administrative acts – without any prior intervention of the court.

[6] Information available at: https://www.schufa.de/en/about-us/company/schufa-facts-figures/inhaltsseite_7.jsp (visited on October 27, 2019).

[7] This «privatization» of the access to information on the debtor's financial situation is a major matter of concern, cf. *Hess*, Juristenzeitung 2009, 662, 664 et seq.

1.3 Legislative Responses to the Information Deficit

Against this background, modern enforcement laws offer different mechanisms to provide the debtor with the needed information. At present, the enforcement laws of EU Member States make (mainly) three different systems available: The first approach is to oblige the debtor to disclose his financial situation by establishing a formal declaration about his financial situation. Under the second approach, third parties (banks, employers) must inform the enforcement organ of the existence of bank accounts or the payment of salaries. According to the third approach, enforcement organs are entitled to access non-public registers (especially tax registers) in order to get the information they need. As I will demonstrate, modern enforcement systems often apply and combine these approaches.[8] As I will demonstrate, national lawmakers recently reformed their enforcement systems in order to enhance the creditor's access to information of the debtor's assets.

In cross-border cases, the EU lawmaker introduced Regulation (EU) 655/2014.[9] Its Article 14 lays down different possibilities to make it possible for the creditor to acquire information about the details of bank account of the debtor in other Member States.[10] This provision permits the creditor to submit a request for the information he needs to the competent authority in the EU Member State of enforcement. A similar system is found in Articles 51(2)(c) and 61–63 of the EU Maintenance Regulation.[11] Here, Central Authorities are entitled to seek for information about the debtor and his assets in other EU Member States for enforcement purposes.

These developments demonstrate that obtaining information on the debtor's financial situation has become a major issue in the contemporary enforcement systems. This development does not come as a surprise. As we all know, the right to effective enforcement is part of the fundamental right of judicial protection.[12] Therefore, States bound by the ECHR and other international human rights instruments are not entirely free when adopting and implementing their respective policies. To the contrary, they must provide for information systems that effectively allow the creditor to acquire

---

[8] See infra at 2.2.

[9] Regulation (EU) No. 655/2014 of the European Parliament and of the Council of 15 May 2014 establishing a European Account Preservation Order procedure to facilitate cross-border debt recovery in civil and commercial matters, OJ 2014 L 189 (EAPO Regulation).

[10] Article 14 reads as follows: (1) Where the creditor has obtained in a Member State an enforceable judgment, court settlement or authentic instrument which requires the debtor to pay the creditor's claim and the creditor has reasons to believe that the debtor holds one or more accounts with a bank in a specific Member State, but knows neither the name and/or address of the bank nor the IBAN, BIC or another bank number allowing the bank to be identified, he may request the court with which the application for the Preservation Order is lodged to request that the information authority of the Member State of enforcement obtain the information necessary to allow the bank or banks and the debtor's account or accounts to be identified.

[11] Regulation 4/2009 of 18 December 2008, OJ 2009 L 7/1 et seq.

[12] *Trocker*, The Right to Effective Enforcement of Civil Judgments and Orders: Lessons from the Case Law of the European Court of Human Rights, in: Stürner/Kawano (ed.), Comparative Studies on Enforcement and Provisional Measures (2011), p. 21 et seq. referring to the landmark decision of the ECtHR, 19/3/1997, *Hornsby v. Greece*, para 40.

the information he or she needs ultimately enforce his or her title. On the other hand, recent developments in data protection and the protection of privacy set limitations to an unfettered right of the creditor to get unlimited access to information about the financial situation of the debtor. All modern systems operate within the framework of these conflicting principles of effective judicial protection and the respect of privacy rights of the debtor.[13]

2 The 2013 Reform of the German Enforcement Law

2.1 A Structural Change of the System

In July 2009, the German lawmaker enacted a law reforming the "Sachaufklärung in der Zwangsvollstreckung" (discovery in enforcement proceedings) that entered into force on January 1st, 2013.[14] The legal literature considers this reform to be the most important reform of enforcement proceedings since 1877 (when the ZPO was enacted).[15] The new system strengthens the bailiff's central position within the enforcement proceedings (sec. 802a ZPO).[16] Accordingly, the bailiff is the competent organ to obtain information from the debtor and third parties regarding the financial situation of the debtor (Sections 802c and 8021 ZPO). The most significant change of the German system relates to the moment when information can be obtained: Under the old legal regime, the bailiff could only order that the debtor issue a declaration on his or her financial situation after an unsuccessful attempt to seize assets at the debtor's domicile.

The new system places the disclosure of the debtor's financial situation at the beginning of the enforcement proceedings: A creditor who does not have sufficient information about the location of assets of the debtor may start enforcement proceedings by requesting that the bailiff obtain information from debtor about his assets via a debtor's declaration (Section 802c ZPO). In this regard, Section 802c (1) and (2) ZPO clearly state the obligation of the debtor to provide for information. It reads as follows:

---

[13] *Hergenröder*, Das Vermögensverzeichnis - Auskunftspflichtige und Auskunftspflichten, DGVZ 2018, 221.

[14] Gesetz zur Reform der Sachaufklärung in der Zwangsvollstreckung (ZwVollStrÄndG) vom 29. Juli 2009, in force since 1 January 2013, BGBl. 2009 I 2258.

[15] Stein/Jonas/*Würdinger*, Vor, Section 802a ZPO (Commentary, 23rd ed. 2017), para 1; *Vollkommer*, NJW 2012, 3681; *Hess*, Juristenzeitung 2009, 662, 664.

[16] However, the German lawmaker refrained from transferring the competence for garnishments to the bailiff. Consequently, the decentralized (and fragmented) structure of the German enforcement organs was maintained, critically, *Würdinger*, Die Sachaufklärung in der Zwangsvollstreckung, Juristenzeitung 2011, 177, 185 seq.; *Hess*, Die Neuorganisation des Gerichtsvollzieherwesens in Deutschland (2006), p. 58 et seq.

> For purposes of enforcing a monetary claim, the debtor is under obligation to provide information to the court-appointed enforcement officer, at the latter's demand, on his financial circumstances and the assets he owns. ... (2) In providing such information, the debtor is to cite all assets belonging to him.

According to its wording, the provision does not entitle the creditor to directly seek information from the debtor: The bailiff, as the competent enforcement organ, is entitled to request the comprehensive information and meeting such request amounts to a procedural obligation of the debtor.[17] Systematically, the lawmaker considers the delivery of this information as an enforcement measure.[18] If the debtor does not comply with this obligation, the enforcement court may impose sanctions, especially detention up to 6 months (Section 802 g and 802j ZPO).

The debtor's assets declaration is not the only way of obtaining information for enforcement purposes. Section 802l ZPO provides for additional ways: if the debtor does not comply with his obligation to disclose his or her financial situation, the bailiff may access registers held by public authorities like the Federal Central Tax Office or the Federal Motor Transport Authority in order to get the details of the debtor's bank accounts and other sources of income.[19] The bailiff may also access these additional sources of information when it is foreseeable that the assets listed in the declaration will not be sufficient to satisfy the creditor's claim. Here again, the creditor does not get direct access to the registers; the bailiff requests the needed information and transmits it to the creditor. In practice, this indirect way of accessing information has proved to be very beneficial—I will come back to this issue in a few moments.

---

[17] Stein/Jonas/*Würdinger*, Section 802c ZPO (Commentary, 23rd ed. 2017), para 1 (Systemwechsel); *Alfasser*, Sachaufklärung in der Zwangsvollstreckung (2018), p. 12 et seq.

[18] This entails that the creditor must explicitly apply for it, cf. *Vollkommer*, NJW 2012,

[19] Section 802l ZPO reads as follows: "(1) Where the debtor does not comply with his obligation to provide information on his financial circumstances and the assets he owns, or if it is foreseeable that the enforcement against the assets listed therein will not achieve the full satisfaction of the creditor, the court-appointed enforcement officer may.

1. Obtain from the statutory pension insurance funds the name, the first names, or the company name of the debtor, as well as the addresses of the current employers in whose services the debtor is working under an employment relationship entailing the obligation to make compulsory social insurance contributions;
2. Request that the Federal Central Tax Office (*Bundeszentralamt für Steuern*) retrieve the data designated in Section 93b (1) of the Fiscal Code (Abgabenordnung, AO) from credit institutions (Section 93 (8) of the Fiscal Code);
3. Obtain from the Federal Motor Transport Authority (*Kraftfahrtbundesamt*) the data on the vehicle and the vehicle keeper pursuant to Section 33 (1) of the Road Traffic Act (Strassenverkehrsgesetz, StVG) for any vehicle regarding which the debtor has been entered as the vehicle keeper.

(2) The court-appointed enforcement officer shall delete or block, without undue delay, any data not required for enforcement purposes. A record is to be prepared of the deletion…".

2.2 *Different Ways of Obtaining Information*

2.2.1 The debtor's Declaration

The 2013 reform of the German enforcement system does not only situate the debtor's declaration at the beginning of the enforcement proceedings. It also reforms the way the declaration is made: The bailiff will summon the debtor to provide the declaration (on a standard form) within 2 weeks or to pay the debt (Section 802f ZPO).[20] The second important part of the reform takes form in the establishment of centralized register of assets declarations that creditors can consult before starting enforcement (Section 802k ZPO). Centralized enforcement courts of the 16 federal states run the debtor registers that are accessible via one central internet portal.[21] The bailiffs are obliged to transmit the debtor's declaration in.pdf format to the respective central enforcement court (Section 802f (4) ZPO). As a result, creditors can easily access all the debtor's declarations rendered in Germany (Section 882f ZPO). This is a major improvement compared to the fragmented situation before the reform, where the local enforcement courts collected the debtors' declarations in local, decentralized registers and creditors had to contact the local courts to access the respective registers.[22]

The transparency of the debtors' assets in enforcement proceedings is, of course, subject to the constitutional principle of proportionality.[23] Therefore, the declaration can only be requested every two years, unless the creditor specifies considerable changes of the debtor's financial situation (Section 802d (1) ZPO). Before summoning the debtor, the bailiff needs to check whether a declaration is already available in the central registers. In this instance, the bailiff immediately transmits the declaration to the creditor (Section 802d (2) ZPO).[24] Furthermore, if the debtor satisfies the claim, the declaration will be removed from the register.

2.2.2 Information from Third Parties

The major improvement introduced with the reform relates to the possibility of the bailiff to request information from third parties (public authorities). According to Section 802l ZPO, the bailiff may access the statutory pension insurance funds to obtain the name and address of the debtor's employer, the Federal Central Tax Office to obtain the details of the debtor's bank account and/or the Federal Motor

[20] The content of the declaration corresponds largely to the former declaration of the debtor (cf. the former sec. 807 ZPO), *Alsfasser*, Sachaufklärung, p. 28 et seq.

[21] https://justiz.de/onlinedienste/vollstreckungsportal/index.php.

[22] In practice, private service provider collected the information held in the decentralized registers and offered it (against payment) to interested creditors, cf. *Hess*, Die Neuorganisation des Gerichtsvollzieherwesens in Deutschland (2006), p. 20 et seq.

[23] *Alsfasser*, Sachaufklärung, p. 48 *et seq*.

[24] *Vollkommer*, NJW 2012, 3681, 3684.

authority to obtain information about the debtor's car. Being a subsidiary means of investigation, this information shall be requested when the debtor does not disclose or only insufficiently discloses his financial situation.[25] However, the creditor may request the bailiff to immediately request information from third parties when it is foreseeable that the debtor's known assets will not suffice to satisfy the claim. Since 2016, the minimum threshold of an enforceable claim of 500 EUR does not longer exist.[26] From its objective, Section 802l ZPO shall not only operate as a source of information for the creditor, it shall also provide the bailiff with additional information to control the appropriateness of the debtor's declaration.

Once the bailiff gets the information, he transmits it to the creditor (Section 802l (3) ZPO). The latter must decide whether he requests the competent enforcement organ (Section 828 ZPO: the court officer) to start garnishment proceedings into the bank account (Sections 829 and 835 ZPO). However, the information about the details of bank account does not imply that there is sufficient money to satisfy the creditor's claim. Once the account has been seized, the bank will be obliged to inform the court officer about the balance (Section 840 ZPO). As a result, the arrest of the account may eventually fail.

However, the bailiff will inform the debtor about the information request only 4 weeks after the transmittal of the information about the account to the creditor. This sequencing allows the creditor to benefit from the "surprise effect" and prevents any warning of the debtor about the imminence of enforcement proceedings.[27]

The practical importance of the new information system is great as it opens up to the creditor the possibility to get comprehensive information about the debtor's bank accounts. This source of information did not exist before leaving the creditors without any possibility of effectively searching the debtor's accounts. Prior to the reform, some debtors tried to overcome the information deficit by requesting the overall seizure of "all accounts of the debtor within all banks located in Frankfurt". However, the Federal Civil Court held that these requests for "search orders" did not sufficiently specify the targeted bank account and were abusive. The legal literature harshly criticised the insufficient protection of creditors in enforcement proceedings.

---

[25] Beck-Online Commentary/*Fleck*, Sec. 802 l ZPO, para 2.

[26] In the practice, the statutory pension fund insurance does not answer to requests for claims below 500 EUR as the Section 74a Sozialgesetzbuch X requires an enforceable claim of more than 500 EUR. Obviously, the German lawmaker was not sufficiently aware of the applicable legal framework, Beck-Online Commentary/*Fleck*, Section 802l ZPO, para 5.

[27] *Vollkommer*, NJW 2012, 3681, 3686.

3 European Developments

3.1 The Maintenance Regulation, Articles 51(2), 61–63 Reg. (EC) 4/2009

The recent reforms at the domestic level largely correspond to parallel developments in European procedural law. Here, the EU lawmaker has highlighted the need for providing for sufficient transparency in enforcement proceedings in order to guarantee the creditor's right to effective judicial protection (Article 47 CFR and Article 6 ECHR).[28] The insufficient situation at the domestic level is much more problematic in cross-border settings. Here, creditors are confronted with the basic situation whereby enforcement proceedings are strictly regulated by national law and, therefore, creditors must access the national procedures in order to get basic information about the debtor's financial situation. As a result, creditors face a double hurdle: first, they need to access the (diverse) national systems on the obtaining of information about the debtor's financial situation. Second, based on the potential information obtained, they must start enforcement proceedings under the (foreign) national laws.[29]

The Maintenance Regulation is the first EU instrument to overcome these practical impediments. This does not come as a surprise: there is a strong interest of the Member States to provide for an effective mechanism to enforce maintenance claims as there is a strong involvement of public authorities in this field of law. Usually, public institutions need to pay maintenance when the maintenance debtor does not pay it: Creditors (especially left alone mothers) do not have any possibility to get support from other persons. Therefore, social welfare steps in and pays the maintenance. In return, the maintenance claim is transferred to the public authority in order to collect it from the debtor. This is the reason why the cross-border recovery of maintenance claims has become a priority for the Hague Conference on Private International Law and for the EU lawmaker.[30]

The 2009 EU Regulation on Maintenance provides for a two-track system to facilitate the cross-border recovery of maintenance claims.[31] On the one hand, it empowers the individual creditor to claim and enforce maintenance obligations within the European Judicial Area. On the other hand, Article 49 et seq. provide for a system of cooperation among central authorities of EU Member States to collect maintenance claims in cross-border settings. In this regard, Article 51 (2) of Reg. 4/2009 states that the Central Authorities have the specific function.

(a) "to help locate the debtor or the creditor, in particular pursuant to Articles 61–63;

[28] *Hess*, Europäisches Zivilprozessrecht (2nd ed. 2020), Section 10 III with further references.

[29] See footnote 28.

[30] *Hess/Spancken*, in: Beaumont et al. (ed.) The Recovery of Maintenance (2015), pp 385–410.

[31] *Hess*, Europäisches Zivilprozessrecht (2nd ed. 2020), Section 7 IV, with further references.

(b) to help obtain relevant information concerning the income and, if necessary, other financial circumstances of the debtor or creditor, including the location of assets, in particular pursuant to Articles 61–63."

Under Articles 61–63, a Central Authority may request that another Central Authority use all appropriate and reasonable means of its national law to obtain the necessary information to effectively enforce the maintenance claim against the debtor. In this regard, the requested Central Authority shall provide for the following information[32]:

(a) the address of the debtor or of the creditor;
(b) the debtor's income;
(c) the identification of the debtor's employer and/or of the debtor's bank account(s);
(d) the debtor's assets.

The requested Central Authority shall transmit this information only to the requesting Central Authority (not to the individual claimant). The information shall be used exclusively for the recovery/enforcement of the maintenance claim at hand. As a matter of principle, the information is obtained according to the domestic information systems of the EU Member States. However, some Member States enlarged the functions of the Central Authorities under national law in order to provide for an efficient system of information gathering. For instance, the German lawmaker empowered the Federal Office for Justice (Bundesamt für Justiz) to request the pertinent information directly from Federal authorities like the Federal Office for Taxes and the Federal Motor Transportation Authority.[33] As a result, German law now provides for a specific mechanism of the public enforcement of maintenance claims available for foreign creditors coming not only from other EU Member States but also from third States.[34]

3.2 The European Bank Account Preservation Order, Article 14 Reg. (EU) 655/2014[35]

3.2.1 The Regulatory Approach

Article 14 of the EAPO-Regulation provides for a similar mechanism. This instrument permits the cross-border attachment of bank accounts located in the European

[32] Cf. Article 61 (2) Regulation 4/2009.

[33] https://www.bundesjustizamt.de/DE/Themen/Gerichte_Behoerden/ZAEK/ZAEK_node.html; jsessionid=982CEA87B557509B1D0EE13C45A52904.2_cid500.

[34] Section 17 Auslandsunterhaltsgesetz, cf. Münchener Kommentar FamFG/*Lipp*, Article 61 EU-Unterhaltsverordnung (2nd ed. 2018), para 16.

[35] This part of the paper is based on empirical research provided by Carlos Santaló Goris, research fellow at the MPI Luxembourg.

Judicial Area.[36] As a matter of principle, a creditor who seeks to attach an account in another EU Member State must specify the account by its IBAN number in the application for attachment (Article 8 no 1 EAPO-Regulation).[37] However, if the creditor does not know the details of the bank account, he or she can apply for a request to investigate the bank account under Article 14 of the Regulation.

The Regulation does not prescribe a specific or language of the application. However, the Implementing Regulation[38] has already integrated a formalised application under Article 14 into the form of the request for a Preservation Order (Article 8). In the application, the creditor must assert that the specific prerequisites of Article 14 of the EAPO-Regulation are met.[39] He or she disposes of an enforceable title; or, in case of a non-enforceable title, the creditor must specify that there is a risk that enforcement is likely to be jeopardized)[40]; and the reasons to believe that there is a bank account of the debtor in the Member State where information is sought. The Regulation does not prescribe the use of any specific language. In practice, many Member States accept requests in English (and in French). The integration of the application for information into the general application form facilitates the usage of Article 14 considerably. The request is filed with the court competent for the issuing of the attachment order. The court assesses the admissibility of the request.

Article 14 requires Member States to designate specific "information authorities"[41] empowered (under national law) to obtain and to transmit the requested information about the bank account. The information authority must not necessarily be a

---

[36] The United Kingdom is not bound by this instrument, creditors located in the United Kingdom are not entitled to make use of the Regulation, see Recital 40.

[37] Article 8 reads as follows: "(1) Applications for a Preservation Order shall be lodged using the form established in accordance with the advisory procedure referred to in Article 52(2). (2) The application shall include the following information: (…).

(a) a number enabling the identification of the bank, such as the IBAN or BIC and/or the name and address of the bank, with which the debtor holds one or more accounts to be preserved;
(b) if available, the number of the account or accounts to be preserved and, in such a case, an indication as to whether any other accounts held by the debtor with the same bank should be preserved;
(c) where none of the information required under point (d) can be provided, a statement that a request is made for the obtaining of account information pursuant to Article 14, where such a request is possible, and a substantiation as to why the creditor believes that the debtor holds one or more accounts with a bank in a specific Member State".

[38] Commission Implementing Regulation (EU) 2016/1823 of 10 October 2016 establishing the forms referred to in Regulation (EU) No 655/2014, OJ 2016 L 283.

[39] Article 14 (2) EAPO-Regulation: "The creditor shall make the request referred to in paragraph 1 in the application for the Preservation Order. The creditor shall substantiate why he believes that the debtor holds one or more accounts with a bank in the specific Member State and shall provide all relevant information available to him about the debtor and the account or accounts to be preserved".

[40] ECJ, Case C-555/18, *K.H.K. (Saisie conservatoire des comptes bancaires)* [2019] ECLI:EU:C:2019:652, Opinion AG Szpunar, para. 7 et seq.

[41] According to Article 50(1)(b), by 17 July 2016, the Member State had to communicate to the Commission "the authority designated as competent to obtain account information." Until today, all Member States but Romania have appointed their respective national information authorities.

central body; several Member States designated bailiffs or the national chambers of bailiffs as information authority.[42] However, most Member States designated central authorities, for instance, Germany the Federal Office of Justice. Creditors can find the pertinent information about the designated authorities at the e-justice portal.[43]

On the substance, Article 14 of the EAPO-Regulation does not intend to harmonize the different systems of the Member States to obtain information about the debtor's assets. The aim of the article is to open up the different national systems in the EU-Member States to foreign creditors. Consequently, Article 14 (5) EAPO refers to the different information systems in the EU Member States. It states:

(5) "Each Member State shall make available in its national law at least one of the following methods of obtaining the information referred to in paragraph 1:

(a) an obligation on all banks in its territory to disclose, upon request by the information authority, whether the debtor holds an account with them;
(b) access for the information authority to the relevant information where that information is held by public authorities or administrations in registers or otherwise;
(c) the possibility for its courts to oblige the debtor to disclose with which bank or banks in its territory he holds one or more accounts where such an obligation is accompanied by an in personam order by the court prohibiting the withdrawal or transfer by him of funds held in his account or accounts up to the amount to be preserved by the Preservation Order[44]; or
(d) any other methods which are effective and efficient for the purposes of obtaining the relevant information, provided that they are not disproportionately costly or time-consuming.

Irrespective of the method or methods made available by a Member State, all authorities involved in obtaining the information shall act expeditiously".

Article 15 of the EAPO-Regulation refers to the different methods to investigate the debtor's financial situation without providing for any minimum standard.[45] The only obligation imposed on the authorities of the Member States is to act "expeditiously." This is generally the case. Most of the EU Member States (Estonia, France, Poland, Ireland) respond to information requests within a couple of days (less than a week). However, the situation in Luxembourg is different, as Luxemburgish law

On 10 October 2019, the European Commission initiated a sanctions procedure against Romania for failing to appoint an information authority.

[42] Especially France and the Netherlands where the bailiffs (organized as liberal professionals) act as the competent organ for all enforcement proceedings.

[43] European Account Preservation Order. National information and online forms concerning Regulation No. 655/2014. <https://e-justice.europa.eu/content_european_account_preservation_order-379-en.do>, accessed on 26 October 2019.

[44] Requesting a declaration from the debtor may deprive the creditor of the "surprise effect" as the debtor gets a warning about the imminent enforcement proceedings.

[45] This vague term contradicts many time limits found in other provisions of the Regulation.

requires the banks to respond within 20 days. The Spanish authorities respond within one months. It has been reported, that the German Federal Office for Justice processes requests within 48 h.

The information provided under Article 14 of the EAPO-Regulation is limited to the identification of the bank account. Usually, the requested authority will provide the name and/or address of the bank nor the IBAN, BIC or another bank number. In practice, many information authorities directly request this information from the banks[46] or from (tax) authorities where all bank accounts are registered.[47] The limited scope of the information mechanism under Article 14 facilitates its effective application in practice. Often, the information is exchanged in an informal way (by fax or e-mail); many authorities permit the use of several languages. Due to its limited scope, Article 14 does not provide for any formal standardization of the procedure. In order to protect the debtor, the information is not given directly to the creditor but to the court issuing the asset preservation order, instead. Once the information has been obtained, the court may immediately seize the targeted bank account.

3.2.2 The Practical Application of Article 14—First Results of an Empirical Enquiry

In the framework of a broader study on the practical application of EU instruments of procedural law[48] a researcher of the MPI Luxembourg investigated the application of Article 14 EAPO-Regulation since January 2017. It does not come as a surprise that the number of requests is still limited, this is mainly due to the lacking familiarity with the new EAPO-Regulation. However, the German authority responded so far to 70 requests, the Spanish authority reported having received about 60 requests, and the Luxembourg authority processed 24 requests. Other Member States (Belgium, Estonia, Poland) received less than 10 requests.

It is certainly too early to draw any far-reaching conclusions from these figures. However, they demonstrate that the EAPO-Regulation and its new information tool are used in practice. However, there is still insufficient knowledge about the new EU instrument in the Member States. In this regard, the information available at the e-justice portal is of great importance. Unfortunately, the portal does not provide for sufficient information about the implementation of Article 14 of the EAPO-Regulation in all EU-Member States. Specifically, the information is not available in all different languages of the Union; sometimes even an English translation is missing.

---

[46] In Luxembourg, the information authority sends a general request by e-mail to all banking institutions in the country.

[47] This is the case in Belgium Bulgaria, Croatia, France, Germany, Italy, Lithuania, Poland and Spain.

[48] IC2BE, cf. Cross-Border Enforcement in Europe: Civil Justice Framework, National Courts and the Court of Justice of the European Union—(JUST-AG-2016–02), https://www.mpi.lu/research/department-of-european-and-comparative-procedural-law/research-projects/ic2be-project/.

4 The Protection of the Debtor: Data Protection, Privacy and Asset Tracing

Finally, the legal protection of the debtor needs to be addressed. Traditionally, the debtor's obligation to disclose all his or her assets was undisputed as the debtor has the obligation to satisfy the enforceable claim of the creditor.[49] Consequently, the debtor's failure to disclose all his or her assets may ultimately be sanctioned with personal arrest.[50] However, the constitutional principle of proportionality limits the debtor's obligation to disclose its financial situation. Under German law, the declaration can only be requested every two years. Eventually, the court must release debtor from the personal arrest after a maximum period of six months. On the other hand, the debtor's obligation to disclose the financial situation does not depend on the value of the enforceable claim. In 2016, the German legislator abolished the minimum threshold of 500,00 EUR.

Furthermore, the protection of the debtor operates through strict procedural requirements (Section 802f ZPO). In this regard, the formal requirements of enforcement proceedings are fully applicable. At all stages of the procedure, the debtor may challenge the legality of the bailiff's actions before the enforcement court (Section 766 ZPO).[51] When the enforcement organ obtains information from third parties, data protection law requires that the organs inform in due time the debtor about the processing of his or her data. Finally, the German lawmaker protects the privacy of the debtor by requiring a legitimate interest as a prerequisite of the (direct) access to the debtor register (Section 882f ZPO).[52] Access to registers held by tax authorities (Section 802l ZPO) is restricted to the bailiff. Similarly, Article 14 EAPO-Regulation restrict the information exchange between the issuing court and the information authority.[53] In this regard, the discovery within the enforcement procedures seems to be much more desirable than the tracing of the debtor's assets by private service providers.

References

Hess (2009) Rechtspolitische Perspektiven der Zwangsvollstreckung. Juristenzeitung 662, 664

Trocker (2011) The right to effective enforcement of civil judgments and orders: lessons from the case law of the European Court of Human Rights. In: Stürner/Kawano (ed) Comparative studies on enforcement and provisional measures, p 21

[49] The critic of *Weiss*, Selbstbezichtigungsfreiheit und vollstreckungsrechtliche Vermögensauskunft, NJW 2014, 503 et seq. is not justified; cf. *Alfasser*, Sachaufklärung, p. 70 et seq.

[50] Bundesverfassungsgericht, 19 October 1982, NJW 1983, 559.

[51] *Vollkommer*, NJW 2012, 3681, 3685.

[52] Alternatively, a limitation of the access to the bailiffs might be an option, *Alfasser*, Sachaufklärung, p. 67 et seq.

[53] This restriction is imposed by data protection.

Burkhard Hess born in Worms, Germany in 1961, became founding and executive director of the Max Planck Institute Luxembourg for International, European and Regulatory Procedural Law in September 2012. He studied law at the Universities of Würzburg, Lausanne and Munich and graduated in Munich in 1990. After being granted Venia Legendi in civil law, civil procedure, private international law, European law and public international law in 1996, he held chairs at the Universities of Tübingen and Heidelberg. He was a guest professor in Beijing, in Paris (Sorbonne) and in Georgetown, and served as a part-time judge at the Court of Appeal of Karlsruhe. Professor Hess often acts as an expert and advisor to the European Commission, the European Parliament, the Council of Europe and national governments. Recently, he has evaluated the European Insolvency Regulation and the Brussels I Regulation. He has also contributed to the drafting of the proposal for the Regulation on the European Attachment of Bank Accounts. He is the author of various books on German and European civil procedural law as well as co-editor of IPRax and of Kölner Kommentar zum Kapitalanleger-Musterverfahrensgesetz. He is President of the ILA Committee on the Protection of Privacy in Private International and Procedural Law.

Effective Rights Protection in Civil Enforcement

Some Comments from a French Point of View

Loïc Cadiet

I will not comment on Burkhard Hess' report that I have just heard, as always, with great interest. This report, however, gives me an opportunity for brief and general observations on the evolution of French law on civil enforcement with regard to the protection of fundamental rights. From this point of view, three kinds of observations can be made, respectively devoted to the meaning of evolution (I), the role of the judge (II) and the notion of trial (III).

1 Meaning of Evolution

From a historical perspective, the evolution of enforcement in civil matters must be considered in comparison with enforcement in criminal matters. This evolution has two stages: a differentiation step (A) and an approximation step (B).

A The *stage of differentiation* starts from the common origin of civil execution and criminal execution. Originally, these two contemporary forms of enforcement are not really dissociated, neither are civil liability and criminal liability, civil procedure and criminal procedure.

For France, differentiation really takes place only during the Ancien Régime and it finds its first normative concretization in the codification of French law carried out in the seventeenth century, under Colbert, Louis XIV's prime minister, with, on the

Professor at the Sorbonne Law School (Paris 1 university) Former IAPL President.

L. Cadiet (✉)
Sorbonne Law School (Paris 1 University), Paris, France
e-mail: Cadiet@univ-paris1.fr

M. Deguchi (ed.), *Effective Enforcement of Creditors' Rights*,
Ius Gentium: Comparative Perspectives on Law and Justice 91,
https://doi.org/10.1007/978-981-16-5609-5_5

one hand, the Civil Ordinance concerning the reform of justice, in April 1667,[1] on the other hand, the Criminal Ordinance in August 1670.[2]

The differentiation process has continued to develop since then until the contemporary period, in a logic of normative autonomy in which the Napoleonic codification has of course played an important role with the promulgation of two different codes. The Code of Civil Procedure of 1806 and the Code of Criminal Procedure of 1808 contain, each of them, specific provisions for the execution of judgments, but this execution is conceived differently. The Code of Civil Procedure devotes to it a full body of specific rules grouped in an whole book, the Book V of the first part, while the Code of Criminal Procedure rules execution with judgment, without considering it separately, at the difference of the current Code of Criminal Procedure, which devotes an entire book, the Book V, to enforcement proceedings (sections 707 to 803-7). In civil matters, the execution even left the Code of Civil Procedure in 2012 to be the subject of a specific code, the Code of Civil Enforcement Procedures (*Code des procédures civiles d'exécution, CPCE*). Enforcement in criminal matters could follow the same trend with the prospect of creating a "penitentiary code" (*Code pénitentiaire*) or an "enforcement code" (*Code de l'exécution des peines*) encompassing all the texts relating to the enforcement of criminal decisions and the adjustment of sentences.

B However, and in a manner that is paradoxical only in appearance, the formal differentiation of civil execution and criminal execution does not exclude some substantive convergences.

The most important convergence is a historical phenomenon of softening of execution, both in civil and criminal matters.

In criminal cases, this phenomenon of softening is illustrated by the paradigmatic abolition of the death penalty, of course, but also by the development of the penalty of fines and alternative penalties to imprisonment, as well as through the tendency to certain forms of decriminalization which give way to civil or administrative sanctions.

In civil matters, the phenomenon is also well known: the execution moved from the body of the person to his property:[3] the debtor is no longer sold as a slave ; he is no longer cut into pieces in case of several creditors; he is no longer imprisoned for debt. The execution is limited to its property and, even on this ground, it comes up against several limits consisting, for example, in the prior use of the astreinte,[4] the unseizability of different kinds of goods,[5] and the hierarchy of seizures like,

---

[1] Ordonnance civile touchant la réformation de la justice, avr. 1667, Saint-Germain en Laye, spéc. Titre XXVII : *De l'exécution des jugements.*

[2] Ordonnance criminelle, août 1670, Saint-Germain en Laye.

[3] On this phenomenon of softening, see J. CARBONNIER, *Droit civil*, volume 2: «Les biens, Les obligations», 2004, PUF, «Quadrige», n° 1281, pp. 2524 et 2525.

[4] CPCE, art. L. 131-1 *sq* and R. 131-1 *sq.*

[5] In its most classical aspects (furniture, food, etc.: CPCE art L. 112-2), up to its contemporary renewal for the benefit of entrepreneurs (with the declaration of unseizability of the principal residence of the individual entrepreneur and his spouse: C. com., art. L. 526-1 *sq*).

for instance, the subsidiarity of seizure of movable goods (saisie-vente) relative to attachment of bank accounts (saisie-attribution).[6]

Here as there is even a phenomenon of contractualisation of the execution.[7] In criminal matters, the execution of the penal sanction can be done in a contractual way, whether it is for example by means of a criminal settlement[8] or by means of a Judicial Convention of Public Interest, which is a kind of Deferred Prosecution Agreement, recently introduced in the Code of Criminal Procedure by a law of 9 December 2016.[9] In civil matters, there is a public policy favoring alternative enforcement on an amicable basis amicable recovery, amicable sale, amicable distribution, amicable execution.

In this evolution, the intervention of the judge played an important role.

2 Role of the Judge

I will focus from here on only on the execution in civil matters.

The time is no longer when, as soon as the judgment was pronounced, the severity of the law fell like lightning upon the person who had been condemned. In addition to the introduction of turnaround times, taking into account the possible appeal period, the civil execution experienced a double process of judiciarization and jurisdictionalisation. Sorry for these neologisms.

Judicialization is defined here as the intervention of a judge specialized in the process of execution of judgments, being specified that the intervention of this judge is not compulsory, in the absence of difficulty in the course of enforcement. In civil matters, the institution of a judge dedicated to enforcement proceedings dates from 1991. A veritable man-orchestrator of the execution, the *juge de l'exécution*, the enforcement judge, is in principle a specialized judge of the court of first instance, whose competence is defined by the Code of the judicial organization.[10]

As for *jurisdictionalization*, it reflects the idea that enforcement decisions are not administrative decisions, but real judgments, with the consequences that this entails from the point of view of respect for the fundamental procedural principles, whether

---

6 CPCE, art. L. 221-2.

7 See espec. about C. civ., art. 1244-4 (issued L. n°2015-990, 6 August 2015), which has been analyzed as a participatory implementation tool: L. LAUVERGNAT, «La procédure simplifiée de recouvrement des petites créances de l'article 1244-4 du Code civil : vers une exécution participative ?», *D.* 2015, pp. 1860 *sq.* The provision of this article was quickly transferred to the Code of Civil Enforcement Procedures: CPCE, art. L. 125-1 (Order No. 2016-131, Feb. 10, 2016), where it is supplementad by regulatory provisions: CPCE, art. R. 125-1 to R. 126-6 (issued D. n° 2016-285, 9 March 2016).

8 « Where the law expressly provides » (CPP - Code of criminal procedure, art. 6, al. 3).

9 CPP, art. 41-1-2, issued L. n° 2016-1691, 9 déc. 2016 on transparency, the fight against corruption and the modernization of economic life, art.22.

10 COJ—Code of the judicial organization (*Code de l'organisation judiciaire*), art. L. 213-5 to L. 213.

during or after the execution procedure. This jurisdictionalization was imposed quite naturally in civil matters. The enforcement judge is exclusively competent to decide on the difficulties relating to the enforceable titles and to the objections raised during the execution, "*even if they relate to the substance of the law*"[11] and the proceedings before the enforcement judge follow, unless otherwise stipulated, the common provisions of the Civil Procedure Code.[12]

In truth, following the judicialization and the jurisdictionalization of the civil enforcement, it is a phenomenon of processualization of the execution of the judgments which is given to see, which leads to the third and last series of remarks, relating to the notion of trial.

3 The Notion of Trial

Processualization means the fact that the execution has become part of the trial. It has not always been so. In the French tradition, the trial refers to the litigation brought before the judge; it is therefore limited to the proceedings, which go from the referral of the judge to the judgment he delivers. Traditionally, what precedes the referral to the judge and what follows the judgment was not included in the notion of trial. In the 1970s, two famous authors, Pierre Catala and François Terré, were still writing: «The trial devotes the right, the execution prolongs the trial»,[13] which meant that the execution was not part of the trial.

But, in truth, as dean Jacques Normand had judiciously observed, "litigation can only be calmed once the decision has been executed".[14] The judgment does not extinguish the dispute, so the trial. Therefore, the execution must be considered as a phase of the trial.

This conception is adopted by the European Court of Human Rights since 1997, in the *Hornsby* case, which has made the right to the effective enforcement of judgments one of the guarantees of the right to a fair trial, hence an element of the trial.[15] It is clear that the right of access to a judge to get a judgment in conditions which

[11] COJ, art. L. 213-6, al. 1, without being able, however, to modify the operative part of the court decision on which the enforcement is based, or to suspend its execution (CPCE, art. R. 121-1, al. 2).

[12] CPCE, art. R. 121-5.

[13] P. CATALA P. and F. TERRE, *Procédure civile et voies d'exécution*, Paris, PUF, 2e éd. 1976, espec. p. 421.

[14] V. J. NORMAND, *Le juge et le litige*, LGDJ, 1965, preface R. PERROT, n° 21 to 24, espec. n° 24. Confer Cass. 1re civ., 12 July 2012, n° 09-11582, *D.* 2012, 2577, note Pailler ; *Gaz. Pal.* 7-8 Dec. 2012, 30, obs. BLÉRY, deciding that the compromise terminates the dispute only subject to its execution.

[15] Since ECHR, 19 March 1997, *Hornsby v. Greece, JCP* G 1997, II, 22949, note DUGRIP et SUDRE ; *D.* 1998, 74, note FRICERO ; *RGDP* 1998, 230, obs. FLAUSS. And then ECHR CEDH, 7 March 2013, n° 10131/11, *RAW v. France, Rev. huissiers* 2014, Dr. proc. intern. 20, n° 13, obs. FRICERO, stating that the non-enforcement of a judgment enshrining a right guaranteed by the Convention constitutes a violation of this right, and not merely a violation of Article 6 (1).

ensure the fairness of the proceedings would be of no avail if the public authorities could impede the execution of the judgment or evade the execution of the judgment. As proclaimed in Article 16 of the French Declaration of human rights, "any society in which no provision is made for guaranteeing rights or for the separation of powers, has no Constitution". It is precisely on the basis of this provision that the French Constitutional Council, in 2015, has constitutionalized the right to the effective enforcement of judgments as part of the right to a judicial remedy.[16]

The circle has been closed.

Loïc Cadiet professor at the Sorbonne Law School of the University of Panthéon-Sorbonne Paris 1 (Paris, France). He studied law in Angers, Nantes and Poitiers where he received his State Doctorate in Law in 1983. Appointed as a Full Professor in 1984, he taught in the faculties of law of Rennes (1984/1992), Nantes (1992/1996) before he was elected at the Sorbonne Law School where he teaches civil procedure, general theory of procedure, ADR, administration of justice system and comparative procedural law. He is Emeritus Senior Member of the Institut Universitaire de France and Honorary President of the International Association of Procedural Law. He founded and directed, with Peter Gottwald, then with Burkhard Hess, the International Journal of Procedural Law (Intersentia). Loïc Cadiet is the author or co-author of several books on procedure and justice (e.g. Droit judiciaire privé, with E. Jeuland, Paris, LexiNexis, 11th ed. 2020; Théorie générale du procès, with J. Normand and S. Amrani-Mekki, Paris, PUF, 3rd ed. 2020; Les modes alternatifs de règlement des conflits, with T. Clay, Paris, Dalloz, 3rd ed., 2019; Perspectivas sobre o sistema da justiça civil francês—Seis lições brasileiras, Apresentação L. Guilherme Marinoni, S. Cruz Arenhart e D. Mitidiero, Sao Paulo, Thomson Reuters, 2017; Itinéraires d'histoire de la procédure civile, with S. Dauchy and J. -L. Halpérin, vol. 1 : Regards français, Paris, IRJS Editions, 2014 and vol. 2 : Regards étrangers, Paris, IRJS Editions, 2020 ; Privatizing Dispute Resolution—Trends and Limits, with B. Hess and M. Requejo Isidro, Baden-Baden, Nomos—MPI Luxembourg, 2019 ; Approaches to Procedural Law—The pluralism of Methods, with B. Hess and M. Requejo Isidro, Baden-Baden, Nomos—MPI Luxembourg, 2017; Procedural Science at the Crossroads of Different Generations, with B. Hess andt M. Requejo Isidro, Baden-Baden, Nomos—MPI Luxembourg, 2015). Loïc Cadiet was the editor of the Dictionnaire de la Justice (Presses universitaires de France, 2004) and he is currently the editor of the Code de procédure civile (Paris, LexisNexis, 34th ed. 2021), the Director of the JurisClasseur de procédure civile, encyclopedia of civil procedure (LexisNexis), and the co-Director of Procédures, monthly journal on proceedings and litigation (LexisNexis). Loïc Cadiet is Chevalier dans l'Ordre national de la Légion d'honneur (France), Académico Honorario de la Real Academia de Jurisprudencia y de Legislación (Spain) and foreign member of the Royal Flemish Academy for Science and the Arts (Belgium).

[16] Cons. const., déc. n° 2014-455 QPC, 6 March 2015, cons. 3.

Comments on Information Concerning the Debtor's Assets for the Enforcement Proceeding

Álvaro Pérez Ragone

Abstract As to the question of who can and should provide factual and evidentiary material about the debtor's assets for the purpose of enforcement activities by enforcement bodies, different systems give different answers. Complete and full knowledge of the debtor's assets facilitates the choice of the most efficient and at the same time proportionate and appropriate enforcement measure, and it permits a coordination of several parallel measures. Each legal system has to balance the creditors' right to an efficient enforcement with the debtors' right to adequate data protection. However, full disclosure is a serious intrusion on the debtor's private or business sphere.

1 Introduction

Complete and full knowledge of the debtor's assets facilitates the choice of the most efficient and at the same time proportionate and appropriate enforcement measure, and it permits a coordination of several parallel measures.[1] Each legal system has to balance the creditors' right to an efficient enforcement with the debtors' right to adequate data protection. However, full disclosure is a serious intrusion on the debtor's private or business sphere.[2] A very common means of disclosure is the debtor's declaration, and only very few legal systems do not provide for this instrument of disclosure. There are many variations in detail: duty to declare at the very earlier phase of enforcement proceedings or after an unsuccessful seizure attempt or

[1] Stürner (2016), p. 6.

[2] Stürner (2016), p. 6.

Á. P. Ragone (✉)
Instituto de Estudios Sociales, Políticos y Culturales de la Universidad de San Pablo-Tucumán, Tucumán, Argentina
e-mail: alvaro.perez01@ucn.cl

Univeresidad Católica del Norte, Antofagasta, Chile

M. Deguchi (ed.), *Effective Enforcement of Creditors' Rights*,
Ius Gentium: Comparative Perspectives on Law and Justice 91,
https://doi.org/10.1007/978-981-16-5609-5_6

already in cases where the probability of success is low; full disclosure or identification of assets sufficient for the creditor's enforcement of his claim only; disclosure once and for all or piecemeal disclosure according to the status of success of the enforcement; written declaration under affidavit only or oral examination and cross examination in a court hearing in appropriate cases; registration of refusal to declare in a public register or in a register with limited access only; forced appearance in court for declaration and imprisonment as sanction of last resort or lack of sanctions working in personam.[3] Some jurisdictions empower execution authorities to ask for assistance of public authorities or private agencies holding records containing information on the debtor's assets (requests for information from social security records or fiscal records; information about the debtor's employment from social insurance records, etc.). In most jurisdictions enforcement authorities are empowered to request disclosure of data from public registers with full or limited access (land registers, motor vehicles registers, commercial registers, population registers, etc.). The development of common principles for asset declarations faces the challenge of reaching a satisfying balanced approach taking into consideration the diverging interests of creditors and debtors.[4] The present development in many legal systems moves towards an increase in disclosure of information, whereas the protection of the debtor's data decreases.[5]

2 Conflicts Between Debtor and Creditor

As to the question of who can and should provide factual and evidentiary material about the debtor's assets for the purpose of enforcement activities by enforcement bodies, different systems give different answers. Does the debtor only have a facultative "burden" or is he really under a duty to cooperate with the enforcement organ to provide all relevant information to facilitate the enforcement proceedings? The information relevant to enforcement, such as details of the debtor's assets, is not used to clarify disputed facts between the parties, as it would be in declaratory proceedings.[6]

Most systems require the debtor to make a statement about his assets, as this is the least expensive method of ascertaining what assets he may own. However, the need for an enforcement organ conducting its own research into the debtor's assets arises where there is an allegation that the debtor's declaration is untrue or that it has not been carried through. Only in these circumstances would it be acceptable to compel the debtor to provide access to certain sources of information. The question

[3] Stürner (2016), p. 6.

[4] Alsfasser (2018), p. 5–25.

[5] Stürner (2016), p. 6.

[6] If it is appropriate, discuss the clarification of facts and proof of execution, where there is opposition or third parties involved, or third parties assert the limited number of remedies made. If enforcement is possible even in the cases where the evidence is necessary to clarify the allegations, the factual scope of discussion is already very limited. Capponi (2001), p. 28.

of requiring a statement to be made by the debtor about his assets raises a number of moral as well as legal dilemmas, including the conflict between the debtor's duty to cooperate and the need to respect his right to silence.[7]

The statement of the debtor can be reached consensually, and need not necessarily be a tool to facilitate enforcement, or a coercive means to ensure the debt is paid. The creditor benefits from obtaining a manifest declaration of the debtor's assets in the early stages of enforcement, thus saving the need for subsequent requests.[8] Seeking an initial statement of the debtor's assets is especially advisable in the cross-border (national, regional and international) context, as this will enable the creditor to seek enforcement in the State where the majority of debtor's assets are concentrated, and where there will be a greater prospect of success. Finally, different systems react differently to a debtor refusing to provide the declaration or concealing of his assets.[9] The debtor may face dissuasive criminal sanctions (for example when held in contempt of court), but other functional devices to encourage compliance include the imposition of fines or periodical penalty payments in favor of the creditor (for example French *astreintes*).[10] The potential for a European declaration of debtor's assets has been discussed at the EU level, and many of the replies in response agreed that such a declaration would be useful. In some jurisdictions, it is still unclear whether the power to imprison a debtor should be viewed as a primary penalty or as a secondary penalty and coercive measure if the debtor refuses to pay the penalty fine. Some systems view the contempt of court measures not as a "debtor's prison" but as direct penalty for failing to cooperate with the enforcement organism.[11] I will return to this subject as it is connected with non-money enforcement and disobedience of courts orders. There I will discuss the coercive measures and their limitation and form.[12]

3 The Role of IT: Register and Database

The computerised systems available to a creditor pursuing a debtor's assets abroad vary from system to system: in states with more modern legislation, the judicial or administrative authority takes the initiative in forcing the debtor to make a statement of assets, and may also conduct searches on public, or even sometimes private, registers. This section considers the current operation of these devices in the various

[7] Stürner (1981), p. 1757, 1760.

[8] Leroy (2000), p. 273.

[9] Alsfasser (2018), p. 20–30.

[10] Kengyel (2014), p. 1–14.

[11] See case *JST BTA Bank v. Solodchenko* (no2) 2011 in (2011) EWHC 2163 (Ch).

[12] Holzapfel (2008), p. 30–45.

systems. It also addresses the optimum configuration for their use, given that the information should be protected to prevent its misuse during enforcement, and especially to protect the personal data of the debtor.[13]

Access to registers and other databases with a public character may be sought either by the creditor, especially if the debt is significant, or by the enforcement organ, either because the system in question does not require the debtor to make a statement, or because relevant sources of information are not open to the public, for example databases managed by the tax authorities, or those that have significant safeguards and regulations in place due to the cooperation of financial institutions. There are additional complications which arise in relation to accessing foreign records. The complex and utopian scenario in which this is always possible remains far from reality. Not only are some opposed to the concept, there are also difficult technical barriers.[14]

The contribution of the new technologies in increasing the efficiency of enforcement and searching for debtor's assets is remarkable. According to the principle of non-discrimination on grounds of nationality, access to records should not be problematic either for national or international creditors. This goal could be achieved simply by ensuring electronic access to records. However, electronic access to records without any control over the enquirer (such as an electronic signature or conditions imposed by the enforcement organism), would make it impossible to verify of the legitimate interests of the person making the enquiry. A judicial order should be required, where appropriate, compelling the enquirer only to use the information obtained for the purposes of formal proceedings.[15]

4 General Conclusions: Open Questions

Civil judgments are not automatically enforced by the enforcement organism because it is necessary for successful parties to make an application to the court for enforcement. It may also be necessary to adopt some provisional cautionary measures in order to ensure a later, successful enforcement, for example in the preventive taking of assets from the debtor by means of a judicial order. Once the judgment is enforceable, the enforcement organ could order all the necessary measures in order to obtain the amount of money that is owed by the debtor (including costs), usually by public auction: the item seized from the debtor is sold, and after deduction of the expenses of execution (costs that should be paid by the enforcement debtor) the judgment creditor is paid, and their rights are satisfied.[16]

[13] For example, the provisions of Directive 95/46/EC.

[14] Cf. Kengyel (2014), 1–14.

[15] For a comparative and general overview see Lupoi (2012), p. 181.

[16] Krings (2000), p. 221.

The constitutionalisation of civil procedure as a whole is a reality, and provides an invitation to discuss the constitutionalisation of enforcement. Which constitutional constraints, requirements and are applicable to enforcement? Let me conclude this General Report with some proposals.

(i) First, there is a constitutional structure and requirements according to which effective right protections need a fully functional enforcement law. In order to respect the fundmental rights of both creditor and debtor, enforcement law is constitutionally required. This relates to requiring full enforcement and implementation as an additional stage, rather than merely having a binding judicial declaration about a substantive right.

(ii) Second, in the course of enforcement proceedings, conflicts between the rights of the creditor and debtor might arise. Are the procedural law regulations sufficient to resolve these conflicts? Would it be better for the Constitutional Law and the rights it protects to be applied directly?

(iii) The third aspect to be considered is the fact that enforcement will always affect and touch the debtor's personal and propriety rights. The principles of enforcement proceedings create a proposal for an intermediate solution, which combines principles of procedural, private and public Law, with an adequate and strong link to Constitutional Law. The constitutional norms should not be directly and exclusively applicable to enforcement, but may be applied on a case by case when enforcement law is not sufficiently clear and complete.[17]

(iv) The proportionality principle is usually ruled with other designation in the enforcement proceedings as balance for the specific application case by case. The proportionality in the enforcement has a double role,[18] first as limitation for the enforcement acts, and second as balance to ponderate the admissibility of the enforcement and each measure. The enforcement acts are under reasonableness control as sub-constitutional law.[19]

In other words, the enforcement barriers determine whether and to what extent at this time to satisfying the claim of the debtor is foreseeable and reasonable. The attachment/ seizure's barriers can eventually be a win–win solution for all parties involved eventually. Many barriers not only ensure the existence of the debtor and his family, but also play a major part in ensuring that the debtor can continue his employment or self activity. This can initially be in the immediate interest of the creditor by him thus for the future in the form of a substrate of income garnishment substrate secured for the future. The fact that the debtor is still actively working is also naturally of economic interest.[20]

There are possible coalitions of various fundamental rights that might be more or less relevant to a specific case of enforcement, depending on the protected debtor's and creditor's interests.[21] Although these principles are in fact general principles not

[17] Verbeke (2001), p. 7.

[18] Stürner (2010), p. 285.

[19] Crivelli (2012), p. 25.

[20] Cf. Super (2013), p. 1773–1780.

[21] Vollkommer (1982), p. 1–9.

only of enforcement but of the legal system in general, the review of State action assumes special features in the enforcement.[22] These must therefore be considered on a case-by-case basis which allows us to differentiate the assumptions in enforcement that are either different or similar to general principles concerning the exercise of force and coercion of the State, for example those addressing the exercise of punitive and preventative provisions. Maybe it is possible to focus on balance and fairness when talking about conflicts between fundamental rights.[23] The fairness principle covers both procedural and material fairness. The procedural fairness in the enforcement process is not identical to fairness required at the trial stage.

References

Alsfasser A (2018) Sachaufklärung in der Einzelzwangsvollstreckung. Mohr Siebeck, Tübingen
Baer S (2009) Dignity, liberty, equality: a fundamental rights triangle of constitutionalism. Univ Tor Law J 59(4):417–468
Capponi B (2001) Alcuni problemi sul contraddittorio e processo esecutivo (alla luce del nuovo art. Ili della Costituzione). Riv Esec Forz 1:28. (et seq)
Crivelli A (2012) (2012) La natura e le fonti dell'essecuzione forzata. In: Crivelli A (ed) Esecuzione forzata e processo esecutivo. Utet, Torino, pp 25–51
Holzapfel C (2008) Sachaufklärung und Zwangsvollstreckung in Europa. Nomos, Berlin
Kengyel M (2014) Transparency of assets and enforcement. Unif L Rev 1–14
Krings E (2000) Le delai raisonnable a la lumiere de la jurisprudence de la Cour de Strasbourg. Vers un droit substantiel a l'execution des decisions de justice. in L'efficacité de la justice civile en europe. Larcier, Brussels 2000:221–245
Leroy É (2000) L'efficacité des procédures judiciaires au sein de l'union Européenne et les garanties des droits de la défense. In: de Leval-MT Caupain (ed) Europe G Transparence patrimoniale, L'efficacité de la justice civile. Litec, Bruxelles, pp. 273–402.
Lupoi M (2012) Enforcement of a claim with the support of the new information technology. In: Nemessányi KM (ed) Protection of the creditor and the debtor. Electronic Technology and Civil Procedure. Springer, Dordrecht, p 181
Stürner M (2010) Der Grundsatz der Verhältnissmässigkeit im Schuldvertragsrecht. Mohr Siebeck, Tübingen
Stürner R (1981) Strafrechtliche Selbstbelastung und verfahrensförmige Wahrheitsermittlung. Neue Juristische Wochenschrift (NJW) 1757:1760
Stürner R (2016) Principles of effective enforcement feasibility study. UNIDROIT 2016 C.D. (95) 13 Add. 2 Original. https://www.unidroit.org/english/governments/councildocuments/2016session/cd-95-13add-02-e.pdf
Super DA (2013) A new property. C Law Rev 113(7):1773–1896
Tarzia G (2002) Il giusto processo di esecuzione. Riv Dir Proc 329. (et seq)
Verbeke A (2001) Execution officers as a balance wheel in insolvency cases. TFLR-Civ Law 7. (et seq)
Vollkommer M (1982) Verfassungsmäßigkeit des Vollstreckungszugriffs. Rpfleger 1–9

[22] Tarzia (2002), p. 329.
[23] Baer (2009), p. 417–468.

Alvaro Pérez Ragone currently works at the Facultad de Ciencias Jurídicas, Universidad Católica del Norte (Chile) as visiting lecturer and at the Universidad San Pablo-Tucumán (Argentina). Alvaro's research fields are Civil Justice, Civil Procedure, Civil Procedure History, Comparative Civil Procedure, Legal Fundaments and Civil Law. I studied at the Universidad Nacional de Tucumán (Argentina) and I hold both my LL.M. and Doctor Iuris degree at University of Cologne (Germany). For more details about the publication please see https://www.researchgate.net/profile/Alvaro_Ragone.

America's BYO Approach to Enforcing Money Judgments

Comment on Rechberger and Hess

Richard Marcus

Abstract The role undertaken by the court in enforcing money judgments varies in different countries. It appears that in Germany and Austria court officials shoulder considerable responsibility in identifying and locating assets of a judgment debtor so that the judgment creditor can initiate execution against those assets to satisfy the judgment. In the US, those who obtain money judgments do not receive such help from bailiffs or other court personnel. But they can use broad American discovery, including discovery from third parties, to locate the assets for themselves, gaining direct access to the information about assets and location. This paper labels the American approach a BYO approach, invoking a term used by American university students to signal in party invitations that people must bring their own liquor if they want to drink at the party. Similarly, American judgment creditors must take the initiative to locate assets subject to execution. To do that, they not only can use official discovery but also various self-help measures. Ultimately, however, US procedure does not regard the enforcement of a money judgment (as opposed to an injunction) as the court's responsibility.

1 Introduction

The problem of enforcing a money judgment exists in every legal system, but the methods and orientation vary significantly. For much of the world. these problems are viewed as a matter of civil procedure, as well they might be since the rest of civil procedure (dealing with the methods available to parties seeking to obtain favorable judgments) would be of limited utility if those judgments could not ultimately be enforced.

As in so many things, America stands somewhat apart in regard to these matters. For example, matters of judgment enforcement are not typically the focus of a basic civil procedure course. Nearly fifty years ago, I enrolled in a different course

R. Marcus (✉)
University of California, Hastings College of the Law, San Francisco, USA
e-mail: marcusr@uchastings.edu

M. Deguchi (ed.), *Effective Enforcement of Creditors' Rights*,
Ius Gentium: Comparative Perspectives on Law and Justice 91,
https://doi.org/10.1007/978-981-16-5609-5_7

entitled 'Creditors' Remedies and Debtors' Protections,' which delved deeply into these matters. But that was not a part of the basic civil procedure course (which seemingly assumed that court judgments would—somehow magically—be enforced once entered unless overturned on appeal). And nowadays even that academic attention probably no longer occurs. At UC Hastings, for example, we have no course that corresponds to the one I took fifty years ago; our only offering is a course in bankruptcy law, which has become much more complicated in the past fifty years.

As profiled below, the approach of much of the rest of the world—certainly the approach of Germany and Austria featured in the contributions by Professors Hess and Rechberger—involves much more assistance by the court system to those who seek to turn their money judgments into money.

In contrast, one way of looking at the American approach is to invoke a phrase familiar to American university students—BYO. That stands for 'bring your own.' It usually means that a party invitation does not promise to provide alcoholic drinks; those who want them should bring their own. As explained below, US courts are usually fairly indifferent to whether money judgments are enforced; that is a problem for the judgment creditor to solve. But American courts also provide the judgment creditor with very effective tools to solve that problem—broad American discovery to locate assets and then, once the assets have been located, public authority to seize and 'monetize' those assets (usually by conducting an auction often known as a 'sheriff's sale').

Lest it seem that American courts are uniquely ineffective in enforcing money judgments, consider what an American journalist wrote about Japanese courts a quarter century ago. He wrote that in Japan, unlike America, redress in the courts was rarely effective: 'Therefore, to collect on an overdue loan, you can hire a member of a yakuza group to stand outside the home of the debtor and hurl obscenities and insults until the debtor caves. Disputed traffic accidents are handled at times by one party hiring a mobster to intimidate the other into agreeing into a resolution.'[1] THAT's truly a BYO system, if it ever really existed. One hopes that access to effective relief in court is more available in Japan than in the past.

2 The Basic Outline of Contemporary Practice in Germany and Austria

The insightful explanations offered by Professors Hess and Rechberger are presented in full elsewhere in this volume.[2] This brief recapitulation therefore attempts only to point up some features of this practice that seem remarkable to American eyes.

[1] Sterngold (1992).

[2] Rechberger (2020); Hess (2020).

2.1 *Fundamental Right to Judicial Enforcement*

Professor Hess stresses that the right to effective enforcement is regarded as a part of the fundamental right of judicial protection under German law. From this fundamental 'human right' he takes the next step to ensuring that the court itself gather the information about the debtor's assets necessary for the judgment creditor to effectuate the judgment. Much the same orientation is reflected in Professor Rechberger's contribution about judgment enforcement in Austria. Indeed, the enforcement process apparently takes place ex officio without even the need for the judgment creditor to apply for that assistance.

2.2 *Broad Judicial Access to Information About Debtor's Assets*

It is not entirely clear, but from an American perspective the range of information sources available to the self-starter German or Austrian court that seeks to enforce a judgment is striking. This effort can inquire into many records of assets held by the debtor, including real property, motor vehicles and the like. But it can go beyond. One focus is often tax return information of the debtor. Another is social security accounts held by the debtor. Sometimes, it seems, that access can be obtained throughout the entire EU by the court official gathering this information.

This access to governmental records of the debtor's asserts stands in remarkable contrast to the American approach outlined below. Tax records are not ordinarily available to governmental officials outside the taxing authority, the Internal Revenue Service (IRS). Even the Federal Bureau of Investigation (FBI) cannot obtain access to IRS records in ordinary circumstances. The notion that the court would gather such information on its own motion to assist a private judgment creditor in executing a money judgment is thus particularly striking.

As we shall see below, however, the US approach is also different in that it empowers private actors to seek out the information that governmental actors obtain in Germany and Austria. Unlike the systems in those countries—which deny the creditor access to the governmental information itself—in the US the discovery method empowers the creditor to obtain the information that can be obtained directly. Moreover, as explained in the last section below, self help outside the governmental sphere also plays a major role in debt collection in the US.

2.3 *Judicial Assistance in Collecting the Assets*

After the assets are located, the American approach resembles the German and Austrian approach more fully. For most assets, an officer of the court is authorized (using information provided by discovery in the US) to seize and realize upon those assets. At that point, the American approach is no longer BYO (though self help may sometimes be employed in place of the public variety).

3 Outline of the US Approach to Judgment Enforcement of Money Judgments

3.1 The 'Hunting License' Approach

One approach to judgment enforcement is to regard that as part of the court's responsibility. The court has, after all, entered the judgment and proclaimed that the defendant owes the plaintiff the stated sum. As Professor Hess suggests, one may regard carrying through with enforcement as a feature of the 'fundamental right of judicial protection.'[3]

That is not the universal approach. For example, Professor Andrews has recently written of the possibility that the lien that gives Legal Aid in the UK priority in claiming the proceeds of the litigation might eat up much or all of the amount recovered with that legal assistance. He cites a recent English case in which, although the defendant paid the entire adjudicated sum, that money 'was then entirely swept away to satisfy the legal aid authority's statutory charge.'[4] So the plaintiff did not receive a penny despite winning the case. The court found that the fact that the entire sum recovered had been consumed by the Legal Aid bill 'did not infringe the right of access to court implicit in Article 6(1) of the European Convention on Human Rights.'[5]

A moment's reflection will illustrate that actual recovery cannot be guaranteed. Suppose that the judgment debtor simply does not have sufficient funds to pay. To use an old American expression, 'you can't get blood from a stone.' Indeed, there might even be a risk that the judgment is collusive; if the court is somehow responsible to make up for the shortfall in the judgment debtor's assets, that could tempt litigants to collude for judgment to be entered against one who cannot pay in order to entitle the other to payment from government funds. The existence of bankruptcy protections (discussed below) shows that there is a remedy for the situation in which the debts exceed the assets, and it is not to assign the court the responsibility to make up the difference.

In the same vein, default procedures could not be as simple as they are were the court responsible to ensure payment. In the US, if the defendant does not respond

---

[3] Hess (2020), p. 6.

[4] Andrews (2019), p. 6.

[5] Id. See also R (Tirkey) v. Director of Legal Aid Casework [2017] EWHC 3403 [2018] 1 WLR 2112 ('No sensible interpretation of Article 6 involves a guarantee that an individual will recover the award of damages').

to the complaint after proper service, entry of default is relatively automatic.[6] From that, it is a short step to entry of a default judgment, which must be done by the clerk (not the judge) when the complaint seeks a sum certain.[7] Even in cases in which the complaint seeks damages to be determined later, the court does limited work to determine whether the evidence fully supports such recoveries. Partly as a result, there have been instances of judgments for very large damages awarded by default against defendants accused of supporting terrorists who have killed or injured American citizens. Ordinarily those judgments prove uncollectible.

Much more generally, however, the fundamental point is that an American money judgment 'is not an *order* to the defendant; it is an *adjudication* of his rights or liabilities. No one may be held in contempt for failing to pay some debt as adjudicated by the law court.'[8] An article in the *American Bar Association Journal* reported in 2011 that 'nearly 80 percent of judgments in the US courts aren't collected.'[9] In a 1999 case, for example, plaintiff obtained a judgment for over $230,000 but collected only some $125,000 by execution and sought a court order to defendant to pay the rest. Although the court recognized that such an order might be supported in 'exceptional' circumstances, it found no basis for doing so in this ordinary case.[10]

3.2 A Different Attitude Toward Debt?

To American eyes, it sometimes seems that the European attitude toward debt includes a moral judgment. In the distant past, in other countries, it may be that the debts of the father often fell on the son. In such an atmosphere, one might expect to find that courts would have some responsibility to enforce money judgments. The American colonies inherited the institution of debtors' prison from Europe, but '[f]ederal law abolished debtors' prisons in 1833, and state laws followed suit shortly after,'[11] though jailing the poor when they cannot post bail after arrest or fail to pay court fees has been attacked as a 'new debtors' prison' in America.[12]

In general, America has taken a different approach to private debts as a philosophical matter. This is not to say that American law does not regard judgments as important public declarations of liability. But what might called a more charitable attitude is reflected in the role of bankruptcy in the US. The idea is that one who

---

[6] See Fed. R. Civ. P. 55(a) ('When a party against whom a judgment for affirmative relief is sought has failed to plead or otherwise defend, and that failure is shown by affidavit or otherwise, the clerk must enter the party's default').

[7] See Fed. R. Civ. P. 55(b)(1) (providing that the clerk must enter judgment when 'the plaintiff's claim is for a sum certain or a sum that can be made certain by computation').

[8] Dobbs (1973), p. 94.

[9] Zahoreky (2011), p. 33.

[10] Baxter State Bank v. Bernhardt, 186 F.R.D. 621 (D. Kan. 1999).

[11] Jerjian (2017), p. 243.

[12] See Jerjian (2017) and Dayen (2018).

gets into a financial hole should get a 'fresh start,' leaving his creditors to fight it out for his non-exempt assets under the administration of a bankruptcy court. With corporate debtors, 'reorganization' under Chap. 11 of our Bankruptcy Act has been employed as a method for very large businesses—General Motors Corporation, for example—to get a 'fresh start' free of their prior obligations, and perhaps freed also of some obligations under collective bargaining agreements with unionized workers.

A somewhat similar attitude can be found elsewhere in American law. For much of the American population, the 'American dream' includes owning a home. Almost always, that involves a loan to buy the home, secured by the collateral provided by the house itself. The lender usually would require the borrower to make a down payment of 20% (sometimes less) so that the collateral would ordinarily exceed the amount of the loan. But at times of economic distress (for example, after the 2008 financial crisis) house values might fall a good deal more than 20%. Then the foreclosing lender might find that much of the loan remained unpaid after the house was sold – a deficiency. Under the law of about a dozen American states, including California,[13] the law forbids the lender to enforce that remaining debt in court. That reflects a judgment that home buyers who suffer the misfortune of depleted home value should not also be forever impoverished by the debt resulting from that misfortune.

This orientation does not mean that American courts shy from enforcing money judgments. To the contrary, for some time they made it strikingly easy for creditors to obtain judgments and secure a right to be paid. For a long time, prejudgment remedies variously labeled attachment, garnishment, replevin and other things enabled alleged creditors to obtain something resembling a post-judgment remedy at the outset of the case. The stated goal was to ensure that assets would be available to satisfy a judgment later entered, and often these remedies could be obtained before the defendant was notified that they had been sought. But these devices could be abused due to the relaxed procedures for obtaining prejudgment relief that sometimes made issuance of the remedies almost automatic. As a prominent member of the US Congress declared in 1968, 'in a vast number of cases the debt is a fraudulent one, saddled on a poor ignorant person who is trapped in an easy credit nightmare.'[14]

Beginning in 1969, the US Supreme Court faced numerous challenges to the use of these prejudgment remedies without notice, or without effective scrutiny of the claims being asserted. After striking down garnishment of wages,[15] the Court in 1972 declared that prior notice and an opportunity to contest the claim were constitutionally required unless an 'extraordinary situation' was presented.[16] Since then, most states have revised their prejudgment remedy statutes to prescribe exacting circumstances for issuance of such prejudgment remedies. Ordinarily the showing required includes demonstrating that, absent the prejudgment remedy, there will be a substantial risk that an eventual judgment will be dishonored. But the point is that the US broadly

[13] See Cal. Code Civ. Pro.' 580.

[14] Remarks of Rep. Sullivan, Chairman of the House Subcommittee on Consumer Affairs, 114 Cong. Rec. 1832 (1968).

[15] Sniadach v. Family Finance Corp., 395 U.S. 337 (1969).

[16] Fuentes v. Shevin, 407 U.S. 67 (1972).

recognizes the right of a potential judgment creditor to secure at the outset the assets needed to satisfy a later judgment if the creditor makes the required showing. The federal courts are to honor and enforce those state laws.[17]

4 A Contrasting Case—Judicial Enforcement of Injunctions

Up to this point, the focus has been on money judgments. As Prof. Rechberger says about Austria, 'the vast majority of enforcement proceedings are money executions.'[18] That is surely true in the US, as well. But a telling contrast in terms of judicial enforcement exists with injunction judgments. It is important to pause briefly to recognize how different injunctive judgments are. It is often said that such relief is available only when the plaintiff can show that a money judgment is inadequate and that an injunction is required to avoid 'irreparable injury.' But a pathbreaking article 30 years ago by Professor Laycock proclaimed that 'our law embodies a preference for specific relief if plaintiff wants it. The principal doctrinal expression for this preference is the rule that damages are inadequate unless they can be used to replace the specific thing that plaintiff lost.'[19]

Although a money judgment is not a judicial order to pay, an injunction most certainly is. On occasion, that means that the judge takes the initiative and sends emissaries (often called 'special masters') into the field to make sure that the injunction is obeyed.[20] That sort of exceptional judicial action occurred sometimes in American courts as a result of what was called 'institutional reform litigation,' in which the courts were asked to enjoin unconstitutional 'cruel and unusual punishment' in prisons or racial discrimination in school systems.[21]

Ordinarily, however, the enforcement method depends in the first instance on action from the plaintiff who obtained the injunction. Then the court may use various sorts of orders holding the defendant in contempt.[22] One of these is known as 'coercive civil contempt,' in which the court orders the defendant imprisoned until he complies with the order. In one case, a divorcing husband was imprisoned for more than five years when he refused to reveal where the couple's assets could be found.[23]

---

[17] See Fed. R. Civ. P. 64(a) ('At the commencement of and throughout an action, every remedy is available that, under the law of the state where the court is located, provides for seizing a person or property to secure satisfaction of the potential judgment').

[18] Rechberger (2020), p. 1.

[19] Laycock (1990), p. 691.

[20] See Berger (1978).

[21] See Buckholtz, Cooper, Gettner & Guggenheimer (1978).

[22] See Dobbs (1971).

[23] Catena v. Seidl, 343 A.2d 744 (N.J. 1975).

In another, IBM was fined $150,000 per day until it complied with the court's order.[24] So American courts may act vigorously to enforce this sort of judgment.

Indeed, the Supreme Court has even ruled that a defendant subject to such an injunction may not avoid contempt sanctions by contending that the injunction was entered in violation of the Constitution. Dr. Martin Luther King planned a civil rights march in Birmingham, Alabama, during Easter weekend, 1965. Two days before the first march was to occur, local authorities obtained an *ex parte* temporary restraining order against the march from a state court judge. Despite that order, the march went forward, and King and others were found in contempt and fined and sentenced to jail. The Supreme Court upheld this finding.[25] It ruled that defendants' complaints that the statute on which the injunction was based infringed their First Amendment free speech rights could not be relied upon as a defense to the contempt charge. Two years later, the Court held that the same statute did violate the First Amendment, but in a case not involving a judicial injunction.[26]

Arguably the two cases involving the Birmingham statute were not consistent with each other. But one may also see that they recognize that it is one thing to say that somebody may disobey an unconstitutional statute and defend against a prosecution on the ground that the statute is unconstitutional. It is quite another to say that every person may judge for himself whether a court's order is proper, and disregard it on concluding that the order is not proper. In any event, the arrest of Dr. King had an ironic consequence. Dr. King used his time in the Birmingham jail to compose his 'Letter from the Birmingham Jail,' one of the most famous documents of the civil rights period.[27]

5 American Discovery to the Judgment Creditor's Rescue

Professors Hess and Rechberger both focus on the responsibility of the bailiff to seek enforcement of the money judgment and to obtain information about the judgment debtor's assets. But the judgment creditor does not obtain direct access to the information gathered by the bailiff.

Consistent with the BYO tradition, the American approach is to empower the judgment creditor rather than place a duty on the court. Rule 69(a)(2) of the Federal Rules of Civil Procedure[28] provides the full panoply of discovery tools ordinarily available to an American litigant for discovery 'in aid of execution.' This includes

[24] International Business Machines Corp. v. United States, 493 U.S. 112 (2d Cir. 1971).

[25] Walker v. City of Birmingham, 388 U.S. 307 (1967).

[26] Shuttlesworth v. City of Birmingham, 394 U.S. 147 (1969).

[27] See Oppenheimer (1993).

[28] Fed. R. Civ. P. 69(a)(2): 'In aid of the judgment or execution, the judgment creditor or a successor in interest whose interest appears of record may obtain discovery from any person – including the judgment debtor – as provided in these rules or in the procedure of the state where the court is located.' For explanation, see Wright et al. (2014) sections 3011–15.

discovery from third parties.[29] Thus the American BYO approach provides judgment creditors with valuable tools to locate assets subject to execution.

As our Supreme Court noted in a 2014 case dealing with enforcement of Rule 69 discovery to enforce a money judgment against the Republic of Argentina: 'The rules governing discovery are quite permissive.'[30] In that case, the Court declined to find that there was a 'sovereign immunity' exception to Rule 69.[31] As a result, the Court rejected Argentina's argument that the discovery could be had only regarding assets in the US, and not those outside the country. It did, however, require that the judgment creditor provide prima facie evidence of potential execution before discovery could occur.

For litigants before non-American tribunals, there is one more avenue of possible American discovery to locate assets. By statute, US federal courts may provide American discovery from any person who 'resides or is found' within a federal district 'for use in a proceeding in a foreign or international tribunal.'[32] The decision whether to provide such discovery is within the discretion of the district court.[33]

As with other discovery, a court order directing discovery is like an injunction in that a party (or nonparty) who refuses to obey the order is subject to contempt sanctions. So though the American judgment debtor may not be jailed for failure to pay a money judgment, he can be jailed for failure to respond to court-ordered discovery about assets potentially subject to execution under the judgment.

When the debtor locates assets subject to execution, he can invoke judicial procedures to have them seized and sold. That can include somewhat unorthodox methods of enforcement. For example, in a 2010 case a US court of appeals in California confronted a judgment entered by a Florida federal court against a judgment debtor that owned interests in Internet domain names. The district court in San Francisco appointed a receiver to obtain and sell some 190 domain names by execution against the official registry of the domain names that was located in the district in which the court sat. The appellate court held that the seizure of this intangible property was justified under California law, and therefore that the appointment of the receiver and sale of the domain names was authorized by Rule 69.[34]

[29] Indeed, there is even a provision permitting enforcement of a judgment against a nonparty in unusual circumstances. See Fed. R. Civ. P. 71.

[30] Republic of Argentina v. NML Capital, Ltd., 134 S.Ct. 2250, 2254 (2014).

[31] Id. at 2256–57. It should be noted that Argentina had waived sovereign immunity more generally in connection with this dispute about bonds it had issued but failed to pay.

[32] 28 U.S.C. section 1782(a).

[33] For discussion of this statute, see Wright et al. (2010) section 2005.1.

[34] Office Depot, Inc. v. Zuccarini, 596 F.3d 696 (9th Cir. 2010).

6 American Self-help Methods

The governmental assistance provided in the US to assist in enforcement generally depends in the first instance on the BYO efforts of the judgment debtor. As noted in the domain names case just above, it may depend also on creative use of the court's enforcement powers once the judgment creditor locates assets subject to execution.

But there are also private providers of pertinent services that should be noted here. Those services fall into three categories – asset location, asset hiding, and self-help collection of debts.

6.1 Asset Location

The Internet provides many services, including asset location. Many people research other people by doing Google searches using the names of the people of interest. The goal may be to check out a blind date, get a feel for a potential business partner, or evaluate a proposed purchaser of a condominium. Usually, these services assure the browser that they have located lots of people with the given name, and provide some details about them (e.g., age, place of residence). Then they offer to provide lots more information for a fee.

A recurrent objective of such online searches is to find assets of the person who is the subject of the search. In this way, even without discovery, one can obtain information somewhat like that available to those who use Rule 69 after obtaining a money judgment. There is no prospect of a court order compelling disclosure, but there is also no need to deal directly with the judgment debtor to get this sort of information. Professor Hess worries that the Schufa AG, established by powerful lending interests, may still possess information about assets not available to others. In the US, these private services claim to provide something similar, but it is probably not as complete.

6.2 Asset Hiding

If there are private services engaged in locating assets, it should not be a surprise that there are also private services that seek to guard assets against execution. The usual theme of these services is that they use legal means to defeat legal process.

This paper does not urge anyone to employ such strategies, but it can report that a Google search of "protect your assets from creditors" produced 18,600,000 responses, mainly from firms seemingly operated by American lawyers. A sampling of the offerings on the first page of hits is as follows:

> Determine whether Advanced Asset Protection and Privacy is for you—Complete the form below by checking the boxes that apply to you to see if your score indicates a need for asset protection services.
>
> Protect Against Lawsuits—Our effective solution can protect you against lawsuits and creditors. Asset protection is most effective when implemented in advance of a lawsuit, judgment, or claim. But even if you have been sued or threatened with a lawsuit, it may be possible to protect your assets. If you are an individual or company at risk from lawsuits or other claims, you should consult with us as soon as possible. Effective asset protection planning against lawsuits involves the use of an offshore asset protection trust. An 'offshore trust' is a trust formed under the laws of a jurisdiction other than the United States. The prospect of bringing a case in the Cook Islands is extremely daunting to most creditors.
>
> Structure your estate so your assets stay where you want them—with you and your family—We live in an age where we must protect ourselves from unforeseen circumstances that can greatly affect our lives and the lives of those around us. Insuring things has become a common practice; why not protect your assets with a form of legal 'insurance'?
>
> Asset Protection After a Lawsuit is Filed—Can you engage in asset protection after a lawsuit is filed? We need to deal with the situation the way it is, not the way we wish it was. Your best defense, is offense. That said, the bottom line is this: yes, you can set up asset protection after a lawsuit is filed. But it is much better to do it before finding yourself in a situation where they are at the mercy of the courts. Consider an Asset Protection Trust as your best way to prevent financial loss, should someone sue you or your company. Even better, consider an Offshore Asset Protection Trust.
>
> Asset Protection Myths—debunks a variety of supposed myths, including: Asset Protection is only for those with very high net worth; On-shore planning is as strong as offshore planning; I will lose control of my money with asset protection; Asset protection is illegal.

Probably similar services exist in other countries, perhaps equally openly. Perhaps some entities provide both asset location services and asset protection services. If so, hopefully they don't do so for the same clients. It is interesting to ask whether the bailiffs in Germany and Austria encounter such devices, and whether they take the steps needed to surmount them.

6.3 Self-help Collection of Debts

The story quoted above about use of yakuza in Japan to collect debts[35] is one version of self help. Judicial enforcement involves court officers like bailiffs executing the judgment. But that is not the only way to obtain relief.

Instead, self help is sometimes another option. Non-judicial foreclosure on mortgages is allowed in many states, including California. Repossession of cars and other items purchased 'on time' has long been an American phenomenon. It's even been the subject of a Hollywood movie—*Repo Man*, in 1984. Repo men are not, of course, clothed with the authority of the court, and if they commit a tort while repossessing

---

[35] See text accompanying note 1 above.

property that can lead to liability.[36] But it is useful to recognize this form of relief to appreciate the entire range of American creditor remedies.

The US Congress has recognized that these self-help efforts can be overdone. It enacted the Fair Debt Collection Practices Act[37] to combat abusive collection practices. The Act regulates communications between a creditor and debtor. It provides that the creditor or its agent may not call the debtor before 8:00 a.m. or after 9:00 p.m., and also forbids calling the debtor at work if the employer forbids such contacts. If the debtor has a lawyer, the creditor may only call the lawyer, not the debtor. It also forbids use during permitted calls of 'language the natural consequence of which is to abuse the hearer.'[38] Debtors who claim a violation of the Act may sue for compensatory damages and recover attorney's fees as well.

Although these are self-help efforts, debt collectors often try to invoke governmental authority to collect debts. For example, in a 2012 story about people who wrote checks that were dishonored for insufficient funds, the *New York Times* reported that debt collectors used the stationary of the public prosecutor for their payment demands. These letters 'bear the seal and signature of the local district attorney's office. But there is a catch: the letters are from debt-collection companies, which the prosecutors allow to use their letterhead.'[39] In some instances, arrests of debtors were used to pressure them to pay.[40]

These efforts by debt collectors to invoke governmental authority may show that more vigorous efforts by the courts would be a welcome alternative. But in the BYO American regime, these sorts of free-wheeling activities have proliferated.

7 Conclusion

This paper provides only a quick look at the American system of judgment enforcement. But it should be enough to show that the US relies more on the judgment creditor and less on the court. It certainly does not accept the idea that the court has a judicial responsibility to make sure that a money judgment is satisfied. It does provide an array of judicial services to the creditor who can identify the debtor's assets—even Internet domain names—but finding those assets is the creditor's problem, not the bailiff's. Ultimately, though they proceed from what might be called different premises, the German and Austrian systems probably work quite similarly to the American system in most cases. And the more vigorous court efforts in Germany and Austria might curtail resort to self-help efforts like those described just above.

---

[36] See, e.g., Clark v. Associates Commercial Prop., 149 F.R.D. 629 (D. Kan. 1991) (suit against lender for injuries sustained in repossession of a tractor).

[37] 15 U.S.C. sections 1692–1692(b).

[38] 15 U.S.C. section 1692d(2).

[39] Silver-Greenberg (2012).

[40] See Silver-Greenberg (2011).

References

Andrews (2019) Developments in english civil justice: judicial proceedings and other civil processes. ZZPInt 2018:1–23

Berger (1978) Away from the courthouse and into the field: the odyssey of a special master. C Law Rev 78:707–732

Buckholtz,, Cooper, Gettner, Guggenheimer (1978) The remedial process in institutional reform litigation. C Law Rev 78:784-929

Dayen (2018) Prosecutors and judges have brought back debtors' prison. Nation Magazine

Dobbs (1971) Contempt of court: a survey. Cornell Law Rev 56:183–284

Dobbs D (1973) Remedies, 1st edn. West Publications & Co., St. Paul

Hess (2020), The effective disclosure of the debtor's assets in enforcement proceedings, in this volume

Jerjian (2017) The debtors' prison scheme: yet another bar in the birdcage of mass incarceration of communities of color. NYU Rev of Law & Soc Change 41:235–76

Laycock (1990) The irreparable injury rule. Harv Law Rev 103:687–771

Oppenheimer (1993) Martin Luther King, Walker v. City of Birmingham, and the letter from the Birmingham jail. UC Davis Law Rev 26:791–834

Rechberger (2020) Clarification of facts in Austrian enforcement law, in this volume

Silver-Greenberg (2012) In prosecutors, debt collectors find a partner, NY times

Silver-Greenberg (2011) Debtor arrests criticized. Wall St J

Sterngold (1992) Japan's rigged Casino, NY times

Wright C, Miller A, Marcus R (2010) 8 Federal practice & procedure, 3rd edn. Thomson Reuters, Minneapolis

Wright C, Miller A, Marcus R (2014) 12 Federal practice & procedure, 3rd edn. Thomson Reuters, Minneapolis

Zahorky (2011) In the judgment trade: law student's website helps bring in the cash. ABA J 33

Richard Marcus was born and raised in San Francisco. He attended Pomona College, where he lettered for four years on the track team, engaged in a variety of 1960s-era political activities and spent a year as president of the student body. He then attended the UC Berkeley School of Law (Boalt Hall), where he was research editor of the California Law Review and elected to the Order of the Coif when he graduated in 1972. Both before and after graduation from law school, Professor Marcus served as law clerk to Justice Raymond Peters of the California Supreme Court. After an around-the-world expedition went awry in a bus accident in Afghanistan, he spent a summer working on the Wounded Knee Legal Defense Committee in Rapid City, South Dakota. Then, during 1973 to 1974, he served as an associate-in-law at Boalt Hall and, in 1974 to 1975, as a law clerk to U.S. District Court Judge Alfonso J. Zirpoli in San Francisco. In 1976 he got a real job, as a litigation associate at Dinkelspiel, Pelavin, Steefel & Levitt (since disbanded) in San Francisco, where he became a partner in 1980. In 1981, Professor Marcus left practice and entered teaching as an associate professor at the University of Illinois College of Law, becoming a full professor in 1984. He was a visiting professor at the University of Michigan Law School in 1986 to 1987. He joined the UC Hastings faculty in 1988, became a Distinguished Professor in 1997, and was awarded the Horace O. Coil ('57) Chair in Litigation in 1999. His teaching has focused on litigation-related areas such as civil procedure, complex litigation, conflicts of law, and evidence, and he has also taught contracts, corporations and remedies. Professor Marcus' writing has focused on litigation-related topics. He is a lead author of the West casebooks Complex Litigation (6th ed. 2015) and Civil Procedure: A Modern Approach (7th ed. 2018). He was elected a member of the International Association on Procedural Law (IAPL) in 1998, and now serves as the Vice President of the IAPL for North America.

Fact Clarification and Effective Legal Protection in Civil Enforcement Law in Japan

Masahisa Deguchi

1 Introduction

The former Code of Civil Procedure (CCP) was enacted in 1890 as the first full-fledged civil procedure law in Japan.[1] It was drafted by the German jurist Hermann Techow,[2] and was reformed in 1926, influenced by the Austrian Law of Civil Procedure. After World War II, the General Headquarters (USA) directed the drastic reform of the civil procedure system in connection with Japanese democratization.[3] For almost 70 years thereafter, the revised code continued to be used with occasional amendments. The most important of these were the adoption of the cross-examination system, the abolition of the supplemental ex-officio examination of evidence by the court, and the exclusion of the alteration of judgment.[4] After some preliminary work beginning in the 1950s, the Ministry of Justice at the end of the sixties, reformed the Code of Execution, which had remained almost unchanged since the 1890s and had become outdated. This reform represented the first step of a longer process, covering the whole field of Civil Procedure Law reform.

[1] Cf. *Taniguchi/Reich/Miyake*, Civil Procedure in Japan, Revised Second Edition, section 1,03[1].

[2] See, in details, *Matsumoto*, The reception and Transmission of the Law of Civil Procedure in Japan-The Experience in Japan-, P.142 in: Masahisa Deguchi/Marcel Strome, The Reception and Transmission of Civil Procedure Law in the Global Society.

[3] The idea was to transform an interrogative approach to a more adversary system which was the hallmark of the american democracy; See in details, *Matsumoto*, supra note 2, p.138.

[4] *Matsumoto*, supra note 2, p.142.

I would like to express my sincere thanks to Professor Jeffrey Lubbers, American University, Washington College of Law, for his careful proofreading.

M. Deguchi (✉)
Ritsumeikan University, Kyoto, Japan
e-mail: mdt00298@law.ritsumei.ac.jp

M. Deguchi (ed.), *Effective Enforcement of Creditors' Rights*,
Ius Gentium: Comparative Perspectives on Law and Justice 91,
https://doi.org/10.1007/978-981-16-5609-5_8

The system of enforcement law, which was implemented by the CCP of 1890, mentioned above, and the Auction Act of 1898, had contained some theoretical discrepancies since its inception. Beyond that there were also practical difficulties such as procedural delays that could not be overlooked. Against this background, in 1968 the legislature began work on a new Enforcement Law. After two preliminary drafts in 1971 and 1973, the Civil Enforcement Act was enacted in 1979. This Act entered into force on 1 October 1980. Subsequently, the provisions on enforcement law were amended in the Sixth Book of the CCP and the Auction Act was repealed. However, the provisions on interim relief in the CCP itself remained almost untouched by this reform. Thus, this area became the subject of the next reform. The original CCP had also included provisions on civil enforcement and civil preservation proceedings, but the Civil Enforcement Act was merged with the now-repealed the Auction Act. In 1989 the Civil Provisional Remedies Act was enacted to cover the issues of interim relief thus allowing the CCP to become an independent separate statute. The new CCP, as opposed to the old CCP, was then reenacted in 1996 as a new law with the aim of creating a proper and expeditious civil procedure system.[5] It entered into force on 1 January 1998. The most important new requirements introduced by the amended CCP have been mainly the following: (i) improvement of the preparatory procedure, (ii) promotion of the exchange of information between the parties, (iii) extension of the procedure for collecting evidence, (iv) introduction of a special procedure involving small amounts in dispute, and (v) limitation of appeals.[6] Indeed, as a result, civil proceedings have become more expeditious. But the enforcement system needs strengthening to make it more effective, especially for creditors, following the model of enforcement systems in other countries. That was a reason why I undertook research on the "Effective Enforcement of Creditor's Right in Civil Execution through Effective Discovery of Debtor's Assets" with my colleagues of the International Association of Procedural Law.

After World War II, the Constitution of Japan was promulgated in 1946 as a charter that provides "fundamental principles of democratic change".[7] Art. 29 of the Japanese Constitution guarantees property rights of the people, as do most of the world's constitutions.[8] The right to legal proceedings is constitutionally secured (Art. 32 of the Japanese Constitution). Self-help is denied to the individual creditor.[9] The state also has the monopoly on authority in the area of civil enforcement.[10] In order to guarantee the citizen's right to an effective procedure, not only the civil procedure must be guaranteed, but it must also be ensured that the civil rights of the citizen are

---

[5] *See, Kakiuchi,* Erkenntnisverfahren, Vollstreckung, einstweiliger Rechtsschutz, p.1290 in: Baum/Bälz, Handbuch des Japanischen Handels- und Wirtschaftsrechts.

[6] *Kakiuchi,* supra note 5, p.1295.

[7] *Matsumoto,* supra note 2, p.142.

[8] *Matsumoto,* Minjishikko Hozennho, p.16; Japanese constitution: http://www.japaneselawtranslation.go.jp/law/detail/?id=174.

[9] *Nakano,* Minjishikkoho, Zohoshintei 6th ed. p.3f.

[10] *Id.* p.3.

effectively implemented.[11] The protection of the constitutional rights mentioned also includes the realization of rights through civil enforcement law.[12] In other words, an effective enforcement system for the enforcement of rights plays a central role in the right of citizens to a judicial proceeding. However, even in carrying out the best of the world's civil procedural laws, in order to guarantee effective protection of creditor's rights, in civil enforcement practice the purpose of the proceedings can only be achieved if the creditor has sufficient information about the debtor's assets.[13] Civil procedure laws around the world now require the effective collection of information in enforcement cases to ensure effective protection of creditor's rights. Ensuring this is a very important legislative task in Europe as well as in Japan. For more than 150 years Japan's civil procedure law has been developed based on the influence of several foreign civil procedure jurisprudences. This issue of enforcement rights is one more issue where that should be the case.

The aim of this article is to attempt to compare the different enforcement rights in Japan, Germany and European countries, in so far as it concerns the fact clarification in civil enforcement law. The focus will be on the effective protection of creditor's rights.[14]

2 Reform Efforts in Japanese Civil Enforcement Law

2.1 Reform of the Civil Enforcement Act in Japan

The Japanese Civil Enforcement Act was passed in 1979 as a new law. It united the law on civil enforcement law in the old code of civil procedure law and the law on auction procedure law in an independent law.[15] However, after the bubble economy[16] collapsed, the malfunction of the auction system became a serious problem. After the Civil Provisional Remedies Act (regulating arrest and injunction in Japan)[17] came into force in 1989, various legal provisions were introduced as measures against disturbing the enforcement of real estate sales.[18] Significant changes to the security

---

[11] Vgl. *Stein/Jonas/Münzberg*, ZPO vor § 704, Rn. 501. The civil enforcement has a kind of general preventive effect in this respect (cf. Lüke, Zivilprozessrecht, 10th ed. Nr.501).

[12] *Matsumoto*, supra note 8, p.17.

[13] *Schlauss*, RIW 2017, 20.

[14] The title of this article is based on "Gesetz zur Reform der Sachaufklärung in der Zwangsvollstreckung " of 29. Juli 2009. In detail, Alsfasser, Sachaufklärung in der Einzelzwangsvollstreckung, 2018, S.3 ff.

[15] *Kakiuchi*, supra note 5, p. 1294.

[16] The Japanese asset price bubble (Baburu Keiki, "bubble economy") was an economic bubble in Japan from 1986 to 1991, in which the real estate and equity market prices were greatly inflated.

[17] Civil Provisional Remedies Act in Japan: http://www.japaneselawtranslation.go.jp/law/detail/?id=2028&vm=&re=

[18] See, *Taniguchi/Tsutsui*, Kaiseitanpo Shikkoho no Kaisetsu, S. 126 ff.

and enforcement system were made in 2003 and 2004 to respond to changes in social and economic conditions and to improve the effectiveness of rights enforcement.[19] As the need for security for the monetary claim was emphasized very strongly, a procedure for the disclosure of the financial situation was introduced for the first time in the civil enforcement law in Japan.[20]

This new procedure was intended to provide the creditor, whose claim had been titled claim through judicial judgment, certain information about the debtor's assets. The legislative purpose was to ensure the effectiveness of the enforcement of money.[21] In civil enforcement practice, however, it is still generally difficult for creditors to explore the debtor's assets. The creditor must also identify the object to be enforced, with the exception of enforcement in movable property (§ 23 and §133 of the Civil Enforcement regulation). To this end, the procedure for disclosing debtors' assets was introduced, the aim of which is to improve the obtaining of information about the debtor's assets and to reduce the difficulties for the creditor in identifying the assets to be enforced.[22]

The new procedure for disclosing the financial situation has now been carried out in practice for almost 17 years in Japan.[23] The sanctions envisaged were often considered inadequate. The number of applications in 2015 was only 791 cases. The practical importance of this Japanese disclosure procedure was not necessarily great.[24] However, in the asset disclosure procedure, the debtor often does not follow the enforcement court's disclosure order, as this behavior only results in a fine (up to 300,000 yen).[25] In September 2016, the Japanese Minister of Justice established a commission to reform the civil enforcement law.[26] Its suggestions led to the Civil Enforcement Act of May 10, 2019.[27]

In the following, the procedure for the disclosure of assets and the information collection system vis-à-vis third parties such as financial institutions (savings bank, giro bank) or public institutions (registrar, city, municipality, social insurance institution) are examined in depth from the point of view of fact clarification in enforcement and effective legal protection.[28]

---

[19] *Nakano*, supra note 9, p.68f.

[20] *Nakano*, supra note 9, p.832 has called this property disclosure procedure only as a preparation for enforcement, not a mandatory procedure.

[21] *Uchiyama*, Zaisankaijitetsuzuki no Jikkousei, Ho to Seiji, Vol. 62 Nr. 4, S. 30.

[22] *Matsumoto*, supra note 8. p.454 criticized in those days this as a legislative loophole since the current law knew no disclosure of debtor's assets apart from the monetary claim.

[23] Cf, *Uchino/ Tomoya/ Yamamoto/ Matsumami*, Minjishikkoho to no Gaiyo, NBL No. 1153, S. 5 ff.

[24] *Koga*, Kinsenshikko no Jitsujyo, in: Koichi Miki Hen, Kinsenshikko no Jitsumu to Kadai, Seirinshiin, 2013, S. 4. Nakamura, Minjishikkohokaisei to Kinyujitsumu he no Eikyo, Gingouhomu 21, Nr. 837, S. 4 ff.

[25] *Koga, supra note 24, p.4.*

[26] Cf, http://www.moj.go.jp/content/001237417.pdf (zuletzt abgerufen am: 11.03.2020).

[27] Cf, *Uchino/Tomoya/Yamamoto/Matsumami*, supra note 16, p.4f.

[28] Cf, *Id*, p.6f.

2.2 *Difficulty in Identifying Monetary Claims*

As already mentioned, the debtor's assets must be specified in the application for enforcement on the basis of monetary claims (§ 23 of the Civil Enforcement Regulation). § 133(2) of the Civil Enforcement Act states that the applicant for the enforcement of money for the purpose of enforcement must state the type and amount of the claim to be attached and sufficient other characteristics of the claim in order to be able to identify the claim. Therefore, if a creditor intends to seize the debtor's property, it is imperative to obtain the debtor's financial information.

In many cases, however, creditors who have already received the judgment or the enforcement order cannot simply exercise their rights because they have no information about the debtor's assets. It is extremely difficult to find the details of the claims at all, since a claim such as intangible assets is not known to the public. One of the triggers for the renewed need to improve the ability to provide information about the debtor's assets prior to enforcement was the Supreme Court Ruling in Japan on September 20, 2011, on the identification of third-party debtor's claims. Until this decision, the creditor was able to request that the identification of the claim be attached to each branch of this bank using a so-called numbering scheme for third-party debtors (banks). The Supreme Court has ruled with regard to § 133(2) of the Civil Enforcement Regulation that this may represent an unreasonable burden for third-party debtors because of the relationship of trust with the bank customer.[29] This decision will make it more difficult to get immediate and effective protection of creditors' rights. It could even encourage debtors to avoid enforcement.[30] This decision has been heavily criticized in the literature because it would cause dysfunction in the civil system of enforcing rights.[31]

2.3 *Improve the Effectiveness of the debtor's Property Disclosure Procedure*

2.3.1 Reform of the debtor's Property Disclosure Procedure

The former Japanese Civil Enforcement Act already contained such a procedure for the disclosure of debtors' assets (§ 196 ff, old version). Under that law, the debtor was obliged to pay due to a loss of lawsuit seeking disclosure of his own assets. However, the procedure only took place under very narrow conditions. In the event of violation of the order, the debtor only had to pay a fine of up to 300,000 yen. Compared to

[29] Minshu Vol. 65, Nr. 6, S. 2710 vom 20. September 2011; Hanrei, Times Nr. 1357, S. 65; Jiho, Nr. 2129, S. 41; cf, *Takada,* Sashiosaerubeki Saiken no Tokutei, Besssatsu Jurist, Nr. 208, S. 103 ff.

[30] *Takada,* supra note 22, p.103.

[31] *Takada,* supra note 22. p.103; Uchida, Yokinsaiken no Tokutei nikansure Saikosaikettei no Igi to Kadai, Law & Practice. Nr. 08 (2014), p.185; Kasuga, Saikosaiminsojireikenkyu, Hogakuj kenkyu Vol. 85, Nr. 8, (2012), p.31f.

South Korea and other countries that have implemented very effective asset disclosure procedure, it is still difficult to say whether the Japanese asset disclosure system is operating effectively.[32] Some lawyers in Japan are reluctant to use this procedure. In fact, since the new law was introduced in Japan, the number of requests to disclose debt has gradually decreased from 1207 in 2010 to 1085 in 2012.[33] Shortly after the reformed procedure for disclosure of debtor's assets came into force in 2003, practitioners demanded that the procedure urgently needed improvement because the effectiveness of this procedure was extremely low.[34]

It is not always easy for a private creditor to obtain a debtor's asset information. This can reduce trust in the judicial system as a whole, since the creditor, after having obtained an enforcement order for his claim—possibly with great difficulty—still cannot realize his right. The debtor is obliged to appear on the day of the disclosure of the assets, to make a declaration, and to swear that it is correct; however, the Japanese disclosure procedure on debtor's assets does not have effective sanctions if the statements are not made or are not made in full.[35] Soon after the introduction of the new proceedings in 2003, this was heavily criticized as a legal structural defect in the new proceedings.[36] Under the old law, there was also no procedure for obtaining asset information from third-party debtors. For this reason, even if the creditor had obtained a successful court decision, the actual debt collection was based on so-called bar association inquiries (§ 23-2 of the Lawyers' Act) or the investigations commissioned by the creditor, unless the debtor had voluntarily fulfilled the obligation. The creditors therefore had to seek the debtor information themselves.

In order to achieve effective protection of the rights of creditors in civil enforcement, corresponding measures to effectively strengthen the disclosure procedure of debtor's assets by the debtor or the asset information of third parties would have to be taken in the new enforcement law.[37]

2.3.2 Review of the Requirements to Disclose the Property by the Debtor

The requirements for the procedure for the disclosure of assets by the debtor were scrutinized. A certain enforcement order is required to initiate a procedure for the disclosure of assets. However, according to the old law, neither the judgment with a provisional declaration of enforcement nor the enforceable deed or the order for payment (§ 197 (1), old version of the Civil Enforcement Act) was sufficient as an enforcement title to file an application for a disclosure procedure. According to the

[32] In Korea there were 127,830 cases of property disclosure in 2010. The Korean asset disclosure procedure has been used much more effectively.

[33] Cf, *Miki Hen*, Kinsenshikko no Jitsumu to Kadai, S. 84, Tabelle ⑧-2.

[34] Cf, *Uchino/Tomoya/Yamamoto/Matsumami*, supra note 23, p.5f.

[35] *Nakano*, supra note 9, p.833.

[36] *Nakano*, supra note 9, p.833.

[37] Cf, *Uchino/Tomoya/Yamamoto/Matsumami*, supra note 23, p.5f.

Reform Act, a procedure for the disclosure of assets can be submitted if one has an enforceable title of obligation with which the monetary claims can be required (§ 197 (1) new version of the Civil Enforcement Act). According to the old law, a fine of only 300,000 Yen was imposed if the person required to disclose did not do so on the due date without a legitimate reason or if he made a false statement. The Reform Act can impose a custodial sentence of up to six months or a fine of up to 500,000 Yen (§ 213 (1) of the Civil Enforcement Act). The sanctions have been tightened by the new law, but the Japanese civil enforcement law still lacks enforcement custody as there is in Germany or Korea.[38]

2.3.3 Gathering Procedure of Third party's Information

The most notable reform of the Civil Enforcement Act is the introduction of a system for acquiring financial information about third-party's debtor assets (the so-called third-party information acquisition procedure for debtors' real estate, wages, and savings).[39] In the reform discussion on the amendment to the Security and Civil Enforcement Act of 2003, the introduction of the asset disclosure procedure of the debtor pointed to the constitutionally questionable possibility that the creditor could use the information requested by the authorities (tax office) for purposes other than the original one.[40] The creditor must therefore always try to obtain financial information about third parties from the financial institutions (or the bank). This was done mainly through inquiries from the Bar Association in accordance with § 23-2 of the Lawyers Act or inquiries to the authority. The debtor's asset disclosure procedure was introduced in 2003 by amending the Security and Civil Enforcement Act. The model, according to which the debtor himself is supposed to declare his assets, has proven to be ineffective.[41]

According to the current enforcement practice, the responsible branch of the bank must be specified when the creditor wants to enforce the bank claims. Therefore, the view prevailed that the practical necessity of collecting bank information is extremely important in the discussion about the introduction of a third party's debtor information collection system. In recent years, however, property ownership has shifted to forms of investment other than savings. Information about debtors' assets such as corporate bonds, investment trusts, stocks and other forms of investment, along with bank claims and reimbursement claims for life insurance have become increasingly important. Therefore, the new information acquisition system for real estate,

[38] According to section 802 g ZPO, the court issues an arrest warrant against the debtor, who does not excuse the deadline for submitting the property information or refuses to provide the property information in accordance with section 802c without reason, at the request of the creditor. In Korea, coercive detention also works as an indirect coercive measure.

[39] Cf, *Uchino/Tomoya/Yamamoto/Matsumami,* supra note 23, p.6f.

[40] Cf, *Kinyutorihikikenkyukai,* Minjishikkohokaisei- Zaisankaijiseido, Ginkohomu 21, Nr. 827, p.38f.

[41] *Koga,* Minjishikkoho Kaiseiyokou no Gaiyo to Jitsumu eno Eikkyo, Business Homu, 2019, 1, p.88.

deposits, and salary of debtors was introduced. It should allow for more effective civil enforcement.

In addition, real estate is generally a valuable asset and should be open to enforcement access. The creditor should therefore also be able to obtain the debtor's information on real estate contained in the register. Since the real estate information of public institutions contains personal data, the use of real estate information for purposes other than the intended purpose is prohibited.

The property disclosure procedure must be strengthened in order to strike a balance between creditor protection and debtor protection. With regard to the support costs claims with an enforceable title of obligation and damages due to injury to human life or the body mentioned in accordance with § 151-2 (1) of the Enforcement Act, the creditor can request information about the debtor's income from cities and municipalities or Japanese pension organizations.[42]

3 Clarification of Fact in the Civil Enforcement in European Countries

In the reform discussion of the Civil Enforcement Act, lawyers and practitioners have been carrying out detailed comparative law studies on the enforcement system in various countries for some time. In addition, the latest developments in the field of clarification of fact in the civil enforcement in Japan and in other European countries are briefly compared.

3.1 Clarification of Facts in German Enforcement Law

First of all, on July 29, 2009, a law was passed in Germany to reform the clarification of fact in the civil enforcement in order to transfer the clarification-of-fact powers to the bailiff and to modernize the enforcement procedure. It entered into force on January 1, 2013.[43] The law has significantly changed the regulations on the disclosure of assets and the list of debtors in Germany.[44] The debtor is now obliged to provide information about his assets at the request of the bailiff and to state her maiden name, date of birth, and place of birth for the purpose of enforcing a monetary claim (§ 802c ZPO). The two-pronged system consists of the debtor's self-disclosure at the beginning of enforcement (§ 802c ZPO) and the subsidiary option to obtain third-party information (§ 802 l ZPO). Central measures for third party information are the acceptance of the asset report after an attempt to seize it (§ 807 ZPO) and enforcement detention (§ 802 g ZPO) to enforce property information. If the debtor

---

[42] *Koga,* supra note 41, p.89.

[43] *Gottwald,* Ritsumeikan Law Review, Nr. 37 (2019), S. 70.

[44] *Gottwald, supra note 43, p.*71f.

provides property information, it is stored electronically by the bailiff in an asset register that is transmitted to the central enforcement courts of the federal states (§ 802f, (5) and (6), § 802 k ZPO).[45] If, for example, they do not provide any financial information, debtors will be entered in the debtor register under further conditions (§ 882b ff. ZPO).[46]

3.2 Clarification of Facts in French Enforcement Law

In France, unlike Germany, there is no disclosure procedure of debtor's asset although the effectiveness of the voluntary disclosure of assets by the debtor can be questionable.[47] However, the information collection system about the third-party debtor's assets was quite extensive. In 1991, the property disclosure procedure was introduced into the Civil Enforcement Act through amended law.[48] After the reform of the Civil Enforcement Act in 2010, the access point was transferred from the public prosecutor to the senior huissier (court officer) and the requirement to first request information from the debtor was removed.[49] L. 152-1 (Code des procédures civiles d'exécution) contains the requirements for the procedure for the disclosure of assets, the institutions concerned, the information concerned etc. L. 152-2 contains the rules for custodian and savings banks and the corresponding one's information about it. L. 152-3 regulates the handling of acquired information and the punishment for violations of these rules in order to reconcile the information gathering of the creditor and the privacy of the debtor. In France, the questioning of the debtor is an essential feature of the factual investigation.[50] If the claim has a value of less than € 535, the debtor is requested to provide information about his employer and accounts with a request for payment, indicating that the public prosecutor will investigate against him if he does not comply.[51] This indicates that the French civil enforcement law does not have a method of disclosing assets, but intends to obtain direct information from debtors. As mentioned above, sanctions are not provided in the event that the debtor does not fulfill his obligation to provide information. Both government agencies and credit companies are required to provide information to French hussiers.[52]

---

45 *Alsfasser,* Sachaufklärung in der Einzelzwangsvollstreckung, p.210.

46 The Japanese new civil enforcement act has not introduced a debtor register.

47 *Yamamoto,* Furansuho karamita Kinsenshikko no Jikkosei, in: Kinyushikko no Jitsumu to Kadai, S. 125.

48 *Id, p.127f.*

49 *Id,* p.127f.

50 *Alsfasser,* supra note 45, p.210.

51 *Id,* p.210. Prosecutors in France have traditionally played a larger role than in Japan in civil matters.

52 *Id,* p.210.

3.3 Clarification of Facts in English Civil Enforcement Law

The English Enforcement Act itself does not have its own fact-finding resources.[53] The debtor is already obliged to provide financial information based on the enforceable title of obligation (rule 71.1 Civil Procedure Rules, CPR).[54] It is not embedded in certain civil enforcement procedures, but set up in early stage. On the one hand, there is the oral examination, i.e. the debtor survey, in which the debtor has to disclose his assets. In an oral procedure, the latter must declare all assets under oath (rule 71.6 (1) CPR) that are relevant for civil enforcement.[55] If the debtor does not meet these obligations and refuses to swear or does not answer individual questions, then he can be ordered to take preventive detention (rule 71.8 CPR).[56]

3.4 Clarification of Facts in Austrian Enforcement Law

The Austrian Execution Act (§ 47 Exectionsordnung: EO) stipulates that the debtor must submit a list of assets in order to increase the transparency of the debtor's assets.[57] The obligation to draw up a list of assets is subsidiary to an unsuccessful attempt to seize assets or to enforce a salary without a third-party's debtor designation (§ 47 (2) EO).[58] If the debtor does not appear on the date for the submission of the property register or if he refuses to produce such a list for no reason, the court must first order the compulsory appearance to the court and impose imprisonment. After § 294a of the Austrian Code of Execution, the creditor can file an enforcement application in which he does not have to indicate either the third-party debtor or the legal reason for the claim, but only the date of birth of the debtor.[59] The execution court determines ex officio and can request information from the main association of Austrian social security institutions.[60]

---

[53] *Id*, p.210.

[54] *Id*, p.211.

[55] *Id*, p.211.

[56] *Id, p.211*; According to section 25.1 (h) and (f) of Civil procedure rules, the creditor is also entitled to the factual clarification of the provisional legal protection (freezing order, disclosure order).

[57] For factual clarification by the Austrian execution law: *Rechberger*, Zur Effizienz der Sachaufklärung in der Zwangsvollstreckung – Das Österreicher Exekutionsrecht - ein Vorbild?, in: FS Schilken, 2015, p. 763, 764.

[58] *Alsfasser*, supra note 45, p.211.

[59] *Rechberger*, supra note 57, p.763, 766.

[60] *Alsfasser*, supra note 7, *p211*.

3.5 *Harmonization in the European Union*

The aim of the preceding discussion was to analyze the status quo of the civil enforcement law in European countries in a simple way. Despite the large differences between European civil enforcement laws, there has been no supranational legislation to fill the gaps in the legal area of the European Union. According to § 36 (1) of Brussels I Regulation, decisions made in one Member State are recognized in the other Member States without the need for a special recognition procedure. A decision made in one Member State, which is enforceable in that Member State, is enforceable in the other Member States without the need for an enforceability declaration (Art. 39 of Brussels I Regulation). However, a requirement for recognition under the Brussels I Regulation is that the enforcement must not "obviously" contradict public policy (Art. 45 para. 1 lit. a) of Brussels I Regulation.[61] To this extent, the enforceability of judgement as such has been Europeanized.[62] However, the enforcement of judgment as such is still left to the Member States.[63] The national enforcement systems of judgment are very different due to the varying historical or constitutional backgrounds. Common to all is the goal of effective creditor satisfaction, which is guaranteed by finding debtor's assets and by fact clarification, what is enshrined at the European level in Art. 47 the Union's Charter of Fundamental Rights; and Art. 6. Para. 1 ECHR in conjunction. Art. 6 para. 1 and 3 TEU.[64]

3.6 *Measures of Europeanizing Fact Clarification*

The civil procedural law is also increasingly under the strong influence of legislation by European Union.[65] With the exception of Art. 55 of Brussels I Regulation, it strictly adhered to the principle of territoriality of civil enforcement and only enabled the recognition and enforcement of titles of obligation, but not civil enforcement itself.[66] The EU Commission tried early on to supplement European procedural law in this area.[67] The European Account Preservation Orders (EAPOs) have been in effect since January 18, 2017 and had an immediate effect in all member states (Art. 288 (2) sentence 2 TFEU).[68] This Regulation established a Union procedure enabling a creditor to obtain a European Account Preservation Order ('Preservation

---

[61] *Lüke,* Zivilprozessrecht I, 11. Aufl. 2020, section 55, Rn. 15.

[62] *Lüke*, supra note 54, section 55, Rn.14f.

[63] *Alsfasser,* supra note 7, p.213.

[64] *Alsfasser,* supra note 7, p.213.

[65] *Lüke,* supra note 53, section 54, Rn. 2.

[66] *Lüttinghaus,* ZZP 129 (2016), 187, 188.

[67] Cf, Id, 187, 189.

[68] Regulation (EU) No 655/2014 of the European Parliament and of the Council of 15 May 2014 establishing a European Account Preservation Order procedure to facilitate cross-border debt recovery in civil and commercial matters.

Order' or 'Order'), which prevents the subsequent enforcement of the creditor's claim from being jeopardised through the transfer or withdrawal of funds up to the amount specified in the Order that are held by the debtor or on his behalf in a bank account maintained in a Member State (Art. 1-1 EAPOs).[69] The Preservation Order shall be available to the creditor as an alternative to preservation measures under national law (Art. 1-2 EAPOs). The aim of the EAPOs is in particular to reduce the risk of unsuccessful enforcement in claims caused by the transfer of assets abroad by simplifying the cross-border attachment of claims.[70] The regulation enables a cross-border attachment order, which can be obtained in all stages of debt collection (Art. 5 EAPOs). Indeed, cross-border enforcement has been extremely important for European economic activity. The area of enforcement law has been called the "Achilles' heel of the European civil law area".[71] The EAPOs does not offer an actual enforcement measure, but only a security measure. Obtaining account information is a correct step for this, because within the framework of the EAPOs this is only possible with regard to the provisional account attachment.[72]

4 Conclusion

If a creditor receives a successful judgment after the civil procedure, the right to claim effective enforcement against the debtor is constitutionally guaranteed for the citizen. It goes without saying that the state would lose its legitimacy to ban self-help if the rights of creditors were not guaranteed. In contrast to the enforcement of furniture or real estate, the enforcement of claims is an intangible property right, and it is extremely difficult for creditors to find the existence and extent of the claims. In order to ensure effective protection of the rights of creditors in civil enforcement praxis, it is essential for creditors to receive information about debtors' assets.

As previously mentioned, the Supreme Court in Japan has ruled that using the so-called numbering scheme to identify debtor assets among third-party debtors (banks) could be an unreasonable burden.[73] However, there was no other effective legal basis for the attachment creditor in Japan to obtain information about the debtor's bank branch. The reform of the civil enforcement law in Japan, along with measures to strengthen the disclosure of debtor's assets or new asset information for third-party debtors such as credit institutions, is a correct step in accordance with foreign enforcement law systems to strengthen creditor protection. With regard to future questions, it is necessary to examine which roles should be assigned to the bailiffs only responsible for the enforcement of furniture and to the enforcement court that is currently responsible for the enforcement of claims. It remains to be discussed

---

[69] *Alsfasser,* supra note 7, p. 214.

[70] *Id. P.214.*

[71] *Lüttinghaus,* supra note 66, 187, 188.

[72] *Alsfasser,* supra note 45, p.215.

[73] Minshu Vol. 65, Nr. 6, S. 2710 on 20th September 2011.

whether and how the enforcement system can be organized uniformly within the judicial system in Japan. The bailiff plays an important role in both Japan and Europe. The question is how bailiffs should be trained in law to increase their ability to make legal decisions in the civil enforcement praxis.[74]

Masahisa Deguchi Professor of Civil Procedural Law at Faculty of Law, Ritsumeikan University, Kyoto/Japan. He studied at Chuo University and Freiburg University (Germany) and got Master of law (Keio University 1988) and Doctor of law (University of Freiburg 1991) through DAAD-Scholarship (1988–1991). Fellow of Alexander von Humboldt Foundation in Freiburg (1994–1995, 2007), Regensburg (2015) and Colon (2015). JaDe-Preis [Die Stiftung zur Förderung japanisch-deutscher Wissenschafts- und Kulturbeziehungen in Köln] (2002). Verdienstkreuz am Bande des Verdienstordens der Bundesrepublik Deutschland (2006). Board Member of Notarial Law in Japan (since 2005). Vice President of International Association of Procedural Law (2007–2015) and Honorary Vice-President of International Association of Procedural Law (since 2015). Member of Judicial State Examination in Japan (2012). President of Freiburg Alumni in Japan (2014), Presidium Member of Freiburg Alumni and Board Member of Alumni Freiburg e.V. (since 2016), Vice President of DAAD-Tomonokai (2019).

[74] Cf, *Walker,* DGVZ 2019, S. 89, 90; *Yanagisawa,* Doitsu niokeru Shikkokanseido no Mineika nikansuru Giron, (3), p.41. Hikakuhogaku, Vol. 42.

Investigation of Debtor's Property in Japan—To Make Claims Truly Enforceable

Hiroshi Tega

1 The 2003 Reform of the Japanese Civil Execution Act

As well as in Germany and in the other countries, creditor's burden of finding debtor's property has been a serious problem in the civil execution system in Japan. Until the beginning of this century, however, a creditor could not obtain any assistance from the execution court about it—he/she had to find property to be seized all on his/her own before filing a compulsory execution for his/her monetary claim. Especially for a creditor who have little information about debtor's property (e.g., maintenance claim creditor, crime victim, etc.), such a burden can be a big obstacle to enforce his/her claim.

It was in the 2003 reform of the Japanese Civil Execution Act (hereinafter "CEA")[1] when the Property Disclosure Procedure (the CEA articles 196 through 203. Hereinafter "Property Disclosure") was introduced as a part of the civil execution system. In the Property Disclosure proceedings, upon a petition by a creditor, a court may order a debtor to appear at the court and to make a statement on his/her property. This reform of the CEA was the first important step for the Japanese civil execution system to ease the creditor's burden to search debtor's property.

The Property Disclosure was designed with so cautious approach for fear of abuse—for example, creditors with some types of title of obligation (a judgement with a declaration of provisional execution, a notarial deed etc.) were not allowed to request the disclosure, that impaired usability and effectivity of the procedure. In

[1] Act No. 4 of 1979. An unofficial English translation of this act can be accessed at Japanese Law Translation (http://www.japaneselawtranslation.go.jp/law/detail/?id=3483&vm=02&re=01&new=1 (Last visited on Sep. 3, 2021)).

H. Tega (✉)
Tokyo Metropolitan University, Hachioji, Japan
e-mail: tega-hiroshi@tmu.ac.jp

M. Deguchi (ed.), *Effective Enforcement of Creditors' Rights*,
Ius Gentium: Comparative Perspectives on Law and Justice 91,
https://doi.org/10.1007/978-981-16-5609-5_9

particular, weak sanction (non-penal fine up to JPY300,000[2]) had caused debtor's disobedience to the disclosure order.[3]

2 Creditor's Efforts to Overcome the Difficulty of Finding Debtor's Property

Creditors (and their attorneys) have tried to explore other measures than the Property Disclosure to overcome the difficulty of finding debtors' property.

One approach was to ease creditor's burden of specifying the property to be seized. Attempts to specify debtor's bank accounts in a comprehensive way, like prof. Hess referred to the German case, were also made in Japan (for example, a creditor filed a seizure of debtor's bank accounts by ranking all the accounts in all the branches of the bank, by the factors such as the number of the branch, the type of the account, and whether or not there was any preceding seizure[4]). These attempts were, however, rejected by the Supreme Court, for the reason that an insufficient specification of accounts to be seized makes the bank's (and other interested persons') status unstable.[5]

Another approach was to obtain information about debtor's property from third parties. The Attorney Act authorizes bar associations to make, upon their member attorney's request relating a case he/she is retained, inquiries to public offices or public or private organizations for necessary information.[6] Creditors' attorneys have tried to obtain information about debtor's property, addresses etc. with this inquiry. The inquired office/organization may, however, refuse to respond to the inquiry if there are legitimate grounds (Banks often claim their duty of confidentiality as the reason of refusal[7]). And, even when the refusal was illegitimate, the inquiring bar

---

[2] CEA (before 2019 amendment) art. 206. JPY300,000 approximates USD 2,727 at the currency rate as of Sep. 2021.

[3] In 2017, Only 686 Property Disclosure cases are filed and only 253 cases were settled with debtors' disclosure of their property. Muneki Uchino et al., *Minji Shikko-ho to no Kaisei no Yoten* [Points of the Amendment of the Civil Execution Act etc.], 2118 Kin'yu Homu Jijyo 36 (2019), at 38.

[4] Nakayama v. Yoshida, 65 Minshu 2710 (Sup. Ct., Sep. 20, 2011). Unofficial English translation of the judgment can be accessed at Courts in Japan (https://www.courts.go.jp/app/hanrei_en/detail?id=1118 (Last visited on Sep. 3, 2021)).

[5] Nakayama v. Yoshida, supra note 7. X v. Y., 1386 Hanrei Taimuzu 182 (Sup. Ct., Jan. 17, 2013).

[6] Attorney Act, Act No. 205 of 1949, art. 23-2. An unofficial English translation of this act can be accessed at Japanese Law Translation (http://www.japaneselawtranslation.go.jp/law/detail/?id=3528&vm=02&re=01&new=1 (Last visited on Sep. 3, 2021)).

[7] Though responding to the bar association's inquiry can be deemed as a legitimate ground to exempt the duty of confidentiality of the inquired office/organization, the inquired has to judge whether its response is within an appropriate range at its own risk—when it disclose too much information about its customers etc., it would be blamed for the breach of confidentiality. It therefore has to be cautious about responding to the inquiry.

association may not compel the inquired to respond, nor they may claim compensation for damages caused by the refusal.[8] This inquiry of bar association, therefore, has also failed to be a definitive solution for creditors.

3 The 2019 Reform of the Japanese Civil Execution Act

The 2019 reform of the CEA[9] made two major changes with respect to a search of debtor's property. The one is the enhancement of the Property Disclosure, and the other is the introduction of new "Procedures for Acquiring Information from a Third Party".

Concerning the Property Disclosure, the range of creditors who can request the disclosure is expanded to include those who have a judgement with a declaration of provisional execution or a notarial deed etc.[10] And debtor's non-disclosure is now subject to the criminal sanctions (imprisonment with work for not more than six months, a penal-fine of not more than JPY 500,000[11]).

The Procedures for Acquiring Information from a Third Party (the CEA articles 204 through 211) allow a court, upon a creditor's petition, to order a third party to provide information about debtor's property. The following table describes three types of the procedure—what type of creditors may obtain what information from what type of third parties (Table 1).

To file the procedure #2 and #3, a creditor has to go through the Property Disclosure in the preceding three years (For the procedure #1, the preceding Property Disclosure is not required considering easiness of transfer of bank deposits, etc.). The ordered third party shall provide the information by means of documents to the court, then

[8] The Supreme Court dismissed an action by a bar association for compensation for damages against a postal service company which claimed confidentiality and refused to respond to the inquiry. Aichi Bar Association v. Japan Post co., 70 Minshu 1725 (Sup. Ct., Oct. 18, 2016). Unofficial English translation of the judgment can be accessed at Courts in Japan (https://www.courts.go.jp/app/hanrei_en/detail?id=1490 (Last visited on Sep. 3, 2021)). In this case, the inquiry was made to obtain the new address of the debtor who secretly relocated while the creditor prepared for filing compulsory execution. There is another judgment on the same case, which dismissed a bar association's action seeking a declaratory judgment of the duty to give a response to the inquiry as unlawful. Aichi Bar Association v. Japan Post co., 72 Minshu 1368 (Sup. Ct., Dec. 21, 2018). Unofficial English translation of the judgment can be accessed at Courts in Japan (https://www.courts.go.jp/app/hanrei_en/detail?id=1627 (Last visited on Sep. 3, 2021)).

[9] See Civil Affairs Bureau, Ministry of Justice of Japan, *Outline of the Act Partially Amending the Civil Execution Act and the Act for Implementation of the Convention on the Civil Aspects of International Child Abduction*, at Japanese Law Translation (http://www.japaneselawtranslation.go.jp/common/data/outline/191217095043_Re_9053101.pdf (Last visited on Sep. 3, 2021)).

[10] CEA art. 197. In these years, a notarial deed is increasingly being used to agree on child support. Satoshi Aoki, *Minji Shikko-ho no Kaisei–Saimusha no Zaisan Jyokyo no Chosa wo Chushin ni* [Reform of the Civil Execution Act–Mainly Focusing on the Investigation of Status of Obligor's Property], 1537 Jurisuto 58 (2019), at 59.

[11] CEA art. 213. JPY500,000 approximates USD 4,545 at the currency rate as of Sep. 2021.

Table 1 Three Types of the Procedure for Acquiring Information from a Third Party

#	Creditor	Third party	Information to be provided
1	Creditor who has a title of obligation for their monetary claim	Financial institution (banks, credit unions, etc.)	Matters necessary to file a petition for compulsory execution or exercise of a security interest for the debtor's claim of deposits, book-entry transfer corporate bond, etc.
2	Creditor who has a title of obligation for their monetary claim or who provide a document proving general statutory lien in the property of a debtor	Registry office	Matters necessary for a petition for compulsory execution or exercise of a security interest to the debtor's lands or buildings
3	Creditor who has a title of obligation for his/her child support or other maintenance claim, or his/her claim to damages for infringement on human life or body	Municipalities, Japan Pension Service, etc.	Matters necessary to file a petition for compulsory execution or exercise of a security interest for a claim pertaining to the debtor's salaries, remunerations etc. (e.g., the place of employment)

the court send a copy of the documents to the creditor and notify the debtor of the provision of the information about his/her property.

Creditors in Japan have long suffered from the burden of finding debtors' property, lacking effective measures to obtain information about it. Now, however, the reformed CEA has just come into force on Apr. 1, 2020. The new system is expected to be a great help for a creditor in finding the debtor's property, like the German system, to make his/her claim truly enforceable.

Hiroshi Tega Associate Professor, Tokyo Metropolitan University Law School. LL.B., 1998; LL.M., 2000, University of Tokyo; Research Assistant, Tokyo Metropolitan University, 2005-06; Academic Assistant, 2006-09; Associate Professor, Tokyo Metropolitan University, since 2009. Author: [3] Civil Provisional Remedies, in 5 Doing Business in Japan §14.08 (LexisNexis, Rel.54, 2013). Co-author: Civil Litigation, in 5 Doing Business in Japan §14.04 (LexisNexis, Rel.52, 2012).

Comment on Civil Enforcement Reforms from a Comparative and Historical Perspective

Omi Hatashin

Abstract Following the 2019 amendment to Japanese Civil Enforcement Act 1979 to provide the courts with the long-awaited 'teeth' with which to commit the obligor to custody who has failed to comply with a disclosure/discovery/searching order, this comment reviews why searching order, general freezing order, civil penalties, prioritisation of earlier enforceable titles (*Schuldtitel*), etc. were deleted during the enactment of Civil Procedure Act 1890, which was otherwise an almost article-by-article translation of German Civil Procedure Code (ZPO). Such blunting of ZPO's teeth can be explained by the surviving influence of pre-modern Japanese practice, somewhat excessive separation of civil procedure from criminal one, the moderation of certain consequences of modernisation, such as the abolition of feudal class system, etc. It is rather surprising to learn of this, because Japan succeeded in persuading Great Britain to give up their extraterritoriality, which guaranteed the security and property of British citizens in Japan, within four years of the enactment of Civil Procedure Act. Japan took from 90 to 130 years to replant and sharpen its teeth. Japanese law does not allow any general freezing order, but it would be the law's "nuclear weapons", along with a searching order. This comment suggests a way forward.

I am invited to give a comment on the international colloquium in Kyoto, 2019, "Effective Enforcement of Creditors' Rights in Civil Execution through Effective Discovery of Debtors' Assets". As a Japanese member of the English Bar, I would like to contribute to the debate from a comparative and historical perspective. My realization that Great Britain was by far the largest trade partner of Japan during the modernisation of its legal system in the nineteenth century and that England and Wales are a common law jurisdiction led to my interest in English legal history, because this may at the time have suggested a potential for Japan to modernise its own customary law, which had developed far away from the sphere of influence of Roman

O. Hatashin (✉)
Osaka Jogakuin (Wilmina) University, Osaka, Japan
e-mail: hatashin@wilmina.ac.jp

M. Deguchi (ed.), *Effective Enforcement of Creditors' Rights*,
Ius Gentium: Comparative Perspectives on Law and Justice 91,
https://doi.org/10.1007/978-981-16-5609-5_10

law. Common law and civil law could have informed the modernisation of existing old Japanese law rather than replacing it. However, that was not the path which Japanese law followed. In theory, the customary laws of Japan still remain a valid source of law, for example, under Commercial Code, but in practice, only a little survived. Why? The British, in 1882, thought that Japan would be better off if it imported French or German laws, which were familiar to the British, partly because English law was more voluminous and complex to export than modern compact codes of civil law; partly because Scotland was and is a partial civil law jurisdiction; partly because localised customary laws of Japan represented impediments to Western access to Japanese market; and partly because the Japanese desired to attain the *sui juris* status among the "civilised" nations as soon as possible (Kayaoglu 2010, pp. 96–97; Jones 1931, p. 95; FO 882/4778 1883).

For Japan, civil enforcement has been a great source of lingering concerns since the enactment of its first Civil Procedure Act 1890. The procedure was regarded as a part and parcel of the wholesale modernisation of Japanese legal system, upon which Japan's earning of the *sui juris* status among "civilised" nations hinged. So eager to delete the mark of its international inferiority, i.e. the extraterritoriality, Japan hired Eduard Hermann Robert Techow from Germany to draft Japan's civil procedure. The outcome was an *almost* article-by-article translation of German Civil Procedure Code (ZPO), which was regarded by many to be the best civil procedure at the time. On 16 July 1894, merely three and half years after the coming into force of Courts Act 1890 and Civil Procedure Act 1890, Japan succeeded in persuading the most powerful, Great Britain, to agree with the annulment of the extraterritoriality in five years, and took the liberty of waging war against China in no time. The brisk and successful conclusion of the limited war by Japan on 17 April 1895 prompted the ratification of the similar treaties with dozens of Euro-American powers. From 1899 onwards, foreigners in Japan were freed from their confined settlements, which were reclaimed from the sea near the designated treaty ports, and to live anywhere in Japan subject to Japanese law. How modern was it in practice, asked the China Association, the most powerful British interest group in the Far East, which had been kept in the dark while White Hall and Kasumigaseki negotiated the terms of their new treaty of commerce and navigation behind the closed doors (FO 881/6582 (1894: 153–154)). The British communities in Japan wanted to wait and see whether or not Japanese codes and courts were adequate and competent enough to guarantee their security and property to their satisfaction (FO 881/6582 (1894: 153–154)).

The deep chasm between London and the reclaimed settlement in Yokohama leads me to wonder which factors contributed more to Japan's rapid rise to the *sui juris* status under positivist international law, its fire power, or civil power. The Civil Procedure Act 1890 seems to suggest that it was the former. The Act looked like a faithful, *almost* article-by-article translation of ZPO. This was somewhat strange not least because Japanese Civil Code 1896 relied on a great variety of civil codes across the globe. On closer examination, Civil Procedure Act 1890 was deprived of its teeth, in other words, lacking provisions guaranteeing obligees'/creditors' rights. The deleted examples include the compulsory retaining of attorneys in the court of first instance and the recovery of attorneys' fees from the losing party; the priority of the first creditor who had secured his enforceable title (*Schuldtitel*) to the other creditors who did so later; the courts' power to compel the obligor to comply with orders; disclosure/discovery of the obligor's assets from which to pay judgment debts where the creditor's enforcement turned out to be ineffective; and a general/abstract freezing order (Sono'o 2009, p. 215; Sono'o 2011, pp. 12–13). Litigants in person tend to delay and confuse the administration of justice and do not serve their own interests either. The denial of the winning party's recovery of attorneys' fees, which, by the English standard, could often amount to no smaller than the sum of judgment debt itself, deterred any litigation. The virtual absence of civil penalties meant that the effectiveness of civil justice depended entirely on the good will of the obligor. The less property, the less fear of enforcement. The more dishonesty, the more advantages for the obligor. The insistence on thorough equality among all kinds of creditors, whether they had secured their enforceable titles or not, served to delay the enforcement proceedings, and denied expeditious administration of justice. The lack of compulsory disclosure of the obligor's assets and the creditor's duty to specify the particulars of any object of a freezing order tended to make the enforceability contingent on many uncertainties.

It is somewhat surprising to learn that the British agreed to give up the extraterritoriality, even though the Japanese civil procedure had provided the courts with such weakened and diminished powers to protect the creditors' rights. It is perhaps even more surprising to learn that it was as late as 1979 that Japan departed from its radical egalitarianism for the priority ("the sooner, the better recovery") principle in enforcement. It was only in 2003 that disclosure orders were enacted to be available, in theory, against the obligor and third parties such as the tax office and the automobile inspection and registration system. In practice, it was only in 2019 (effective from 1 April 2020) that the courts were provided with a tooth in their proceedings, i.e. the power to commit the obligor to custody up to six months for failure to comply with a disclosure order (§213, Civil Enforcement Act 1979 as amended in 2019). It must be all the more astonishing to remember that Japan experienced periods of rapid industrial developments before and after the Second World War without the enactment of Civil Enforcement Act 1979. Indeed, it looks to be the case that the Japanese civil procedure had little to do with their modern industrialisation. It is intriguing as to what enabled the Japanese to develop the size of their economy to a greater extent than that of the Germans in the Federal Republic without effective civil enforcement mechanisms, which were expected to underpin the security of modern business transactions.

It is difficult to give satisfactory answers to this riddle. The Japanese had larger demographic dividends than the Germans in the relevant periods. The ways in which business trust is being built in Japan is said to be largely different from Germany and the United States, and it tends to take much longer for strangers to enter into closed Japanese society to win very personal trust. Business profile does not seem to matter so much in Japan. This is arguably a symptom of a society where court is not particularly trusted. Perhaps because the resort to court is a kind of salvage operation after something goes wrong, civil enforcement reforms are more likely to be conducted at the time of economic difficulties than at the time of economic boom.

Why were the said enforcement provisions of Civil Procedure Act 1890 so radically different from ZPO 1877? The first difference related to attorneys was caused by the underdevelopment of professional bar in Japan by the late 1880s, because Japan used to admit only litigants in person in principle. The concept of attorneys as officers of court was entirely new to Japan. By contrast, the virtual loss of civil penalty was partly attributable to Western overinsistence on the separation of civil procedure from criminal procedure. The pre-modern Japanese authorities discharging judicial functions were far more rigorous to "enforce" their orders, in the sense that non-compliance would be met with a range of sanctions from chains and detention, on the one hand, to the seizure and sale of property on the other, and the latter was not necessarily limited by the rationale of enabling the recovery of debts, but designed to deprive the non-complying party of his property (*shindai kagiri*). As regards the denial of the priority principle in enforcement, which similarly marked a striking departure from Japan's pre-modern practice, Sono'o Takashi, a former senior judge of Tokyo Court of Appeal, offers the following explanation. The abolition of feudalism meant that upper classes were no longer immune from courts' sanctions. No bankruptcy protection was available for debtors yet. It seems to be most likely that Yamada Akiyoshi, the Justice Minister as of early 1889, who rose from the ranks of warrior class and was apparently unable to free himself from Confucian prejudice against merchant class, found it necessary to deter 'usury' creditors from exploiting the law machine and punishing the poor for greed (Sono'o 2011, pp. 13–14). Sono'o attributes the unavailability of disclosure/search in enforcement proceedings to the then unavailability of bankruptcy protection, too (Sono'o 2009, p. 217). When it came to the creditor's duty to specify the particulars of any object of a freezing order, which survives to this day under Civil Preservation Act 1989, Sono'o attributes the duty to pre-modern Japanese practice, where the relevant authorities were minded to protect debtors from fishing expedition by 'usury' creditors (Sono'o 2009, pp. 183–184).

So, some parts were due to the surviving influence of Japan's pre-modern practice, and some were new, designed to moderate the consequences of the abolition of feudalism for the interests of the poor. It took nearly 90 to 130 years for Japanese Diet to give the courts those powers which were denied back in 1890.

As far as the freezing order is concerned, its English counterpart, the *Mareva* (freezing) injunction ([1975] 2 Lloyd's Rep 509) does not necessarily require the specification of the particulars of the object, and it is normally combined with the *Anton Piller* (searching) order ([1976] Chap. 55). These demand the *ex parte* applicant Counsel to be most carefully and professionally prepared to assure the judge in chambers that there is neither abuse such as fishing expedition nor error (Forrester 2020). These are the English "law's two nuclear weapons" ([1985] F.S.R. 87, 92 per Lord Donaldson MR) and as such, call for utmost caution on the part of the judge. This caution seems to have led the United Kingdom to opt out of its EU version, European Account Preservation Order, after preparing for it (Rechberger 2019). Judges in some of the EU members, for example, Germany, may be qualified to grant it, but from the UK point of view, it is still premature to adopt at the EU level.

Judge Sono'o, as of 2011, similarly observed that it was still necessary in contemporary Japanese society to deter greedy creditors from persecuting the poor through the law machine and to maintain Japan's 'traditional good morals and fair customs' (Sono'o 2011, pp. 14–16). Such concerns are hardly unique to Japan. However, the court may also be invited to vindicate and enforce the right of a poor mother and infants against a rich father in default of his maintenance duties, dissipating and hiding his assets, for example. Japan's problem seems to be that judges are chronically overburdened with hundreds of backlog cases per person at one time, without much assistance from attorneys on both sides. The separation of procedural judges and trial judges may be useful in striking out unmeritorious claims sooner. There seems to be significant room for improvement in terms of efficient allocation of time and resources to judges and attorneys in administering justice, so that they can give due undivided attention to meritorious claims. This may pave the way for Japan to enable judges in the future to grant an abstract freezing order, coupled with a searching order.

References

Japanese Statutes

Civil Procedure Act 1890 (Meiji 23, Horitsu No. 29)
Civil Enforcement Act 1979 (Showa 54, Horitsu No. 4)
Civil Preservation Act 1989 (Heisei 1, Horitsu No. 91)
Civil Procedure Act 1996 (Heisei 8, Horitsu No. 109)

English Cases

Anton Piller KG v Manufacturing Processes Ltd [1976] Ch. 55, CA
Bank Mellat Iran v Nikpour [1985] F.S.R. 87, CA
Mareva Compania Naviera SA v International Bulkcarriers Ltd [1975] 2 Lloyd's Rep. 509, CA

British Foreign Office Archives

FO 882/4778 (1883)
FO 881/6582 (1894: 153–154)

Unpublished Sources

Forrester I (2020) Reply to the present author's intervention after his lecture entitled. "The European Account Preservation Order", on 17 February at Ritsumeikan University

Rechberger W (2019) Intervention after the present author's intervention in the Q&A session after Professor Dr. Bart Krans's presentation entitled, "European Account Preservation order (EAPO): a view from the Netherlands", at the International Colloquium, on 8 November at Ritsumeikan University

Published Sources

Jones FC (1931) Extraterritoriality in Japan and the Diplomatic Relations Resulting in its Abolition, 1853–1899, New Haven, CAT: Yale University Press

Kayaoglu T (2010) Legal Imperialism: sovereignty, extraterritoriality in Japan, the Ottoman Empire and China, Cambridge: Cambridge University Press

Sono'o T (2009) Minjisosho, Shikko, Hasan-no Kingendaishi, Tokyo: Kobundo

Sono'o T (2011) "Kingendai Hoseishi-kara mita Yusenshugi to Byodoshugi (Ge)", Hanrei Times, No. 1339, pp 5–16

Omi Hatashin born 1966, B.A. in law 1991, University of Tokyo; Ph.D. 1999, Lancaster University; call to the English Bar by the Inner Temple, 2003; Senior Visiting Fellow, St. Antony's College, Oxford University, 2004; Comparative European Law, Oxford University, 2008. In 2010, he became a part-time lecturer at the School of International Liberal Studies, Waseda University. Since 2016 he has been teaching at Osaka Jogakuin (Wilmina) University and College.

Proposal for a Procedure to Strengthen Creditor's Claims While Protecting Debtor's Quality of Life and Privacy in Japan

Study Group for Improvement of Civil Enforcement Law

Hiroko Namura and Shigehide Koyanagi

Abstract We are members of the study group for Improvement of Civil Execution Procedures. We consider the inefficiency of the civil enforcement law in Japan as a cause for frustration of creditors who have obtained a monetary judgment. After visiting and learning from the procedures in European countries, we decided to propose a new enforcement procedure called Enforcement Executive (the "EE"). The EE, we propose, is an attorney at law who is appointed by a court upon at the request of a creditor. The EE may have access to all the information of the assets of the debtors, which should not be shared by the creditor. The EE may choose the asset of the debtor to enforce. The EE may enforce directly when the asset the EE chooses is a third-party debt. If the asset is movable, the EE files the motion to attach to an enforcement officer. If the asset is a real estate, the EE will apply the judgement lien. We are also thinking to empower to the EE to offer an installment payment plan to the creditor. With this new enforcement procedure, we may escape from the dilemma between the requirement of creditors' access to debtors' asset information

---

Members: Shigehide Koyanagi, Attorney at Law (Senior Researcher); Hiroko Namura, Attorney at Law (Reporter); Prof. Dr. Masahisa Deguchi; Katsuhisa Masuda, Attorney at Law; Hirofumi Ata, Attorney at Law; Kenya Nagashima, Attorney at Law; Prof. Yoshihisa Hayakawa. Only the co-authors have the responsibility regarding this legal essay, however, all the members discussed and made great effort to consider how to renovate the civil enforcement procedure in the Japan as written in this essay.

We felt honored to have the opportunity to attend and introduce our study at the colloquium on November 8th, 2019 where highly esteemed academics and practitioners gathered on the campus of Ritsumeikan University under the great coordination by Professor Masahisa Deguchi.

H. Namura (✉)
Osaka, Japan
e-mail: namura@namura-law.jp

S. Koyanagi
Yokohama Minato Law Office, Yokohama, Japan
e-mail: office@minato-law.jp

M. Deguchi (ed.), *Effective Enforcement of Creditors' Rights*,
Ius Gentium: Comparative Perspectives on Law and Justice 91,
https://doi.org/10.1007/978-981-16-5609-5_11

for effective enforcement and protecting debtors' privacy from creditors and give an opportunity to a debtor to restructure his/her life.

1 The Purpose of Our Study Group

We are members of the *Study Group for Improvement of Civil Execution Procedures*. The members share the common understanding that the civil enforcement law in Japan does not function effectively and creditors who have obtained a monetary judgment are quite frustrated since they are not able to collect all of the payment from his/her debtor even when trying to enforce the money judgment.

One of the reasons for such frustrations is that the assets of the debtors are not disclosed to the creditors in effective ways although Japan has implemented a procedure of debtors' assets information. Thus, we think a new procedure should be introduced for creditors while protecting the debtors' privacy and their lives.

2 The Newest Amendment from the Old System of the Civil Enforcement Act of Japan

The Civil Enforcement Act of Japan, however, has been continuously amended to provide disclosure procedures to satisfy creditors who desire access to their debtors' assets while balancing the protection of the privacy of the debtors and excessive enforcement against them.

We would like to precede the newest amendment from the old system of the Civil Enforcement Act of Japan before stating our proposal for the procedure of enforcement executives.

3 The Legislative Process of Investigating Debtor's Property

3.1 Property Disclosure Procedure

The Civil Enforcement Act of Japan requires creditors to specify the properties of their debtors in petitions of compulsory execution. Thus, to clarify the specific assets of debtors is material to start compulsory execution.

In 2003, "the property disclosure procedure" was introduced[1] to the Civil Enforcement Act of Japan for the first time as a procedure for obtaining information about

[1] This procedure came into force in 2004.

debtors' properties by the debtors' own statements. It was modeled on the German system.[2] However, it employs the old German system in which the court, not the executive officer, has jurisdiction over the Property Disclosure Procedure.[3] Therefore, in Japan, courts have jurisdiction over the property discovery procedure.[4]

The process of the property disclosure procedure before the 2019 revision is as follows.[5]

3.1.1 The Requirements for a Petition

The title-of-obligation which makes this procedure available is restricted to a final and binding judgment, a settlement record that has the same effect as a judgment, etc., and excludes a judgment with a declaration of provisional execution, execution deed, and demand for payment.

3.1.2 Requirements of Such as Un-successful Compulsory Execution to Be Shown[6]

For filing the petition, it is necessary that any compulsory execution ends up unsuccessfully or, a prima facie evidence should be produced that the petitioner is unable to obtain full performance even by implementing compulsory execution against the known property (hereinafter referred to as "Requirement of Ineffective Execution.").

---

[2] Section 807 ZPO former version before 2009 (Section 802 c Vermögensauskunft des Schuldners ZPO current version).

[3] In Germany, the executive officer has jurisdiction over property discovery procedure since the Second Compulsory Execution Amendment Act (BGBI.I.S.3039), which was enacted in 1997 and came into effect in 1999.

[4] Article 196, Civil Execution Act (Japan). The following are the article of the Civil Enforcement Law of Japan unless otherwise specified.

[5] Shigehide Koyanagi, Zaisankaiji no Jitsumu to Riron(Practice and Theory of Property Disclosure Procedure), p. 7–35,67–103.

[6] This requirement is also stipulated in Article 197 (1) and (2) of the Civil Enforcement Law in the current law as follows.

Article197 (1) When the petitioner was unable to obtain full performance of said monetary claim in the procedure of liquidating distribution, etc. (excluding a procedure that was terminated by at least six months prior to the day of filing the petition) in compulsory execution or exercise of a security interest. (2) When prima facie showing was made that the petitioner is unable to obtain full performance of said monetary claim even by implementing compulsory execution against known property.

(http://www.japaneselawtranslation.go.jp/law/detail/?re=01&ky=release&ia=03&page=16&la=01&ja=04, **last visited September 23, 2020).**

3.1.3 Hearing

Upon a creditor's appropriate petition, the court summons the debtor who is requested to make a statement regarding his/her property on a property disclosure hearing date which is not held publicly.

3.1.4 Means to Ensure Effectiveness

In the following events, a non-penal fine of up to 300,000 Yen may be imposed on a debtor:

1. Failure to appear on the property disclosure hearing date,
2. Refusal to swear under oath, or
3. Rejection to make a statement or making a false statement at the hearing.

    (a) 2019 amendments to Property Disclosure Procedure

However, the number of filings did not reach 1000 annually contrary to the expectation of the legislators. We think creditors hesitated to file the procedure because of many tough requirements for filing. Therefore, it was necessary to improve the effectiveness of the investigation procedure about the debtor's property.

In 2019, two material revisions were made to this procedure. The first one is reviewing requirements for the application of such a disclosure procedure. The limitation to the titles-of-obligation, which was criticized, was abolished. Thus, a creditor who has any kind of title of obligation may apply a petition of the property discovery procedure. The second is the review of penalties for procedural violations. The non-penal fine of 300,000 yen was changed to imprisonment of 6 months or less or a criminal fine of 500,000 yen or less. However, a kind of hurdle, the Requirement of Ineffective Execution still remains as a requirement to the application of disclosure procedure.[7]

(b) Introduction of the new procedures for obtaining information on debtor's property from third parties

Three different kinds of procedures have been implemented by the revision in 2019 as follows.[8] The district court shall have jurisdiction over these three procedures (Article 204).

For filing these three kinds of petitions, the Requirement of Ineffective Execution is necessary for each of them.

---

[7] In Germany, Requirement of Ineffective Execution was abolished by the revision in 2009.

[8] The following procedures b. and c. came into effect in April 2020.

(i) Acquisition of Information on Real Property of Obligor (Article 205[9])

A creditor with a title of an obligation of monetary payment may request a registry office of real estate to disclose the real estate owned by his/her debtor. Filing this petition should be applied within three years after the property disclosure procedure is carried out.

(ii) Acquisition of Information on Salary Claim of Obligor (Article 206)

The information on a salary is acquired from municipalities, the Japan Pension Service, etc. This procedure is limited to a creditor who has a title-of-obligation related to child supports or claims for damages based on life/physical injury. The same procedural requirements as the above procedure in the item are required.

(iii) Acquisition of Information on Claim of Deposits or Savings, etc. of Obligor (Article 207)

The information on claims of such as Deposits is acquired from Financial Institutions, etc.

A pre-property disclosure procedure is not required to obtain such deposits information. This is a measure to improve the effectiveness of seizure of deposits since the money in them can be drawn easily.[10] This is a unique character of Japanese legislation.[11]

4 Remaining Issues of the Amendment in 2019

4.1 Property Disclosure Procedures

The court is still hosting the discovery process, which remains a heavy process.

Requirement of Ineffective Execution is still required.

One of the court cases clearly shows that the Requirement of Ineffective Execution is a burden on a petitioner by reversing the district court decision which had dismissed the application)[12] (the "Decision").

[9] This procedure is scheduled to come into effect in April 2021. Since construction of a system took time, effecting is overdue.

[10] Kazuo Imai et al., kaiseiminjisikouhou jitumukaisetu (Revised Civil Enforcement Law, Practical Commentary), pp. 84–86.

[11] In Germany, only after the debtor does not comply with his obligation to disclose his or her financial situation, the bailiff may access the Federal Central Tax Office in order to get information of the debtor's bank accounts, (ZPO8021).

[12] Appeal against a Disposition of Execution filed against the decision to dismiss the petition for the property discovery procedure, Osaka High Court 2009 (La) No. 1166, dated as of January 19, 2010.

The Legislative Council insisted that the problem of the severe burden shown in the Decision changed the practice to reduce the burden on petitioners to ease them to apply the property disclosure investigation, therefore, the abolition of the Requirement of Ineffective Execution[13] would be postponed,

Nonetheless, the abolition of the Requirement of Ineffective Execution in Germany affected the way of Japanese property investigation procedure significantly. The investigation procedure came to be used to search assets of debtors before the execution of titles of creditors. The investigation procedure had been allowed to apply after a creditor tried to execute his/her title before the amendment.[14]

We believe that in Japan as well, the Requirement of Ineffective Execution should be abolished in order to position the property investigation procedure first.

4.2 Procedures for Obtaining Information from Third Parties

The property disclosure procedure must conclude unsuccessfully in order to request information of the registry offices of real estates and municipalities and the Japan Pension Services.

Both the preceding property disclosure procedure petition and the subsequent information acquisition procedure from a third party require the Requirement of Ineffective Execution to make a petition. We have the concern that this element makes the structure complicated and this burden to the petitioning creditors tends to make them give the petition up.

Only a creditor who has a title of obligation related to child support or damages based on life/physical injury can access information on salaries of his/her debtor. However, all creditors who have any kind of title of an obligation of monetary payment need such information.

In Japan there is no central organization like that in Germany or France which has control of the information owned by all the banks, therefore, a creditor must make inquiries to each bank.[15]

The information of a debtor is quite limited. Information related to any other assets like cancellation refund of insurance or information related to unregistered real estate owned by governmental offices should be more accessible.

Eiji Uchiyama,Toshio Uehara et al., Hanrei Hyakusen Minjisikkou-Hozen (100 Selections of Civil Enforcement and Conservation Judgments), p. 172 (2012) (Author Koyanagi acted as an agent).

[13] Kazuhiko Yamamoto et al., Ronten kaisetu Reiwa gannen kaisei minjisikouhou (Explanation of Issues, Revised Civil Enforcement Law of Reiwa 1 Year), pp. 24–27(2020).

[14] See. Hess, pp. ??–??.

[15] Muneki Uchino et al., Q & A reiwa gannen kaisei minnjisikkouhousei (Revised Civil Enforcement Legislation of Reiwa 1 Year, p. 113–114.

5 The Purpose of Our New Proposal

We hope you could see how the Civil Enforcement Act of Japan has been amended to strengthen the enforcement of monetary judgments. However, we are afraid that the various procedures implemented in the Civil Enforcement Act are still not enough to realize a title of obligation in effective ways.

This thought motivated us so much to research and study whether any good measure can be introduced that we visited Luxembourg, Austria, Switzerland, and Germany in the summer of 2018 (cooperated by Professor Deguchi).

We visited Professor Burkhard Hess and Dr. Veerle Van Den Eeckhout at the Max Planck Institute Luxembourg. We learned from them about European Account Preservation Order Regulation ("EAPO"). We also discussed with Professor Cunibert regarding the EAPO and the measures to investigate assets of debtors in France.

Then we moved to Austria and in Wien we met Dr. Franz Mohr,[16] the chief of the No. 15th department at Federal Legal Ministry (Justizministerium) which has authority for civil enforcement proceedings and Mr. Robert Gleixner[17] at the position of supervising enforcement officers there. Furthermore, we visited Professor Walter H. Rechberger[18] and Professor Andreas Konecny[19] at the faculty of law at Wien University. Then, we attended a meeting with Attorney Florian Masser, who is an expert in civil enforcement proceedings at the Austrian Bar Association. After that, we also visited the Wien District Court to meet with Judge Michael Schaumberger who is the authority on civil enforcement proceedings there. He explained the measure to find assets of debtors in Austria.

In Switzerland, we met with Professor Samuel P. Baumgartner and Mr. Thomas Winkler, an enforcement officer (Betreibungsbeamter)[20] at Zurich University and Professor Daniel Staehelin at his law offices in Basel. We learned from them the measures of collecting monetary debts in Switzerland, the Civil Procedure Law and Enforcement and Bankruptcy Law in Switzerland (Bundesgesetz über Schuldbetreibung und Konkurs [SchKG[21]]).

In Freiburg in Germany, we visited the District Court Freiburg to meet with Dr. Thomas Kummle, the chief of the court, and Ms. Katharina Matzken, a court clerk

---

[16] Exekutionsverfahren zuständigen Abteilungsleiter im Bundesministerium für Justiz.

[17] The former chairperson of German Civil Procedure Leitungseinheit Gerichtsvollzug, Mitglied der FEX-Planungs- und Leitungseinheit beim OLG Wien,Trainer im Justizbildungszentrum Schwechat,Sachverständiger in der Arbeitsgruppe Exekutions- und Insolvenzrechtfür den Zentralausschuss beim BMJ.

[18] Vice chairperson of the study group of the officers in charge of German Civil Procedure and an author of a hornbook of civil procedure.

[19] Head of the Institute for Civil Procedure Law at the University of Vienna (2000–2009). Deputy Head of the Institute for Civil Procedure Law (2010~).

[20] Betreibungsbeamten is an officer belonging to an administrative organization which has a jurisdiction to collect third party debts.

[21] Articles 149–149a and 265 of the Federal Code on the Enforcement of Money Judgments and Bankruptcy, SchKG , available at https://www.admin.ch/opc/de/classified-compilation/18890002/201901010000/281.1.pdf, last visited September 23, 2020.

(Rechtspflegerin). Ms. Matzken kindly gave us a presentation regarding the measure to find assets of debtors in Germany and then a Q & A session was held as joined by Professor Dieter Leipold[22] and Professor Alexander Bruns.[23]

6 Proposal of New Procedure of Enforcement Executive

Now, we would like to introduce our proposal to strengthen and innovate civil enforcement. We named this procedure as the procedure of the Enforcement Executive. The name of this EE is our tentative proposal and if a good naming suggestion is made, we are willing to adopt such an alternative. We consider the naming as important to make a procedure attractive and effective. Until then we will keep the name "EE" from now on.

What we propose is a kind of officer called the EE who will be authorized to coordinate the entire civil enforcement process. We suggest that the EE may make an investigation of the debtor's property and realize such discovered property by the power to apply compulsory execution. The procedures of EE and the powers we think the EE should be granted are explained as follows.

6.1 *Appointment of an Enforcement Executive*

1. First step is that a creditor who has a title-of-obligation files a petition to a district court which has the jurisdiction to his/her debtor for this procedure. This petition should be simple so that creditors who have a title of obligation may apply it by themselves. In the near future, when such filing can be done online by entering the necessary information in the form prepared by the district court, a creditor may easily file it by himself or herself. Such simplicity should make this procedure very practical.
2. Upon the filing, the court appoints an EE in charge of satisfying the title-of-obligation the applicant creditor owns. We propose that the EE should be an attorney at law with expertise in bankruptcy proceedings.
3. The EE investigates the debtor's property and makes a concrete plan to satisfy the title-of-obligation of the applicant creditor.

---

[22] The legendary authority of civil procedure academism in Germany who served as the chairperson of the study group of the officers in charge of German Civil Procedure.

[23] LL.M. at Duke University in North Carolina in the US. The chairperson legal policy association (Mitglied des Präsidiums der Gesellschaft für Rechtspolitik).

6.2 Compulsory Execution to Assets of a Debtor

The EE should be authorized to perform compulsory execution against property owned by the debtor.

1. The most effective and easiest measure is the seizure of third-party debtors. Therefore, we think the seizure of debts owed by such a third party can be performed by the EE with its own power.
2. For movables, a compulsory execution sometimes requires physical enforcement power to which an attorney at law is not an expert. Thus, we think what an EE can do to movables is filing a petition to a court and the appointed court execution officer will execute the movables in the same manner as the officer does for the current proceeding system.
3. For real property; it is a serious decision to perform a compulsory sale of the real property since it causes a material impact on the life of the debtor. Furthermore, such compulsory sale of real estate may cost the applicant creditor. Thus, we propose it should be appropriate to grant a limited power to the EE just to establish a title-of-obligation-mortgage to real property owned by the debtor (ex. judgment lien). The Civil Enforcement Act of Japan does not provide such a judgment lien; such a procedure should be provided there. After the EE establishes the mortgage, the EE should inform the creditor regarding the mortgage to the real property of the debtor and let the creditor decide the subsequent execution procedure.

6.3 Recommendation of a Settlement Between a Creditor and a Debtor

We also propose to grant the EE the power to make recommendations for a kind of settlement between such creditor and the debtor.

1. Even if the properties the EE finds in his/her investigation are not enough to satisfy all the debts to the applicant creditor, the EE may make a payment plan (in installments) based on the debtor's proposal.
2. When the EE concludes that the debtor is insolvent and the debtor is not willing to pay his/her debt by installment, the EE notifies and reports to the creditor in writing that the title-of-obligation is unable to be fulfilled.
3. After that, when the creditor seeks an adjudication of the debtor into bankruptcy by using the above report, we propose that the fee for such a bankruptcy procedure that the creditor pays to court will be reduced from the regular fee without the EE Procedure.

7 The Good Points of the Procedure of Enforcement Executive

7.1 *To Make a Balance of Satisfying Title-of-Obligation and Protecting the Private Information of a Debtor*

Different from the current procedure where a creditor obtains the property information of his/her debtor, only the EE receives the information from third parties or the debtor about such information. Thus, third parties do not need to be cautious about the invasion of the privacy of the debtor. We think it may make third parties more cooperative to the EE. By that, we think the investigation of the debtor's property becomes fast and effective as a preparatory act for compulsory execution.

7.2 *Simple Proceeding for a Creditor*

Once an EE is appointed, there is no need for the applicant creditor to make any other proceeding. The EE will request the disclosure to the debtor and proceed compulsory execution immediately after the discovery of the debtor's property without any measure by the creditor. As I mentioned above, the application for an EE may be structured in a quite simple form since only a creditor is just proving he/she has the title of obligation.

7.3 *Protection of a Debtor's Quality of Life*

The EE may support a debtor who is willing to pay his/her debts by offering installment payment plans. Thus, a debtor has an opportunity to keep his/her current quality of life even after the compulsory execution has started.

7.4 *Smooth Transition to a Bankruptcy Proceeding*

Finally, an EE's report about the insolvency of the debtor allows a smooth transition to bankruptcy proceedings.

However, what by "smooth" we do not mean a bankruptcy proceeding as a direct result as the Swiss SchKG does.[24] It means to make the information of assets of a

[24] In Switzerland, monetary claims collection and bankruptcy proceedings are stipulated in one law, Bundesgesetz über Schuldbetreibung und Konkurs (SchKG).

debtor found in an EE proceeding available in the latter bankruptcy proceeding for the debtor. The process is as follows.

When the EE finds the assets of the debtor are insufficient to satisfy the debts against the applicant creditor and the debtor has no plan to pay the debt by installment, the EE reports his/her investigation to the applicant creditor.

If the creditor decides to file a bankruptcy proceeding against the debtor, the creditor may attach the report of the EE to prove the elements for adjudication of the debtor into bankruptcy. We consider the filing fee for bankruptcy may be discounted since the bankruptcy trustee may be the same person as the EE and may save his/her time to spend on the investigation of the debtor's assets.

On the other hand, it may allow the debtor to reset his/her situation by a bankruptcy proceeding. Such debtor may be indemnified from over loans or heavy debts and restart a new life.

8 The Procedures in Other Countries Giving Inspirations to the EE Procedure

We structured our EE Proceeding by discussing how to coordinate the excellent proceedings we learned in the study in Europe in 2018 to the current proceedings in Japan.

8.1 EE's Power to Investigate a Debtor's Properties and Performing Compulsory Execution

The EE will be granted the power to investigate the debtor's properties and is authorized to proceed with compulsory execution by him/herself. The model of this power and authorization is the procedure in Switzerland and in Germany.

In Switzerland, an executive officer (Betreibungsbeamter) investigates a debtor's property by having the debtor disclose the assets or contacting the third parties (Article 91SchKG). Then, the executive officer selects a target from all the assets found and seizes it to realize the selected object.

In Germany, it is possible for enforcement officers to (a) make payment plans, (b) file for property disclosure procedures, (c) obtain information from third parties, (d) seize and realize**re** movables, and (e) delegate prior seizures(Section 802a ZPO).

For the avoidance of doubt, we are not copying the proceeding in Germany where the authority of the enforcement officer is empowered, since the Japanese enforcement officers are not in charge of investigating the properties of the debtors as well as executions of the claim to third party debtors in the current procedure. We are trying to make a new quasi officer, "EE", like a bankruptcy trustee to be appointed by a court. We consider it better to establish a new system of EE instead of granting enforcement officers other authorities since the attorneys who work as bankruptcy trustees are accustomed to such work.

8.2 EE's Power to Establish a Payment Plan by a Debtor

In Germany, it has been reported that a system for temporary suspension of execution by planning payment installments based on the debtor's proposal is functioning effectively (Section 802b ZPO).

In Switzerland, there is also a procedure called a settlement contract (Article 293 SchKG).

We arranged these procedures to grant the EE the power to try to mediate the settlement regarding the payment by a debtor.

8.3 Title-of-Obligation-Mortgage to Real Property

We referred to what is called a Judgement Lien, in which a security interest is set on the debtor's real property based on a final judgment which originated in Austria (Section 87 EO) and was developed in the United States.

8.4 The System to Protect the Debtor's Privacy

The EE controls information of a debtor which prevents creditors from directly obtaining such information. Under the current Civil Enforcement Act of Japan, a creditor collects the debtors' information, but in Germany and France,[25] court enforcement officers collect such information.

8.5 Relationship with Bankruptcy

In Switzerland, an administrative enforcement officer's procedure is well connected with bankruptcy. For example, the Betreibungsbeamter can shift from enforcement to bankruptcy proceedings without any petition.

---

[25] Articles L152-1~3 Code de la Procedure civile d'execution (France), available at https://www.legifrance.gouv.fr/codes/section_lc/LEGITEXT000025024948/LEGISCTA000025025755/#LEGISCTA000025026669, last visited September 23, 2020.

The property information of the debtor who was investigated under the EE procedure can be transferred to bankruptcy proceedings. Such transfer may reduce the cost of bankruptcy proceedings.

9 Cost, Multiple Creditors, and Multiple Debts Against the Same Creditor

9.1 *Fee for the EE*

9.1.1 Introduction

The matter of cost should be structured with various viewpoints of fees to establish the system and the relation with other proceedings as well as the fee for the proceeding.

Let us consider this matter with some cues by comparing it with the systems in other countries, like Germany where enforcement officers are granted to obtain information from the third parties regarding the financial situation of the debtor (Section 802c and 802 l ZPO), and Switzerland where administrative enforcement officers (Betreibungsbeamte) can not only collect information but also execute to the properties of the debtor and claims to third party debtors.

In Japan, the enforcement officers are in charge of the execution of movables and the execution of building eviction, for example, and cannot collect the debtor's financial information or execute against a claim.

Enforcement officers are applied by the retired court clerks. Thinking about their career, it takes time and cost to prepare an adequate number of enforcement officers who have the expertise to find the assets of debtors which is not the role of court clerks. Also, establishing an independent organization in charge of executing against a claim to a third-party debtor should be more costly in Japan.

Thus, it is more cost-effective to establish a system of enforcement executives who are attorneys at law with enough knowledge and experience as bankruptcy trustees. Also, it will not take a long time to initiate such a system.

Also, by mimicking the bankruptcy trustee training system, we can develop a skilled EE at a reasonable cost.

On the other hand, for the fee for each application of civil enforcement after the system is established, it is possible to keep the cost relatively low if the executive officer or the collection officer (Betreibungsbeamter) carries out the procedure. Thus, to request such a proceeding to EE, the civil professionals, looks more costly at a glance.

However, we think we may institute the system with a reasonable cost when we consider that the EE performs all the proceedings like the investigation of the assets of the debtor, compulsory execution against a claim, and recommendation of settlement.

9.1.2 Examples

To analyze this more specifically, let us show some examples.

We think the basic court filing fee for an EE procedure is between 150,000 and 200,000 Japanese Yen (about 1000 or 1500 Euro) depending on the number of claims, with a success fee equivalent to 3 to 5% of the collected amount.

There would be less resistance to pay the success fee when the EE succeeds at collecting money, however, if it is concluded that the title-of-obligation cannot be realized at all, the applicant creditor will not be able to collect the basic filing fee.

In the current civil enforcement proceedings, even though creditors usually engage with attorneys at law to apply any of the enforcement proceedings, most of such proceeding ends up unsuccessfully.

For example, the investigation proceeding does not reveal any asset of the debtor even though the creditor engages with an attorney at law to proceed to the disclosure proceeding,

Or in spite of the efforts of the attorney who is hired to enforce the title of obligation, he/she discovers that nothing remained in the bank account of the debtor. Such a creditor has to pay attorney fees, but gained nothing.

As written in the introduction, we propose to make the filing system for EE proceedings simple in order for a creditor to apply and file an EE proceeding without the support of an attorney.

It would be even better if a creditor may file it online by checking boxes in an application form. In that case, a creditor does not need to hire attorneys to enforce the title of obligation. We can think of the fee for an EE as an alternative to the attorney fee. We hope you understand that the amount we are proposing is not unreasonably expensive compared to the current system.

9.2 *Multiple Creditors*

We consider that other creditors may join in the ongoing EE procedure as follows;

1. Before payment planning is settled.
2. Before the EE seizes specific claims (third party debts).
3. After the EE files a petition for execution against movables and before such movables are transferred to others.
4. After the EE registers mortgage against real property and the creditor executes the mortgage, and before the end of the demand for liquidating distribution set by an execution court.

9.3 *Multiple Title-of-Obligations Owned by a Creditor*

The same EE may execute the procedures for multiple titles-of-obligation. The EE may establish a payment plan to satisfy multiple titles-of-obligation.

10 Conclusive Remarks

Ultimately, we would like to emphasize again that a reform to satisfy the title of obligation is an urgent issue. Without such a reform the frustration of the creditors who can not realize their titles of obligation may cause the loss of credibility in the judicial system. One of the grounds that makes such a realization difficult is the rapid deterioration of the value of movables like furniture and household appliances. Another is the difficulty to enforce execution to the financial assets which are of various kinds and for which the debtors' personal **information**, which is more sensitive to obtain currently, is necessary for execution. These matters are commonly understood in many countries as well as in Japan. We think professionals can perform their roles as a balancer to enforce the title of obligation effectively while protecting the interest of the debtors.

This legal essay is our challenge trying to propose an effective procedure by making the professionals work efficiently in Japan. We hope this proposal will add momentum to further discussions.

Hiroko Namura born in Kyoto, Japan in 1960, the representative attorney at law of Namura and Partners from 2000. She studied law at Osaka University and later finished LL.M. at University of Chicago in 1996. She is qualified as an attorney at Osaka Bar association and NY State Bar Association. Her areas of practice are international transactions, intellectual properties, bankruptcy including international corporate bankruptcy cases, antitrust defense, merger & acquisition, civil litigations and international arbitrations.

Shigehide Koyanagi born in Nagasaki, Japan in 1964, became the director of the Yokohama Minato Law firm in 2007. He studied law at the University of Chuo, and graduated in 1990. He became a judicial apprentice in 2004 and became a lawyer after undergoing practical training. He belonged to the Kanagawa Bar Association and served as the vice chairperson of the Japan Federation of Bar Associations' Committee on Civil Trial Procedures. He was a part-time lecturer in the Constitution at Izumi Junior College in 2011. He belongs to a research group on civil enforcement law and has visited countries such as the United States, Germany, France, South Korea, Austria, Luxembourg and Switzerland. He has written books and several treatises on property discovery. Since 2018, he has been a senior researcher at the Study Group on Improving the Effectiveness of Civil Enforcement Procedures.

Some Comments on the Proposals of the Study Group from a German Perspective

Wolfgang Lüke

1 Efficient Proceeding and the Recent Reform of the German Enforcement Law

As a person that is not familiar with the Japanese enforcement law and its shortcomings, I probably should not give any comments on that. The only reason, why I dare to do the contrary, is the fact, that the proposal the study has presented, is also referring to the German enforcement law. Especially in the field of information about the debtor's seizable assets the current Japanese law is to a certain degree similar to the German law, that has served as a model. Furthermore, the shortcomings in both laws are or have been partly similar. At the end, the study group is trying to improve the enforcement proceeding by making it more efficient. Both laws are trying to achieve more efficiency in the field of enforcement law. There are different ways to increase the efficiency of the enforcement proceeding: e.g., to strengthen the possibilities for the creditor to get information on the debtor and his assets or improving the enforcement proceeding itself, to name just two. This is true for Germany as it is for Japan.

2 The Problem of Disclosure

The study group has discovered different reasons for the inefficiency of the enforcement proceeding. The lack of information on the seizable assets of the debtor causes unsuccessful attempts to get satisfied by enforcing a title. As the study group is stating, one of the main reasons why creditors are frustrated of the enforcement

W. Lüke (✉)
Leipzig University, Leipzig, Germany
e-mail: lueke.pulsnitz@web.de

M. Deguchi (ed.), *Effective Enforcement of Creditors' Rights*,
Ius Gentium: Comparative Perspectives on Law and Justice 91,
https://doi.org/10.1007/978-981-16-5609-5_12

proceeding in Japan is the fact, that the assets of the debtor are not disclosed to the creditors enforcing. Although the current Japanese enforcement law includes a disclosure procedure, this proceeding is used very rarely. The study group considers the prerequisites of the procedure to be tough, even though the legislator has tried to improve the regulation in 2019: Now the proceeding is open even for small claims[1] and the sanctions for not disclosing the property are now a lot more severe than before. Consequently, the study group is proposing a reform of that part of the Japanese enforcement law.

In general, one can say, an efficient enforcement proceeding requires—among others—for the creditor a solid knowledge of the assets to seize. In order to get that knowledge, there are different possible ways one can choose: One can solve this problem by way of substantive law, as it is the case in the law outside the enforcement world. For instance, in the relationship between agent and principal: if it is the duty of the agent to bring his principal and third parties into a contractual relationship. Instead in the context of enforcement law the procedural frame offers a possibility to get access to information in a less cumbersome way.

The study Group proposes different measures in order to improve the enforcement proceeding. Since its members consider the prerequisite of an unsuccessful execution in order to file a petition for disclosure, as one of the reasons, why many creditors refrain from filing a petition for enforcement, it is convincing, if the study group proposes to abolish that requirement.[2] The same is true for the access to information concerning salaries. So far, this is open only to creditors of maintenance claims and certain damage claims. The proposal is suggesting to make that information accessible for just any creditor.[3] Besides that, the study group is proposing to broaden the scope of the information. It would clearly make sense to oblige the debtor to disclose all the seizable assets, no matter whether movables, immovable, claims, titles or other rights. All these suggestions will most likely increase the efficiency and the attractiveness of the enforcement proceeding.

---

[1] There was such a limit also in the German law in regard to the information gained from third persons, § 802l ZPO. That access to information was not open for creditors of small claims (on the amount of less than 500,00 EURO). That limitation was abolished in the year 2016, BGBl 2016, I, p. 2509.

[2] This was a mandatory requirement also in the German law according § 807 Abs. 1 No. 1 ZPO (former version); today it is also possible to ask the debtor to disclose his or her assets before starting the enforcement, § 802c ZPO. Instead, the creditor can file a petition to the bailiff to start the enforcement into the seizable chattels and in case, that is unsuccessful, also to disclose his or her assets.

[3] In regard to this information in Germany the bailiff can ask under certain circumstances defined governmental entities for information on facts, which are specified in the regulation, § 802l ZPO; this regulation is considered to be compatible with the constitutional protection of privacy; cf. BVerfG NJW 2007, 2464.

3 The Enforcement Executive as Enforcement Manager

While the proposals above mentioned fall within the frame of the German proceeding, that has been changed fundamentally in 2013,[4] the study group goes far above that, developing the idea of an enforcement executive (hereinafter: EE). That person is supposed to be the main person in the enforcement proceeding, appointed by the court after a petition of enforcement has been filed. The EE is in charge for the coordination of the enforcement, investigating the property of the debtor, also asking third persons for information on that; furthermore the study group is suggesting that the EE may be empowered to seize a claim of the debtor against third parties. He can open the seizure of movables by filing a petition. Regarding immovables the EE has the power to establish a title of obligation mortgage. Then, it will be up to the creditor to proceed with the enforcement. The EE can also recommend settlements between the creditor and the debtor, such as installment plans. The EE may also notify the creditor that the debtor is unable to fulfill the executory title. His report will form the basis of a possible bankruptcy proceeding and reduce the fees paid to the court in such a proceeding.

The EE should be appointed by the district court once a petition for enforcement has been filed. The study group is suggesting, the EE should be an attorney at law, with good expertise in the field of bankruptcy law. It is pointing out that it should not be a state or court official in contrast to different European legal systems but an attorney.

As I understand the proposal, the EE is to a certain degree functionally the equivalent to the German bailiff. However, in contrast to German bailiff, the EE has more of a leading function within the enforcement proceeding than the bailiff in the current German law. In this regard, the proposal is very different from the current German law. In Germany, in general it is the creditor, who is deciding what measure should be taken within an enforcement proceeding, by filing a corresponding petition. There is a number of petitions or motions, which a creditor may file within the proceeding; often without the help of a lawyer or a legally well informed person the creditor will not be able to make a deliberate decision on which steps should reasonably be taken next. However, it is considered to be consistent with the current law if the creditor is giving just a general order to the bailiff by filing a not very specific petition to enforce, leaving the rest up to the bailiff who is implementing the creditor's discretion.

Apparently, it is the idea that the proceeding is going to be more efficient, if it is in the hand of one person, who is in charge of the enforcement management. The proposal leaves that up to the EE. According the German law this power remains at the creditor. Even in Germany, there is a strong opinion, which considers the concentration of the enforcement proceeding on one person as a way to increase the efficiency of the proceeding. Currently it is discussed to transfer the leading role to the bailiff as the main person implementing a kind of claim management and to

[4] Gesetz zur Reform der Sachaufklärung in der Zwangsvollstreckung vom 29.7.2009, BGBl. I p. 2258, in force since Jan. 1, 2013.

empower him to seize also claims and titles and other rights.[5] According the current law this power lies still with the court of enforcement.

If one agrees with the idea, that in an enforcement procedure a convergence of all the responsibilities in mainly one person will lead to a more efficient procedure, the limitations of powers of the EE proposed by the study group will again cause inefficiencies. Maybe these limits are from the viewpoint of the Japanese law unavoidable, if the proceeding is transferred to an attorney, but at least from the perspective of efficiency, it is desirable to leave as much as possible in the hand of one organ, which can decide what measure to take.

4 Attorney's Exercising Sovereign Power

In Germany the enforcement will start seizing an asset of the debtor. That seizure which will create a security right[6] based on an execution order is considered as a sovereign act.[7] The seizure will be done by the enforcement court, bailiff, or the land registry office. They are all part of the judiciary at least in a broad sense.[8] Therefore, if one would try to implement the proposal of the study group into the German law, it would require to assign such power to an attorney as a private person. In that regard the situation is quite different to the current German enforcement law. At the moment, all the enforcements acts are carried out by officers or clerks of the courts. As state officers they all have the power to undertake sovereign acts. Therefore, under the current law the question to be empowered to act as a sovereign is not raised.

The situation is also not comparable to the bankruptcy proceeding where the bankruptcy court is rendering the decision to open an insolvency proceeding. As the consequence of that opening decision all the debtor's assets are garnished. The trustee, regularly an attorney, is in charge to administrate the debtor's estate, already garnished by the court.

Even though it is possible to entrust private persons with public powers, it is a rare exception in German law. But in the year 2010 the legislator introduced a proposal[9] to change the status of the bailiff from a civil servant to a private person empowered to perform sovereign acts. One of the main reasons for that proposal was to avoid the costs for the bailiff, since the fees are not covering the costs he is causing.[10] That proposal was considered to be inappropriate and therefore rejected by the federal government[11] with the result that until today the bailiff is still a public servant.

[5] *Walker*, DGVZ 2019, 89; it would, however, possibly require, that the bailiffs would need a different legal education.

[6] So called Pfändungspfandrecht, § 804 ZPO.

[7] The same is true for the realizing of the pledged goods.

[8] Even though they do not act as courts in the constitutional sense.

[9] BT-Dr 16/5727, p. 1 ff.

[10] BT-Dr 16/5727, p. 35.

[11] BT-Dr 16/5727, p. 110.

Apparently, the proposal expects a more efficient proceeding if it is run by attorneys. If that is true, one has also to decide whether the surveillance of the attorneys for that part of their work is sufficient. At least in Germany one would have also to create new regulations on personal liability for that field of legal work, as it is true for lawyers working in the field of public notary.[12]

At the end, in Germany the fees of this kind of measures would have to be raised, since at the moment the measures of the bailiff are not covered by the fees. It is very likely, that attorneys would try to avoid this kind of working unless it is providing for a decent income.

Wolfgang Lüke Prof. Dr., LL.M. (Chicago) holds the Chair of Civil Law, Civil Procedure Law, Notarial Law and Comparative Law at the University of Leipzig. His doctoral thesis was on "Die persönliche Haftung des Konkursverwalters" (Munich, 1986). He obtained the academic degree of a Master of Laws at the University of Chicago Law School (1986/1987). After completing his habilitation in 1991 (with a thesis on "Die Beteiligung Dritter im Zivilprozeß", Tübingen, 1993), he was bestowed the venia legendi for Civil Law, Civil Procedural Law and Comparative Law. In 1992, he was appointed to one of the five founding professorships at the Faculty of Law of the TU Dresden. There, he acted as Dean from April 1995 until June 1997. Between 1996 and 2009, he acted as a judge (part time) at the Court of Appeal in Dresden. Subsequently, from May 2009 to June 2011, after a leave of absence was granted, he worked full time as Attorney at law in a law office in Munich. After that, he resumed his work at his chair in Dresden. On September 01, 2018, Prof. Lüke switched to the Faculty of Law at the University of Leipzig.

[12] Cf. § 19 DNotO.

Comment on "A Proposal of a Procedure to Strengthen Creditor's Claims While Protecting Debtor's Quality of Life and Privacy in Japan" by the Study Group for Improvement of Civil Enforcement Law

Hans-Peter Marutschke

The subject dealt in the above-mentioned paper has gained in importance, since the corona pandemic changed daily life circumstances worldwide. Most dramatic changes can be witnessed in the economy, with especially medium and small companies or self-employed people, who run very small businesses in order to earn their livelihood. After half a year of severe restrictions set up by the government, many companies etc. struggle to survive or went bankrupt, despite the massive financial support policy. In consequence, creditors have difficulties to collect their debts, like rental fees and unpaid bills for delivered goods, and debtors look to get rid of their debts—which is not easy because it would need to carry out a bankruptcy procedure.

A similar situation applies to private people who lost their job and now as well are not able to pay back depts or bank loans.

With regard to the actual situation, this comment will concentrate on describing legal instruments recently set up in Germany to cope with the controversial interests of creditors and debtors facing the corona-crises.

In this context I would like to refer to the various countermeasures taken in Germany to minimize the economic and social consequences of the COVID-19 pandemic, especially with the respective law, enforced end of March 2020 under the title "Gesetz zur Abmilderung der Folgen der COVID-19 Pandemie im Zivil-, Insolvenz und Strafverfahrensrecht" (Act to mitigate the consequences of the covid19-pandemic in private law, insolvency law and criminal procedure law).

This law sets up in Art. 5 a payment moratorium for existing continuing obligations in favor of consumers and small businesses. According to this regulation, private households and small businesses can suspend payment for electricity, gas and district heating supplies for a maximum of three months if the payment difficulties are due

H.-P. Marutschke (✉)
Doshisha Law School, Kyoto, Japan
e-mail: hmarutsc@mail.doshisha.ac.jp

M. Deguchi (ed.), *Effective Enforcement of Creditors' Rights*,
Ius Gentium: Comparative Perspectives on Law and Justice 91,
https://doi.org/10.1007/978-981-16-5609-5_13

to the circumstances of the Corona crisis. In the commercial customer area, the right to withhold performance expressly applies only to very small companies and is not applicable to small, medium-sized and large commercial and industrial entities. This means that the contractual and civil law termination and retention rights apply without restriction to this group of customers in the event of default in payment.

Although the law refers expressively to the interests of companies of general interest (creditors) and their customers (debtors), the principles laid down in this law, especially with regard to the duty of customers to disclose the facts and reasons for their inability to perform payment, will apply adequately to other legal relationships.

Furthermore, Article 1 of the legislative package suspends the obligation to file for insolvency until September 30, 2020 for companies with payment difficulties. In the course of this, the right to avoid insolvency was severely restricted so that in later insolvency proceedings the insolvency administrator cannot contest payments made during this period on energy and water supplies. According to this, in addition to the payment in accordance with the contract, payment facilitation and performance in lieu of performance or on account of performance as well as payments by a third party on the instruction of the debtor are expressly insolvency-proof.

The aim of the package of measures is to enable and facilitate the continuation of companies that have become insolvent or have economic difficulties as a result of the pandemic. The companies concerned and their organizational representatives should be given time to take the necessary precautions to eliminate the bankruptcy, in particular to apply for state aid for this purpose or to make financing or restructuring arrangements with creditors and investors. For consumers and small businesses, it should be ensured that they are not cut off from services of general interest such as electricity, gas, heat or drinking water if they are unable to meet their payment obligations due to circumstances that can be traced back to the pandemic.

The law does not establish an automatic deferral of the payment obligation, but the contractual partner must expressly invoke the right to refuse performance and demonstrate that the requirements are met. In the explanatory memorandum for the law, this is made clear with the following words: "The right to refuse performance must be asserted as an objection. The debtor who cannot afford payment because of the pandemic must therefore expressly invoke the right to refuse performance and, in principle, also prove that he cannot afford to pay precisely because of the pandemic. In practice, this will be particularly important if the creditor doubts that the debtor is not able to provide his services due to the pandemic."

The utility company is therefore not obliged to automatically defer payment for the due claim or to proactively inquire about the reasons for the arrears in payment. There is also no legal obligation to inform customers about the possibilities of the right to refuse performance. It is therefore at the discretion of the respective utility company whether and how such notices are included in the warning letters or on the company's website. This means that as long as a consumer or a micro-enterprise does not explicitly invoke the right to refuse performance–be it in advance or on the occasion of a reminder–the regular insolvency procedure of the utility company takes place in the event of default in payment.

From the point of view of data protection law, the utility company is entitled to request the information that is required to clarify the legal requirements of the right to refuse performance. With the self-declaration the customer guarantees the correctness of his information. As part of the organization under data protection law, the utility company must ensure that the personal details used to demonstrate the right to refuse performance are not used for other purposes and are deleted when the purpose is no longer applicable.

The new regulation has effect on the insolvency procedure:

Article 1 of the COVID-19 Insolvency Suspension Act (COVInsAG) contains a temporary amendment to the Insolvency Code (InsO), according to which the obligation to file for insolvency (Article 15a InsO) is suspended for companies with payment difficulties until September 30, 2020. The suspension does not apply if the bankruptcy cannot be attributed to the effects of the COVID-19 pandemic or if there is no prospect of eliminating an insolvency that has occurred. However, since it may be unclear whether the bankruptcy is due to the effects of the COVID-19 pandemic or not and, given the uncertainties, it is difficult to make forecasts, companies that were already insolvent as of December 31, 2019 are still obliged to file for bankruptcy. This fact is also of particular importance for the limitation of the obligation to file for insolvency.

To sum up, we can say that the new regulation in German insolvency law tries to keep a balance between the interests of creditor and debtor in these difficult times, by setting a time frame within which the debtor can try to recover from payment difficulties, but has to reveal or disclose all circumstances of his financial and economic situation, so that the pandemic can not be used as an excuse to get rid of debts at the expense of the creditor. The position of the creditor has been strengthened, because he can enforce the disclosure. It might be interesting for Japan to have a look from the point of view of comparative law with regard to a respective legal reform.

Hans-Peter Marutschke Prof. Dr., studied law in Tuebingen (Germany) and Geneva (French part of Switzerland) and passed the First Barexam in 1976. From 1976 to 78 he was a Monbusho/DAAD-Scholar at Tokyo University, Faculty of Law and passed the Second Barexam in Germany in 1981. From 1983 to 89 he held a position as DAAD-Lecturer for German Law at Kobe University, Osaka University and Osaka City University and was nominated Associate Professor at Kobe University in 1985. Back in Germany in 1989 he established a Distance Learning Course for Japanese Law at Hagen University, which became the first, only and still ongoing possibility for fundamental and comprehensive studies of Japanese Law in German Language. In 1992 he got his Ph.D (Dr. iur.) Degree from Hagen University, and published on top, in 1996 a dissertation on comparative Japanese, German and French Law, earning the Degree of Habilitation with teaching qualification in Japanese Law, Comparative Law, German Civil Law and Japanese Legal and Social History. He became Director of the new founded Institute for Japanese Law at Hagen University in 2002, and responded in 2004 to a call for professorship at the newly founded Law School at Doshisha University, Kyoto, to teach Comparative Legal Culture, European Law, as well as German Law at the Doshisha Faculty of Law and Business Law at Doshisha Business School. As Director of the EU-Research Center from 2005 to 2009 and of the Institute for Comparative Studies from 2010 to 2014 he organized numerous international symposia, lecture sessions and seminars on comparative law. For consecutive 12 years he organized as well two weeks Study tours to Europe for students of Doshisha and Kyoto University Law Schools, was active in various functions in Japanese-German- Exchange Organizations and received funding from the Japanese Ministry of Education, Culture, Sports, Science and Technology (Monkasho) for a research project on the History of Japanese Legal Scholars in Germany. He retired from Doshisha Law School in March 2021.

The European Account Preservation Order in Dutch Practice

Bart Krans and Pauline Ribbers

1 Introduction

Times change. In May 1980, the European Court of Justice decided that judicial decisions authorizing provisional or protective measures, which are delivered without the party against which they are directed having been summoned to appear, and which are intended to be enforced without prior service, do not come within the system of recognition and enforcement of the European Communities.[1] Twenty-six years later, in October 2006, the European Commission published a Green Paper in which it launched a consultation on the need for a uniform European procedure for the preservation of bank accounts and the possible features of such a procedure.[2] On 25

[1] Court of Justice 21 May 1980 (*Denilauler v. SNC Couchet Frères*), Case C-125/79, EU:C:1980:130, p. 1572, cf. Opinion of Advocate General Szpunar, delivered on 29 July 2019, Case C-555/18 (ECLI:EU:C:2019:652), para 1. Cf. CJEU 7 November 2019 (*K.H.K. v. B.A.C. and E.E.K.*), Case C-555/18, ECLI:EU:C:2019:937.

[2] Green Paper on improving the efficiency of the enforcement of judgments in the European Union: the attachment of bank accounts {SEC(2006) 1341}/*COM/2006/0618 final*/, Brussels, 24 October 2006.

Bart Krans is full professor of private law and civil procedure law at Leiden University (the Netherlands). Pauline Ribbers is a PhD-fellow at Leiden University (the Netherlands). This chapter was finished in June 2020.

B. Krans (✉) · P. Ribbers
Leiden University, Leiden, Netherlands
e-mail: h.b.krans@law.leidenuniv.nl

P. Ribbers
e-mail: p.l.f.ribbers@law.leidenuniv.nl

M. Deguchi (ed.), *Effective Enforcement of Creditors' Rights*,
Ius Gentium: Comparative Perspectives on Law and Justice 91,
https://doi.org/10.1007/978-981-16-5609-5_14

July 2011, the Commission presented a proposal for a Regulation creating a 'European Account Preservation Order' to facilitate debt recovery in civil and commercial matters.[3] On 17 July 2014, Regulation No. 655/2014 (hereinafter: the (EAPO) Regulation), establishing a European Account Preservation Order procedure, entered into force.[4] This procedure enables the creditor of one Member State to protect the future enforcement of his claim by preventing his debtor from withdrawing and/or transferring funds held on bank accounts maintained in another Member State.[5]

In this contribution, the following subjects will be discussed: the EAPO in general (no. 2), with a particular focus on the subject of the request for the obtaining of account information (no. 3). After some general information will be given with regard to the enforcement and prejudgment attachment in the Netherlands (no. 4), the Dutch implementation Act on the EAPO will be discussed (no. 5), (again) with a particular focus on the request for account information (no. 6). Subsequently, Dutch case law on the EAPO will be discussed (no. 7). In short, judgments have been delivered on the subjects of security to be provided by the creditor (no. 8), the request for information (no. 9), and on the subjects of jurisdiction and the revocation of an EAPO (no. 10). Lastly, some final remarks will be given (no. 11).

2 The EAPO in General

Before the entering into force of the Regulation, a creditor who wanted to seize funds on a bank account in another Member State had to turn himself to a court in the country where the bank account was held. This procedure had several complications, in particular when the creditor wanted to preserve funds on several bank accounts that were maintained in several Member States. In short: judicial decisions authorizing provisional or protective measures were not covered by the system of recognition and enforcement provided for by the European Union: the European Court of Justice ruled so in 1980 in its landmark case *Denilauler*, and later this rule was laid down in Article 2 of the Brussel I bis Regulation.[6] This changed, however, with the entering into force of the EAPO Regulation. Not without reason, the Regulation is referred to as a huge

---

[3] Proposal for a Regulation of the European Parliament and of the Council–Creating a European Account Preservation Order to facilitate cross-border debt recovery in civil and commercial matters, COM(2011) 445 final, Brussels, 25 July 2011.

[4] Cf. Art. 54 Regulation (EU) No. 655/2014 of the European Parliament and of the Council of 15 May 2014 establishing a European Account Preservation Order procedure to facilitate cross-border debt recovery in civil and commercial matters. The Regulation applies from 18 January 2017 (Art. 54). Legal basis: Art. 81(2) TFEU.

[5] G. Cuniberti & S. Migliorini, *The European Account Preservation Order Regulation: A Commentary*, Cambridge University Press 2018 (online), p. 10.

[6] Denilauler: see footnote 1. Brussel I bis Regulation in full: Regulation (EU) No. 1215/2012 of the European Parliament and of the Council of 12 December 2012 on jurisdiction and the recognition and enforcement of judgments in civil and commercial matters (recast).

step forward compared to the *ex ante* situation.[7] The EAPO Regulation established a uniform procedure on seizure of bank accounts. Previously the European Order for Payment and the Small Claims procedure established uniform procedures on respectively payment orders and small claims.[8]

The scope of the EAPO Regulation, however, is limited in several ways. In the first place, the Regulation is a European Union instrument that only applies in Member States.[9] Besides, the Regulation only applies to pecuniary claims in civil and commercial matters in cross-border cases.[10] The restriction to civil and commercial matters excludes inter alia administrative and social security matters, insolvency and arbitration.[11] A case can be qualified as 'cross-border' if, inter alia, it is one in which the bank account or accounts to be preserved by the Preservation Order are maintained in a Member State other than the court of the Member State in which the creditor is domiciled.[12] By way of example, a German court can issue such an order for a bank account in Belgium or in the Netherlands.[13]

The purpose of the Regulation, in short, is preservation, in cross border cases, in an efficient and speedy way, of funds held in bank accounts.[14] By making use of this Regulation, creditors can protect future cross border enforcement of their claim(s) by freezing money on bank accounts.[15] In order to freeze the funds on the bank account, a Preservation Order must be obtained.[16] The application for such an order can be lodged by using a special form.[17] In the proceedings to obtain a Preservation Order legal representation by a lawyer or another legal professional is not mandatory.[18] A court in a Member State can issue ex parte a Preservation Order freezing a bank account that is maintained in another Member State.[19]

An important condition for issuing a Preservation Order is the so-called 'urgent need for a protective measure in the form of a Preservation Order'.[20] The court shall

---

[7] See for example *C. Santaló Goris, 'First impressions from Kirchberg on the EAPO Regulation–Opinion of AG Spuznar in Case C-555/18', in June 2020 consulted on* conflictoflaws.net/2019/first-impressions-from-kirchberg-on-the-eapo-regulation-opinion-of-ag-szpunar-in-case-c-555–18/.

[8] Regulation (EC) No. 1896/2006 of the European Parliament and of the Council of 12 December 2006 creating a European order for payment procedure and Regulation (EC) No. 861/2007 of the European Parliament and of the Council of 11 July 2007 establishing a European Small Claims Procedure.

[9] It does not apply in Denmark.

[10] Art. 2(1) EAPO Regulation.

[11] Art. 2(2) EAPO Regulation.

[12] Art. 3 EAPO Regulation.

[13] There is a special rule on jurisdiction in Article 6 of the EAPO Regulation for cases where the debtor is a consumer who has concluded a contract with the creditor, cf. no. 10 of this contribution.

[14] Cf. recital 5 of the preamble of the EAPO Regulation.

[15] Cuniberti & Migliorini 2018, p. 10.

[16] See EAPO Regulation, Chap. 2 ('Procedure for obtaining a Preservation Order').

[17] Art. 8 EAPO Regulation.

[18] Art. 41 EAPO Regulation.

[19] Art. 11 EAPO Regulation.

[20] Art. 7(1) EAPO Regulation.

issue a Preservation Order only when the creditor has submitted sufficient evidence to satisfy the court that there is such an urgent need. This condition comes down to it that there must be a real risk that, without such a protective measure, the subsequent enforcement of the creditor's claim against the debtor will be 'impeded or made substantially more difficult'.[21] Where the creditor has not yet obtained in a Member State a judgment, court settlement or authentic instrument requiring the debtor to pay the creditor's claim, the creditor shall also have to submit sufficient evidence to satisfy the court that he is likely to succeed on the substance of his claim against the debtor.[22]

3 The Request for the Obtaining of Account Information

It is very well possible that a creditor does not know the name of the bank of the debtor and/or the number of the debtor's bank account. According to the Regulation, the creditor may request the court to request that the information authority of the Member State of enforcement obtains the information necessary to allow the bank(s) and the debtor's account(s) to be identified. The Regulation requires that each Member State makes available in its national law at least one of the several methods of obtaining that information.[23]

The option to request for the obtaining of account information is an important subject. If creditors do not have sufficient information about the whereabouts of the bank account(s) of the debtor, the option to freeze bank accounts may turn out to be merely theoretical. In other words, one cannot take blood from a stone, but one must also know where the money can be found.[24] Article 14 of the Regulation provides the option to request for information. If the creditor has obtained an enforceable judgment in a Member State, he can request the court to request that the information authority of the Member State of enforcement obtains the information necessary to allow the bank or banks and the debtor's account(s) to be identified.[25] According to Article 14(2) of the Regulation, the creditor shall substantiate why he believes

[21] Art. 7(1) EAPO Regulation.

[22] Art. 7(2) EAPO Regulation.

[23] Art. 14(5) EAPO Regulation.

[24] So, with good reason that this topic was already addressed in the rapport by Burkhard Hess of 2004, see: B. Hess, Study No. JAI/A3/2002/02 on making more efficient the enforcement of judicial decisions within the EU: Transparency of a Debtor's Assets, Attachment of Bank Accounts, Provisional Enforcement and Protective Measures, 18 February 2004.

[25] Art. 14(1), first subparagraph of the Regulation reads as follows: 'Where the creditor has obtained in a Member State an enforceable judgment, court settlement or authentic instrument which requires the debtor to pay the creditor's claim and the creditor has reasons to believe that the debtor holds one or more accounts with a bank in a specific Member State, but knows neither the name and/or address of the bank nor the IBAN, BIC or another bank number allowing the bank to be identified, he may request the court with which the application for the Preservation Order is lodged to request that the information authority of the Member State of enforcement obtain the information necessary to allow the bank or banks and the debtor's account or accounts to be identified.'.

that the debtor holds one or more accounts with a bank in the specific Member State and shall provide all relevant information available to him about the debtor and the account or accounts to be preserved.

It is up to the court where the application for a Preservation Order is lodged to consider whether the creditor's request is sufficiently substantiated.[26] When the court is satisfied that the creditor's request is well substantiated and that all the conditions and requirements for issuing a Preservation Order are met, except for the information requirement, and, where applicable, the security requirement pursuant to Article 12 of the Regulation, the court shall transmit the request for information to the information authority of the Member State of enforcement in accordance with Article 29 of the Regulation.[27] So then the request is brought to the information authority of the other Member State.[28]

4 Enforcement and Prejudgment Attachment in the Netherlands

Enforcement measures (in Dutch: *dwangmiddelen*) are laid down in the Dutch Code of Civil Procedure (hereinafter: CCP).[29] The main coercive measure is the attachment in execution (*executoriaal beslag*).[30,31] Other coercive measures are the committal for failure to comply with a judicial order (*lijfsdwang*[32]) and the incremental penalty payment (*dwangsom*[33]).[34] In general, two conditions have to be met in order to be entitled to use coercive measures: i) the creditor has to be entitled to enforcement,

[26] Art. 14(2) EAPO Regulation.

[27] Art. 14(3) EAPO Regulation.

[28] In no. 6 of this contribution, the question of how this request is dealt with in the Dutch EAPO implementation Act will be discussed.

[29] In Dutch: *Wetboek van Burgerlijke Rechtsvordering*, see for the text of the Code: wetten.overheid.nl/BWBR0039872/2019-01-01.

[30] See: Article 439 et seq. CCP, cf. e-justice.europa.eu/. The attachment in execution has to be distinguished from the prejudgment or conservatory attachment (Art. 700 et seq. CCP, *conservatoir beslag*), an example of a so-called 'preservative measure' (*conservatoire maatregel*), which is taken pending the obtaining of a title to enforcement.

[31] Three categories of execution can be distinguished: i) right to redress without the need of a title, see, inter alia, Article 3:248 Dutch Civil Code (*parate executie*); ii) forced execution of one or more assets of the debtor in order to collect a monetary claim, Article 3:276 DCC (*verhaalsexecutie*); iii) execution for specific performance, Articles 3:297–301 Dutch Civil Code and Articles 491–500 CCP (*reële executie*).

[32] Art. 585–600 CCP.

[33] Art. 611a-611i CCP.

[34] These two coercive measures are also labelled as 'indirect' (because there is a certain 'incentive' to the debtor to comply with the judgment) means of enforcement (*indirecte executiemiddelen*), whereas attachment is an example of a 'direct' (because no cooperation by the debtor is needed) mean of enforcement (*direct executiemiddel*).

in other words: the creditor is in possession of a title to enforcement[35]; ii) the title to enforcement has to be served in advance on the party against whom the enforcement is aimed.[36] Service will take place by a bailiff (*deurwaarder*).[37]

When the creditor has not yet been entitled to enforcement, protective measures by attachment (*conservatoir beslag*, hereinafter: prejudgment attachment) are available which anticipate a judgment.[38] The main purpose of prejudgment attachment is to prevent the debtor from alienating the attached asset(s) before or during legal proceedings against this debtor.[39] In order to be able to levy a prejudgment attachment, the preliminary relief judge of the competent District Court has to be requested to grant leave (*verlof*) to prejudgment attachment.[40] To obtain this leave, the applicant has to present a (written) petition (*verzoekschrift*) to the preliminary relief judge.[41] The petition has to contain the following information: the nature of the attachments to be made, the legal basis of the underlying claim(s) and—if it concerns a money claim—the estimated amount of the underlying claim(s).[42] The request will be dealt with only summarily[43]; in general, the debtor will not be notified of the request and no hearing will be held.[44] As soon as[45] the leave for a prejudgment attachment is granted, the leave and the petition, together with the writ of attachment, have to be served by a bailiff to the debtor.[46] However, as *conservatoir beslag* is a protective (and therefore temporarily) measure, the leave is given under condition that the applicant (i.e. the creditor) will initiate proceedings on the merits against the debtor within a

---

[35] Art. 430(1) CCP. E.g. the first enforceable authenticated copy (*grosse*) of a judgment (*vonnis*) delivered in the Netherlands, a decision (*beschikking*) of a Dutch court or an authentic deed executed in the Netherlands.

[36] Art. 430(3) CCP.

[37] Article 430(3) CCP in conjunction with Article 45(1) CCP.

[38] See Art. 700 et seq. CCP. See, in general, e.g. A. Steneker, *Mr. C. Assers Handleiding tot de beoefening van het Nederlands Burgerlijk Recht. Procesrecht. 5. Beslag en executie*, Deventer: Wolters Kluwer 2019; GS Burgerlijke Rechtsvordering, commentaar op titel Vierde titel Rv, in: P. Vlas & T.F.E. Tjong Tjin Tai (ed.), *Groene Serie Burgerlijke Rechtsvordering*, Deventer: Wolters Kluwer (online).

[39] Cf. Art. 1(1) EAPO Regulation: '(…) which prevents the subsequent enforcement of the creditor's claim from being jeopardised through the transfer or withdrawal of funds up to the amount (…)'.

[40] Art. 700(1) CCP. See also: the attachment syllabus (*beslagsyllabus*), version February 2020 (source: www.rechtspraak.nl/sitecollectiondocuments/beslagsyllabus.pdf). This syllabus contains requirements that seizure assessments must comply with in order to sufficiently inform the preliminary relief judge. The syllabus is published under the responsibility of 'Landelijk overleg Vakinhoud Civiel, Kanton en Toezicht van de rechtbanken' (which can be translated as: 'National Consultation Course Content Civil, District and Supervision of the District Courts').

[41] Article 700(2) in conjunction with Article 700(1) CCP.

[42] Art. 700(2) CCP.

[43] Art. 700(2) CCP: '(…) De voorzieningenrechter beslist na summier onderzoek. (…)'.

[44] Asser Procesrecht/Steneker 5 2019, nos. 197, 198.

[45] This can be very soon as it concerns preliminary relief proceedings.

[46] Art. 702 CCP.

certain period of time,[47] i.e. a period of at least eight days after the attachment.[48] If these proceedings are not initiated within this period of time, the seizure is lifted.[49] The prejudgment attachment automatically converts into an attachment in execution if the creditor obtains a title to enforcement.[50]

Although the debtor has no possibility to appeal the given leave to prejudgment attachment,[51] he can seek relief from this attachment. On the one hand, the debtor has the possibility to initiate preliminary relief proceedings and to seek the lifting of the prejudgment attachment.[52] On the other hand, without the need to bring (preliminary relief) proceedings, the debtor can offer the creditor security in advance, i.e. a bank guarantee, for the payment of the (alleged) claim(s).

5 The Dutch Implementation Act

In the Netherlands, the implementation of the Regulation has taken shape with an implementation Act (hereinafter: the Act) of 14 November 2016.[53,54]

The Act only implements those provisions in the Regulation that needed implementation.[55] The following parties have been asked for advice: the Dutch Association

47 The preliminary relief judge will determine this period.

48 Art. 700(3) CCP: 'Tenzij op het tijdstip van het verlof reeds een eis in de hoofdzaak is ingesteld, wordt het verlof verleend onder voorwaarde dat het instellen daarvan geschiedt binnen een door de voorzieningenrechter daartoe te bepalen termijn van ten minste acht dagen na het beslag. (…)'.

49 Art. 700(3) CCP.

50 Art. 704(1) CCP. Nevertheless, the title to enforcement has to be served on the debtor (Art. 704(1) CCP).

51 Art. 700(2) CCP.

52 Art. 705(1) CCP, cf. Art. 705(2) CCP.

53 In full: Wet van 14 november 2016, houdende uitvoering van Verordening (EU) nr. 655/2014 van het Europees Parlement en de Raad van 15 mei 2014 tot vaststelling van een procedure betreffende het Europees bevel tot conservatoir beslag op bankrekeningen om de grensoverschrijdende inning van schuldvorderingen in burgerlijke en handelszaken te vergemakkelijken (*PbEU* 2014, L 189) (Uitvoeringswet verordening Europees bevel tot conservatoir beslag op bankrekeningen). See for (the text of) the implementation Act: wetten.overheid.nl/BWBR0038749/2017–01-18. See, in general, Explanatory Memorandum of the implementation Act (*Kamerstukken II* 2015/16, 34 462, 3, p. 1–21), see also: C.E. Oudshoorn, *Grensoverschrijdend bankbeslag op geldvorderingen*, Deventer: Wolters Kluwer 2018, no. 4.3.3.7.

54 Cf. the degree implementing this Act stating that the implementation Act entered into force on 18 January 2017 (Besluit van 17 november 2016 tot vaststelling van het tijdstip van inwerkingtreding van de Uitvoeringswet verordening Europees bevel tot conservatoir beslag op bankrekeningen, see: zoek.officielebekendmakingen.nl/stb-2016–441.html).

55 *Kamerstukken II* 2015/16, 34 462, 3, p. 8: 'Dit wetsvoorstel geeft daarom alleen uitvoering aan bepalingen die uitvoering behoeven'. See for an overview, the appendix to the Explanatory Memorandum (ibid. p. 18–21). Interesting is the expectation, expressed by the Dutch legislator in the Explanatory Memorandum, that the legislative proposal will lead to a change in the workload of the judiciary; the Council for the Judiciary (Raad voor de rechtspraak) expected the total workload consequences for the procedure to be € 269,512 per year (from 2017) (ibid. p. 10).

for the Judiciary,[56] the Royal Professional Organization of Judicial Officers in the Netherlands,[57] the Council for the Judiciary,[58] the Dutch Banking Association[59] and the Advisory committee for civil procedure.[60,61] The Act has fifteen provisions.

In the Explanatory Memorandum of the implementation Act,[62] the Dutch legislator stated that the Act will tailor the European procedure as closely as possible to the national procedure on prejudgment attachment.[63] However, this was not possible on every aspect. The Dutch legislator illustrated this by making a reference to the European requirement of security in a case where the creditor has not yet obtained a judgment, court settlement or authentic instrument; (only) by way of exception, a court may dispense with the requirement if it considers that the provision of security is 'inappropriate' in the circumstances of the case.[64] In Dutch law, a court has the power to give leave subject to the provision of security.[65] In practice, little use is made of this.[66] Therefore—according to the Dutch legislator—it was to be expected that in the European procedure security will be required from a creditor more often than in the national procedure.[67] Another difference is the (total) amount of the attachment. In both the European and the national procedure, the permission to attach up to a certain amount is based on the amount of the principal claim of the creditor and of expected additional interest and costs.[68] Pursuant to Article 24(2) of the Regulation, the amount preserved is the amount included in the Preservation Order. Under Dutch law, on the contrary, the attachment is levied on all claims that the debtor has against third parties or will obtain directly from an already existing legal relationship.[69,70] Where the Regulation makes an explicit reference to the national law of

---

56 Nederlandse Vereniging voor Rechtspraak.

57 Koninklijke Beroepsorganisatie van Gerechtsdeurwaarders.

58 Raad voor de rechtspraak.

59 Nederlandse Vereniging van Banken.

60 Adviescommissie voor burgerlijk procesrecht.

61 *Kamerstukken II* 2015/16, 34 462, 3, p. 10.

62 See: zoek.officielebekendmakingen.nl/kst-34462–3.html.

63 *Kamerstukken II* 2015/16, 34 462, 3, p. 8: 'Het wetsvoorstel laat de Europese procedure zo veel mogelijk aansluiten bij de nationale procedure voor het leggen van conservatoir beslag', cf. ibid. p. 9: 'Het wetsvoorstel zorgt ervoor dat de Europese procedure zoveel mogelijk aansluit bij de nationale procedure'.

64 See: Art. 12(1) EAPO Regulation, cf. *Kamerstukken II* 2015/16, 34 462, 3, p. 8.

65 See: Art. 701(1) CCP.

66 *Kamerstukken II* 2015/16, 34 462, 3, p. 8: 'In de praktijk wordt hier weinig gebruik van gemaakt'.

67 Ibid. p. 8.

68 Ibid. p. 8.

69 See: *Kamerstukken II* 2015/16, 34 462, 3, p. 8 with a reference to Article 718 CCP in conjunction with Article 475 CCP.

70 Other differences are, inter alia, different terms and different conditions under which the parties can be heard, see: *Kamerstukken II* 2015/16, 34 462, 3, p. 8–9 and C.G. Van der Plas & D. Beunk, 'Het Europees bankbeslag in de Nederlandse praktijk. Een herijking van beslagroutes in grensoverschrijdend verband', *Tijdschrift Financiering, Zekerheden en Insolventierechtpraktijk* 2018, issue 6, p. 34–40.

the Member States, (further) implementation by the Dutch legislator was required.[71] For instance, according to Article 4(14) of the Regulation, Member States are free to designate the 'competent authority', i.e. the authority or authorities which a Member State has designated as competent for receipt, transmission or service.[72] In Article 2(1) of the implementation Act, the Dutch legislator designated the bailiff as competent authority.[73] Bailiffs are also the designated information authorities to submit a request to banks, established in the Netherlands, for information about the bank account(s) of the debtor.[74] Bailiffs are allowed to submit requests to several banks at the same time.[75] The bank, which has provided information, does not have to inform the debtor of the request for account information until the injunction has been executed by the bank.[76] In this regard, the Dutch legislator did not adopt the idea of the European Commission on a central register of banks.[77] In addition, the legislator did not opt for the possibility of giving the information authority (i.e. the bailiffs) access to information that public authorities or administrations keep in their registers. The Explanatory Memorandum explained this possibility to be 'not very effective'.[78] Another option that is not used is the possibility for the courts to oblige the debtor to disclose with which bank(s) in its territory he holds one or more bank accounts, as this currently does not fit into the Dutch system.[79]

Where the creditor has not yet obtained a judgment, court settlement or authentic instrument, jurisdiction to issue a Preservation Order shall, pursuant to Article 6(1) of the Regulation, lie with 'the courts of the Member State which have jurisdiction to

[71] Cf. Oudshoorn 2018, no. 4.3.3.7. Cf. Art. 46(1) EAPO Regulation: 'All procedural issues not specifically dealt with in this Regulation shall be governed by the law of the Member State in which the procedure takes place'.

[72] Pursuant to Articles 10(2), 23(3), (5) and (6), 25(3), 27(2) and 28(3) and the second subparagraph of 36(5) of the EAPO Regulation.

[73] The bailiff as defined in the Bailiffs Act, see: *Kamerstukken II* 2015/16, 34 462, 3, p. 10–11. So, the bailiff will serve the Preservation Order to the bank, as is currently also the national procedure (ibid. p. 11).

[74] Art. 5(2) implementation Act, cf. Art. 14(5) EAPO Regulation. See with regard to the procedure: *Kamerstukken II* 2015/16, 34 462, 3, p. 13–14. See also Van der Plas & Beunk 2018, p. 38–39. See with regard to the costs of such an information-request: Art. 11 implementation Act.

[75] *Kamerstukken II* 2015/16, 34 462, 3, p. 13.

[76] 'bevel tot conservatoir beslag', Art. 5(3) implementation Act, cf. Art. 14(8) EAPO Regulation.

[77] Article 14(5) of the EAPO Regulation gives Member States a number of options for ensuring that account information can be obtained. See: *Kamerstukken II* 2015/16, 34,462, 3, p. 12: 'Het strekt te ver om een dergelijk register op te tuigen voor deze Europese procedure met beperkt toepassingsgebied'. See also, inter alia, Th. P. Ten Brink, M.H. Gardien & S.E. Poutsma, 'Het Nederlandse bankbeslag; Hoe kunnen de knelpunten worden opgelost?', in: S.J.W. van der Putten & M.R. van Zanten (ed.), *Compendium Beslag- en executierecht*, Den Haag: Sdu 2018, p. 594–596; O.J. Boeder, 'Het Europese bankbeslag creëert rechtsongelijkheid', *Tijdschrift voor de Procespraktijk* 2016, afl. 4, p. 91–92. Cf. Art. 14(5) (a) EAPO Regulation.

[78] *Kamerstukken II* 2015/16, 34 462, 3, p. 12: '(…) De mogelijkheid om de deurwaarder toegang tot informatie van het UWV te geven, zal dus weinig doeltreffend zijn. (…)'. Cf. Art. 14(5) (b) EAPO Regulation.

[79] Ibid. p. 12: '(…) In Nederland kennen we een dergelijk systeem niet. (…)'. Cf. Art. 14(5) (c) Regulation.

rule on the substance of the matter in accordance with the relevant rules of jurisdiction applicable'. The Dutch legislator decided to authorize the court in preliminary relief proceedings of the competent District Court in this regard.[80] This assignment is in line with the Dutch procedure regarding prejudgment attachment.[81] According to the Dutch legislator, it seemed obvious to let preliminary relief judges deal with requests for an European Preservation Order as these judges already have experience in considering requests for prejudgment attachment.[82]

6 The Dutch Implementation Act and the Request for the Obtaining of Account Information

How does the Dutch implementation Act deal with the request for information, as prescribed by the Regulation? The Regulation mentions several methods of obtaining the information. Member States shall make available in its national law at least one of the methods mentioned in the Regulation.[83]

The Netherlands did not have a pre-existing central information authority that was authorized to obtain all the information on bank accounts. During the legislative process concerning the Dutch Act to implement, it was considered to set up a central register for all bank accounts. The Dutch legislator, however, denied this idea, stating that the costs of such a register would be disproportional, especially with a view to an expectation that this instrument would not be used very often. If, at some point in the future such a register would be set up for national procedures, it could be—according to the Dutch legislator—decided whether such mechanism would be used for the EAPO as well.[84] At this stage the Dutch legislator has chosen to make use of the bailiff.[85]

With regard to the request for the obtaining of account information, the Explanatory Memorandum to the implementation Act provides the following example.[86] A creditor turns himself to a German court and requests a preservation order. He also makes clear in that request that he wants to obtain information on a bank account and substantiates why he believes that a debtor has a bank account in a certain Member

---

[80] Art. 3 implementation Act, see also: *Kamerstukken II* 2015/16, 34 462, 3, p. 11.

[81] See: Art. 700(1) CCP, see also: *Kamerstukken II* 2015/16, 34 462, 3, p. 11.

[82] *Kamerstukken II* 2015/16, 34 462, 3, p. 11: '(…) Omdat de voorzieningenrechter van de rechtbank al ervaring heeft met het beoordelen van verzoeken om conservatoir beslag, ligt het voor de hand om deze rechter ook verzoeken om een Europees beslagbevel te laten behandelen. (…)'.

[83] Art. 14(5) EAPO Regulation.

[84] Explanatory Memorandum to the implementation Act, see: *Kamerstukken II* 2015/16, 34 462, 3, p. 12.

[85] The bailiff is the information authority as mentioned in the Regulation; the Netherlands have chosen to use the method as mentioned in Article 14(5) under d EAPO Regulation.

[86] See for this example the Explanatory Memorandum to the implementation Act (*Kamerstukken II* 2015/16, 34 462, 3, p. 13).

State.[87] The creditor must provide necessary and relevant information on the debtor and the bank account. If the German court rules that the requirements for the request are met, the court can send this request for information to the information authority of the relevant Member State, for example the Netherlands. Then a Dutch bailiff must try to obtain the information, by turning himself to banks and ask for information. He can ask several banks at the same time whether the debtor has an account at that bank. If the creditor has mentioned a specific bank, the bailiff must ask at least that specific bank. If the creditor has not mentioned a specific bank, according to the Dutch legislator it makes sense that the bailiff turns himself to the five largest banks in the Netherlands. A bank that has received such a request, must answer it as soon as possible. If the bailiff gets the information the court requested, he passes it on to the court that requested it.[88] The bank is not entitled to inform the debtor on the request for information until the order to freeze the account is executed.[89] If the bailiff does not get the information, he has to tell that to the court that requested it that he did not get the information.

In short, the possibility of a request for the obtaining of account information can be considered to be a step forward for creditors who seek to obtain information on the bank accounts of their debtor(s) as before the entering into force of the Regulation, in the Netherlands there existed only some general obligations to provide information.[90]

[87] Art. 8(2) under f EAPO Regulation.

[88] The EAPO Regulation wants to make sure that banks do not pass on the request for information to the debtor. In this contribution, the question whether the general bank terms in the Netherlands need to be adjusted, is not discussed, because it may be that general bank terms contain(ed) a clause that the banks have to inform the debtors in case of a request for information.

[89] Art. 5(3) implementation Act.

[90] On the basis of Article 475g(1) CCP, a general obligation for the debtor exists to 'declare his sources of income', if so requested by a bailiff. With a reference to this article, in 1991 the Dutch Supreme Court ruled that a debtor had an obligation to provide information to the creditor in the execution phase (Supreme Court 20 September 1991, ECLI:NL:HR:1991:ZC0338, *NJ* 1992/552 (*Tripels v. Masson*), para 4.1); in September 2018, the District Court of Amsterdam held that the obligation to provide information also applied in the conservatory phase (District Court Amsterdam 18 September 2018, ECLI:NL:RBAMS:2018:6641, para 4.4). The obligation to provide information arises from the principle of 'reasonableness and fairness' (Art. 6:2 and 6:248 Dutch Civil Code)) (see: Annotation J.B.M. Vranken, Supreme Court 20 September 1991, *NJ* 1992/552, no. 9). However, the obligation to provide information is not unlimited; the Dutch Supreme Court (also) ruled in 1991 that the obligation did not go that far that the debtor can, in fact, be held accountable for his own financial position (para 4.1). In addition, the obligation did not go that far as to require the debtor to (documented) account for the amount of the income he had received (Court of Appeal Leeuwarden 30 March 2010, ECLI:NL:GHLEE:2010:BL9953, para 11). In short: the extent of the obligation may vary from case to case (cf. District Court Limburg 17 April 2018, ECLI:NL:RBLIM: 2018:3649, para 4.5). Any bailiff, who is entitled to seize against a debtor, is authorized to ask the person, he assumes making or arguably making periodic payments to the debtor, whether this is the case (Art. 475g(2) CCP).

7 Dutch Case Law on the EAPO: General Remarks

From August 2017 to June 2020, Dutch courts delivered twelve judgments in which the EAPO Regulation played a role. It seems likely to us that more than twelve judgments were given, but these twelve are the ones that were published on the official website of the Dutch Judiciary.[91] Based on this published case law, the number of Dutch cases in which the EAPO is brought forward is limited.

What does this case law deal with? It seems that this (first) case law mainly deals with two subjects: security to be provided by the creditor and requests for the obtaining of account information. To a lesser extent jurisdiction and the revocation of an EAPO have also been addressed.[92] We will briefly discuss the published judgments so far based on these four subjects. Attention will not only be paid to the relevant legal consideration(s), but also to the facts that underlie each case. We will start with the discussion of the subjects of providing security (no. 8) and the request for information (no. 9). Subsequently, the subjects of jurisdiction and revocation will be discussed (no. 10). It is clear that this order does not fit to the procedural order of these topics, but the order we have chosen is based on the attention to the topics in the Dutch case law so far.

8 Case Law on Security to Be Provided by the Creditor

A first decision (*beschikking*) that was delivered in which a court required a creditor to provide security was delivered by a preliminary relief judge of the District Court of Gelderland in March 2018.[93] In the underlying proceedings, applicant based her claim on the fulfilment by the interested party of payment obligations on which an agreement for the supply of goods was based.[94] Applicant stated inter alia that, due

[91] In the Netherlands, Dutch case law will be published on the official website of the Dutch judiciary: www.rechtspraak.nl. However, not all judgments that are delivered, are published on this website. In a decision, the 'Besluit selectiecriteria uitsprakendatabank Rechtspraak.nl', a description of the categories and/or characteristics of judgments that will be published on www.rechtspraak.nl, is given. On enquiry (by e-mail) at the Council for the Judiciary (*Raad voor de rechtspraak*) in June 2020, it turned out that no (more) quantitative information in this regard was available. Cf. Van der Plas & Beunk 2018, p. 30: 'In heel Nederland zouden er in totaal (slechts) 26 bevelen zijn uitgevaardigd.$_{11}$'; in their contribution, authors quote from an unpublished decision of the District Court of Amsterdam (from this decision it would follow that the District Court gave precedence to the EAPO Regulation over the Brussels I bis Regulation) (ibid. p. 33–34).

[92] In several of these cases more subjects come across, but we have categorized this case law so far based on these four main subjects.

[93] District Court Gelderland 1 March 2018, ECLI:NL:RBGEL:2018:1217. See also: Asser Procesrecht/Steneker 5 2019, no. 210; M. Zilinksy, GS Burgerlijke Rechtsvordering, aanhef EAPO-Vo, note 22 (online, updated until 4 November 2019); Oudshoorn 2018, no. 7.5.2.2; Van der Plas & Beunk 2018, p. 30, 36.

[94] Ibid. para 1.7.

to her precarious financial situation, she was unable to provide security.[95] The judge did not concur with her and considered as follows. In order to qualify for exemption from the provision of security, applicant had to convince the judge that she had 'a particular strong case'[96] that her claim in the principal action would be allowed.[97] However, it followed from e-mail correspondence between applicant and the interested party, submitted by applicant as evidence, that the interested party alleged to have a counterclaim against applicant and has provided applicant an overview with supporting documents.[98] As applicant did not submit this overview nor these documents, the persuasiveness of the evidence provided was affected.[99] In addition, from other evidence submitted, it could be deduced that the interested party also alleged to have other counterclaims against applicant.[100] In sum, the judge was not convinced that applicant had a particular strong case and rejected the application for a Preservation Order.[101]

A second decision on the provision of security was delivered in November 2018. A preliminary relief judge of the District Court of The Hague (Den Haag) rejected an application for a Preservation Order as the condition for issuing such order laid down in Article 7(2) of the Regulation was not met.[102] To substantiate their application, two applicants (a Spanish and a Dutch company) argued that respondent has deceived one of the applicants, because respondent—by means of a construct—would have paid out itself an amount that should have been paid to four (other) advisers; respondent would therefore owe applicant an amount of € 5,300,000.[103] The judge was not convinced: it considered, inter alia, that the course of events, put forward by applicants, in determining the amount to be due was not apparent from the submitted documents.[104] In addition, the judge considered it to be important that applicant ultimately had agreed to the amount she already received; applicants did not substantiate their claim that this would have been the result of a wrongful act of respondent.[105] The same consideration also held true for the statement of applicants that the amount of € 5,300,000 was not paid to four (other) advisers, but to respondent.[106] Taking the above into consideration, the judge concluded that applicants did not provide

---

[95] As required by the preliminary relief judge in February 2018 (ibid. para 1.3).

[96] Cf. recital 18 of the preamble of the EAPO Regulation.

[97] District Court Gelderland 1 March 2018, ECLI:NL:RBGEL:2018:1217, para 1.6.

[98] Ibid. para 1.7.

[99] Ibid. para 1.7.

[100] Ibid. para 1.7.

[101] Ibid. paras 1.7, 2.

[102] District Court Den Haag 2 November 2018, ECLI:NL:RBDHA:2018:14523, paras 2.6, 3, see also ibid. para 2.3.

[103] Ibid. para 2.4.2. Due to its (unintentional) share in the unlawful conduct of the respondent, the other applicant argued that she incurred considerable damage to her reputation, as a result of which she was dealing with loss of income (ibid. para 2.4.2). In paras 2.1–2.3 the judge gave an outline of the legal framework (i.e. Art. 7(1) and (2) EAPO Regulation).

[104] Ibid. para 2.5.

[105] Ibid. para 2.5.

[106] Ibid. para 2.5.

sufficient evidence to conclude that their claims in the main action would be uphold with the required degree of likelihood.[107] Another (brief) decision has been delivered in November 2018 by a preliminary judge of the District Court of Rotterdam. In these proceedings, applicant (a Dutch company) submitted an application for a Preservation Order.[108] As applicant had not yet obtained a title to enforcement,[109] the judge required her, pursuant to Article 12(1) of the Regulation, to provide security amounting to 30% of the principal claim, i.e. (rounded to) € 40,250.[110] Although the registrar requested applicant to provide this security (both by telephone and (then) by e-mail),[111] applicant did not provide the requested security.[112] The judge therefore rejected the application.[113]

The two most recent (published) decisions on this subject are delivered by a preliminary relief judge of the District Court of Noord-Holland in mid-January 2020.[114] The decisions are interesting as the judge determined the amount of security to be provided by applicants in both cases at nil.[115] In both cases, applicants submitted an application for a Preservation Order in order to seize before judgment bank accounts in Lithuania.[116] After making a reference to recitals 14 and 18 of the preamble of the Regulation as well as to Article 12(1) and (3) of the Regulation,[117] the judge posed itself the question in which case a judge could derogate from Article 12(1), first subparagraph of the Regulation, and thus in which case reliance on (the exception of) the second subparagraph of this subsection[118] would be successful.[119] In this context, the judge sought a link with recital 18 of the preamble of the Regulation which states, inter alia, that a court should dispense with the requirement of security only exceptionally if it considers that such security is inappropriate, superfluous or disproportionate in the circumstances of the case.[120] In the underlying

[107] Ibid. para 2.6.

[108] District Court Rotterdam 27 November 2018, ECLI:NL:RBROT:2018:9770, para 1.1. See also: R.E. van Esch, *Giraal betalingsverkeer/Elektronisch betalingsverkeer*, Deventer: Wolters Kluwer 2019, no. 13.2.2. Applicant already submitted this request in September 2018 (ibid. para 1.1).

[109] Ibid. para 1.2.

[110] Ibid. para 1.3.

[111] Ibid. para 1.4.

[112] Ibid. para 1.5.

[113] Ibid. para 1.5.

[114] District Court Noord-Holland 15 January 2020, ECLI:NL:RBNHO:2020:1471 and ECLI:NL:RBNHO:2020:1472.

[115] See (both decisions): para 3.1.

[116] See (both decisions): para 2.1.

[117] See (both decisions): para 2.2.

[118] Art. 12(1), second subparagraph EAPO Regulation: 'By way of exception, the court may dispense with the requirement set out in the first subparagraph if it considers that the provision of security referred to in that subparagraph is inappropriate in the circumstances of the case'.

[119] See (both decisions): para 2.3.

[120] Such circumstances could be, for instance, that the creditor has a particularly strong case but does not have sufficient means to provide security, that the claim relates to maintenance or to the payment of wages or that the size of the claim is such that the Order is unlikely to cause any damage

proceedings, applicants put forward that they were unable to provide security due to their precarious financial situation.[121] As a response to this, the judge decided to hear one of the applicants and asked for an explanation why he was unable to provide security.[122] Subsequently, applicants provided documents to substantiate this statement.[123] The judge held that applicants had convincingly demonstrated that they did not have the financial means to provide security.[124] Besides, the judge considered, in view of the submitted documents and given explanation, that applicants had a particularly strong case and the judge was 'convinced' that their claims needed, as a matter of urgency, to be protected in court.[125] It followed from the above that applicants had a particularly strong case but did not have sufficient means to provide security, that the enforcement of a future judgment would most likely be impeded and/or made substantially difficult, and that there existed a real risk that respondents would have withdrawn their funds by the time that enforcement would be possible.[126] Therefore, the judge decided that the amount of security to be provided by applicants in both cases had to be determined at nil.[127]

In sum, on the subject of the provision of security by the creditor, five cases have been discussed. In two of these cases, the preliminary relief judge considered that applicants did not provide sufficient evidence to conclude that they had 'a particular strong case', i.e. that their claim in the principal action would be allowed. In one case, applicant was requested (both by telephone and by e-mail) to provide security, but did not provide this. In the other two cases, the preliminary relief judge decided that the amount of security to be provided by applicants had to be determined at nil. The mean consideration of the judge was as follows: applicants had a particularly strong case but did not have sufficient means to provide security, the enforcement of a future judgment would most likely be impeded and/or made substantially difficult, and there existed a real risk that respondents would have withdrawn their funds by the time that enforcement would be possible.

---

to the debtor, for instance a small business debt, see (both decisions): para 2.3 (and recital 18 of the preamble of the EAPO Regulation).

[121] See (both decisions): para 2.4.

[122] See (both decisions): para 2.4.

[123] See (both decisions): para 2.5.

[124] See (both decisions): para 2.5.

[125] See (both decisions): para 2.6. Cf. ibid. para 2.7 in which the judge made a reference to the draft summons of applicants.

[126] See (both decisions): para 2.8.

[127] See (both decisions): para 3.1.

9 Case Law on the Request for the Obtaining of Account Information

In April 2018 a preliminary relief judge of the District Court of Rotterdam gave a decision with regard to an application for a Preservation Order as well as to a request for the obtaining of information on the bank account of respondent.[128] The judge partly granted the application which would take place in a separate standard form,[129] but refused the request of applicant (a Dutch company) to obtain information on the bank account of respondent (an Indian company) in other Member States than Germany.[130] The judge considered that applicant did not properly substantiate or argued convincingly that in other Member States such as Belgium, France or Italy bank accounts in the name of respondent existed.[131] The mere circumstance, as applicant had argued, that respondent is, or was, doing business with companies that were located in these states, was insufficient to substantiate the presumption that respondent held a bank account in these places; in international payment transactions it would not be necessary to have a bank account in the country of the trading partner since payments to and from foreign banks are possible and in many sectors are also common practice.[132] The same preliminary relief judge gave another decision with regard to a request for the obtaining of information on the bank account of respondent in May 2018.[133] The decision was brief and to the point: having regard to the fact that, in April 2018, applicant did not take advantage of the opportunity to respond to a statement from the Spanish authorities that respondent (who has not been heard in these proceedings) did not hold a bank account in Spain,[134] there was no evidence that respondent held a bank account in Spain and the judge refused the request for information.[135]

In February 2019 a preliminary relief judge of the District Court of Den Haag considered an application for a Preservation Order and a request for the obtaining of information on the bank account of respondent (residing in France).[136] The judge

---

[128] District Court Rotterdam 4 April 2018, ECLI:NL:RBROT:2018:3235. See also: Asser Procesrecht/Steneker 5 2019, no. 264; M. Zilinksy, GS Burgerlijke Rechtsvordering, aanhef EAPO-Vo, note 33 (online, updated until 4 November 2019); Van der Plas & Beunk 2018, p. 30, 31, 38.

[129] Ibid. para 2.3. The judge made a reference in this regard to the implementing regulation (ibid. para 2.3).

[130] Since no standard form has been established for the refusal of these requests, the refusal has, according to the judge, to be included in a decision (and not in a judgment) (ibid. para 2.4).

[131] Ibid. para 2.5.

[132] Ibid. para 2.5.

[133] District Court Rotterdam 23 May 2018, ECLI:NL:RBROT:2018:6658. See also: Van der Plas & Beunk 2018, p. 30, 38.

[134] Ibid. para 2.3.

[135] Ibid. para 2.4.

[136] District Court Den Haag 13 February 2019, ECLI:NL:RBDHA:2019:1289. See also: Van Esch 2019, no. 13.2.2.

granted the application to issue a Preservation Order,[137] but rejected the request to obtain information as this request was, in accordance with Article 14(2) of the Regulation, not sufficiently substantiated.[138] To substantiate his request to obtain information on the (French) bank account(s), applicant put forward, inter alia, that respondent had his fixed place residence in France for some time, that respondent owned real estate in France and that respondent had worked in France for a number of years in the past.[139] The judge considered that these circumstance were not sufficient to assume that respondent also held one or more French bank accounts; in any event, the circumstances did not make this necessary.[140]

In sum, on the subject of the request for the obtaining of account information, three cases have been discussed. The outcome of all three cases is the same: the preliminary relief judge(s) refused the request for information as applicant(s) did not properly substantiate or argued convincingly that bank accounts, held by respondent(s) in other Member States, existed.

10 Case Law on Jurisdiction and the Revocation of an EAPO

10.1 Jurisdiction

The first published judgment on an EAPO was delivered by the Court of Appeal's-Hertogenbosch in August 2017.[141] On appeal, the Court of Appeal considered the question whether the preliminary relief judge in the first instance had jurisdiction to issue a Preservation Order. The facts underlying these proceedings can be summarized as follows. In September 2015, a Belgian company (hereinafter: X) sold three cars to a Dutch buyer (total amount: € 300,000).[142] The cars, by the parties referred to as 'restauration projects', were in a shed in Belgium.[143] On 9 February 2017, the judge in preliminary relief proceedings of the District Court of Zeeland-West-Brabant issued a Preservation Order against X under Article 17(4) of the Regulation

[137] Ibid. para 2.3. The judge made a reference to the (separate) standard forms in which the granting would take place (para 2.3).

[138] Ibid. paras 2.4, 2.5, see also: para 3.1.

[139] Ibid. para 2.6.

[140] Ibid. para 2.7.

[141] Court of Appeal's-Hertogenbosch 29 August 2017, ECLI:NL:GHSHE:2017:3764. See also: Asser Procesrecht/Steneker 5 2019, no. 168; M. Zilinksy, GS Burgerlijke Rechtsvordering, aanhef EAPO-Vo, notes 15, 21 and 28 (online, updated until 4 November 2019); Oudshoorn 2018, nos. 5.4.2, 7.5.2.2; Van der Plas & Beunk 2018, p. 30.

[142] Ibid. para 3.1.1.

[143] Ibid. paras 3.1.1, 3.1.2.

up to an amount of € 186,000.[144] Subsequently, the bailiff had a garnishee order issued (*bewarend derdenbeslag*) against a bank in Belgium.[145]

In the underlying proceedings, X tried to lift the attachment on the basis of Article 33(1) of the Regulation.[146] In this regard, she argued, while making a reference to Article 6 of the Regulation, that the judge in preliminary relief proceedings had no jurisdiction to issue a Preservation Order.[147] By judgment of 27 March 2017, however, the preliminary relief judge rejected her request.[148] Although the Court of Appeal's-Hertogenbosch, on appeal, considered that it had jurisdiction to hear the request for revocation of the attachment,[149] the court agreed with X in her assertion that the judge in preliminary relief proceedings had no jurisdiction to issue a Preservation Order.[150] The Court of Appeal firstly considered, briefly summarized, that the main rule of Article 6 of the Regulation did not apply if a buyer could rely on Articles 17 and 18 of the Brussels I bis Regulation allowing a consumer to bring proceedings against the other party in the courts for the place where the consumer is domiciled.[151] In this regard, the court reflected extensively on the notion of 'consumer'.[152] Subsequently, it ruled—with a reference to the factual circumstances of the case[153]—that the buyer in the present case could not be qualified as consumer.[154] Therefore, he could not rely on Articles 17 and 18 of the Brussels I bis Regulation.[155] The buyer's reliance on Article 7 of the Brussels I bis Regulation was also untenable; under applicable Belgian law, the delivery took place in Belgium so that no jurisdiction of the Dutch court(s) could be derived.[156] Based on the aforementioned, the Court of Appeal concluded that the judge in preliminary relief proceedings had no jurisdiction to issue a Preservation Order.[157] Therefore, according to Article 33(1) (a) of the Regulation, the Preservation Order had to be revoked as the conditions set out in Article 6 of the Regulation were not met.[158] Lastly, the Court of Appeal agreed with X that the Dutch buyer had not

[144] Ibid. para 3.1.3.

[145] Ibid. para 3.1.4. The Dutch buyer submitted his claim in the principal action in February 2017; he based this claim on the fact that X failed in the performance of its obligations (ibid. para 3.1.6).

[146] Ibid. para 3.2.1.

[147] Ibid. paras 3.2.2, 3.7.

[148] Ibid. para 3.4.

[149] Ibid. paras 3.6–3.6.6.

[150] Ibid. para 3.16.

[151] Ibid. paras 3.9–3.9.2.

[152] Ibid. para 3.9.3. In para 3.9.4, the Court of Appeal made reference(s) to case law of the Court of Justice of the European Union in this context.

[153] Ibid. paras 3.10–3.11.10.

[154] Ibid. para 3.11.11.

[155] Ibid. para 3.11.11.

[156] Ibid. paras 3.12–3.13.

[157] Ibid. para 3.16.

[158] Ibid. para 3.16.

provided, in accordance with Article 7(2) of the Regulation, 'sufficient evidence' to satisfy the court that he was likely to succeed on the substance of his claim.[159]

In June 2020, another decision on (inter alia) the subject of jurisdiction has been delivered by the Court of Appeal of Arnhem-Leeuwarden.[160] The facts underlying these proceedings can be summarized as follows. From 2 July 2019 up to and including 6 September 2019, appellant deposited various amounts into one (or more) bank account(s) of respondent, a company established in Cyprus (hereinafter: X), up to an amount of € 66,050.[161] On 19 November 2019, appellant summoned X and submitted before the District Court of Noord-Holland a claim to declare in law that the agreement concluded between the parties had been annulled extrajudicially, or that the District Court would annul the agreement, or that the District Court would declare that X had acted unlawfully towards appellant, so that X would be obliged to repay appellant.[162] By decision of 16 April 2020, the preliminary relief judge of the District Court of Noord-Holland rejected a request of X to issue a Preservation Order.[163] In short, the judge considered that the request was not sufficiently substantiated.[164]

In the underlying proceedings, appellant tried (inter alia) to annul this decision and requested again a Preservation Order.[165] Before the Court of Appeal took a look at the contested decision, it considered the question whether it had jurisdiction to issue an EAPO.[166] In short, the court held that appellant could be qualified as consumer for the purposes of the Brussel I bis Regulation (cf. Art. 17(1) under c Brussel I bis Regulation).[167] The court qualified the contract concluded between the parties as a consumer contact because appellant was employed as an employee, he invested his savings with X and because he did not pursue a 'business purpose' with his investments but he wanted to increase his private assets.[168] Under Article 18(1) of the Brussel I bis Regulation, a consumer may bring proceedings against the other party to a contract in the court for the place where the consumer is domiciled; given the fact that appellant lived in the Netherlands, the Dutch court therefore had jurisdiction.[169] With regard to the statement of X that parties agreed on a choice of forum (Art. 25 Brussel I(bis) Regulation), the court considered that a choice of forum was not allowed as the provision of Article 18(1) may only be departed from by an agreement which was entered into after the dispute has arisen (Art. 19 under 1 Brussel I bis Regulation); the underlying choice of forum was agreed before the

[159] Ibid. paras 3.17–3.25.

[160] Court of Appeal Arnhem-Leeuwarden 5 June 2020, ECLI:NL:GHARL:2020:5062.

[161] Ibid. para 3.1.

[162] Ibid. para 3.1.

[163] Ibid. para 3.2.

[164] Ibid. para 3.2.

[165] Ibid. para 3.2.

[166] Ibid. paras 3.5–3.11, cf. paras 3.3–3.4.

[167] Ibid. para 3.8 in conjunction with para 3.7.

[168] Ibid. para 3.8 in conjunction with para 3.7.

[169] Ibid. para 3.9.

dispute has arisen.[170] In sum, the Court of Appeal concluded that it had jurisdiction.[171] Furthermore, given the fact that appellant provided security on the basis of Article 12 of the Regulation,[172] and that the court was sufficiently convinced that appellant was likely to succeed on the substance of his claim against X (Art. 7(2) Regulation)[173] as well as that there was a real risk that the subsequent enforcement would be impeded or made substantially more difficult,[174] the Court of Appeal decided to annul the decision of 16 April 2020 and to issue a Preservation Order.[175]

10.2 Revocation of an EAPO

In March 2018, a judgment has been delivered by a preliminary relief judge of the District Court of Rotterdam on the revocation of a Preservation Order.[176] In the underlying proceedings, two claimants—a Dutch company and a Polish company—submitted, inter alia, a claim to revoke a Preservation Order that has been issued by a preliminary relief judge of the District Court of Rotterdam in March 2018 for a claim estimated at an amount of € 17,250,000.[177] After the judge considered their claim to lift the prejudgment attachments made according to Dutch attachment law,[178] the judge considered the allowability of revoking the Preservation Order. As claimants filed their claim in the first instance (only) by means of a summons, while the application for the remedy of revocation shall be made using the remedy form (see Art. 36(1) Regulation),[179] the judge offered claimants the opportunity to submit this form at the hearing.[180] The judge decided to adopt its earlier consideration with regard to the Dutch prejudgment attachments; in its consideration it was implied that the conditions under Article 33(1) (a) of the Regulation were not met, and in particular that defendant 'ultimately' failed to convince the judge that she had a particular strong case.[181] In addition, the judge adopted its consideration with regard to the

170 Ibid. para 3.10.

171 Ibid. para 3.11.

172 Ibid. para 3.12.

173 Ibid. para 3.13.

174 Ibid. para 3.14.

175 Ibid. paras 5.1–5.2, cf. para 4.

176 District Court Rotterdam 28 March 2018, ECLI:NL:RBROT:2018:2712. See also: Van Esch 2019, no. 13.2.2; Oudshoorn 2018, no. 7.5.2.2; Van der Plas & Beunk 2018, p. 30, 35.

177 Ibid. paras 2.14, 3.1.

178 Ibid. para 4.1–4.15.

179 Ibid. para 4.18.

180 Ibid. para 4.19. The judge considered defendant not to be prejudiced in her defense due to the late submission of the form as defendant could expect the other party to contest the attachment at law. In addition, defendant had been offered sufficient opportunity to respond to this remedy at the hearing (ibid. para 4.20).

181 Ibid. para 4.23. The judge made a reference to Article 7(2) of the Regulation in conjunction with Sect. 6.1.1.5 of the model form.

balancing of interests; the seizure of bank account weighted disproportionately heavy on claimants.[182] Furthermore, the legal principle of proportionality, which had—according to consistent case law of the Court of Justice of the European Union—to be complied with, would be unduly violated if the seizure of bank account would not be withdrawn.[183] Lastly, the judge held that it would notify the Polish authorities as soon as possible of this decision.[184]

In June 2020, another judgment on the subject of revocation has been delivered by a preliminary relief judge of the District Court of Midden-Nederland.[185] In the underlying proceedings, claimant (a company established in Cyprus) submitted, inter alia, a claim to revoke a Preservation Order that has been issued by a preliminary relief judge of the District Court of Midden-Nederland in January 2020 for an amount of € 352,610.37.[186] To substantiate her claim, claimant stated, inter alia, that the Preservation Order should be revoked because the conditions and/or requirements set out in the Regulation were not met (Art. 33(1) Regulation).[187] In short: she argued that the institution (Wirecard) under which the prejudgment attachment had been made against her was not a 'bank' within the definition of Article 4 under 2 of the Regulation,[188] that the preliminary relief judge of the District Court did not have jurisdiction as parties agreed on a choice of forum in Cyprus and that defendant was not a 'consumer' within the meaning of Article 17 of the Brussel I bis Regulation,[189] that there was no urgent need for a protective measure in the form of a Preservation Order because there was no real risk that the subsequent enforcement of the claim would be impeded or made substantially more difficult (Art. 7(1) Regulation),[190] that defendant did not submit sufficient evidence to satisfy the preliminary relief judge that defendant was likely to succeed on the substance of his claim against claimant (Art. 7(2) Regulation),[191] as well as that defendant should have been required to provide security or to provide a higher security than has been required (Art. 12 Regulation).[192] In addition, claimant stated that the documents were not served on her in due time in accordance with Article 33(1) under b of the Regulation[193] and

[182] Ibid. para 4.24.

[183] Ibid. para 4.24.

[184] Ibid. para 4.25. Cf. the following, interesting, consideration of the preliminary relief judge; since there was no separate model form for the decision (in the present case: *beslissing*) to be taken on the remedy to revoke or modify a European bank attachment, the decision (*beslissing*) will be recorded in the present judgment as it concerned a remedy (ibid. para 4.21).

[185] District Court Midden-Nederland 24 June 2020, ECLI:NL:RBMNE:2020:2301.

[186] Ibid. para 2.4.

[187] Ibid. para 3.1 in conjunction with para 5.1 under a.

[188] Ibid. para 5.2 in conjunction with paras 5.3, 5.4.

[189] Ibid. para 5.2 in conjunction with para 5.6.

[190] Ibid. para 5.2, cf. para 5.8.

[191] Ibid. para 5.2, cf. para 5.11.

[192] Ibid. para 5.2 in conjunction with para 5.13.

[193] Ibid. para 5.1 under b (cf. under c) in conjunction with para 5.17.

that the preserved amounts exceeding the amount of the EAPO were not released in accordance with Article 27(2) of the Regulation.[194]

The preliminary relief judge was not convinced. With regard to the first allegation, the judge considered that claimant failed to demonstrate sufficiently why Wirecard could not be qualified as 'bank' under the Regulation.[195] In addition, the judge made a reference to a judgment in the proceedings on the merits that was delivered on the same day as the present judgment: in this judgment the District Court held that defendant could be qualified as consumer.[196] Therefore, the District Court had jurisdiction and, as a result, the preliminary relief judge in the underlying proceedings also had jurisdiction (Art. 6 Regulation).[197] With regard to the third argument, the judge considered (inter alia) that claimant had impeded the subsequent enforcement of defendant's claim by contacting Wirecard to inform Wirecard that the funds on her bank account would belong to third parties.[198] Subsequently, on the basis of the evidence submitted by defendant, the judge considered it sufficiently likely that defendant's claim would be allowed on the basis of aggressive business practices by claimant.[199] Lastly, the judge considered the (form of) security to be provided by defendant in accordance with Article 12(3) of the Regulation as the subsection provided the Member States with discretionary power in relation to the forms of security acceptable.[200] With regard to the allegation of the not-in-time-service, the judge allowed the reliance on Article 33(3) of the Regulation as defendant demonstrated that she had taken all the steps she was required to take to have the initial service of the documents effected.[201] Finally, the judge considered that the situation referred to in Article 27(2) of the Regulation did not currently arise.[202]

11 Final Remarks

Before the EAPO Regulation entered into force, a creditor who wanted to seize funds on a bank account in another Member State had to turn himself to a court in the Member State where this account was held. With the EAPO Regulation, life looks more easy to creditors as they can obtain an EAPO from a court in their own state to freeze funds in the account of their debtor in another Member State.

In this contribution, light has been shed on the first experiences with the EAPO in the Netherlands. Firstly, the Dutch Act on the implementation of the EAPO had

---

194 Ibid. para 5.1 under d, cf. para 5.22.

195 Ibid. para 5.5.

196 Ibid. para 5.7.

197 Ibid. para 5.7.

198 Ibid. para 5.10, cf. para 5.9.

199 Ibid. para 5.12.

200 Ibid. para 5.14.

201 Ibid. para 5.20.

202 Ibid. para 5.23.

been discussed. Although the Dutch legislator stated that the implementation Act would tailor the European procedure as closely as possible to the national procedure on prejudgment attachment, it turned out that this was not always possible. For instance, with regard to the requirement of security to be provided by the creditor in cases where the creditor had not yet obtained a judgment, a court settlement or an authentic instrument, differences exist between the European and the Dutch procedure. Another difference relates to the (total) amount of the attachment; under Dutch law, the attachment is levied on all claims that the debtor has against third parties or will obtain directly from an already existing legal relationship, whereas the amount preserved in the European procedure is the amount included in the Preservation Order. The possibility of a request for the obtaining of account information is interesting as the Netherlands did not have a pre-existing central information authority that was authorized to obtain all the information on bank accounts.[203]

Dutch case law on the EAPO had been discussed in this contribution as well. From August 2017 to June 2020, Dutch courts delivered at least twelve judgments in which the Regulation played a role. In these judgments four different subjects played a role: security to be provided by the creditor, the request for the obtaining of account information, jurisdiction and the revocation of an EAPO. Taking into consideration the relatively low number of judgments in which the EAPO played a role,[204] one can look for an explanation. An explanation may be rather simple: unfamiliarity with the EAPO.[205] However that may be, times may change in this regard as well.

References

Boeder OJ (2016) Het Europese bankbeslag creëert rechtsongelijkheid. Tijdschrift voor de Procespraktijk issue 4

Cuniberti G, Migliorini S (2018) The European account preservation order regulation: a commentary. Cambridge: Cambridge University Press 2018 (online)

Oudshoorn CE (2018) Grensoverschrijdend bankbeslag op geldvorderingen. Deventer: Wolters Kluwer

[203] In Dutch literature, however, it has been argued that this creates legal inequality, see: Boeder 2016, p. 89: 'Die bevragingsbevoegdheid bestaat niet voor een Nederlandse beslaglegger die ten laste van een Nederlandse schuldenaar bankbeslag legt. De Verordening is alleen van toepassing op grensoverschrijdende inning van schuldvorderingen. Dit creëert rechtsongelijkheid en is daardoor schadelijk voor de civiele invordering.'.

[204] Cf. the 'Besluit selectiecriteria uitsprakendatabank Rechtspraak.nl'.

[205] See: Van der Plas & Beunk 2018, p. 40: 'Onbekend maakt onbemind. Het EAPO lijkt hiervan een sprekend voorbeeld. In de praktijk wordt het EAPO nog weinig toegepast, terwijl het EAPO bij de gelijktijdige beslaglegging van verschillende bankrekeningen in diverse lidstaten wel degelijk interessante voordelen biedt ten opzichte van de lokale- of de Brussel Ibis-route. (…) Voor beslaglegging op in Nederland gelegen bankrekeningen zullen vooral de verplichte zekerheidstelling en de beperkte omvang van het EAPO reden zijn voor een schuldeiser om toch te kiezen voor een Nederlands conservatoire derdenbeslag.'.

Ten Brink ThP, Gardien MH, Poutsma SE (2018) Het Nederlandse bankbeslag; hoe kunnen de knelpunten worden opgelost? In: van der Putten SJW, van Zanten MR (eds) Compendium Beslag- en executierecht, Den Haag: Sdu 2018

Van der Plas CG, Beunk D (2018) Het Europees bankbeslag in de Nederlandse praktijk. Een herijking van beslagroutes in grensoverschrijdend verband. Tijdschrift Financiering, Zekerheden en Insolventierechtpraktijk, issue 6

Bart Krans defended his Ph.D. (on Compensation for breach of contract) in Leiden in 1999. He then worked as a practicing lawyer at Pels Rijcken & Droogleever Fortuijn in The Hague. In August 2005 he was appointed as full professor in Private law, in particular civil procedural law, at the University of Groningen. In the academic year 2010–2011 he was a guest professor at the TPR chair at Ghent University (Belgium). In 2015 he was visiting professor at Ghent University. Krans is interested in civil procedural law, contract law and liability law. The Europeanisation of civil procedural law is one of his research topics. In 2016 The European Union and National Civil Procedure (editors prof. dr. A. Nylund, University Tromso and prof. dr. Bart Krans), Intersentia was published. Krans wrote the monograph Nederlands burgerlijk procesrecht en materieel EU-recht (Deventer–Kluwer 2010); a book on Dutch civil procedural law and substantive EU law. Krans is–with prof. dr. M.H. Wissink and dr. G.T. de Jong-author of the book Verbintenissenrecht algemeen (Studiereeks Burgerlijk Recht); a book on the Law of Obligations. Krans writes case notes for the leading Dutch case note journal Nederlandse Jurisprudentie (NJ). Krans teaches in the fields of substantive civil law and civil procedural law. In 2018 he received the price for the best teacher of Leiden Law School for the academic year 2017/2018. In 2019, 2018, 2017 and 2106 he has received the price from Leiden Law School for the best evaluated lecture for law professionals.

Pauline Ribbers graduated from Leiden University with a degree in Civil Law and a degree in European Law. At the time of writing this contribution, Ribbers was a Ph.D.-candidate and a teacher at the Institute of Private Law at Leiden Law School.

The Investigation into the Debtor's Assets in Civil Enforcements Proceedings

(Comments on the Report of Prof. Krans)

Guillermo Ormazabal

Abstract My comment will discuss some points concerning the investigation into the debtor's assets in civil enforcements proceedings inspired by the insightful report of Prof. Krans. I will confine myself to outline, without referring to specific national legal systems, the key requirements or elements which a reasonable enforcement system should meet in this area.

1 Introduction

First of all, let me thank and congratulate the organization on the initiative of having summoned us to hold this colloquium. It is just a happy coincidence and a good opportunity to celebrate the birthday of our colleague Masahisa Deguchi. So dear colleague: you don't have to worry about the years rolling by since you retain your characteristic good mood and this open-mindedness, friendliness and cordiality which we, especially south Europeans, so much appreciate. Thank you, Masahisa, and warm congratulations! I hope you keep being as you are for many, many years!

My comment will discuss some points concerning the investigation into the debtor's assets in civil enforcements proceedings inspired by the insightful report of Prof. Krans. I will confine myself to outline, without referring to specific national legal systems, the key requirements or elements which, from my point of view, a reasonable enforcement system should meet in this area.

G. Ormazabal (✉)
University of Girona, Girona, Spain
e-mail: guillermo.ormazabal@udg.edu

M. Deguchi (ed.), *Effective Enforcement of Creditors' Rights*,
Ius Gentium: Comparative Perspectives on Law and Justice 91,
https://doi.org/10.1007/978-981-16-5609-5_15

2 Investigations into Debtor's Assets and the Right to a Fair Trial

To begin with, I have the impression that when dealing with this topic we are again facing the classic and pervasive problems raised by the enforcement procedure in general, namely, the need to strike the right balance between the imperative creditor's recovery while causing minimum damage to the debtor's assets and respecting his right to be heard and oppose his defenses in due course.

The lack of a reasonably exhaustive ways to carry out an investigation into the debtor's assets would deadly impair the effective enforcement of judicial decisions which constitutes a human right, according with the view of the European Court of Human Rights. In *Hornsby v. Greece*,[1] the court concluded that,

> according to its established case-law, Article 6 para. 1 (art. 6-1) secures to everyone the right to have any claim relating to his civil rights and obligations brought before a court or tribunal; in this way it embodies the "right to a court", of which the right of access, that is the right to institute proceedings before courts in civil matters, constitutes one aspect (see the Philis v. Greece judgment of 27 August 1991, Series A no. 209, p. 20, para. 59). However, that right would be illusory if a Contracting State's domestic legal system allowed a final, binding judicial decision to remain inoperative to the detriment of one party. It would be inconceivable that Article 6 para. 1 (art. 6-1) should describe in detail procedural guarantees afforded to litigants - proceedings that are fair, public and expeditious - without protecting the implementation of judicial decisions; to construe Article 6 (art. 6) as being concerned exclusively with access to a court and the conduct of proceedings would be likely to lead to situations incompatible with the principle of the rule of law which the Contracting States undertook to respect when they ratified the Convention (see, mutatis mutandis, the Golder v. the United Kingdom judgment of 21 February 1975, Series A no. 18, pp. 16–18, paras. 34–36). Execution of a judgment given by any court must therefore be regarded as an integral part of the "trial" for the purposes of Article 6 (art. 6); moreover, the Court has already accepted this principle in cases concerning the length of proceedings (see, most recently, the Di Pede v. Italy and Zappia v. Italy judgments of 26 September 1996, Reports of Judgments and Decisions 1996-IV, pp. 1383–1384, paras. 20–24, and pp. 1410–1411, paras. 16–20 respectively).

At least in Europe, the general opinion seems to be that there is still room to press the uncooperative debtor to uncover his assets without affecting his rights in an abusive manner. To put it another way, the scale still should tip in favor of the creditor's right of recovery to the detriment of the debtor's interest. Of course, putting the emphasis on creditor's recovery does not mean underestimate sensitivity towards situations and risks of social exclusion. To be more precise, the more the law introduces effective devices to affect the goods of the debtor, the more urgent to overhaul the legal minimum standards to prevent the debtor from falling in a situation of irreparable indigence or pauperization. It is more than likely that many European civil procedure laws have not risen to this demand in the years of the great economic crisis in the first decades of the current century.

---

[1] Case number 107/1995/613/701, 19 March 1997. See also Würdinger, M., *Die Sachaufklärung in der Einzelzwangsvollstreckung. Informationsgewinnung des Vollstreckungsgläubigers de lege lata et ferenda*, Juristen Zeitung 4/2011, p. 178.

Back to the need for improving debtor's recovery, I may be wrong, but I have got the impression that countries where the research of the debtor's assets collides with major obstacles, international transactions and the trust of the markets use to be seriously impaired. The proof that this is not an unrealistic view is that at least in Europe numerous and substantial legal reforms have been carried out in past years to enhance transparency in this area. European regulations, directives or, in general, international treaties on recognition and enforcement of judgements would be for little use if, at the same time, national laws did not improve the instruments to allow an adequate investigation into the debtor's assets. With the Regulation, on one hand, about the European Account Preservation Order to facilitate cross-border debt recovery and, on the other hand, with the reforms to the regulation on recognition and enforcement of judgments in civil and commercial matters, I believe that this parallel evolution in Europe is, generally speaking, taking place in the right way.

3 Interim Measures as the Most Effective Way to Carry Out Investigations

Indeed, the most effective device to ensure the success of the enforcement proceedings is an adequate system of protective, provisional or interim measures, which includes most especially the freezing of assets or provisional attachment of goods before initiating the declaratory proceedings or at least while pending those procedures. As it is commonly said, better safe than sorry. A protective measure of that kind taken at the right time can effectively avoid arduous investigations in the debtor's assets in the enforcement stage and save the administration of justice the cost and efforts necessary to carry out such investigations.

It seems to me, for that reason, that the precedent set by the European Account Preservation Order (EAPO), established by the Regulation 655/2014[2] is one of the most valuable contributions in this direction at supranational level. It allows issuing a protective order to attach the accounts of the debtor even when the creditor who has obtained in a Member State an enforceable judgment, court settlement or authentic instrument in order to obtain the information necessary to allow the bank or banks and the debtor's account or accounts to be identified.

But for one particular reason this European instrument represents a critical landmark, namely that it does not only allow issuing a protective order to attach the accounts of the debtor in every European Member State (which would on itself constitute a big deal) but also carrying out a genuine investigation activity in the debtor's assets when there are reasons to believe that he holds accounts with a bank in a specific Member State, but it is not known neither the name and or address of the bank nor the IBAN, BIC or another bank number allowing the bank to be identified.

[2] Regulation (EU) No 655/2014 of the European Parliament and of the Council of 15 May 2014, establishing a European Account Preservation Order procedure to facilitate cross-border debt recovery in civil and commercial matters.

In this case, the creditor may request the Member State of enforcement to obtain the information necessary to identify the bank and the debtor's accounts.

In so doing, the Member States may use different methods:

- imposing a disclosure obligation on all banks in its territory,
- Allowing the access to the relevant information where that information is held by public authorities or administrations,
- Empowering its courts to oblige the debtor to disclose the bank with which he holds the accounts accompanying that obligation by an *in personam* order prohibiting the withdrawal or transfer the funds
- Or any other efficient methods for the purposes of obtaining the relevant information, provided that they are not disproportionately costly or time-consuming.

4 No Automatic Issuance of the EAPO. The creditor's Burden of Proof

The issuance of an EAPO is not an automatic result of a creditor's simple request. The order should qualify as a necessary measure and the European Regulation doesn't spare the creditor's efforts to prove certain requirements.

More specifically, art. 7.1 of the Regulation 655/2014 establishes that the creditor must demonstrate the urgency to adopt the measure. This proof may in general terms be provided by the very ease existing in current times to move money between accounts placed in banks based in different countries.[3] However, the said need cannot be general, it must rather be related to a real cause or causes that affect the specific case, ad ex. the creditor having evidence that the debtor has carried out some kind of move or operation related to his assets hinting at the intention of concealing them.[4]

The creditor must also prove that without the adoption of the order, the enforcement of the resolution will be impossible or more difficult. This requirement of the Regulation imposes on the creditor the burden of bringing evidence about the real risk the debtor not being able to face the debt. The creditor has to prove a real, concrete risk, not a hypothetical or generic one. This shows that issuing the order is not a sort of automatism, but rather the result of a decision reached by the court after weighing the circumstances that the creditor has proven such as ad. ex., the behavior of the debtor before the commence of the process and his creditworthiness; the nature of the assets he or she possesses, if they have any charge or encumbrance; the debtor's background, his credit history or his performance in a previous situation etc.[5]

[3] Antón Juárez, I., *La orden europea de retención de cuentas: ¿adiós a la dificultad que plantea el cobro de la deuda transfronteriza en la UE?*, Cuadernos de Derecho Transnacional (marzo 2017), Vol. 9, No 1, pp. 16–17.

[4] Ibidem, p.17.

[5] Ibidem, p.17.

5 Judicial Control of the Investigation Activities and the Increasing Dejudicialization of the Enforcement Proceedings

Despite of these considerations, we should also bear in mind that introducing more effective instruments to investigate the debtor's assets implies greater judicial control, since the effectiveness of those instruments also entails a higher impact on certain fundamental rights of the debtor.

But it turns out that in most countries precisely the opposite tendency is predominant, namely, the tendency to "dejudicialize" civil enforcement proceedings. In other words, to transfer enforcement activities from judicial hands to those of certain officials in the service of the administration of justice (court clerks, sheriffs, the German *Gerichtsvollzieher* or *Rechtspfleger*, *Letrados de la Administración de Justicia* in Spain). In Spain, for example, even notaries are increasingly taking on enforcement roles. Obviously, the decisions of those authorities or professionals are usually subject to judicial review. However, there are well founded fears that judges, overwhelmed with increasingly overburdened dockets, be progressively taking distance from enforcement tasks, which, de facto, may end up practically as a sovereign territory monopolized by the aforementioned authorities, who, let us remember, by the way, don't generally depend hierarchically on the judiciary, but on the executive branch.

6 The Need of Binding Case-Law in Enforcement Proceedings

Intensification of judicial review would also require extending the jurisdiction of the national courts entrusted with producing binding case-law to issues arising from enforcement proceedings, which does not actually happen or not, at least, in in due measure, in many legal systems.[6] Indeed, it is difficult to avoid the suspicion that many law makers consider civil enforcement as a minor or secondary issue, not deserving the attention of the highest judicial spheres. Which is deeply worth deploring, since, as we know, when a legal system relegates civil enforcement to the background, it commits a major error and probably jeopardizes the arduous work that courts have previously done to render a fair final decision. Furthermore, the consolidation of a uniform case law reinforces the legal certainty and confidence of international actors who must commence enforcement proceedings in a given country.

On the other hand, when the tools provided by the justice system to investigate the debtor's assets do not work properly, a kind of injustice may arise which is especially outrageous but regrettably not uncommon, namely the fact that the average citizen frequently fails in his attempt to ferret out the debtor's assets while powerful creditors

[6] See about Hess, B., *Rechtspolitische Perspektiven der Zwangsvollstreckung*, JZ (Juristen Zeitung) 13/2009, p. 664.

manage to reap great success, sometimes through scanned screens and confidential information acquired at a high price from top bank employees.

7 Resorting to Private Actors: The Flourishing of the Credits Bureaus or Data Collection Agencies Gathering Account Information and Providing Other Kinds of Data About the Financial Solvency of the Debtors

Without resorting to the use of those unlawful means, it is clear that in recent years the so-called credits bureaus or data collection agencies gathering account information and providing other kinds of data about the financial solvency of the debtors have exuberantly flourished. This proliferation may be irreproachable or blameless, but it is crucial to guarantee that this kind of services meet the data privacy requirements and in particular that operate with special sensitivity in the handling of personal data. They also should commit themselves to store data exclusively on servers located in their own states and to conduct their business activities in accordance with the General Data Protection Regulations and under the control by the competent data protection authorities, who should have unrestricted access to all processes and procedures relevant to data protection.

The considerations explained so far clearly signal a dramatic increase of the private investigation activities in the field of civil enforcement, which does not but reinforce the common place or cliché that justice is predominantly at the service of the well-off and rich people who can afford such expenses. In addition, this state of things confirms the aforementioned trend of dejudicialization or outsourcing of the traditional tasks of the justice system. It is not only, as has been said, that civil enforcement is becoming a kingdom under the rule of clerks and civil servants, functionally subject but not organically ascribed to the judiciary branch. That could be in part understandable but also clearly shows that the limelight is increasingly shifting to private players.

8 Using Criminal and Other Punitive Devices to Compel the Uncooperative Debtor

Dealing with the means available to creditors in order to investigate the assets of the debtor under enforcement proceedings also means referring to the response of the criminal law to the debtor's moves or strategies seeking to conceal their assets, transfer them to other people or, in general, frustrate the interest of the creditor through other kind of fraudulent behavior. In fact, the threat of a reasonably severe criminal law through subpoenas and effective prosecution in case of failure to accomplish is a major guarantee to prevent the debtor to engage in such behaviors.

It is not uncommon, however, that criminal laws don't live up to these needs, allowing certain room for maneuver to the uncooperative debtor. In some countries, penalties imposed for such conducts are rather lenient or courts and public prosecutors might be reluctant to actually conduct criminal investigations against unruly debtors. In my country, like in many others, the debtor is obliged to submit a sworn statement or affidavit of his assets and incomes. If he fails to do so, he may commit a crime of disobedience to the authority in the following cases: if he doesn't submit a list of assets or incomes; if he includes a list of assets that are not owned by him; intentionally excluding own assets subject to seizure; or intentionally omitting charges and encumbrances currently weighing on his goods. Nevertheless, thou increasing in number, initiation of criminal proceedings in those cases use to be in practice rather unusual.

Imposing periodic penalty payments by the court to the uncooperative debtor is also common practice in many countries. It could be a useful device to compel the debtor to provide information about his assets when he refuses, prevaricates or procrastinates in discharging his duty of transparency. This kind of penalties has often been criticized on account of the lack of determination of his limits and the vagueness of the criteria to fix their amounts, since they use to leave a large margin of discretion to the non-judicial authorities. However, it is also true that they have proven much more effective than criminal penalties, which require commencing prosecution and cause therefore more delay, nuisance and trouble to the creditor.

9 Extending the Duty of Cooperation with the Judiciary Including Both Public and Private Persons

Eventually, to conclude my reflections let me add that in order ensure an effective investigation, it is not enough to exhaust the means to compel the debtor to disclosure his assets, but it is also necessary the procedural laws to provide the possibility of requiring third parties to share the information they hold about the debtor's assets. This duty of cooperation with the judiciary must include both public and private persons and must also be backed or endorsed with the power of imposing sanctions on those who refuse to provide their collaboration or refuse complying with the court's requirement. These duties of disclosure of third parties, furthermore, should not be limited to the assets located in the forum but also to those located in other jurisdictions.

References

Antón Juárez I (2017) La orden europea de retención de cuentas: ¿adiós a la dificultad que plantea el cobro de la deuda transfronteriza en la UE?, Cuadernos de Derecho Transnacional (marzo 2017), vol 9, no 1, pp 16–17

Hess B (2009) Rechtspolitische Perspektiven der Zwangsvollstreckung, JZ (Juristen Zeitung) 13/2009, p 664
Würdinger M (2011) Die Sachaufklärung in der Einzelzwangsvollstreckung. Informationsgewinnung des Vollstreckungsgläubigers de lege lata et ferenda, Juristen Zeitung 4/2011, p 178

Guillermo Ormazabal Sánchez is a Professor of Procedural Law at the University of Girona (Spain) where he teaches civil and criminal procedure. His civil procedural research focuses on comparative Law, evidentiary issues in civil procedure, collective actions, electronic evidence and arbitration. In the field of criminal procedure, the author has specialized in the right against self-incrimination and in the European Judicial Area in criminal matters. He was elected vice-rector of the University of Girona and Dean of its Law School. He was awarded a Humboldt Stiftung Fellowship to develop his research at the Institut für die gesamten Strafrechtswissenschaften, Rechtsphilosophie und Rechtsinformatik of the Ludwig Maximilian Universität de Munich and a Salvador de Madariaga Fellowship to do research about comparative civil procedure at of the Fordham University School of Law. He is also a former Fellow of the German Academic Exchange Service and has delivered conferences and seminars at various Spanish and universities in Europe and South America. Currently he serves as chief director of REDIJEA (Red Interuniversitaria para el Dialogo Jurídico entre Europa y América), an interuniversity academic network to promote the juridical dialogue between Europe and America.

Towards More Effective Enforcement Proceedings Through More Effective Asset Discovery

Fernando Gascón-Inchausti

Abstract This chapter addresses the relevance of the discovery of the debtor's assets to ensure the effectiveness of enforcement proceedings. It deals, firstly, with the general issues on this topic, which have an impact on the success of enforcement. It then focuses on the discovery of assets as such, analyzing who should gather and who should provide the information. Finally, it addresses two cross-cutting issues: the use of ICT and cross-border situations.

Effectiveness of enforcement proceedings is crucial to ensure full access to justice. This chapter will focus on the relevance of an effective discovery of the debtor's assets. It will first address some general issues, with potential consequences when analyzing the problem of effectiveness of enforcement proceedings (1). Then, it will focus on the debtor's assets discovery, from two different interplaying perspectives: who is expected to gather the information and from whom may the information be gathered (2). It will finally deal with some cross-cutting issues, directly linked to recent legal evolutions whit impact in this field (3).

[1] Among many others, see K.D. Kerameus, "Chapter 10. Enforcement proceedings", in *International Enciclopedia of Comparative Law. Vol. XVI (2). Civil Procedure* (ed. M. Cappelletti), Tübingen-Leiden-Boston, 1987, 10–1 to 10–146; W. Kennett, "General Report: Enforcement", in *Procedural Laws in Europe* (ed. M. Storme), Maklu, Antwerpen-Appeldoon, 2003, 81–111; B. Hess, *Making more efficient the enforcement of judicial decisions within the European Union: Transparency of a Debtor's Assets, Attachment of Bank Accounts, Provisional Enforcement and Protective Measures (Study No. JAI/A3/2002/02)*, available online at http://www2.ipr.uni-heidelberg.de/studie/General%20Report%20Version%20of%2018%20Feb%202004.pdf). More recently, Y. Taniguchi, "Enforcement of judgments", in *Civil Litigation in Comparative Context* (eds. O. G. Chase, H. Hershkoff, L.J. Silberman, J. Sorabji, R. Stürner, Y. Taniguchi, V. Varano), 2nd ed., St. Paul, 2017, 595–642.

F. Gascón-Inchausti (✉)
Complutense University, Madrid, Spain
e-mail: fgascon@ucm.es

M. Deguchi (ed.), *Effective Enforcement of Creditors' Rights*,
Ius Gentium: Comparative Perspectives on Law and Justice 91,
https://doi.org/10.1007/978-981-16-5609-5_16

1 General Approach to the Topic: Commonalities and Divergences in Enforcement Proceedings with Potential Consequences on Their Effectiveness

Enforcement proceedings are embedded in legal tradition and culture more than any other piece of civil procedure. A comparative overview shows very—and radically—different approaches, even between countries that are geographically and culturally very close to each other.[1] This might look astonishing, since the problems are exactly the same all around the world; but the ways to cope with them serve to mirror the way each society tries to find a balance between confronting rights and interests.

1.1 Convergence and Similarities

We can detect, nevertheless, at least three points where convergence and similarities prevail.

1.1.1 The Pro Creditore Approach

There is, in the first place, a common idea underlying every contemporary system of civil enforcement: the «*pro creditore* approach». Enforcement proceedings are a field of civil procedure where overarching principles operate in a very peculiar manner: regulation of enforcement proceedings are not structured in a "neutral" manner, but starting from the assumption that the enforceable title allows the public authority to presume that the creditor is entitled to the relief he/she is seeking. In other words, it is not reasonable to address enforcement proceedings with the same perspective as declaratory proceedings. In the case of declaratory proceedings, the aim should be to design a regulation allowing the parties to put the judge in the best position to make the best possible decision. When we look at enforcement, the merits of the case cease to be the nuclear point, and procedural fairness by itself takes the lead: enforcement proceeding must ensure satisfaction of the creditor's interest, but securing at the same time fairness regarding the debtor's position, i.e., offering him/her reasonable possibilities to defend himself.

1.1.2 The Constitutionalization of Enforcement Proceedings

In strict relation to the above, a second common spot is the constitutionalization of enforcement proceedings.

- On the one hand, the creditor's right to enforcement proceedings is to be considered as part of the fundamental right of access to justice, which would be delusory if litigants were to be entitled only to receive a judgment on the merits: this view prevails in any advanced legal system and has been clearly endorsed many times by the European Court of Human Rights as being part of Article 6.1 ECHR.[2] This means, in turn, that the creditor has a right to *efficient* enforcement proceedings and to have the enforceable title executed within a reasonable deadline.[3]

- On the other hand, the debtor involved in enforcement has the right to fair proceedings, also in the sense of Article 6.1 ECHR and of national constitutions: he/she shall be in a position to avail him/herself of reasonable remedies to challenge enforcement proceedings and/or enforcement measures.[4] And, of course, other fundamental rights of the debtor do not just simply «vanish» or «fade away» when enforcement commences: freedom of movement, privacy and data protection, for instance, may entail hurdles to the effectiveness of enforcement proceedings.[5]
- This confrontation between the opposing creditor/debtor interests shall be solved in the light of the principle of proportionality,[6] which lies also in the basis of any reasonable regulation of enforcement proceedings.

---

[2] Article 6(1) ECHR: "In the determination of his civil rights and obligations or of any criminal charge against him, everyone is entitled to a fair and public hearing within a reasonable time by an independent and impartial tribunal established by law (…)".

[3] Since *Hornsby v. Greece* (Application no. 18357/91, Judgment of 19 March 1997: at Section 40 the Court clearly stated the following:

> The Court reiterates that, according to its established case-law, Article 6 para. 1 (art. 6–1) secures to everyone the right to have any claim relating to his civil rights and obligations brought before a court or tribunal; in this way it embodies the "right to a court", of which the right of access, that is the right to institute proceedings before courts in civil matters, constitutes one aspect (see the Philis vs. Greece judgment of 27 August 1991, Series A no. 209, p. 20, para. 59). However, that right would be illusory if a Contracting State's domestic legal system allowed a final, binding judicial decision to remain inoperative to the detriment of one party. It would be inconceivable that Article 6 para. 1 (art. 6–1) should describe in detail procedural guarantees afforded to litigants—proceedings that are fair, public and expeditious—without protecting the implementation of judicial decisions; to construe Article 6 (art. 6) as being concerned exclusively with access to a court and the conduct of proceedings would be likely to lead to situations incompatible with the principle of the rule of law which the Contracting States undertook to respect when they ratified the Convention (see, mutatis mutandis, the Golder vs. the United Kingdom judgment of 21 February 1975, Series A no. 18, pp. 16–18, paras. 34–36). Execution of a judgment given by any court must therefore be regarded as an integral part of the "trial" for the purposes of Article 6 (art. 6).

[4] The ECtHR, for instance, has explicitly addressed the need to serve on the debtor a seizure or any similar enforcement measure, in order to enable him/her to react before forced and irreversible transmissions are made: see *Tsironis v. Greece* (Appl. no. 44584/98), judgment of 6 December 2001(Section 27) and *Société Anonyme Thaleia Karydi Axte v. Greece* (Appl. no. 44769/07), judgment of 5 November 2009 (Section 25).

[5] For a very comprehensive update, see M.L. Villamarín López, "Access to Justice under European Case Law", *International Journal of Procedural Law*, Vol. 7, 2017–1, 130–155.

[6] Operating on the basis of the principle of proportionality when fundamental rights confront is a technique enshrined in Article 52.1 of the Charter of Fundamental Rights of the European Union, pursuant to which «Any limitation on the exercise of the rights and freedoms recognised by this

1.1.3 The Practical Relevance of Monetary Enforcement

A third common point is, of course, the perception that monetary enforcement is still the core of enforcement proceedings. There are obviously many kinds of judicial relief and final injunctions are becoming increasingly common, especially in legal fields where we are experiencing very important developments (for instance, when it comes to the enforcement of judicial decisions relating to the infringement of IP rights). Nevertheless:

- In practice, monetary claims are still the most frequent ones before civil courts, which means that money judgments are the ones most needed of enforcement; in addition, non-judicial enforceable titles are usually confined to money claims.
- Injunctions are usually accompanied by orders to pay sums of money (such as orders to pay costs or compensations for damages).
- Enforcement of injunctions may, in the end, need to be transformed in monetary enforcement, in case it gets impossible to obtain full performance and/or if fines are imposed to the unwilling debtor.

In other words, enforcement is in the end of the day a question of money; and money can only be gathered if the assets are located.

1.2 Divergences

From that point on, divergences among legal systems arise: time limits for voluntary compliance; statutes of limitation to engage into enforcement proceedings; remedies available to the debtor are just a few examples thereof. In practice, the most «visible» difference—and the one with the biggest repercussions for this topic—regards the authority in charge of enforcement. A look at the situation within the "most integrated region" in the legal field, that is, the European Union, shows very relevant divergences.[7]

Whereas in some Member States enforcement will be granted and directed by a court (Austria, Ireland, Italy, Malta, Slovenia, Spain), in others the bailiffs are the competent authorities (Cyprus, Estonia, Finland, Greece, Romania, Slovakia). In addition, the notion or "bailiff" or "enforcement agent" is not univocal. Bailiffs may be court-appointed officers (Belgium, Denmark, Germany, Latvia, Lithuania, The

---

Charter must be provided for by law and respect the essence of those rights and freedoms. Subject to the principle of proportionality, limitations may be made only if they are necessary and genuinely meet objectives of general interest recognised by the Union or the need to protect the rights and freedoms of others.»

[7] See on this F. Gascón Inchausti and M. Requejo Isidro, "A Classic Cross-Border Case: The Usual Situation in the First Instance", in B. Hess and P. Ortolani (eds.), *Impediments of National Procedural Law to the Free Movement of Judgments. Luxembourg Report on European Procedural Law. Volume I*, Munich, 2019, 70–73.

Netherlands, Sweden, UK), but they can also act as private practitioners (Luxembourg), or both (Bulgaria). In some Scandinavian systems enforcement is entrusted to public bodies (ie, administrative, non-judiciary ones). Notaries are sometimes entrusted with enforcement-related tasks (e.g. enforcing extrajudicial titles in Croatia and Hungary—also in Spain, under certain conditions—, conducting auctions in Greece and Italy). Moreover, in some Member States the authority in charge of enforcement changes depending on the enforcement measure, on the type of asset subject to enforcement, or even on the choice of the applicant. Examples are France (the usual enforcement authority is the bailiff, but some enforcement measures will require a judicial decision and fall under the competence of the enforcement judge or another first instance judge), Luxembourg (where the enforcement authority is essentially the *huissier de justice*, but enforcement over immovable property also heavily involves courts), Germany (local courts are responsible for execution proceedings concerning enforcement against claims and other property rights and enforcement against real estate), or the Czech Republic (where a creditor can choose whether to obtain satisfaction of his claim by means of judicial enforcement of a decision, i.e. by a judicial enforcement agent, or by means of execution by a judicial executor).

This issue is very relevant when it comes to the problem of discovering the debtor's assets: it is an activity requiring sometimes public authority—*imperium* in a classical sense—and bailiffs do not always have it.

2 Discovering Debtor's Assets: Main Problems and Some Examples of Solution

No matter who the competent authority is, a recurrent problem for the success of monetary enforcement is the difficulties to locate the debtor's assets. In 2002 Prof. Burkhard Hess undertook for the EU Commission a Study entitled "Making more efficient the enforcement of judicial decisions within the European Union: transparency of a Debtor's assets; attachment of bank accounts; provisional enforcement and protective measures".[8] The panorama might have a changed a little, but not too much, at least when it comes to identifying the key elements, the shortcomings and possible solutions.

Two factors intersect in this field: who can gather the information and from whom can it be retrieved.

2.1 Who is Entitled to Gather the Information?

On the one hand, as previously mentioned, it is necessary to identify who is entitled to gather the information and/or who bears the burden to do it. Two possible—and

[8] Supra note 1.

compatible—answers emerge: the creditor and the authority in charge of enforcement proceedings (court, bailiff, and/or notary).

Many legal systems assume that it is the creditor's task to identify the assets to be seized: from such a perspective, the authority in charge of enforcement proceedings would only assist him if necessary, i.e., it would play an ancillary role, so the failure to identify the assets would be the creditor's failure. In this vein, many legal systems establish the burden of the creditor to identify in his claim for enforcement—or similar document—the assets to be seized by the court.

It is this author's view, however, that exacerbating the burden of the creditor to retrieve the information would not be a reasonable approach:

- Firstly, because of the limited means and powers in the hand of the creditor to overturn such a heavy burden: the creditor could only gather by himself information from entities obliged to provide it, which would help discovering immovable property, for instance, and maybe cars, but not much more.
- Moreover, the creditor, as mentioned before, has a fundamental right to effective enforcement proceedings, and this right involves the legitimate expectance to get from the judicial system not just as many assistance as necessary, but a real involvement, so that a failure to identify the assets would be a system's failure. In other words, a too passive role of the public authority could be seen as a denial of justice, i.e., as the infringement of a fundamental right. This approach underpins the possibility to demand legal changes from domestic lawmakers (e.g., from the European Union). And, in those systems where enforcement is not in the hand of courts or public bodies or public officers, it also demands that those authorities are sufficiently empowered to perform or to boost the tasks required to an efficient location of the debtor's asset.

In other words, an effective system of debtor's assets discovery requires a real involvement of the authority in charge of enforcement proceedings. And this, in turn, means that the authority in charge of enforcement proceedings must be sufficiently empowered.

This involvement, of course, is not incompatible:

- either with the possibility of the creditor to carry on his own investigations; party autonomy is of course at the core of civil enforcement and it would be paternalistic to prevent any creditor's initiative, which would unclutter the justice system or reduce the costs of private bailiffs.
- nor with the possibility for the lawmaker to throw upon the creditor the burden of conducting a first investigation into the debtor's assets, as it would be a proportionate measure, especially in times of austerity, where public resources are limited.

2.2 *From Whom May the Information be Validly Retrieved?*

On the other hand, as mentioned earlier, apart from determining who is in charge of the assets discovery, it is crucial to examine from whom may the information be validly retrieved: this issue contains also the question on how this task is to be performed. Two possible answers appear here: the debtor himself and/or third parties—in a very broad sense—.

2.2.1 The Debtor

Many national systems establish the possibility to question the debtor directly about his assets.[9] This debtor's declaration may be made in different forms: sometimes it may be carried out in a similar way to testimony, at an oral hearing before the judge or a court officer; it is however more frequent—since it requires less effort from the system—to arrange things in written form, normally requiring the debtor to submit a form and, if necessary, producing documents.

Regarding the extent of the declaration, in many legal systems the debtor is required to make full disclosure of all his assets. In other jurisdictions, on the contrary, the duty to disclose is limited to assets, the value of which would be sufficient for the enforcement of the creditors claim.

Both options entail pros and cons. Full disclosure prevents the debtor to keep away from enforcement valuable assets, whose enforcement would be faster and easier than that on the identified assets. It could also be the basis to build a sort of database which could be used in further procedures, following the German example. Limited disclosure, on the other hand, if properly carried out, seems more respectful to the principle of proportionality and to data protection.

Whatever is the national lawmaker's choice, the main problem remains in establishing the possible means to compel the debtor to make a full and frank disclosure, either in full or in part. The possibilities managed by legal systems are here again diverging in nature and/or intensity.

First of all, it is important to define who would be empowered to request such a declaration. If it is in the hands of the court or of a public body, a higher degree of coercion may be used; in the hands of the creditor or of bailiffs acting without any public authority support, the debtor will certainly feel less compelled to fulfill the duty—unless a US-style discovery device is available—. At most a legal system may throw upon the creditor the burden to make a first attempt; but the right must be ensured to demand from a public authority (the court, as a rule) to end up requesting the assets declaration from the debtor –even if this may break the convenient surprise effect.

As far as coercive means available to the court are concerned, some possibilities appear in the comparative landscape:

[9] B. Hess, supra note 1, 35–38.

- The most aggressive one is the threat of criminal prosecution (i.e., by means of contempt of court or equivalent offence). Many legal systems establish it, although it is sometimes difficult to implement, especially if the debtor does not explicitly refuse to submit the declaration, but submits an incomplete one; and it may also be pointless if the debtor is a legal person. Anyway, if it comes to this point, a sanction will not be useful to the creditor.
- Many legal systems establish the threat to impose the debtor a fine or an *astreinte* or similar sanction in case of non-submission. Here, again, it is like a snake biting its own tail: it is not useful to the creditor and, of course, if the fine is charged by the public Treasury, then it would compete with the creditor.
- By contrast, drawing adverse inferences is not a useful possibility, since in the framework of enforcement proceedings there is not the expectance of a decision on the merits where this might be anyhow useful to the creditor.

To sum up, collecting the information from the debtor is a useful possibility when things «run smoothly», i.e., when the debtor collaborates with the person or authority seeking the declaration, either because he is interested in it, or because he is afraid of the consequences. Otherwise, it may prove fruitless and even detrimental to the enforcement's effectiveness.

2.2.2 Third Parties

All legal systems rely on information retrieved from third parties—in a very broad sense—to gather information on the debtor's assets. Comparative analysis shows how these third parties could be included under the following headings/categories, each one entailing potential different difficulties. In general terms, it should be noted that there is a general duty to collaborate with a sound administration of justice, conceived in many legal systems as a public duty, established in Constitutions and statutory law. This general duty concerns not only, e.g., the duty to give testimony or to produce documents when requested by a court, but should also encompass enforcement proceedings.

(a) Public registers

Public registers are a traditional and reliable source of information, usually accessible to anyone showing an interest, including hereunder the creditor or a bailiff, apart from court officers and other public bodies.

The organization of public registers is far from being harmonized, even in the context of the European Union. In general terms, public registers help detecting immovable property, cars, ships or similar assets subject to registration (either mandatory or voluntary). In some jurisdictions these registers are centralized, enabling a quick and efficient search. In other places, however, lack of centralization and coordination makes it harder to ensure a full search.

Securing centralized information and public—and free or at least cheap—access to public registers is a measure which would foster more efficient enforcement proceedings.

(b) Public bodies in the possession of financial information

No one has a better image of a person's financial situation than the tax administration. The tax administration knows the assets of each taxpayer and, thus, is in an optimal position to determine which are liable to seizure. In addition, the tax administration is frequently itself a debtor's garnishee, i.e., it is a debtor of the debtor: this is namely the case with VAT refund claims, which are frequently seized.

Another interesting public body holding relevant information is the social security or similar authority, i.e., the public entity in charge of controlling contributions to the public social security system, where this exists. These bodies have information of employers and employees, allowing identifying if the debtor has a salary that could be seized—in whole or in part—. Apart from this, and similarly to the tax administration, these public entities are sometimes debtor's garnishees (again, when the debtor is entitled to some refund on the basis of specific bonuses or benefits).

Two problems have arisen in practice with these public bodies:

- On the one hand, they manage sensitive information, which they are not enabled to share openly or even to any person showing a legitimate interest. A legal provision determining who is empowered to obtain information from them is therefore required; and, given the need to make a balance of proportionality, only judicial authorities (judges or court clerks) and bailiffs acting as public authorities will be in the end enabled to «access the gate».
- On the other hand, these entities tend sometimes to be reluctant to share information for enforcement purposes, probably for budgetary reasons.

Ensuring full cooperation from these public bodies is crucial for a successful assets' discovery. If necessary, legal reforms should be enacted in order to establish an express duty to cooperate with court authorities, and to do it in the shortest deadlines.

(c) Financial entities

Banks and equivalent financial entities also hold relevant information on the debtor's assets. Indeed, bank accounts are among the most desired items to be seized, for obvious reasons that need no further explanation.

Sometimes the creditor himself knows of their existence, due to the preexistent commercial relationships with the debtor. But this does not mean much, due to privacy policies of banks, who cannot—and will not—provide the creditor with information on the subsistence of the account and of its amount. These are, once again, third parties that will only abdicate from their professional secret duties if a statutory provision compels them to do so, on the basis of a judicial or public warrant. The notion of banking secrecy and the feeling that banks owe themselves in the first place to their clients—and only secondly to other interests, including public interests—sustains the fear for shortcomings in this field.

Moreover, due to the high volatility of amounts deposited in bank accounts, time is here of the essence: requests for information should be answered without delay, in order to enable immediate seizure of the sums.

The best example of a model regulation coping with these issues is, undoubtedly, the relatively recent European Account Preservation Order (EAPO, hereinafter),[10] already addressed in other chapters of this book. The focus will be put later on other aspects of this institution, but now it is important to emphasize some relevant features of its Article 14, under a very eloquent title: «Request for the obtaining of account information».

1. "Where the creditor has obtained in a Member State an enforceable judgment, court settlement or authentic instrument which requires the debtor to pay the creditor's claim and the creditor has reasons to believe that the debtor holds one or more accounts with a bank in a specific Member State, but knows neither the name and/or address of the bank nor the IBAN, BIC or another bank number allowing the bank to be identified, he may request the court with which the application for the Preservation Order is lodged to request that the information authority of the Member State of enforcement obtain the information necessary to allow the bank or banks and the debtor's account or accounts to be identified. Notwithstanding the first subparagraph, the creditor may make the request referred to in that subparagraph where the judgment, court settlement or authentic instrument obtained by the creditor is not yet enforceable and the amount to be preserved is substantial taking into account the relevant circumstances, and the creditor has submitted sufficient evidence to satisfy the court that there is an urgent need for account information because there is a risk that, without such information, the subsequent enforcement of the creditor's claim against the debtor is likely to be jeopardised and that this could consequently lead to a substantial deterioration of the creditor's financial situation.
2. The creditor shall make the request referred to in paragraph 1 in the application for the Preservation Order. The creditor shall substantiate why he believes that the debtor holds one or more accounts with a bank in the specific Member State and shall provide all relevant information available to him about the debtor and the account or accounts to be preserved. If the court with which the application for a Preservation Order is lodged considers that the creditor's request is not sufficiently substantiated, it shall reject it.
3. When the court is satisfied that the creditor's request is well substantiated and that all the conditions and requirements for issuing the Preservation Order are met, except for the information requirement set out in point (d) of Article 8(2) and, where applicable, the security requirement pursuant to Article 12, the court

[10] Established by Regulation (EU) No 655/2014 of the European Parliament and of the Council of 15 May 2014 establishing a European Account Preservation Order procedure to facilitate cross-border debt recovery in civil and commercial matters (OJ L 189, 27.6.2014, p. 59–92).

shall transmit the request for information to the information authority of the Member State of enforcement in accordance with Article 29.

4. To obtain the information referred to in paragraph 1, the information authority in the Member State of enforcement shall use one of the methods available in that Member State pursuant to paragraph 5.
5. Each Member State shall make available in its national law at least one of the following methods of obtaining the information referred to in paragraph 1:

   (a) an obligation on all banks in its territory to disclose, upon request by the information authority, whether the debtor holds an account with them;
   (b) access for the information authority to the relevant information where that information is held by public authorities or administrations in registers or otherwise;
   (c) the possibility for its courts to oblige the debtor to disclose with which bank or banks in its territory he holds one or more accounts where such an obligation is accompanied by an in personam order by the court prohibiting the withdrawal or transfer by him of funds held in his account or accounts up to the amount to be preserved by the Preservation Order; or
   (d) any other methods which are effective and efficient for the purposes of obtaining the relevant information, provided that they are not disproportionately costly or time-consuming.
   Irrespective of the method or methods made available by a Member State, all authorities involved in obtaining the information shall act expeditiously.

6. As soon as the information authority of the Member State of enforcement has obtained the account information, it shall transmit it to the requesting court in accordance with Article 29.
7. If the information authority is unable to obtain the information referred to in paragraph 1, it shall inform the requesting court accordingly. Where, as a result of the unavailability of account information, the application for a Preservation Order is rejected in full, the requesting court shall without delay release any security that the creditor may have provided pursuant to Article 12.
8. Where under this Article the information authority is provided with information by a bank or is granted access to account information held by public authorities or administrations in registers, the notification of the debtor of the disclosure of his personal data shall be deferred for 30 days, in order to prevent an early notification from jeopardising the effect of the Preservation Order."

As a tool to reinforce the effectiveness of the EAPO, this provision is meant to work in cross-border settings—a very reduced "corner" of litigation—. However, it is important to highlight four elements of the Regulation, which seem to have been identified by the European lawmaker as "best practices" in this field and which should be usable generally when dealing with the problem of discovering the debtor's assets in any framework—i.e., not only in cross-border litigation:

(i) The EAPO Regulation makes it clear that there is a duty of the courts to collaborate with creditors in gathering information: the creditor is entitled to activate the mechanism of Article 14, it is not just a discretionary decision from the court.

(ii) It might not be reasonable to force the court to provide such collaboration in the manner of a "fishing expedition"[11]: in other words, the EU lawmaker has preferred to be more cautious and exclude a general duty to launch indiscriminate investigation orders. Therefore, the creditor is expected to show a prima facie case: he/she shall substantiate why he believes that the debtor holds one or more accounts with a bank in the specific Member State and shall provide all relevant information available to him/her about the debtor and the account or accounts to be preserved.

In this author's view, this limitation may be justified in cross-border contexts, where the rules on banking secrecy and data protection[12] are not fully harmonized; it seems also sensible to limit the possibility of a wide disclosure when the purpose of the request is to ensure the effectiveness of a provisional measure, since the creditor's right has not been endorsed by the court. However, in purely domestic settings, and for the purpose of enforcement of a judgment or an enforceable title, it would be more convenient to opt for the "fishing expedition" possibility, especially if it is not technically cumbersome.

(iii) National legal systems are expected to have methods of obtaining information on bank accounts. The Regulation offers a sort of free choice, provided that they are effective and efficient and that they are not "disproportionately costly or time-consuming". Three possibilities are described as examples:

   - The obligation on banks to disclose, upon request by a so-called "information authority", whether the debtor holds an account with them: it is important to note that Member States are free to decide who is the "information authority" [in Spain, for instance, it is a Directorate General within the Ministry of Justice, not a court, empowered for the purposes of implementing the EAPO provisions to request an information that, in internal cases, could only be required by a court or a court clerk]. This option is an example of a direct duty to collaborate with the enforcement.
   - If bank account information is held by public authorities or administrations in registers or otherwise, the "information authority" shall have access. This option, differently, shows that collaboration with enforcement operates in an indirect manner, on the basis of a previous duty to provide information to public authorities or administrations.

[11] See G. Cuniberti and S. Migliorini, *The European Account Preservation Order Regulation. A Commentary*, CUP, 2018, 178.

[12] On the data protection concern, again G. Cuniberti and S. Migliorini, supra note 11, 183–186.

- The possibility for the courts to oblige the debtor to disclose with which bank or banks he holds one or more accounts, provided that such an obligation is accompanied by an in personam order by the court prohibiting the withdrawal or transfer by him of funds held in his account or accounts up to the amount to be preserved by the Preservation Order.

These three options are not just "ideas" or "suggestions" of the European lawmaker; they represent, differently, a choice among the preexisting methods already used by domestic legislations to deal with this issue. Anyway, the EAPO Regulation establishes the duty of Members States to adapt, if necessary, their domestic legislation in order to stick to one of those options. It is, therefore, a "European standard" that should foster the improvement of domestic legislation with a potential impact on purely internal settings: if such measures have to be enacted in order to increase the effectiveness of an EAPO, it would not be justifiable not to use them in support of national enforcement proceedings—it would generate a sort of internal legal inequality between cross-border and domestic litigation.

(iv) The fourth relevant "best practice" regards the need to address the *periculum in mora* problem, i.e., the risk linked to the high volatility of amounts in bank accounts. The Regulation establishes here that "the notification of the debtor of the disclosure of his personal data shall be deferred for 30 days, in order to prevent an early notification from jeopardising the effect of the Preservation Order". It is, of course, one of the possibilities: deferring the moment the debtor is informed of the disclosure, as an exception to the general rights and duties under the relevant provisions on data protection. Regardless which solution is preferred, it is important to stress the legal awareness of the necessity to prevent these risks: here again, the pro creditore approach is visible; the debtor's protection is secondary and possible only after allowing the creditor a reasonable deadline to secure the effectiveness of the preservation order (i.e., the enforcement measure).

To sum up, it could be said that, here again, effective enforcement depends on a proper regulation on the duties of banks and equivalent financial entities to collaborate in a quick and truthful manner with enforcement authorities.

(d) Employers

Another potential source of information is the debtor's employer, which enables to seize the debtor's salary—to the extent, of course, it is admissible—. The social security administration can provide the information on whether the debtor is an employee or not, but maybe not a full picture of the salary, which may only be known by the debtor and his/her employer. In case there is not a traditional "labor law" relationship with the employer, it will be even more difficult to find out if there is an equivalent to an employer from whom the information might be sought.

Here again, the main issue is confidentiality and data protection, which justifies the employers' refusal to hand over information to the creditor and/or to some types of bailiff. And, here again, two principles should apply:

On the one hand, there is the constitutional right to enforcement, which empowers the creditor to request the court's assistance—or a public authority's assistance—in order to gather this sort of information.
- On the other hand, the general duty to collaborate to a sound administration of justice, which underpins the duty of the employer to give this kind of information upon request of a public authority, giving hence priority to enforcement over the debtor's privacy rights.

Also in this field, therefore, efficient enforcement requires legal provisions ensuring the employers' cooperation, not only as debtors' garnishees, but also previously providing the enforcement authority with information on the debtor's salary.

(e) Other debtor's garnishees

The situation is similar when there are reasons to believe that there are other debtor's garnishees, different from public authorities, banks and employers. This may be the situation, e.g., when the debtor owns a property that he has rented to a third party: the rent is seizable and seizure thereof may prove to be more efficient or proportionate than the seizure of the property itself. It may also be the case when the creditor knows that the debtor has a monetary claim against a third party.

Once again, data protection and potential confidentiality agreements may prevent the creditor to obtain the information from that third party.

And, here again, the solution has to be found in the light of the role of enforcement authorities activating the general duty to collaborate with a sound administration of justice.

(f) Witnesses in general

Finally, it should be recognized that other subjects, other than those listed so far, may have information about the debtor's assets. Those persons may be qualified in a broad sense as witnesses, i.e., as persons in the possession of relevant information. Some legal systems, indeed, are aware of this fact and lawmakers have included general clauses and provisions establishing the general duty of any person to inform the enforcement authority of any assets of the debtor they might be aware of.

Determining who these witnesses are is, of course, a task which is attributed to the creditor or to a bailiff, especially when the latter works on behalf of the former. Depending on the source of the information, the witness may be entitled to refuse giving information (again, on the basis of data protection duties or confidentiality agreements) or may be free to deliver it without fear to subsequent consequences. In the first situation, the creditor or the bailiff should be entitled to avail themselves of the enforcement authorities to request the witness to produce information.

To sum up, an effective enforcement system should not give up the possibility of gathering information on the debtor's assets wherever it might be: the powers of the enforcement authorities and the general duty to collaborate should be used in a proportionate manner, also in those systems where this issue does not find a clear regulation.

3 Two Cross-Cutting Issues

The last part of this report will deal with cross-cutting issues directly linked to recent legal developments.

3.1 The Use of ICT Devices

ICT devices have proven very efficient in the field of enforcement proceedings[13]: the best examples are electronic auctions, which are currently the rule in many legal systems. And all legal systems should be aware of their usefulness also when it comes to performing the necessary tasks to carry out the discovery of assets. The information in public registers should be made available through electronic means, as well as that in the possession of public bodies and financial entities. This would allow sparing time, something which is of the essence if we want to avoid assets to "vanish" as soon as the debtor has the suspicion that the creditor might be starting enforcement proceedings against him.

An interesting model is offered by the Spanish legal system, with the establishment ten years ago of an electronic platform, the so-called "*Punto Neutro Judicial*" (Judicial Neutral Spot, in a very rough translation).[14] This platform connects the court system to most relevant stakeholders in the field of assets discovery: public registers, banks, tax and social security administration, and police authorities.

When court clerks are required by the creditor to perform an investigation on the debtor's assets, they just need to enter the platform and introduce the debtor's official identification number and launch a search with all relevant entities. The request will be automatically transferred to the electronic files of those entities, which will in turn deliver the information they are holding regarding immovable property, cars, bank accounts, and so on. The system is not perfect, especially regarding bank accounts, because it does not allow any sort of on-line access to the debtor's bank account, but only to monthly or quarterly reports. As compensation, the system allows the

---

[13] M.A. Lupoi, "Enforcement of a Claim with the Support of the New Information Technology. Protection of the Creditor and the Debtor", in M. Kengiel and Z. Nemessányi (eds.), *Electronic Technology and Civil Procedure. New Paths to Justice from Around the World*, Dordrecht-Heidelberg-New York–London, 2012, 181–209, specially at 188–196. Addressing the Spanish developments, see P. Peiteado Mariscal, "Posibles aplicaciones telemáticas en el proceso civil", in C. Senés Motilla (ed.), *Presente y Futuro de la e-Justicia en España y la Unión Europea*, Pamplona, 2010, 251–277; C. Senés Motilla, "El embargo telemático de cuentas bancarias", in A. De la Oliva Santos, F. Gascón Inchausti and M. Aguilera Morales (eds.), *La e-Justicia en la Unión Europea. Desarrollos en el ámbito europeo y en los ordenamientos nacionales*, Pamplona, 2012, 175–195.

[14] See J.M. González García, "El Punto Neutro Judicial: una herramienta al servicio de la mayor eficacia de la Administración de Justicia española", in A. De la Oliva Santos, F. Gascón Inchausti and M. Aguilera Morales (eds.), supra note 13, 197–215.

court clerk to launch an immediate seizure of the bank account—provided that there are sufficient funds—. The system is still far from perfect, but from now it is just a question of progressively improving its quality and potentialities.

3.2 The Cross-Border Dimension

Cross-border litigation and cross-border enforcement are becoming increasingly normal. Even in cross-border settings, enforcement proceedings remain in principle strictly national: European law and international law regulate the mechanisms to grant enforceability abroad and establish the possible grounds for the debtor to refuse enforcement linked to its cross-border nature. But the unfolding itself of enforcement proceedings is a matter of domestic procedural law,[15] including the search of the debtors' assets.

In practice, this means that a foreign creditor envisaging starting enforcement proceedings in a different jurisdiction must rely on the mechanisms existing in that jurisdiction to discover assets: the divergences appear here sometimes as hurdles, sometimes as advantages. But common ground already exists and, as described above, it is common to most legal systems that court and sometimes other public authorities are empowered to gather information from the debtor and from relevant third parties. The question arises then immediately: would it be possible to expand the mechanisms of international judicial cooperation also to this field? Within the EU and other regional contexts, for instance, tax and other public administrations cooperate already, transferring data and information, sometimes even on a spontaneous basis.[16]

It should be, therefore, feasible to imagine a cross-border access to the information on debtors' assets: it would be a very useful tool to prevent unnecessary costs for the creditor, because it would prevent him to engage into cross-border enforcement if there is not a clear expectance to collect any sum of money due to the lack of identified assets.

The clearest step in this direction is the above mentioned Article 14 of the EAPO Regulation[17]: as has already been mentioned, it requires Member States to establish efficient and effective methods to gather information on bank accounts, at least with

[15] This is a recurrent idea, for instance, in the case law of the Court of Justice of the European Union addressing recognition and enforcement of foreign judgments (see, for instance, case C-139/10, *Prism Investments*).

[16] See, in this vein, the Council Directive 2010/24/EU of 16 March 2010 concerning mutual assistance for the recovery of claims relating to taxes, duties and other measures (OJ L 84, 31.3.2010, p. 1–12).

[17] It is not, however, the first one. The EU Maintenance Regulation (Council Regulation (EC) No 4/2009 of 18 December 2008 on jurisdiction, applicable law, recognition and enforcement of decisions and cooperation in matters relating to maintenance obligations, OJ L 7, 10.1.2009, p. 1–79) already established in 2009 a system of cooperation of national Central Authorities. Pursuant to Article 61.2 of the Maintenance Regulation, Central Authorities shall be empowered to use all appropriate and reasonable means to obtain certain information, among which (c) "the identification

the purpose to make it available to a foreign judicial authority, who is in turn acting "on behalf" of a creditor. The system works in a very simple manner:

- Each Member State shall establish and identify a so-called "information authority", empowered to activate the available methods to collect information—whose existence is mandatory.
- The creditor, showing prima facie evidence of the existence of a bank account in a different Member State, may request from the competent judge in his territory to launch a search for information on bank accounts in those Member States where there are reasonable grounds to believe that the debtor holds bank accounts. This request for information is ancillary to the application for the issuing of a European Account Preservation Order, aimed at securing the amounts to be found.
- The competent court will send the request to the "information authority" where the debtor appears to hold a bank account.
- The "information authority" will activate the search using the mechanisms foreseen in its legal system and will send the result in the shortest deadline, ensuring in the meanwhile confidentiality vis a vis the debtor for a 30 days period.

It is easy to grasp that it is clearly just a first trial, limited to a very specific type of asset, bank accounts. But it represents also the scaffolding on which to build a much more interesting and advanced system, which includes other types of assets, with the potential to be applied in a general way, not only internally but, also, as a model to articulate cross-border cooperation outside the scope of the European Union.

References

Cuniberti G, Migliorini S (2018) The European account preservation order regulation. A Commentary. CUP, p 178

Inchausti FG, Requejo Isidro M (2019) A classic cross-border case: the usual situation in the first instance. In: Hess B, Ortolani P (eds) Impediments of national procedural law to the free movement of judgments. Luxembourg Report on European Procedural Law, vol I, Munich, pp 70–73

Kennett W (2003) General report: enforcement. In: Storme M (ed) Procedural laws in Europe storme

Kerameus KD (1987) Chapter 10. Enforcement proceedings. In Cappelletti M (ed) International Enciclopedia of Comparative Law. Civil procedure, vol XVI, no 2, Tübingen–Leiden–Boston, pp 10-1–10-146

Lupoi MA (2012) Enforcement of a claim with the support of the new information technology. protection of the creditor and the debtor. In Kengiel M, Nemessányi Z (eds) Electronic technology and civil procedure. new paths to justice from around the world. Dordrecht, Heidelberg, New York, London, pp 181–209

Peiteado Mariscal P (2010) Posibles aplicaciones telemáticas en el proceso civil. In Senés Motilla C (ed) Presente y Futuro de la e-Justicia en España y la Unión Europea, Pamplona, pp 251–277

of the debtor's employer and/or of the debtor's bank account(s)" and, more broadly "the debtor's assets".

Senés Motilla C (2012) El embargo telemático de cuentas bancarias. In De la Oliva Santos A, Gascón Inchausti F, Aguilera Morales M (eds) La e-Justicia en la Unión Europea. Desarrollos en el ámbito europeo y en los ordenamientos nacionales, Pamplona, pp 175–195

Taniguchi Y (2017) Enforcement of judgments. In: Chase OG, Hershkoff H, Silberman LJ, Sorabji J, Stürner R, Taniguchi Y, Varano V (eds) Civil litigation in comparative context (eds) 2nd edn., St. Paul, pp 595–642

Villamarín López ML (2017-1) Access to justice under European Case Law. Int J Procedural Law 7:130–155

Fernando Gascón-Inchausti 09/24/1972, Guernica (Vizcaya), EDUCATION 1997 Ph.D. in Procedural Law (cum laude), Law School, Complutense University (Facultad de Derecho, Universidad Complutense de Madrid) [Extraordinary Doctorate Award]. 1995 J.D., Law School, Complutense University (Facultad de Derecho, Universidad Complutense de Madrid), Madrid, Spain [Extraordinary Graduate Award]. PROFESSIONAL EXPERIENCE Fernando GASCÓN INCHAUSTI 2 2016—Full Professor (Catedrático) of Procedural Law (Civil and Criminal Procedure), Universidad Complutense de Madrid Law School. Secretary General of International Association of Procedural Law.

Finding Defendant's Assets in Proceedings to Enforce Money Judgments in Switzerland

Samuel P. Baumgartner and Martin Heisch

Abstract If a debtor fails to pay, knowing his assets is crucial to enforcing the debt. Finding these assets, however, can be a challenge. Swiss law offers some features with regard to the discovery of debtor's assets as well as with regard to the enforcement of judgments and debts in general that are unique in comparative perspective. The result is a procedure that is quite efficient and effective at enforcing debts while also protecting the interests of the debtor. This contribution presents and analyzes these features of Swiss enforcement procedure and reproduces some statistical data that provide at least a general impression of how these procedures work in practice.

1 Introduction

If a debtor fails to pay, knowing his assets is crucial to enforcing the debt. Finding these assets, however—if there are any left—can be a challenge. Swiss law offers some features with regard to the discovery of debtor's assets as well as with regard to the enforcement of judgments and debts in general that are unique in comparative

[1] One potential interest of the debtor, the interest in a "fresh start" (*see* Marcus 2020), is, however, protected in only a very limited fashion. Unless the debtor can negotiate such a fresh start with some or all creditors—be it out of court, be it as part of a reorganization procedure—he will have to pay up eventually. If there is not enough money to satisfy the debt in an enforcement or in a bankruptcy proceeding, the creditor can start new collection proceedings for up to twenty years thereafter (articles 149–149a and 265 of the Federal Code on the Enforcement of Money Judgments and Bankruptcy, *SchKG*). Nevertheless, after a bankruptcy proceeding, the creditor will first have to prove that the debtor has acquired new assets that go beyond the minimum needed for a basic standard of living (article 265a *SchKG*).

S. P. Baumgartner (✉)
University of Zurich, Zurich, Switzerland
e-mail: samuel.baumgartner@rwi.uzh.ch

M. Heisch
Attorney at Law, Zurich, Switzerland
e-mail: martin.heisch@prager-dreifuss.com

M. Deguchi (ed.), *Effective Enforcement of Creditors' Rights*,
Ius Gentium: Comparative Perspectives on Law and Justice 91,
https://doi.org/10.1007/978-981-16-5609-5_17

perspective. The result has been a procedure that has led to the efficient enforcement of debts in most cases, while also protecting the interests of the debtor in the process.[1] It is a pleasure to be able to contribute to this *Festschrift* for Masahisa Deguchi by discussing some of these aspects of Swiss enforcement procedure.

2 Procedure to Enforce Money Judgments in Switzerland

The first unique feature of Swiss law is that collection proceedings begin with a preliminary phase, the purpose of which is to establish whether the creditor—more precisely the person who claims to be the creditor—possesses an enforceable judgment or, if he does not, whether the would-be debtor objects to the claim. In other words, the creditor does not need to have reduced his claim to a judgment to begin enforcement proceedings. If the debtor does not contest the claim, the proceeding allows the creditor to advance to enforcement without having to obtain a judgment first—an efficient way to enforce uncontested debts.

2.1 *Preliminary Proceedings*

In Switzerland, the enforcement of money judgments and monetary debts is governed by the Federal Act (or Code) on the Enforcement of Money Judgments and Bankruptcy of April 11, 1889 (Bundesgesetz über Schuldbetreibung und Konkurs; in short *SchKG*).[2] A (would-be) creditor can initiate preliminary proceedings against the person he claims to be the debtor by filing an enforcement request (*Betreibungsbegehren*) with the competent debt enforcement office and by paying the appropriate fee.[3] According to article 67 *SchKG*, the creditor's request must identify the following:

1. name and domicile of the creditor;
2. name and domicile of the debtor;
3. the amount of the claim;
4. the document evidencing the claim and its date or, in the absence of such document, the grounds for the claim.

[2] The enforcement proceedings of the *SchKG* apply not only to money judgments and monetary debts between private persons, but also to money judgments and monetary debts arising from administrative proceedings, taxes, and criminal fines. In contrast, the enforcement of non-money judgments and decrees is governed by articles 335 *et seq.* of the Swiss Civil Procedure Code.

[3] The personal jurisdiction of the enforcement office is determined by articles 46–55 *SchKG*. Generally, proceedings are to be conducted at the domicile of the debtor, though there are a number of exceptions, particularly if the debtor is a foreign person or entity.

Thus, the creditor need not provide either an enforceable judgment or any evidence supporting the existence of the claim in order to initiate the preliminary proceeding—though the debtor may later demand that the creditor make such evidence available at the debt enforcement office for his inspection (article 73 *SchKG*).[4] Upon receipt of the enforcement request, the debt enforcement office issues a payment order (*Zahlungsbefehl*; article 69 *SchKG*). The officer does not and may not make a determination on whether the claimed debt is based on a valid judgment or whether it is justified on the merits. If the creditor's request contains all the information mentioned above, the office must issue the payment order.

The payment order informs the debtor that he has three options. He can either (1) pay the debt plus interest and costs within twenty days; (2) object to the proceedings within ten days; or (3) do nothing, in which case the creditor may initiate actual enforcement proceedings anywhere between twenty days and one year after service of the payment order (article 69 *SchKG*). If the debtor objects—which he can do, without any explanation, by simply putting a check mark in the appropriate box on the payment order[5]; by writing "object" thereon; or orally with the enforcement office—the proceedings are suspended (article 78 *SchKG*). Again, the enforcement office may not assess whether the debtor has a valid defense. If the debtor files such an objection within ten days, the case is suspended. Thus, the would-be debtor can bring the proceedings to a halt as easily as the would-be creditor can initiate them, which is especially important if the debtor is of the view that the debt does not exist or that it is not (yet) enforceable.

If the debtor objects, the creditor has three potential ways to have the preliminary proceedings reopened. All three options require a court decision—the first time a court may get involved in this phase of the enforcement proceedings. First, the court, upon petition of the creditor, will order a reopening (*definitive Rechtsöffnung*) on the basis of a valid and enforceable judgment,[6] unless the debtor can prove by documentary evidence that, since entry of the judgment, the debt has been paid or deferred, or that the statute of limitations has run. In the case of a foreign judgment, the debtor can also raise one or more of the objections available against the recognition and enforcement of the foreign judgment by treaty or Swiss private international law (article 81 *SchKG*).[7] Second, if the creditor holds a promissory note or other written

[4] The purpose of this is to enable the debtor to decide whether to object to the claim. *See*, e.g., Ammon and Walther (2013), Section 17 note 17.

[5] See the official form provided by the Swiss government: <https://www.bj.admin.ch/content/dam/data/bj/wirtschaft/schkg/musterformulare/form/03-d.pdf>.

[6] Pursuant to article 80 para. 2 *SchKG* the following are equivalent to a court judgment (including a criminal judgment imposing a fine): in-court settlements or recognitions of debt; enforceable official records pursuant to article 347 *et seq.* of the Swiss Civil Procedure Code; orders of Swiss administrative authorities and judgments of Swiss administrative courts.

[7] According to article 25–27 of the Swiss Act on Private International Law, a foreign judgment can be recognized and enforced in Switzerland if it is final, the foreign court had personal jurisdiction over the defendant, the defendant was properly served with process, the foreign proceedings did not violate essential tenets of Swiss procedural fairness, and the foreign judgment is not manifestly incompatible with Swiss public policy. For more detail *see* Baumgartner (2008), pp. 219–227.

acknowledgement of debt that is notarized or signed by the debtor, he can obtain a provisional court order to reopen the proceedings (*provisorische Rechtsöffnung*) unless the debtor can provide (documentary) evidence that immediately casts significant doubt on the existence of the debt ("*sofort glaubhaft machen kann*", article 82 *SchKG*). This order to reopen is provisional in the sense that it only becomes effective if the debtor fails, within twenty days of the order, to file a complaint with the court, seeking a declaration that he does not owe the creditor the claimed amount (*Aberkennungsklage*, article 83 *SchKG*), or if such a complaint remains unsuccessful. However, during the deadline for the filing of an *Aberkennungsklage* and while an *Aberkennungsklage* is pending, the creditor may obtain a (provisional) attachment or a provisional inventory of the debtor's assets to secure the debt (article 83 para. 1 *SchKG*). Finally, if the creditor has neither an enforceable judgment nor a written or notarized acknowledgment of the debt in hand, he can only proceed by filing a complaint seeking a money judgment (*Anerkennungsklage*, article 79 *SchKG*). If the court grants the judgment, it will reopen the enforcement proceedings as well, permitting the creditor to continue with the next phase of enforcement. *Aberkennungs-* and *Anerkennungsklage* thus both have a double function. With them, the plaintiff—the debtor in the case of the *Aberkennungklage*, the creditor in the case of the *Anerkennungsklage*—obtains both a judgment on the merits and a court order to reopen or not, as the case may be, the stayed enforcement proceedings.

If the debtor does not contest the claim upon service of the payment order, this procedure offers the creditor a fast and efficient path to enforcement. At the same time, the opportunity to object provides the debtor with a simple and easy means to terminate unjustified enforcement proceedings or at least to force the creditor into full or partial litigation if the claim has not yet been adjudicated. Germany (with the *Mahnverfahren*),[8] Austria (with the *Zahlungsbefehlsverfahren*),[9] and the EU (with the European Order for Payment procedure)[10] have similar proceedings. But these tend to be more limited in their scope of application and are, at least conceptually, organized as judicial proceedings, at the end of which there is an enforceable court judgment. By setting the order-of-payment procedure up as part of the enforcement process, Swiss law gains additional efficiency compared to these approaches in neighboring countries,[11] while making it clearer to the lay debtor that the order does not come from a court, has not been adjudicated and, thus, really can be objected to.[12]

In the Canton of Zurich, one of the few cantons in which detailed statistics are available, the percentage of cases in which an objection is filed has remained fairly

---

[8] Sections 688 *et seq.* German Code of Civil Procedure.

[9] Sections 244 *et seq.* Austrian Code of Civil Procedure.

[10] Regulation (EC) No. 1896/2006 of the European Parliament and of the Council of December 12, 2006, creating a European order for payment procedure, OJ L-399, 1 (2006).

[11] *See* Baumgartner (2019), pp. 30–31.

[12] To make sure the debtor is informed of his right to object to the claim, the payment order must be personally served on the debtor by the enforcement officer, a mail carrier, or, if the debtor attempts to evade delivery, by a police officer. Simply putting the payment order into the debtor's mailbox or delivery by registered mail will not do (article 72 *SchKG*; BGE 117 III 7).

constant over the last few years, at about nine percent.[13] In the remaining 91% of cases, therefore, the debtor either paid, reached a settlement with the creditor, or let the creditor file for actual enforcement .[14]

2.2 *Enforcement*

Once the creditor has successfully completed the preliminary phase (i.e. the debtor has neither objected nor paid or the court has ordered a reopening of the proceedings after objection), he may request enforcement of the claim (*Fortsetzungsbegehren*, article 88 *SchKG*). Enforcement occurs either by seizure or by (liquidation) bankruptcy. The latter happens if the debtor is listed as an entrepreneur or a commercial entity in the register of commerce, the former if this is not the case (article 39 *SchKG*).[15] Seizure involves the marking, taking, and ultimately the sale of sufficient property to satisfy the debt to this particular creditor, including interest and costs of the enforcement proceeding. Bankruptcy results in the liquidation of all of debtor's assets for the benefit of all current creditors. If the debt is secured by a mortgage, a third type of procedure, the procedure to sell the mortgaged property, applies (*Betreibung auf Pfandverwertung*, article 151 *et seq. SchKG*), even if the debtor is listed in the commercial register as an entrepreneur or a commercial entity and thus would otherwise be subject to enforcement by liquidation bankruptcy. Thus, in Switzerland, liquidation bankruptcy occurs not only in cases of insolvency, but also whenever a creditor enforces a debt against a business or a business owner with an entry in the register of commerce and the debtor fails to pay or to mount an adequate defense within the preliminary proceedings.

2.2.1 Seizure (Article 89 *et seq. SchKG*)

If the debtor is subject to seizure, the enforcement office must carry out the seizure immediately upon receipt of the creditor's enforcement request (article 89 *SchKG*). However, the enforcement office must first notice a visit for purposes of determining

[13] Source: <https://www.betreibungsinspektorat-zh.ch/deu/documents/Statistik.2019ListeABetreibungsamter.pdf>.

[14] On the enforcement proceedings, *see* Sect. 2. For the statistics *see* Sect. 4. Another possibility is that the creditor abandoned the proceedings after service of an unobjectet-to order of payment. But given the low fee for an application to begin enforcement and the efficiency of the proceeding, this is an unlikely scenario.

[15] There are exceptions to this rule. Pursuant to article 43 *SchKG*, enforcement by bankruptcy is excluded and, instead, enforcement by seizure applies with certain kinds of debts, including taxes, customs duties, criminal fines as well as recurrent family law maintenance and assistance obligations. On the other hand, individuals not listed in the register of commerce can be subject to bankruptcy proceedings, for instance, by declaring themselves insolvent (article 191 *SchKG*) or in the cases of article 190 *SchKG*. On the latter *see infra* fn. 29.

which property to seize, which it must do at least one day prior to the visit (article 90 *SchKG*). In this notice, the debtor is informed that he must be present for the visit and disclose his assets. Ideally, therefore, the visit takes place on the premises of the debtor. This is particularly true if the enforcement office does not yet have knowledge of the debtor's financial circumstances and assets.[16] During the visit, the officer must find out what assets are available and estimate their value, if necessary with the assistance of an expert.[17] He then decides which assets to seize in order to satisfy the claim with interest and costs (article 97 para. 2 *SchKG*). There are further rules for the enforcement officer to follow, such as the rule to seize movable before immovable property, dispensable before less dispensable property, and movables with a clear market value before others (article 95 *SchKG*). One of the options enforcement officers often choose because of its simplicity is the garnishment of future wages. It is permitted to the extent the wages are not needed for a minimum standard of living (article 93 *SchKG*) and if seizure of other pieces of property is not likely to lead to much faster satisfaction of the creditor than multiple monthly payments from the garnished wages.[18]

The act of seizure consists in a declaration by the enforcement officer to the debtor that the identified assets are henceforth seized and may no longer be disposed of (article 96 para. 1 *SchKG*). With the exception of cash, bearer securities, jewelry and other valuables, the seized objects are usually left with the debtor (article 98 *SchKG*). The debtor is, however, prohibited, under threat of criminal sanctions, from disposing of the seized assets without the consent of the enforcement office (article 96 *SchKG*). In the case of garnishment of wages and other claims against third parties, the third-party debtor is informed that he can henceforth validly pay the debt only to the enforcement office (article 99 *SchKG*).

One month (or up to one year) after the seizure, the creditor can request the sale of the seized movable property. In the case of immovables, he can request the sale six months (or up to two years) after the seizure (article 116 para. 1 *SchKG*). The sale usually occurs by public auction, in specific cases by private contract with specific interested buyers (article 125 *et seq. SchKG*). After covering the costs of the collection proceedings, the proceeds of the sale, up to the value of the claim plus interest, are released to the creditor (article 144 *SchKG*). If the proceeds fail to cover the claim plus interest and costs and there is no other property to seize and sell, the creditor receives a certificate for the uncovered debt (*Verlustschein*). The certificate tolls the statute of limitations and permits the creditor to pursue further enforcement

---

[16] Baumgartner and Heisch (2019), pp. 581–582.

[17] Article 92 *SchKG* lists several assets that are exempt from seizure, such as objects for the personal use of the debtor and his family (i.e. clothes, personal effects, household appliances, furniture or other things) insofar as they are indispensable, objects necessary for the exercise of his profession, and certain social security and pension entitlements.

[18] In the 1997 reform of the *SchKG*, the wording of its article 95 para. 1 was changed so as to make clear that the garnishment of wages is one of the first options for the enforcement officer to consider rather than being something that is only permissible if no other assets can be found, as had been the practice before. *See*, e.g., Foëx (2010), article 95, note 3.

proceedings for the uncovered amount at a later stage, among other things (article 149-149a *SchKG*).[19]

2.2.2 Competent Authorities

As is apparent from the above, seizure visit, seizure, as well as enforcement sale are exclusively for the enforcement office to conduct.[20] No court order is necessary to get the proceedings started or to approve the seizure, as is the case in some countries.[21] Moreover, the enforcement office is not only responsible for the seizure itself, but also for finding the debtor's assets, another unique feature of Swiss law. The creditor does not need to help in that task, though it may be useful, if he has any knowledge thereof, for him to point out existing assets to the enforcement office.[22]

Of course, debt enforcement officers must follow the law. Anyone claiming to have their rights affected by a decision of the enforcement office—for example the debtor, a creditor, or a third party—may appeal that decision on the grounds of incorrect application of the law or inappropriate exercise of the enforcement office's discretion (*Beschwerde*, article 17 *et seq. SchKG*). The appeal is free of charge and must be filed within ten days of the appellant becoming aware of the grounds for objection. The appeal must be filed with the supervisory authority, which, for these purposes, is usually a court.[23] The decision of the supervisory authority is appealable all the way up to the Swiss Supreme Court (article 72 para. 2(a) of the *Bundesgerichtsgesetz*).

2.2.3 Costs

Throughout the enforcement proceedings, the creditor must advance the costs. These costs are determined by ordinance.[24] They are quite low and set as a fraction of the value of the claim. To illustrate, the fee for the issuance of a payment order is CHF 20—for a claim between CHF 100—and CHF 500—or CHF 190—for a claim

---

[19] *See also supra* note 1.

[20] Pursuant to article 1 *SchKG*, the cantons are required to form one or more enforcement districts. Each debt enforcement district has a debt enforcement office under the direction of an enforcement official (article 2 *SchKG*).

[21] *See, e.g.*, Massachusetts Rule of Civil Procedure 4.2(c) (requiring court approval for an attachment); Section 829 of the German Code of Civil Procedure (requiring a court order for the garnishment of debts). *But see* Section 845 of the same Code (allowing for an attachment by the *Gerichtsvollzieher* to secure a later seizure by the court).

[22] Baumgartner and Heisch (2019), p. 580; *see also*, Ammon and Walther (2013), Section 22 note 26.

[23] In a few cantons, an administrative authority is responsible for supervision. But article 75 para. 2 of the *Bundesgerichtsgesetz* (*BGG*; Act on the Federal Supreme Court) requires the cantons to provide a state high court ultimately to decide these matters, since they can be appealed to the federal Supreme Court.

[24] *Gebührenverordnung zum Bundesgesetz über Schuldbetreibung und Konkurs* (in short: *GebVSchKG*).

between CHF 100′000—and CHF 1 million.[25] For the seizure, the fee is CHF 25—for a claim between CHF 100—and CHF 500—or CHF 190—for a claim between CHF 100′000—and CHF 1 million.[26]

3 Discovering Defendant's Assets

3.1 Obligations of the Debtor

Pursuant to article 91 para. 1(1) *SchKG*, the debtor must be personally present for the seizure visit or ensure that a representative will be there. During the visit, he must reveal all his assets, including those in possession of others, as well as rights against third parties, all as far as needed to cover the creditor's claim plus interest and costs (article 91 para. 1(2) *SchKG*). This disclosure obligation is quite comprehensive and includes assets located abroad and assets formerly owned by the debtor.[27] It is not for the debtor to decide which assets are to be seized and which are not and thus to disclose only those assets he considers seizable or those he prefers to have seized first. However, once he has disclosed sufficient seizable movable property to cover the claim with interest and costs, the debtor is not obliged to make any further disclosure of his financial circumstances.[28]

If the debtor is absent from the seizure visit and is not represented by someone knowledgeable about his assets, or if he refuses to open doors and containers, the enforcement officer can request the assistance of the police (article 91 para. 2 and 3 *SchKG*). Furthermore, failure to be present at the seizure visit and/or failure to reveal all of one's assets are federal misdemeanor offenses (*see* article 323, nos. 1–2 of the Swiss Criminal Code), while the fraudulent attempt to hide or fictitiously reduce assets is a federal felony (article 163 no. 1 Swiss Criminal Code). Moreover, the attempt to hide assets is grounds for immediately opening (liquidation) bankruptcy proceedings, even if the debtor is not listed in the commercial register und thus is not ordinarily subject to bankruptcy enforcement and irrespective of whether the debtor is insolvent.[29]

---

[25] For the complete table of costs see article 16 para. 1 *GebVSchKG*.

[26] For the complete table of costs see article 20 para. 1 *GebVSchKG*.

[27] BGE 129 III 239 E. 3.2.1; but see BGE 107 III 73 E. 3 (does not apply to cash amounts owned years ago, as they would be difficult to prove). The purpose of the obligation to reveal assets formerly owned by the debtor is to permit the creditor to sue against the third-party owner for retroactive seizure of the property in appropriate cases (*Pauliana* or *Anfechtungsklage*, articles 285 *et seq. SchKG*, which is akin to the avoidance powers in bankruptcy law).

[28] Baumgartner and Heisch (2019), p. 585.

[29] Pursuant to article 190 para. 1 no. 1 *SchKG*, a creditor may request the court to open bankruptcy proceedings without first conducting preliminary proceedings against any debtor (1) whose whereabouts are unknown, (2) who has fled in order to avoid fulfilling his obligations, or (3) who has acted fraudulently or concealed assets in seizure proceedings.

3.2 Obligations of Third Persons

Article 91 para. 4 *SchKG* states that third persons who have custody over assets belonging to the debtor or who owe him money have the same obligation of disclosure as the debtor himself. This means that banks, trustees, lawyers and employers, among others, must reveal—under threat of criminal sanctions—all of the debtor's assets that they hold when asked by an enforcement officer. The enforcement office expressly informs the persons involved of their obligations and of the criminal sanctions applicable in case of noncooperation (article 91 para. 6 *SchKG*). Banking secrecy laws do not apply, as the debtor would have to disclose the relevant information to the authorities himself.[30] The same goes for privileges and data protection provisions.[31] However, fishing expeditions are not permitted. There must be some reason for the enforcement office to believe that the third person holds assets belonging to the debtor.[32] Such a reason may be present, for example, if the enforcement office is aware that the debtor previously had business relations with the third party, for instance by long having been a customer at a particular bank. Generally speaking, the office's enforcement actions—including requests to reveal against third persons—must be proportionate and take into account all competing interests.[33]

3.3 Obligations of Authorities

Finally, authorities, too, are required to provide information to the same extent as the debtor (article 91 para. 5 *SchKG*). This is true for all authorities, federal, state or local. Tax authorities are probably the main target of the enforcement officials.[34] However, social security offices, motor vehicle bureaus, or residents' registration offices may also be considered. Again, data protection laws and privileges do not apply, since the obligation of the authorities to provide information does not go beyond that of the debtor.[35]

---

[30] BGE 51 III 37, 39 *et seq.*, a decision the Swiss Supreme Court has since regularly confirmed.

[31] Baumgartner and Heisch (2019), p. 587.

[32] KGer SG, GVP-SG 2009 Nr. 88 p. 211 et. seq.; KGer BL, 420 16 455, E. 2.3; Winkler (2017), art. 91, note 36.

[33] Baumgartner and Heisch (2019), pp. 588–589; Müller-Chen (2000), pp. 208, 211–214.

[34] For an example, *see* BGer 5A_800/2010.

[35] BGE 124 III 170 E. 5a. This decision of the Federal Supreme Court has, however, been subject to some criticism. *See* Fey (1998), pp. 1247 *et seq.*

4 Finding Debtor's Assets in Bankruptcy Proceedings

Generally, in bankruptcy proceedings the same disclosure obligations apply as in seizure proceedings.[36] Thus, pursuant to article 222 *SchKG*, the debtor is obliged to declare all assets to the bankruptcy office and to hold himself at the office's disposal. If the debtor is deceased or has fled, his duty falls to those adult persons who shared his household. Third parties and authorities have the same obligation to disclose information as the debtor (article 222 paras. 4 and 5 *SchKG*). Failure to comply with these disclosure obligations may result in the same criminal sanctions as failure to comply with the disclosure obligations in seizure proceedings.[37]

However, bankruptcy law goes even further: Pursuant to article 232 para. 1 *SchKG*, the bankruptcy office publicly announces the opening of the bankruptcy proceeding. This public announcement is usually made in the Swiss Official Commercial Gazette and in the official paper of the canton in question.[38] The announcement calls on creditors of the debtor and all persons having claims to objects in the debtor's possession to file such claims with the bankruptcy office within one month of the announcement (article 232 para. 2 *SchKG*). The announcement further includes a call on persons in possession of things belonging to the debtor, as holders of security rights or for other reasons, to deliver those things to the bankruptcy office (article 232 para. 4 *SchKG*). This means that any third person (such as a bank or a trustee) must provide the relevant information, even if he is subject to professional secrecy, and submit the things in their possession to the bankruptcy office.[39] The bankruptcy office need not ask; the public announcement of the bankruptcy itself triggers the obligation. The obligation of third persons in bankruptcy proceedings thus goes further than in seizure proceedings, where third persons have a duty to disclose only when asked by the enforcement office whether they are in possession of debtor assets.[40]

5 Enforcing Support Payments

Debts arising from support obligations are enforced the same way as are all other debts in Switzerland. However, the cantons offer creditors of family support obligations, such as children and (former) spouses generally free help with enforcement (*Inkassohilfe*) or, alternatively, the option of state payments for debts in arrears (*Alimentenbevorschussung*) (articles 130 and 130a of the Civil Code (*ZGB*)). In the latter case, the state subrogates into the claim and enforces it against the debtor according to the procedures described above. This way, creditors of family support

---

[36] The sanctions are the same as those discussed *supra*, II. 2.

[37] *See supra*, II. 2.

[38] *See* article 35 *SchKG*. Where circumstances so require, publication may be effected by other means.

[39] Ammon and Walther (2013), Section 44, note 32; Bovey (2009), p. 74.

[40] *See supra* III. b.

obligations do not have to chase after the debtor themselves. However, this is a matter regulated by cantonal law and thus the cutoffs, if any, for state payments can vary considerably from canton to canton.

6 Statistics

The following general statistics on enforcement proceedings are available for all of Switzerland[41]:

Bankruptcy proceedings	2016	2017	2018
Bankruptcy proceedings opened	14′860	15′269	15′291
Bankruptcy proceedings closed	13′290	13′794	13′023
Bankruptcy proceedings completed[42]	5′475	5′514	5′069
Total amount lost by creditors (in million CHF)	2′556	1′700	2′028

Enforcement proceedings	2016	2017	2018
Payment orders	2′939′178	2′929′998	2′967′555
Seizures/garnishments	1′574′305	1′710′834	1′775′151
Proceedings with enforcement sale	610′356	649′572	690′072

More specific data are available for the Canton of Zurich, the most populous canton in Switzerland[43]:

Enforcement proceedings	2018	2019
Payment orders	396′319	446′848
Objections to payment order	34′873	37′960
Bankruptcy announced[44]	10′035	9′774

(continued)

[41] Statistics available at: <https://www.bfs.admin.ch/bfs/de/home/statistiken/industrie-dienstleistungen/unternehmen-beschaeftigte/unternehmensdemografie/konkurse.html>.

[42] The number of bankruptcy proceedings closed is larger than the number of proceedings completed since a considerable number of bankruptcy proceedings are closed soon after opening because of a lack of debtor assets to cover the costs of such proceedings, let alone to satisfy any non-secured the creditors.

[43] Statistics available at: <https://www.betreibungsinspektorat-zh.ch/deu/documents/Statistik.2019ListeABetreibungsamter.pdf>.

[44] Recall that actual enforcement of the debt proceeds either by seizure or by bankruptcy. *See supra* II. 2. If the debtor is subject to enforcement through bankruptcy, the creditor can ask the bankruptcy office, after successfully concluding the preliminary proceedings, to send the debtor a bankruptcy announcement, informing him that, after twenty days, the creditor can obtain a court order to open bankruptcy proceedings (article 160 *SchKG*). The purpose of the announcement is to give the debtor one last chance to pay the debt and thus to avert bankruptcy.

(continued)

Enforcement proceedings	2018	2019
Seizures	199′018	198′869
Seizures where no seizable property found	83′358	83′116
Seizure sales	105′633	101′603
Seizure sales with full coverage of claim	41′091	42′095

These statistics for the Canton of Zurich show that among the enforcement cases filed (as evidenced by an issued payment order), roughly 10% led to enforcement with full satisfaction and 15% to enforcement with partial satisfaction of the claim. But the level of full or partial recovery is likely considerably higher. In another 50% of cases, the creditor did not even request a seizure or the opening of bankruptcy proceedings, as the case may be. This includes the 8% or so of cases in which the debtor objected to the payment order, in which the creditor did not or could not overcome the objection by one of the avenues described in Sect. 2.1.[45] This means that the claim, not yet reduced to a judgment, either did not exist or was difficult to prove, thus necessitating ordinary litigation or a settlement with the debtor. What remains are still 42% of cases with a payment order in which the creditor chose not to seek seizure or the opening of bankruptcy proceedings even though the debtor failed to object or the creditor overcame the objection with a court order by one of the avenues described in Sect. 2.1. Usually, this happens because the debtor either pays or is able to negotiate a settlement with the creditor, having been spurred into action by the payment order. Add to that the 3% or so of cases in which the creditor abandoned enforcement after a successful seizure. That likely happens only if the debtor pays in full or reaches a settlement with the creditor so as to avert a sale of the seized property.

In sum, we know that, at least in the Canton of Zurich, seizure leads to full or partial recovery in at least 25% of cases, though the level of full or partial recovery is likely to be closer to 70% (25 + 42% abandoned after service of payment order +3% abandoned after successful seizure, all probably because of at least partial payment by debtor). The percentage of cases with full or partial recovery may be even higher than 70%: As mentioned, there are close to 8% of cases in which the creditor abandoned the proceedings after the debtor objected to the payment order. In these cases, the creditor either had no claim. If he did, he did not possess enough

[45] In about 9% of cases with a payment order, the debtor objected. In a bit more than 1% of cases with a payment order (or in about 13% of the cases in which the debtor objected to the payment order), the courts of the Canton of Zurich granted a provisional or a final reopening of the enforcement proceedings. *See* the statistics of the Supreme Court of the Canton of Zurich (https://www.gerichte-zh.ch/fileadmin/user_upload/Dokumente/obergericht/Rechenschaftsberichte/Rechenschaftsbericht_2018.pdf), p. 122, according to which there were 4′828 and 4′950 provisional and definitive reopenings of enforcement proceedings handed down by Zurich courts in 2017 and 2018, respectively. That leaves about 8% of cases, in which the creditor did not or could not obtain a judicial reopening of the enforcement proceedings after the debtor had objected to the payment order.

proof to overcome the debtor's objection or settled with the debtor, or both.[46] Plus, there are the 3% or so of cases that lead to the opening of a bankruptcy proceeding—about one third of which, that is, 1% of all cases, lead to the (partial) satisfaction of the creditor.[47]

On the other hand, about 20% of cases lead to unsuccessful enforcement due to lack of any assets found at the seizure visit. Another 2% or so lead to bankruptcy proceedings in which there are too few debtor assets left for any of the unsecured creditors to obtain any recovery.[48]

While these statistics do not tell us how many debtors who think the claim is not justified fail to object, these statistics do suggest—together with the ease with which an objection can be filed—that a large number of claims filed are probably not really contested and thus that the Swiss enforcement proceedings provide an efficient way for creditors to get their money.

7 Conclusion

There are two unique features of Swiss law that are primarily responsible for an enforcement procedure that leads to both efficient and quite effective enforcement of a claim for the creditor while adequately protecting the interests of the debtor. The first is a preliminary proceeding that allows a person who believes to have a claim against another to initiate enforcement proceedings without first obtaining a judgment in the matter. If the would-be debtor fails to object, the creditor can move for the appropriate enforcement to take place. The second is a seizure procedure that relies on the enforcement office to find appropriate property of the debtor to seize and provides the enforcement office with the necessary powers to do so.

Both anecdotal evidence and the statistics reproduced above support the proposition that this has resulted in quite effective enforcement. The statistics and analysis presented above further suggest that most claims in enforcement proceedings are probably not contested and that in these uncontested cases, the Swiss proceedings provide an efficient means for the creditor to collect on the debt. However, there are questions that remain. For instance, it is unclear how many debtors—especially one-shot players,[49] such as consumers, who have no experience with the litigation system—decide to pay under threat of enforcement, even though they have good reason to contest the claim and could thus easily file an objection, yet fail to do

[46] *See supra* note 45 and accompanying text. There is also the very real possibility of the creditor initiating preliminary proceedings for harassment purposes only, knowing that the debt does not exist. The debtor can easily stop such shenanigans by objecting to the claim.

[47] *See* the statistics of the Supreme Court of the Canton of Zurich (https://www.gerichte-zh.ch/fileadmin/user_upload/Dokumente/obergericht/Rechenschaftsberichte/Rechenschaftsbericht_2018.pdf), pp. 93–94.

[48] *See supra* note 47 and accompanying text.

[49] On one-shot players as opposed to repeat players *see* Galanter (1974).

so for whatever reason.[50] On the other hand, the tools described above to help the enforcement office find defendants' assets need to actually be used by the office to be effective. Unfortunately, actual practice seems to vary. For instance, there appear to be enforcement offices that routinely conduct seizure "visits" at the office rather than by visiting the debtor at his premises.[51] This makes it considerably easier for the debtor to hide assets if the office is not already familiar with the debtor's property from earlier visits.

Finally, even Swiss law cannot guarantee that all assets will be found. Especially fraudulent activities are not always easy to detect. In addition, there is a large number of debtors who simply do not have much of any seizable property left when enforcement proceedings are commenced.[52] Though the standard of living is high for most of the population in Switzerland, a considerable number of people appear to live beyond their means. Similarly, many businesses in distress muddle on for far too long before they seek (reorganization) bankruptcy relief. Thus, once liquidation bankruptcy proceedings are opened, there are few assets left to satisfy non-secured creditors.[53] Hence the 22% or so of enforcement cases mentioned in Sect. 6 that result in the creditor(s) walking away empty handed.

References

Ammon K, Walther F (2013) Grundriss des Schuldbetreibungs- und Konkursrechts, 9th edn. Stämpfli, Bern

Baumgartner S (2008) How well do U.S. judgments fare in Europe? 40 Geo Wash Int'l L Rev 173

Baumgartner S (2019) Die Betreibungsregistereinsicht zum Zweck des Kreditschutzes. In: Portmann W et al (eds) Gedenkschrift für Claire Huguenin, Dike, Zurich/St. Gallen, pp 29–46

Baumgartner S, Heisch M (2019) Ermittlung schuldnerischen Vermögens im Pfändungsverfahren. In: Arnet R et al (eds) Der Mensch als Mass, Festschrift für Peter Breitschmid, Schulthess, Zurich/Basel/Geneva, pp 577–591

Bovey G (2009) L'obligation des tiers de renseigner l'office des poursuites et des faillites (art. 91 al. 4 et 222 al. 4 LP), JdT 1/2009 II, pp 62–77

Fey M (1998) Bundesgericht, Schuldbetreibungs- und Konkurskammer, 24.3.1998 i.S. Betreibungsamt Zürich 4 c. den Beschluss vom 17.11.1997 des Obergerichts des Kantons Zürich, II. Zivilkammer, als oberer kantonaler Aufsichtsbehörde über Schuldbetreibung und Konkurs, Beschwerde; BGE 124 III 170, AJP 1998, pp 1245–1249

Foëx B (2010) Article 95. In: Staehelin A et. al., Basler Kommentar zum Bundesgesetz über Schuldbetreibung und Konkurs I (Art. 1–158 SchKG), vol I, 2nd edn. Helbing Lichtenhahn, Basel

Galanter M (1974) Why the "Haves" come out ahead: speculations on the limits of legal change. Law Soc Rev 9:95

Haas U (2019) § 64. In: Baumbach A, Hueck A (eds) GmbHG, 22d edn. Beck, München

[50] *See* Baumgartner (2019), pp. 37–40.

[51] Baumgartner and Heisch (2019), pp. 590–591.

[52] Baumgartner and Heisch (2019), p. 591.

[53] *See*, e.g., Kunz (2014), pp. 182–183; Rüetschi (2014), p. 26. In this, Switzerland is certainly not unique. For Germany, *see, e.g.*, Haas (2019), Section 64, note 144.

Kunz P (2014) Sanierungen von Kapitalgesellschaften: Wann und wie kann oder muss saniert werden? recht 2014, pp 175–185

Marcus R (2000) America's BYO approach to enforcing money judgments: comment on Rechberger and Hess (in this volume)

Müller-Chen M (2000) Die Auskunftspflicht Dritter beim Pfändungs- und Arrestvollzug. BlschK 2000:201–232

Rüetschi D (2014) Das neue Sanierungsrecht—Ein Rückblick auf die Entstehungsgeschichte. In: Europa Institut Zurich, Nr. 153, Sanierung und Insolvenz von Unternehmen V, Das neue Schweizer Sanierungsrecht, pp 7–28

Winkler T (2017) Article 91. In: Kren Kostkiewicz J, Vock D (eds) Kommentar zum Bundesgesetz über Schuldbetreibung und Konkurs, 4th edn. Schulthess, Zurich/Basel/Geneva

Samuel P. Baumgartner Professor of civil procedure, bankruptcy, debt collection, private law, and mediation at the University of Zurich, Switzerland. Studied law at the University of Bern, Switzerland (LL.B. 1990); attorney at law Canton of Bern (1990); M.L.I. (1993) and LL.M. (1995), University of Wisconsin, Madison; Dr. iur. (2003), University of Bern, Switzerland. Assistant lecturer (1990–92, 1996–98) and associate lecturer (1998–2001), University of Bern. Director of Studies, Hague Academy of International Law (summer 2001). Deputy Head, Section of Private International Law, Swiss Department of Justice (2001–2004). Adjunct lecturer, University of Lucerne (2002–2004).Visiting Professor, Cornell University (Spring 2003). Associate Professor (2004–2011), Professor (2011–2016), Director of Faculty Research and Development (2011–2013), University of Akron Law School. Professor, University of Zurich (since 2016).

Martin Heisch doctoral candidate and research assistant at the chair of Prof. Samuel P. Baumgartner (University of Zurich), civil procedure and comparative civil procedure, attorney at law since 2017 (Zurich), graduate of University of Zurich, member of the board Institut für zivilgerichtliches Verfahren Zurich. Publications include: Ermittlung schuldnerischen Vermögens im Pfändungsverfahren. In: Arnet R et. al, FS Breitschmid, Schulthess (2019), pp. 577–591 (together with Prof. Samuel P. Baumgartner).

Searching Assets and Pressuring the Debtor for an Effective Enforcement: An Overview of the Brazilian Execution Proceedings

Antonio Cabral

Abstract In Brazilian Civil Procedure, the search for debtors' assets is viewed as primarily the creditor's responsibility. But whenever the creditor has exhausted the means to search for assets, the law provides for a subsidiary state activity: the judge or other court personnel can help in order to provide effective relief in execution proceedings. On the other hand, the new Code of Civil Procedure enacted in 2015 has strengthened the debtor's procedural legal duties of disclosing the existence and location of assets, and established general clauses of coercion that allow the judge to force and pressure the debtor to comply, and many other methods that might help to achieve a more efficient enforcement proceeding such as notarized notices of dishonor, the register of money judgments in bad debtor's lists and creditwatch services, litigation agreements regarding assets, sales by private initiative, etc. In comparative perspective, the Brazilian new legal system seems to be a middle way between many other jurisdictions and so far has proven to be more effective than the format that existed prior to the reforms.

1 Introduction

This presentation wishes to highlight some of the latest trends in execution proceedings in Brazilian Civil Procedure. Our main focus will be the instruments to balance the rights of debtor and creditor, attempting to achieve efficiency without harm to fundamental constitutional guarantees.

Indeed, one of the main problems of execution proceedings in Brazil (and throughout the world) is effectiveness. Execution and enforcement proceedings in

---

This article was produced for a conference held at the Ritsumeikan University in Kyoto, Japan, in November 2019. I would like to thank Professor Dr. Masahisa Deguchi for his honorable invitation.

Present Address:
A. Cabral (✉)
University of Rio de Janeiro State, Rio de Janeiro, Brazil
e-mail: antoniocabral@uerj.br

M. Deguchi (ed.), *Effective Enforcement of Creditors' Rights*,
Ius Gentium: Comparative Perspectives on Law and Justice 91,
https://doi.org/10.1007/978-981-16-5609-5_18

Brazil last twice longer than cognitive proceedings,[1] and some of the main problems faced in Brazil are the difficulties of finding the debtor and her assets, as well as bringing the procedure to an end in reasonable time, with full payment of the creditor and avoiding depreciation of the assets market value.

Well, in order to make proceedings more expedite and efficient, enforcement of judgments has gone through significant changes in the last years in Brazilian Civil Procedure. This movement began with the approval of statutes nº 11.232/2005 and nº 11.382/2006, that have modified many rules concerning execution proceedings. In 2015, after four years of debate through several commissions, a new Code of Civil Procedure was approved in the Brazilian Parliament and brought some innovation since it came into legal force in March 2016.[2]

In Brazil, there are several different proceedings that vary depending on the nature of the asset and the type of execution. There is, for example, execution proceeding to collect a sum of money (article 523 until 527 and 824 and following); proceedings to enforce obligations to do something or to deliver or hand over a specific movable good (articles 536 and following and articles 814 until 821); proceedings to collect child support or alimony (articles 528 until 533 and 911 until 913); and proceedings regarding execution against the State or state companies (article 910).[3]

Before the recent legislative modifications, in any case it was necessary an autonomous judicial process for enforcing any judgments and a special procedure was required for this purpose. The general rule for the enforcement of judicial decisions is currently based on the idea of a *syncretic* process, in which enforcement has become an additional stage of the cognitive proceeding and there is no need for bringing up a new action to enforce the judgment.

---

[1] The National Council of Justice (an administrative body that organises Civil Justice in Brazil) publishes yearly a report (Justice in Numbers or "Justiça em Números"). The report, of 2017 says that in total, the new cases filed regarding execution are 6.900.525 (almost 7 million). In the last 5 years, almost 25 million new cases. Execution proceedings not only last longer in Brazil than cognition proceeding, but they also tend to burden the Judiciary much more. More than half of all pending procedures in the country relate to execution. In most cases, the main difficulty is to find the debitors assets.

[2] There is an English translation of the new Brazilian Code of Civil Procedure, which is available at my profile at the website academia.edu at the following link: https://www.academia.edu/34624319/Brazilian_Code_of_Civil_Procedure_-_Translated_to_English. Accessed 07 January 2020. In the same webpage there is a Spanish version of the Code as well.

[3] The main differences are the execution measures that can be used in either one; and the possibilities for the judge to act on her own motion.

However, in some other cases, as enforcement of extrajudicial titles[4] and the judgments in which a State organ (administrative bodies or government agencies) is a party, the autonomous enforcement process is still required.

2 Parameters in Comparative Perspective: Who Should Be in Charge of Searching for Debtor's Assets

A quick comparative glance at legal systems all around the globe will show that the search of debtor's assets is a big problem to enforcement and execution proceedings in almost every jurisdiction.

The main questions for a precise comparison seem to me to be the following:

(1) Are there obligations of the individuals to declare the existence, possession and location of their assets prior to the lawsuit (for example to a government body or agency)?
(2) Is there a public record (whether or not digitalized and/or centralized) containing this information?
(3) Is finding assets.

    (3.1) a duty of state bodies? or is it.
    (3.2) an obligation of the creditor?

    If 3.1 applies, how and when can or must the judge pressure the debtor to disclose his assets?

    If 3.2 is correct, how far can the business of disclosure go?[5]

(4) Are these public and private initiatives related?

---

[4] The list of executive titles in Brazil is very generous. Article 515 of the Code of Civil Procedure lists the titles of judicial origin, such as decisions, sentences and the judicial confirmation of transactions or agreements betwenn the parties. And article 784 lists titles of contractual basis. These comprehend checks, lettres, duplicates, warrants, and some types of contracts (as long as they are in written terms, with 2 witnesses, or signed by members of the Public Prosecution Office or Public Defender Service). Brazilian Law also provides for a proceeding called "ação monitória", similar to european *Mahnverfahren*, by which the creditor files a complaint with written proof of the credit (articles 700 until 702 of the Code of Civil Procedure). The judge issues a payment order against the debitor and, depending on the debitors atitude (if she does not oppose to it), this order becomes an executive title and the proceeding follows an enforcement track. If the debitor opposes to it, defending against the payment order, the proceeding follows a cognitive track similar to a normal lawsuit for the decision about the existence of the debt.

[5] In this volume we can find an overview of several different types of enterprises that provide this kind of service, like the German Schufa-kind companies or the *common law* discovery or self-help mechanisms to work on the "asset's hunt" that the creditor has to deploy, as Richard Marcus referred to the activity of finding the debtor's assets. See Marcus (2020); Hess (2020).

And of course, as we take a closer look in each legal system, different scenarios appear. Some jurisdictions, like the U.S.A., view the task of finding debtor's assets as one of *exclusively private* initiative.

Some other countries tend to an approach that is more state-centered. In Poland, for instance, the reports are that this activity is *primarily* public and judges take on a major role in finding debtor's assets.

In another group of jurisdictions, the search of debtor's assets is a task that is conceived as *primarily* a *private* matter but with *subsidiary* activity of the judge to help the creditor whenever she cannot succeed in finding debtor's assets. These seem to be the legal systems of Germany, Japan, Austria and my country, Brazil. Their differences depend on what triggers the state force (a simple unsuccessful attempt of the creditor, if proven by documents; the prior use of other—private—means of execution; etc.).

3 Constitutional Limitation on the Enforcement of Judgments by Preventing Some Assets of Ever Being Seized or Attached

The limitations on enforcement of judgments in Brazil are focused in the protection of the individual, guided by the general principle of human dignity, that has constitutional status (art.1 of the Brazilian Federal Constitution) and protects the minimum necessary for the existence of a human being (in Germany known as *Existenzminimum*).[6] As an outcome of this constitutional norm, execution of judgments in Brazil has to develop itself respecting the so-called principle of the "least onerous means of enforcement", (article 805 of the new Code of Civil Procedure). The principle states that enforcement has to be carried out in the least burdensome way possible for the debtor and applies to any type of procedural act at any stage of judicial proceedings.[7] Of course it should only apply if more than one means to enforce has efficacy.[8] On the other hand, the liability of the creditor for the wrongdoing at enforcement proceedings is due to strict liability (that is without consideration of fault) and eventual undue losses suffered by the debtor have to be refunded by the creditor.[9]

Along with article 5th, that establishes a general principle of good faith in civil procedure, article 805 of the Code of Civil Procedure protects the good-faith and prevents the abuse of rights by the creditor. However, the principle has to be interpreted in balance with the article 797 of the Code of Civil Procedure, that entails a clear message that the goal of execution is to enforce and give full effect to the "title" (the name the roman tradition uses to refer to an execution instrument, either a

[6] An influence of the *favor debitoris* that has its origins in roman Law. See Silva (1998), pp.91–100.

[7] Dinamarco (2009), p.62.

[8] Didier Jr. et al. (2012), p.56.

[9] Art.520 and 776 of the Code of Civil Procedure. Didier Jr-Cunha-Braga-Oliveira. *Curso de Direito Processual Civil, cit.*, p.63.

judicial decision or a document that the law attributes force to start the enforcement proceeding regardless of a previous cognitive proceeding[10]) in favor of the creditor. Therefore, there ought to be an equilibrium between both ideas of effectiveness of the enforcement measures and the debtor's dignity in the proceeding.

4 Specific Performance and Court Injunctions. The Revolution of the General Clauses for Coercion and Induction

Brazilian Civil Procedure foments specific performance in enforcement proceedings, that is the search of a most adequate and precise execution means to enforce the execution instrument.[11] The main idea behind this is that the right to access to justice encompasses the effective relief in execution proceedings. In order to achieve this goal the judge is to avoid converting all obligations into an equivalent monetary sum, and is allowed to manage and adapt the execution measures to an optimal result, also using injunctions to force and pressure the debtor to comply with coercive (and often indirect) measures.[12]

Nevertheless, it is worth mentioning that coercive measures in enforcement proceeding in Brazil were eminently monetary in nature, with very limited possibility of personal constraint.

The Brazilian Federal Constitution establishes in article 5th, LXVII, a clear prohibition of the civil imprisonment by reason of debt, except to the charge of voluntary and inexcusable breach referring to the payment of alimony or in the case of the "unfaithful depositary in breach of duty" (also called "faulty bailee", that is the case of the individual who was in possession and responsible for the safekeeping of goods that were not his property and does not regularly comply with the obligation). In reference to the latter, after some decisions, in 2009 the Supreme Court edited its binding precedent statement nº 25 and determined that this case of civil imprisonment is unconstitutional because it was an excessive (and thus not proportional) means to achieve compliance of a debt.

Nowadays, the sole case in which personal coercion by imprisonment is allowed is the execution for collecting child support or other family support. These type of proceedings in Brazil are very rigorous to the debtor as the creditor can ask for the arrest of the debtor. This is the only type of civil procedure in which the party can be arrested due to a debt (article 528, CPC). But there is a time limit to this arrest, that can be imposed from 1 to 3 months.

The greatest and most interesting innovation of the Code of Civil Procedure in this regard are the general clauses established in articles 139, IV, 536 §1°and 537 (the last two specific for enforcement proceedings), that allow the judge to order,

---

[10] Cãndido Dinamarco. *Instituições de Direito Processual Civil, cit.*, p.207.

[11] See Shimura (2005).

[12] Talamini (2003), pp.230, 336.

by court injunctions, measures to force the debtor to pay the debt and to comply to judicial commands. Since these rules are general clauses, they do not restrain the possibilities and open a big room for judicial discretion.

So far, we have seen judges determining the apprehension of passports, driver's license and imposing limitation on the exercise of the debtor's rights, such as prohibitions to participate in public working sites, prohibitions to contract with public organs and institutions, restriction to obtain loans, and the like. With regard to failure to comply with court orders, some enterprises have had their activities temporarily suspended.[13]

The Superior Court of Justice—the second highest court in the country—has ruled that the apprehension of passport is unconstitutional because it would harm one's freedom to come and go as pleased, including leaving the country. But the same court found that the apprehension of a person's driver's licence is valid, because at the end of the day, one could still be free to go everywhere by other means of transportation.

Nevertheless, since the Code of Civil Procedure is still very new, Brazilian case-law has been still struggling to handle with these provisions, and we cannot estimate to which extent the higher courts in the country will permit the use of such measures against the debtor. This is a question that will have to wait for the developments of the topic in the future.

5 The Indication of Debtor's Assets in the Initial Filing: Primarily a Problem of the Creditor and the Means to Obtain This Information

Turning back to the traditional enforcement proceeding applied to the execution of monetary sum against private individuals, articles 523 and 829 of the Code of Civil Procedure state that the enforced party (the defendant) has to pay the debt as determined by the judgment or title.

In the case of article 523, which is applicable for the cases that do not require an autonomous proceeding for enforcement (that is, enforcement of judicial decisions in which execution is a second phase of a unique process intertwined with the cognitive phase), the deadline for payment is 15 days after being notified by the judge. On the other hand, in the case of the article 829, applicable for extrajudicial titles (documents) and other cases of specific and autonomous enforcement (such as the proceeding for collecting child or other family support), the debtor has 3 days after the court service to perform payment.

One key element is that service is combined with a writ or order of attachment. If the debtor does not pay within the prescribed term, the clerk shall immediately effect the seizure of property and its evaluation, communicating the defendant of the

[13] The most debated case is that of the telephone app called WhatsApp. The enterprise who owns the app refused to obbey to court orders to identify users and provide messages, and therefore had been temporalily suspended and the app was shut down for some days.

seizure on the same occasion. The goal was to seize assets before any opportunity for the debtor to move assets from her account to others, or to try to avoid payment by disposing of property (sometimes in a fraudulent way).

But in order to know which are the debtor's assets and where they are located, the creditor must indicate the assets of the debtor which are going to be seized. The creditor has to do so in the petition that begins the proceeding. This represents a change in the Brazilian legal order after the reform of the enforcement procedure brought by statutes n° 11.382/2006 and n° 11.232/2005. Prior to this reform, the debtor had 24 h after service to indicate his own assets for seizure, which was a prerogative very criticized. On the one hand, the law was designed to offer this opportunity as a debtor's *legal right*, and not as a procedural legal duty. On the other hand, the debtor usually adopted a "wait and see attitude", waiting for the court to determine the seizure and (not rarely) gaining some time to transfer funds from her bank accounts, selling real state or engaging in many other types of fraud to avoid execution.

The reformed rule, which was maintained in the Code of Civil Procedure of 2015, determines that the creditor has to indicate the debtor's assets that are going to be seized in the pleading that starts the enforcement proceeding. The creditor has the obligation to nominate which assets of the debtor should preferably be seized or attached in the initial filing (articles 524 and 798, II, letter "c" of the Code of Civil Procedure).

So, as I highlighted before, the Brazilian legal system establishes the task of searching for debtor's assets as primarily a creditor's problem.

One could ask by which method may a creditor obtain information regarding the debtor's assets. Well, it is possible for a creditor to search such information using the name of a debtor through databases owned by the government, if such information is not protected by bank or fiscal secrecy. The creditor can also go to the notary, pay a fee and obtain a certified document that shows the property chain and the actual owners of a certain immovable good, car or boat, their description and location.

6 The Subsidiary Help of the Judge in Finding and Seizing Debtor's Assets. Electronic Seizure and Attachment of Bank Accounts. Requirements in Statutory Law and the Legal Duties of the Debtor to Disclose Assets and Their Location

If the creditor could not find assets, which was a problem in the past, is now practically solved by a various number of measures the judge can impose upon the debtor.

The rules are applicable to the enforcement of both judicial decisions and extra-judicial instruments. But for these norms to apply, the creditor has to prove to have taken all possible measures to identify and to locate the debtor assets. If the creditor shows that she has tried to find assets in public records and notary services, but this search was unsuccessful, this is enough for the Judiciary to order the debtor to disclose them.

The new Code of Civil Procedure also establishes intense duties of debtors to disclose the location of goods, including bank accounts. According to article 847 §2º of the Code of Civil Procedure, if the debtor does not pay voluntarily and his assets are not found, after being notified by the judge, the debtor has the procedural *legal duty* to present information as to the identification and location of his property.

The judge will fix a term for the debtor to comply (art.774, V), and noncompliance will be considered an act offensive to the "dignity of justice" (somehow similar to contempt of court in common law systems, but without imprisonment).[14] It is understood that the debtor does not need to indicate all assets of her property, but has to indicate assets that are able to cover the debt and also to provide information as to where the assets can be found.[15] If she does not comply with the obligation, there is a sanction provided in article 774, sole paragraph, of the Code of Civil Procedure: the debtor will have to pay a huge fine and this sum is in favor of the creditor.

As an extension of the duty of acting in good-faith in enforcement proceedings, there are some other situations in which the debtor can practice such an act of disobedience or contempt. Article 847, §2º states clearly that it is a legal duty of the debtor, within the term prescribed by the court, to indicate assets subject to enforcement, showing proof of his property and, if applicable, the "certificate of negative charge", a notary certificate that the real state is free of any claims by a third-party. The debtor has also a duty to refrain from doing anything that would obstruct the seizure or any other execution act, in accordance to the general duty of good-faith established in articles 5th and 77 §2º of the Code of Civil Procedure. Failing to comply with those norms can lead to huge fines imposed by the judge on the debtor.

If the debtor provides false statements in a judicial process, or obstructs the judicial activity, she might be committing a criminal offence, and could be criminally prosecuted (article 347 of the Criminal Code: the crime of "fraud in a judicial process").

There is another rule in the Code of Civil Procedure (article 828) that allows the registration of the seizure of an asset in the notarial real state register, which is important to protect the good faith of a third-party and also guarantees an eventual preference (priority) in sale, in case of multiple enforcements or bankruptcy.[16]

Upon identification of the assets, the judge can electronically attach assets and seize property, and can also order third-parties to reveal such assets if they so know or if debtor's assets are registered in records administrated by third-parties. Both public institutions (including notary services) and private organizations (such as banks and financial institutions in general) are subjected to property inquiry and

---

[14] Dinamarco (2009), p.80.

[15] Didier Jr. et al. (2012), pp.328–329.

[16] Assis (2007), p.260, 441.

must collaborate and comply with court orders. If they do not comply, they could be fined or even shut down.[17]

7 Sales by Private Initiative

Some contemporary changes in Brazilian Civil Procedure represent another useful tool to put pressure on debtor's assets. The latest reforms in execution proceedings provided for the modernization of sales and auctions, that can now be done by private initiative.

The judicial sale of seized assets was traditionally carried out by public services of the Judiciary. New rules allow the sale by private initiative since 2006 (now provided for in article 825, II and 880 of the Code of Civil Procedure of 2015). The possibility entitles the creditor to ask the judge for the sale or auction to be implemented by herself or by a professional third party (accreditor broker). The legislator had aimed efficiency in these cases, considering that public auctions can be often inefficient and expensive to the parties.

However, to ensure due process, article 880 §1° determines that the judge shall fix the term within which the sale must be made, the form of publicity, the minimum price, the payment terms and guarantees, as well as, if applicable, the brokerage commission.

This is understood as a tool that allows sales to be much more efficient, since a better auction (carried out by professionals) tends to obtain a fair market value, which of course speaks in favor of the creditor; but it is also an instrument that is deemed to favor the debtor, as obtaining the optimal result of the auction will at the same time allow full payment of the debt and guarantee that the sale was not underpriced.

8 Other Trends of the New Code of Civil Procedure of 2015. Notarized Notice of Dishonor ("Protesto") and the Use of "Bad Debtors Lists"

All of the previous evolution in execution proceedings was operated by punctual modifications of the former Code of Civil Procedure. Since 2010, a draft of a new Code of Civil Procedure has been debated in the Brazilian Parliament, and the path towards approval came to an end in March 2015. The new Code came into legal force in March 2016.

[17] However, there are some information that are protected by bank secrecy. Banks must inform on the existence of assets (for example, the existence of bank accounts) and the amount of money deposited (article 854 of the Code of Civil Procedure). Banks are not obliged, though, to present the full records of transfers, persons that deposited etc., for these specific records the Judiciary must issue a specific order to unveil bank secrecy.

Some of the reformed rules provide for alternatives to judicial execution were strengthened. Brazilian courts have been admitting for quite some time the use of a notice of dishonor ("protesto") of judicial sentences before notary service as a means to force the debtor to pay. The notarized notice of dishonor makes it difficult to the debtor to obtain credit in the financial market or prevents a person (whether an individual or an enterprise) to engage for example in public competitions to contract with an organ of the Executive or a body or branch of public administration, because one needs proof of being free of any debt. Once the debtor is pressured with a notarized notice of dishonor, and plans to participate in public contracts, she would rather pay the debt than resist a judicial execution. So, for quite some time this practice has grown in Brazil.

The new Code of Civil Procedure turned this into a formally admissible procedural alternative (article 517). The creditor herself can bring a certified copy of the sentence to the notary and ask for the notice of dishonor. The only condition is that the judicial decision must be final (*res iudicata*). The notice shall be cancelled by order of the judge if the debt is fully payed.

Another means that will function as pressure on the debtor to pay are the possibilities to include her name in public "bad debtors lists" or "credit score public records" financed and maintained by services similar to others around the world such as creditorwatch, creditor protection service, credit bureaus, credit reference agency and so forth. The so-called "lists of credit protection" are normally private registers maintained by private pools of enterprises that share among each other and with the general public (by payment of a small fee) information about anyone that has not fully payed his debts after being adequately notified.

The new Code of Civil Procedure allows debts determined by judicial decisions and that have not yet been payed to be included in those lists (art.782 §3º). This measure will be immediately cancelled if the debt is payed or if the execution proceedings come to an end by any reason, even on procedural grounds.

9 Litigation Agreements and Their Usage Regarding Debtor's Assets and Their Sales

Last, but not least, the new Code of Civil Procedure innovates a lot in terms of contract procedure, that is, agreements about procedural norms and procedural legal situations.[18] Article 190 establishes a general clause of procedural negotiation: "If the cause deals with rights that admit agreements, the parties, if fully capable, are entitled to stipulate changes in the proceeding to fit the specifics of the cause and may agree upon their powers, faculties and procedural obligations, prior to or during the judicial process".

[18] See Cabral (2018); Cabral and Nogueira (eds.) (2017); Cabral (2016a), pp.773–793. The influence of the German literature and the French praxis in Brazil's new Code of Civil Procedure regarding contract procedure is highlighted in Cabral (2015), pp.381–395; Cabral (2016b), pp.629–648.

This general provision will allow parties to agree upon a large number of situations and norms in execution proceedings, many of which can be related to the debtor's assets and the form of their disposal or sale. The parties can agree, for instance, upon: seizable assets; forms of service and notifications in general; the choice of specific private companies or persons to sell debtor assets; the collaborative shaping of a calendar for the procedural acts and follow-up measures[19]; and even, some might argue, if a certain document could be enforced as an execution instrument, regardless of a statutory provision.[20]

10 Conclusive Remarks

This essay intended to highlight some of the latest trends in execution of proceedings in Brazilian Civil Procedure, not only of the latest reforms and tendencies of case-law, but also the provisions of the new Code of Civil Procedure. Our main focus were the instruments to search, seize and attach assets, but also measures to pressure the debtor to disclose information on the existence and location of her assets.

The idea of the Brazilian legal system is that this task should be primarily attributed to the creditor, but if she fails to find assets, the judge can act to order the debtor and seize/attach property. Litigation agreements, especially if contractually established (therefore agreed previously to the lawsuit) can also play a strong role in defining a list of seizable/attachable assets and the proceeding for their sale.

In comparative perspective, the Brazilian new legal system seems to be a middle way between many other jurisdictions and so far has proven to be more effective than the format that existed prior to the reforms.

References

Assis A (2007) Manual da Execução, 11th edn. RT, São Paulo

Cabral A (2015) Der Einfluss des deutschen Rechts auf die neue brasilianische Zivilprozessordnung. Zeitschrift Für Zivilprozess International 20:381–395

Cabral A (2016a) Accordi processuali nel diritto brasiliano. Rivista di Diritto Processuale, LXXI, pp 773–793

Cabral A (2016b) Les conventions sur la procédure en droit processuel brésilien. Rev Int Droit Comp (3):629–648

Cabral A (2016) Vollstreckungsverfahren im Widerstreit zwischen Effizienz und Grundrechten: Einige Anmerkungen zu den jüngsten Reformen des brasilianischen Zivilprozessrechts. Zeitschrift Für Zivilprozeβ International 21:289–303

Cabral A (2018) Convenções processuais. Salvador, 2nd edn. 2018

Cabral A and Nogueira P (eds) (2017) Negócios processuais, 3rd edn. JusPodivm, Salvador.

---

[19] Didier Jr. and Cabral (2018), p.193–228.

[20] Cabral (2016c), pp.297, 301–302; Cabral (2018), p.316–317; Carvalho F. (2015), p.1772.

Carvalho F (2015) Comentário. In: Wambier T et al. (eds) Breves comentários ao Código de Processo Civil. RT, São Paulo. pp 865–876, 1166–1173
Didier F Jr, Cabral A (2018) Negócios jurídicos processuais atípicos e execução. Rev Proc 43(275):193–228
Didier F, Cunha L, Braga P, Oliveira R (2012) Curso de direito processual civil, vol 5, 4th edn. JusPodivm, Salvador
Dinamarco C (2009) Instituições de direito processual civil, vol 4, 3rd edn. RT, São Paulo
Hess B (2020) The effective disclosure of the debtor's assets in enforcement proceedings, in this volume
Marcus R (2020) America's BYO Approach to Enforcing Money Judgments: Comment on Rechberger and Hess, in this volume.
Shimura S (2005) Título executive, 2nd edn. RT, São Paulo
Silva O (1998) Jurisdição e execução, Forense, São Paulo
Talamini E (2003) Tutela relativa aos deveres de fazer e não fazer, 2nd edn. RT, São Paulo

Antonio Cabral Professor of Civil Procedural Law at the University of Rio de Janeiro State (UERJ), where he teaches at the undergraduate, master's and doctorate levels, in addition to being coordinator of the Center for German and Comparative Law Studies. He holds his venia legendi (*Habilitation*) from the University of São Paulo (USP). Ph.D. in Procedural Law from UERJ, in cooperation with the University of Munich, Germany (Ludwig-Maximilians-Universität). Master in Public Law by UERJ. Post-doctorate at the University of Paris I (Panthéon-Sorbonne). Visiting Professor at the Universities of Passau (2015), Kiel (2016), Germany, and at Ritsumeikan University, Kyoto, Japan (2018). Senior Lecturer at Peking University, Beijing, China (2019). Vice-President of the International Association of Procedural Law. Vice-Director of International Relations at the Brazilian Institute of Procedural Law. Member of the Iberoamerican Institute of Procedural Law, of the German-Brazilian Association of Jurists and of the *Wissenschaftliche Vereinigung für Internationales Verfahrensrecht*.

Polish Enforcement Law in Civil Cases General Characteristics and Directions of Development

Piotr Rylski and Karol Weitz

1 Introduction: General Characteristics of Polish Enforcement Law

Enforcement proceedings in Polish law have been regulated in the Civil Procedure Code (CPC) since the interwar period, together with the examination proceedings, interim remedy proceedings and issues relating to international civil procedure.[1] The model of the Polish enforcement law, similarly to the examination proceedings, was developed based on German- and Austrian solutions.[2] Russian law had a much lesser influence.[3] The doctrine distinguishes between a broader and a narrower sense of the term "enforcement proceedings". Enforcement proceedings in a broader sense include proceedings aimed at issuance of a writ of execution for an enforcement order and the actual enforcement proceedings; enforcement proceedings in a narrower sense of the term refer only to the actual enforcement proceedings. Proceedings for the issuance of a writ of execution aim at obtaining a general permission to execute a

[1] The first Polish code of 1930–32. The currently effective Code of 1964. For more information on the Polish enforcement proceedings in general, cf. T. Ereciński, *Civil procedure*, [in:] Introduction to Polish Law, ed. T. Frankowski, Hague 2005, pp. 141–145; F. Zedler, *Civil Procedure*, [in:] Handbook of Polish Law, eds. W. Dajczak, A.J. Szwarc, P. Wiliński, Warsaw 2011, pp. 644–651.

[2] K. Weitz, *Die Bedeutung der Rezeption für die Entwicklung des polnischen Zivilprozessrechts*, Ritsumeikan Law Review. International Edition, 2010, no. 27, p. 141ff.

[3] P. Rylski, K. Weitz, *The Impact of the Russian Civil Judicial Proceedings Act of 1864 on the Polish Civil Proceedings*, Russian Law Journal 2014, no. 4, p. 78.

P. Rylski (✉) · K. Weitz
Faculty of Law and Administration, University of Warsaw, Warsaw, Poland
e-mail: p.rylski@wpia.uw.edu.pl

K. Weitz
e-mail: k.weitz@wpia.uw.edu.pl

M. Deguchi (ed.), *Effective Enforcement of Creditors' Rights*,
Ius Gentium: Comparative Perspectives on Law and Justice 91,
https://doi.org/10.1007/978-981-16-5609-5_19

given enforcement order, whereas the purpose of the actual enforcement proceedings is to effect the enforcement.[4]

As a rule, the enforcement order (e.g. a final and binding judgment or a notarial deed wherein the debtors subjected themselves to enforcement proceedings) with a writ of execution (Articles 776 and 777 of CPC) forms the basis for enforcement. The writ of execution is issued either upon request or—*ex officio* in exceptional cases—by the court or by a court clerk. Once the writ of execution has been issued, the enforcement order becomes an enforceable title and the basis for enforcement. Enforcement is generally initiated upon the request of the creditor; in exceptional situations, it is initiated by the court acting *ex officio* or upon the motion of a competent authority (e.g. upon the motion of a prosecutor, Article 796 of the CPC). The motion for initiating enforcement needs to be filed with the enforcement authority; it should identify the obligation to be fulfilled and it should be accompanied by the enforceable title (Article 797, Section 1 of the CPC). The motion for initiating enforcement allows for conducting enforcement with any acceptable methods. Special rules apply only in case of enforcement against immovable property. In the motion for initiating enforcement, the creditor may, but is not required to, indicate the enforcement method or methods; the enforcement authority should, however, use an enforcement method that is the least burdensome for the debtor (Article 799 of the CPC).[5]

Depending on the subject matter of enforcement, there is enforcement of monetary obligations (Articles 844–1040 of the CPC), enforcement of non-monetary obligations (Articles 1041–1059 of the CPC) and enforcement in order to terminate joint ownership of immovable property by way of a public sale (Articles 1066–1071 of the CPC).[6] Different enforcement methods may be applied in case of enforcing monetary obligations; the methods depend on the source of satisfaction for the creditor. Notably, enforcement against movable assets, enforcement against salary, enforcement against bank accounts, enforcement against other debt claims, enforcement against other property rights, enforcement against immovable property, enforcement against a fraction of a movable property, enforcement against perpetual usufruct, simplified enforcement against immovable property or enforcement against seagoing vessels. In case of enforcement proceedings involving entrepreneurs, enforcement methods also include enforcement by administrative receivership and enforcement by way of selling an enterprise or a farm. Enforcement of maintenance has a special place in case of enforcement of monetary obligations. By contrast, enforcement of non-monetary obligations covers the enforcement of release of a movable property, surrender of an immovable property, of a ship or vacating of premises, taking the so-called substitutable action, taking the so-called non-substitutable action, refraining from an action or not interfering with the action taken by the creditor. The methods

[4] A. Marciniak, *Sądowe postępowanie egzekucyjne w sprawach cywilnych [Court enforcement proceedings in civil cases]*, Warsaw 2019, p. 23.

[5] Cf. K. Weitz, *Probleme der Vollstreckung aus polnischer Sicht*, in: *Grenzüberschreitende Vollstreckung in der Europäischen Union*, eds. M. Kengyel, V. Harsági, München 2011, pp. 184–185.

[6] A. Marciniak, *Sądowe* ..., pp. 31–32.

of enforcing non-monetary obligations include: taking away the object of the obligation from the debtor and releasing it to the creditor, fulfilling the obligation at the expense of the debtor and applying coercive measures against the debtor such as a fine or arrest, or ordering the debtor to pay the creditor a specific sum of money (the mandatory sum).[7]

Under the Polish Civil Procedure Code, competence in enforcement matters is divided between the court and the judicial enforcement officer. As a rule, judicial enforcement officers are the primary enforcement authority (Article 759, Section 1 of the CPC). Therefore, enforcement activities are within the remit of judicial enforcement officers, unless the statute provides that a given matter is within the remit of the court as the competent enforcement authority. A district court is an enforcement authority in a situation concerning the disclosure of the debtor's property (Articles 913–920^{1} of the CPC), and also in case of enforcing non-monetary obligations by performing a substitutionable action (Article 1049 of the CPC), by performing non-substitutable action (Article 1050 of the CPC), refraining from taking an action or not disturbing the action taken by the creditor (Article 1051 of the CPC). The court, as an enforcement authority, is also responsible for enforcement by administrative receivership (Articles 1064^{1}–1064^{13} of the CPC) and enforcement by way of selling an enterprise or a farm (Articles 1064^{14}–1064^{23}). The actions that are within the remit of the court as an enforcement authority may be performed by a court clerk, subject to certain exceptions. For example, the court clerk must not apply coercive measures, state expiration of effects of adjudication and loss of guarantee, run cases regarding enforcement by administrative receivership or cases regarding enforcement by way of selling the enterprise or a farm (Article 759, Section 1^{1} of the CPC). It needs to be emphasised that a district court may act in a role other than an enforcement authority in the enforcement proceedings. In that case the court is referred to as the enforcement court. As the enforcement court, the court is responsible for supervision over the judicial enforcement officer and recognising complaints concerning the activities taken by the judicial enforcement officer.[8]

A complaint (*skarga* in Polish) concerning the activities of the judicial enforcement officer is the basic measure of appeal that may be used by the parties to and participants of those proceedings, including the debtor and the creditor (Article 767 of the CPC). There is a rule that a complaint may be filed in regard to any activity taken or omitted by the judicial enforcement officer, unless the statute provides otherwise. The said complaint is dealt with by the court as the enforcement court. An interlocutory appeal (*zażalenie* in Polish) may be filed in regard to the rulings of the court as an enforcement authority or as the enforcement court in cases indicated in the statute (Article 767^{4}, Section 1 of the CPC). Where an action is taken by a court clerk, a complaint may be filed about the court clerk's ruling; the complaint is recognised according to the rules applicable in the case of an interlocutory appeal

[7] A. Marciniak, *Sądowe* ..., pp. 31–32.

[8] J. Misztal-Konecka, *Postępowanie zabezpieczające i egzekucyjne w sprawach cywilnych [Interim remedy proceedings and enforcement proceedings in civil cases]*, Warsaw 2019, p. 201ff.

(Article 767[3a] of the CPC). No cassation complaint may be filed with the Supreme Court in enforcement proceedings; the proceedings may not be resumed either.

Separate actions, commonly referred to in the literature as anti-enforcement actions, are used for subject-related defence of the debtor or third parties in relation to enforcement proceedings and enforcement (Articles 840–843 of the CPC). Those actions in Polish law were modelled on solutions employed in Germany and Austria; however, they are slightly different.[9]

The action to cancel the enforceability of the enforceable title is the first type of the anti-enforcement action; it is referred to as the opposition action (*powództwo opozycyjne* in Polish) and it is used for protecting the debtor's rights (Article 840 of the CPC). In case of this action, the debtor challenges the admissibility of enforcement pursuant to a given enforceable title for reasons relating to the creditor's right to receive the obligation. The debtor may demand that the enforceability of the enforceable title be cancelled if: (1) s/he denies facts on whose basis a writ of execution was issued (e.g. when s/he challenges the legal succession of the creditor who is in charge of the enforcement versus the person who has previously obtained the enforceable titles, or—in case of enforceable titles other than a court ruling—s/he challenges the existence of the duty to perform; (2) an event took place after the enforceable title was established, as a result of which an obligation expired or may not be enforced (e.g. s/he claims that s/he had performed the obligation; the effects of *res judicata* apply to court rulings, therefore the debtor may not invoke events that took place before the case was closed; (3) the debtor's spouse against whom the court issued a writ of execution proves that the creditor is not entitled to the obligation subject to enforcement (e.g. s/he claims that the obligation must not be enforced against the joint property of the married couple).[10] The opposition action is brought by the debtor against the creditor.

The second type of anti-enforcement actions is the so-called "intervening action" (*powództwo eksydencyjne* or *powództwo interwencyjne* in Polish); it is used for protecting third party's rights which are violated during enforcement proceedings against the debtor (Article 841 of the CPC). A third party may bring an action and demand that the attached thing be exempt from enforcement if enforcement against that thing violates the third party's rights. A classic example of such situation is where the thing against which enforcement was commenced is in the debtor's possession but it is the property of a third party. The so-called intervening action is brought by a third party against the creditor and also against the debtor if the debtor denies the third party's right.

[9] A. Marciniak, *Sądowe* ..., p. 315ff.; J. Misztal-Konecka, *Postępowanie* ..., p. 314ff.

[10] Under Polish law and within certain limits, a writ of execution may be issued for an enforcement title to also include the debtor's spouse, which means that enforcement may be (also) conducted against the joint property of the spouses.

2 Recent Changes to the Enforcement Law

Improving the effectiveness of enforcement proceedings in civil cases has been a major problem since the political breakthrough in 1989. Enforcement was considered to be ineffective, and the legal solutions were considered to be one of the sources of that ineffectiveness. In parallel to the reforms of the examination proceedings in civil law which were commenced in Poland after 1989,[11] there were also attempts at improving enforcement proceedings, also by way of legislative actions. In terms of the system, the most important changes affected the position of the judicial enforcement officer as an enforcement authority.[12] They involved changes in regulations concerning the costs of enforcement proceedings. In 2004,[13] there was a very extensive reform that tackled the provisions regulating the interim remedy proceedings and the enforcement proceedings. In the enforcement area, the changes included the fundamentals of enforcement (enforcement orders and enforceable titles), the disclosure of the debtor's property and the judicial enforcement officer's obtaining information on that property, a system of means of appeal in enforcement and anti-enforcement actions, modification of existing enforcement methods and implementing new ones.[14] The issue of computerisation and the use of new techniques of communication and of recording enforcement activities proved to be a major challenge in the development of the regulations concerning enforcement proceedings, as was the case with the civil procedure in general. The process of computerisation of enforcement proceedings was initiated in 2009[15]; more reforms were implemented as a result of its continuation, particularly in 2015.[16] Most recently, the legislator focused on the issues of debtor's protection and on obtaining information on the debtor's assets.[17] Changes in regulations concerning the implementation of foreign enforcement orders were a separate issue. Changes in that regard were aimed at

[11] For more information see: K. Weitz, *Die Entwicklung des polnischen Zivilprozessrechts nach der politischen Wende im Jahre* 1989, ZZPInt 2006, Vol. 11, p. 89ff; K. Weitz, *Reformen des Zivilprozessrechts in der Dritten Polnischen Republik*, in: *Die Entwicklung des Zivilprozessrechts in Mitteleuropa um die Jahrtausendwende. Reform und Kodifikation—Tradition und Erneuerung*, ed. Th. Sutter-Somm, V. Harsági, Zürich, Basel, Genf 2012, p. 189ff.; P. Rylski, *Polish Civil Procedure: Yesterday, Today and Tomorrow—Some Remarks About Recent Changes of Procedural Law in Poland*, Bratislava Law Review 2019, no. 1, p. 139ff.

[12] It began with the Judicial Enforcement Officers and Enforcement Act of 29 August 1997. It was repealed in 2018. Cf. comments below.

[13] Civil Procedure Code's and Certain Other Acts' Amendment Act of 2 July 2004.

[14] K. Weitz, *Czy nowa kodyfikacja postępowania cywilnego? [New codification of the civil procedure?]*, Państwo i Prawo 2007, No. 3, p. 17.

[15] Pursuant to the Civil Procedure Code's and Certain Other Acts' Amendment Act of 9 January 2009.

[16] Civil Code's, Civil Procedure Code's and Certain Other Acts' Amendment Act of 10 July 2015.

[17] Cf. in particular the Civil Procedure Code's Amendment Act of 10 May 2013 and the Civil Procedure Code's and Certain Other Acts' Amendment Act of 4 July 2019.

supplementing or implementing adequate regulations of the European Union law, particularly those creating the "European" enforcement titles.[18]

It is impossible to present, in these general comments, the detailed changes that Polish enforcement proceedings underwent as a result of legislative actions taken after 1989. While characterising those changes in general, it should be emphasized that, on the one hand, there was a visible intent to improve and increase continually the effectiveness of enforcement, especially in the earlier years. It fits into the process of enforcement computerisation. On the other hand, it is impossible not to notice, especially in the case of the most recent amendments, that that original intention, which was right, somehow crumbled. It is evident in the case of certain normative solutions which are being introduced and which frequently result from the politicians' response to reports about cases of abuse in practice; those solutions reinforce the protection for the debtor in enforcement proceedings, frequently in violation of seemingly fundamental assumptions relating to the enforcement proceedings and to the actions taken by enforcement authorities.

In order to illustrate the current trends in the development of Polish enforcement law, the subsequent comment will focus on a few selected groups of issues or on a few selected issues. The first issue to be tackled is the issue of transformations in terms of the systemic position of a judicial enforcement officer as an enforcement authority. The second issue to be presented is the solutions in Polish law that apply to obtainment of information (in a broad sense of the term) in enforcement proceedings, including in particular information on the debtor's property. The third topic to be specified is the extent and the form in which enforcement proceedings in Poland are computerised. The fourth topic to be discussed is the newest regulations on debtor protection in the enforcement proceedings. And the fifth, and final topic to be presented is a new method of enforcing non-monetary obligations, which was implemented fairly recently; as part of that method, the debtor is required to pay the creditor an adequate sum (the mandatory sum); the method is inspired by solutions applied in Romanic countries.

3 Systemic Position of a Judicial Enforcement Officer in Poland

Initially, a judicial enforcement officer in Polish law had the status of an employee of the competent court (the district court) where s/he acted; s/he acted on behalf of and was supervised by that court. The supervision was exercised by the Court President; it could not be judicial supervision that covered specific enforced actions of the judicial enforcement officer and that was exercised by the enforcement court. Pursuant to the Act of 1997, judicial enforcement officers became independent officers within the

[18] For more details see *Egzekucja sądowa w świetle przepisów z zakresu międzynarodowego postępowania cywilnego* [*Court enforcement proceedings in light of provisions under international civil law*], ed. A. Marciniak, Sopot 2016, pasim.

organisational structure—they were no longer employees of the court where they operated; they became independent public officers running their own businesses.[19] As public officers, judicial enforcement officers took enforcement activities and were subject to judicial supervision of the enforcement court; the judicial enforcement officers were subject only to the rulings of the enforcement court and to the statutes. Because the judicial enforcement officers acted as sole traders, they did not receive a typical remuneration from the State; rather, they earned their income from the fees for enforcement activities which they charged in the course of enforcement. The surplus of those fees above the costs of running the judicial enforcement officer's office was the net income of the judicial enforcement officer. The President of the district court continued to exercise administrative supervision over the judicial enforcement officers; however, that supervision did not concern the subject-related activity of the judicial enforcement officers, i.e. the area of judicial supervision. In addition, as members of the judicial enforcement officers organisation, judicial enforcement officers were also subject to the supervision by the professional self-government of judicial enforcement officers.

A few years ago, the position of judicial enforcement officers in the system, particularly their far-reaching organisational independence, became the object of criticism. It was due to cases of abuse by some judicial enforcement officers of their executive powers in relation to enforcement activities they took which were a manifestation of state coercion. The political authorities acted on it and reformed the judicial enforcement officer profession and the issue of judicial enforcement officer costs in the enforcement proceedings. Pursuant to two statutes of 2018[20] judicial enforcement officers were subjected to much more extensive and multi-level administrative supervision by the Minister of Justice and presidents of courts at all levels (the appellate court, the regional court and the district court). Under the new statutes, judicial enforcement officers kept their status as public officers; however, the status has largely become a hybrid, i.e. it is partly similar to the status of a court employee. For example, judicial enforcement officers have certain employee rights (such as the right to rest), and their remuneration is commission-based—it covers a specific percentage share of enforcement fees they charge.[21]

Notwithstanding the foregoing, it is of key importance that an judicial enforcement officers act as an enforcement authority in the enforcement proceedings. Judicial enforcement officers have their own executive powers; within the scope of activities performed as part of the enforcement proceedings, the statue treats judicial enforcement officers as a public authority. While performing enforcement activities, judicial enforcement officers may use the assistance of other public authorities (e.g.

[19] K. Weitz, *Probleme* …, p. 186.

[20] Judicial Enforcement Officers Act of 22 March 2018 and Enforcement Costs Act of 28 February 2018.

[21] See E. Staszewska, *Quasi-pracownicze uprawnienia komornika na gruncie ustawy o komornikach sądowych [Quasi-employee rights of judicial enforcement officers under the Judicial Enforcement Officers Act]*, in: *Komornicy sądowi i egzekucja sądowa w nowej rzeczywistości prawnej [Judicial enforcement officers and court enforcement proceedings in a new legal reality]*, ed. R. Kulski, Sopot 2019, p. 17ff.

the Police, Article 765 of the CPC). Judicial enforcement officers have their own enforcement power and they do not need to obtain any additional authorisation in order to take the individual enforcement activities. Judicial enforcement officer's general authorisation to carry out enforcement upon the creditor's motion for initiating enforcement results from the enforcement order with a writ of execution. That is why judicial supervision exercised over the judicial enforcement officers by the competent district court acting as an enforcement court is so important. The court's review of complaints about the activities taken by the judicial enforcement officers is the basic form of that supervision (Article 767 of the CPC).[22] Another form of judicial supervision exercised by the enforcement court involves the court's right to issue *ex officio* orders to judicial enforcement officer aiming to ensure a proper enforcement and remedy the ascertained shortcomings. The legal assessment expressed by the court in the orders shall be binding for the judicial enforcement officers (Article 759, Section 2 of the CPC). In practice, there are concerns about the separation of the scopes of application of those two forms of judicial supervision exercised by the court over the enforcement activities taken by the judicial enforcement officers.[23]

It should be noted that judicial enforcement officers in Poland who act at the competent district courts are assigned areas in which they are authorised to act (the so-called *rewiry* in Polish, or court enforcement areas). However, since 1997, creditors have been given the ability (to a certain extent) to select a judicial enforcement officer who will be in charge of enforcement proceedings (Article 759^1 of the CPC). This refers to the ability to indicate a judicial enforcement officer who does not have jurisdiction according to the statutory rules laid down in the relevant provisions. The creditor may select a judicial enforcement officer within the jurisdiction of the appellate court where the judicial enforcement officer has his/her office. The ability to select the judicial enforcement officer is excluded in case of certain enforcement methods (e.g. in the case of enforcement against immovable property). Because the ability to select the judicial enforcement officer was abused in practice and led to disproportions among the individual judicial enforcement officer offices, the right of choice was subjected to certain additional restrictions in the statues of 2018.

4 Obtaining Information in Enforcement Proceedings

Obtaining information required to conduct enforcement proceedings, including in particular information on the debtor's assets, is extremely important in enforcement. Polish enforcement law provides for numerous regulations in that regard that have

---

[22] A. Marciniak, *Sądowe* ..., p. 110.

[23] Cf. A. Marciniak, *Sądowe* ..., pp. 111–113; T. Zembrzuski, *Zarządzenia sądu z urzędu a odpowiedzialność odszkodowawcza komornika sądowego i Skarbu Państwa [Court rulings ex officio vs liability of judicial enforcement officers and State Treasury for damages]*, in: *Sądowe postępowanie egzekucyjne [Court enforcement proceedings]. Nowe wyzwania i perspektywy [New challenges and perspectives]*, ed. J. Jagieła, Warsaw 2020, p. 145ff.

been elaborated on in recent years. In practice, their effectiveness may be evaluated as moderate; however, there are concerns about the correlations between those regulations.

It needs to be emphasised that, in the motion for the initiation of enforcement, the creditor may, but is not required to, indicate the debtor's assets from which his/her claim may be satisfied. If the creditor fails to do it, the burden of the activity rests with the judicial enforcement officer to a large extent (Article 801, Section 1 of the CPC). In such a situation, the judicial enforcement officer shall *ex officio* first: (1) determine the debtor's assets within the scope known to him/her based on other proceedings conducted, or based on publicly accessible sources of information or records to which s/he has electronic access, or (2) call on the debtor to submit a list of assets.

As far as the first scope is concerned, the enforcement authority, including the judicial enforcement officer, has a very important right to demand explanations from the participants of the enforcement proceedings, which includes primarily the parties to the proceedings, that is the creditor and the debtor (Article 761, Section 1 of the CPC). Furthermore, the enforcement authority may demand information on the debtor's material status or information that allow for the identification of the individual assets and address details as necessary to ensure proper conduct of the proceedings from various institutions, including public administration bodies, tax authorities, disability pension authorities, banks and other private entities upon the pain of a fine (Article 761, Section 1^1 and Article 762 of the CPC). The motion in that respect may be filed by the creditor; however, the motion may not be filed solely for the purpose of harassing the debtor (Article 801, Sections 2 and 3 of the CPC).

As regards the list of assets, the debtor is required to provide that list to the judicial enforcement officer either verbally on record or in writing, along with a statement to confirm that the list is true and complete subject to penalty of perjury. If a debtor fails to submit the list of assets with the relevant statement without a justified cause or fails to give answer to a question directed to him/her, the judicial enforcement officer may impose a fine on the debtor, or even order compulsory appearance of the debtor in court to submit the list (Article 801^1 of the CPC). The list of assets, referred to herein, is described as "judicial enforcement officer-mandated" disclosure of assets; however, it differs from the disclosure of assets mandated by the court. First of all, the list is submitted before the enforcement proceedings as part of (already) pending enforcement proceedings; meanwhile, disclosure of assets may be initiated even before such proceedings are initiated and after they have been concluded. Second, the judicial enforcement officer orders the submission of the list of assets *ex officio*, whereas the disclosure of assets takes place upon the motion of the creditor.[24] Despite those differences in construction, there is a possibility that those two constructs might overlap.

[24] Cf. A. Laskowska-Hulisz, *Złożenie przez dłużnika wykazu majątku komornikowi sądowemu w postępowaniu egzekucyjnym w sprawach cywilnych (art. 801^1 k.p.c.) [Debtor's filing a list of assets to a judicial enforcement officer in enforcement proceedings in civil cases (Article 801^1 of the CPC)*, in: *Sądowe postępowanie* …, pp. 120–121.

The creditor's ordering the judicial enforcement officer to look for debtor's assets is the third method of obtaining information on those assets. The creditor has such an ability, unless the judicial enforcement officer determined the debtor's assets based on other proceedings conducted, or based on publicly accessible sources of information or records to which s/he has electronic access (Article 801^2 of the CPC). The creditor must order the judicial enforcement officer to look for the debtor's assets if they want to continue enforcement in a situation where the debtor's assets at an amount that would allow for covering at least the enforcement costs have not been determined, despite the enforcement of debtor's assets indicated by the creditor, arriving at findings pursuant to other proceedings conducted or pursuant to publicly accessible sources of information or records to which the judicial enforcement officer has electronic access, and despite the receipt of the list of assets from the debtor (Article 801, Section 4 of the CPC). An enforcement fee is always charged for the order to look for the debtor's assets. The judicial enforcement officer is bound by such an order and must not deny it if the premises for submitting such an order have been met. The judicial enforcement officer is required to take certain action even though the law does not specify them. The activities taken by the judicial enforcement officer are not based on a civil law agreement between the judicial enforcement officer and the creditor, but rather they are based on the motion for commencing the search which is a type of motion submitted in the course of the enforcement proceedings.[25]

Court-mandated disclosure of assets is a separate stand-alone method of obtaining information on the debtor's assets (Articles 913–920^1 of the CPC). Under that regulation, the creditor may ask the court for an order requiring the debtor to submit a list of their property, including the list of individual assets and their location. The debtor submits such a list to the court subject to criminal liability for making false statements—the court advises the debtor of such liability before accepting the list. The motion for disclosure may be filed even before the enforcement proceedings have been initiated. If the debtor fails to appear in court, without a justified cause, to submit the list or take an oath, or if the debtor appears in court but fails to submit the list or refuses to answer a question asked or refuses to take an oath, the court may impose a fine on the debtor or order compulsory appearance; the court may also order the arrest. The court-mandated disclosure of assets is not very effective in practice as there are problems determining the whereabouts of the debtor and the procedure is highly formalised.

[25] Cf. M. Cichorska, *Poszukiwanie majątku dłużnika przez komornika [Search of debtor's property by judicial enforcement officer]*, in: *Komornicy sądowi i egzekucja sądowa w nowej rzeczywistości prawnej [Judicial enforcement officers and court enforcement proceedings in a new legal reality]*, ed. R. Kulski, Sopot 2019, pp. 279–284.

5 Computerisation of Enforcement Proceedings in Poland

Computerisation of the proceedings is an important aspect of the most recent changes in civil procedure, including the enforcement proceedings.[26] Electronic procedure by writ of payment was implemented in Polish civil procedure in 2010. An electronic writ of payment is issued upon the completion of the procedure (Articles 505^{28}–505^{39} of the CPC).[27] In case of such a writ of payment, the decision on the issuance of a writ of execution is issued without a separate operative part of the judgment; in such a case, the writ of execution is posted in the ICT system with the qualified electronic signature of the court or court clerk who issues the decision (Article 783, Section 3^1 of the CPC). The decision on the issuance of the writ of execution remains only in the ICT system. That possibility also applies to other electronic enforcement titles although, other than in the case of the electronic procedure by writ of payment, it is not very common in Poland yet. The reason for that is that there is no uniform ICT system in Polish courts that would serve all court proceedings.[28]

The motion for initiating enforcement in case of an "electronic" enforceable title is also filed with the judicial enforcement officer via the ICT system (Article 797, Section 2 of the CPC). In such a case, the motion for initiating enforcement proceedings or the demand for conducting enforcement proceedings *ex officio* is accompanied by a document from the ICT system that enables the enforcement authority to verify the existence and the content of that title; where a motion for initiating enforcement proceedings is filed via the ICT system, the enforceable title is indicated (Article 797, Section 3 of the CPC). In such a case, the judicial enforcement officer is required to verify the content of the document obtained from the ICT system and presented to him/her, and mark the fact that enforcement was conducted pursuant to that title in the system. Where enforcement was conducted pursuant to the electronic enforceable title, the enforcement outcome is recorded in the ICT system (Article 816, Section 3 of the CPC). The electronic data created as a result of those actions taken by the judicial enforcement officer are approved with the qualified electronic signature.

As already mentioned, since 1 January 2019, upon the initiation of enforcement proceedings, the judicial enforcement officer determines the debtor's assets within the scope known to him/her based on other proceedings conducted, or based on publicly accessible sources of information or records to which s/he has electronic access. In general, no additional fee is due to the judicial enforcement officer for the fulfilment of that duty. It refers to the use of any databases, such as register of vehicles, data on bank accounts or land and mortgage register, which are available to the judicial enforcement officer electronically.

In order to control whether the activities taken by the judicial enforcement officer are correct, as of 1 January 2019 judicial enforcement officers are required to record

[26] For more general information on computerisation see P. Rylski, *Polish Civil...*, pp. 140–142.

[27] R. Kulski, *Some Remarks on the Course od Polish Electronic Proceedings by Writ of Payment, [in:] Electronic and Justice – Present and Future*, Pecs 2010, p. 17.

[28] Cf. P. Rylski, *Covid-19 and the Civil Justice in Poland*, Septentrio Reports (2020), no 5, pp. 43–44, https://doi.org/10.7557/7.5469.

a number of their activities outside their office using an audio and video recording device (Article 809[1] of the CPC). Those activities include, among other things, activities taken by the judicial enforcement officer with the participation of the debtor in order to determine the debtor's assets, attachment of movable assets, auction of movable assets excluding electronic auction, inspection of immovable property, vacating the premises or removing things from the premises, surrender of movable assets and immovable property. The judicial enforcement officer also records the activities if such a request is submitted by at least one party to the proceedings. The judicial enforcement officer stops the recording of the activities performed at the place of residence of the debtor or of a third party if the debtor, or that third party, object thereto.

The possibility of sale by electronic auction as part of enforcement against movable assets was introduced on 1 March 2017 (Articles 879[1]–879[11] of the CPC). In general, that method of selling movable assets is applied upon the request of the creditor submitted after the attachment of the things. Sale by electronic auction takes place through the ICT system where the notice of auction is posted. In such a case, the person entering the tender procedure also submits a guarantee via the ICT system. The judicial enforcement officer sets the starting and ending dates of the electronic auction so that the electronic auction lasts at least seven days and so that it ends during business hours of the district court at which the enforcement officer operates. Immediately upon the end of the electronic auction, the judicial enforcement officer awards the bid to the person who offered the highest price as at the moment of ending it. The bid is awarded in the ICT system. The purchaser is required to pay the purchase price on the day following the date of service of the notification of bid award, during the business hours of the judicial enforcement officer's office or to the enforcement officer's bank account until 6 p.m. the next day. If that day falls on a Saturday or a statutory holiday, the payment is to be made on the day following the day or days off. The purchase price may be paid through the ICT system.

Apart from the said elements of computerisation of the enforcement proceedings, the legislator also permitted the possibility for the tax authority attaching receivables on account of tax overpayment or tax refund to contact the judicial enforcement officer via electronic means (Article 902[2] of the CPC).

6 Protection of the Debtor

The most recent changes to enforcement proceedings also aim at considerable reinforcement of the debtor's position and at strengthening his/her protection. Unfortunately, it is often at the expense of the debtor's interests and it often leads to undermining the effectiveness of the enforcement.

As of 1 January 2019, judicial enforcement officers have the right to refuse to initiate enforcement if the creditor's motion was only filed to harass the debtor (Article 801, Section 3 of the CPC). With the implementation of those regulations, the legislator assumed that they would be a manifestation of debtor's protection against abuse from the creditor when directing motions to initiate enforcement and other motions to initiate certain enforcement activities. Interpretation of that provision is controversial.[29]

Judicial enforcement officers also have the duty to check, *ex officio*, whether the limitation period for the claim covered by the enforceable title expired; if so, judicial enforcement officers refuse to initiate the enforcement (Article 804, Section 2 of the CPC). That solution is extremely difficult to be implemented in practice because the judicial enforcement officers only have the enforceable title and not the court case file. Furthermore, the duty is in conflict with the cardinal rule of enforcement law, whereby an enforcement authority is not entitled to examine the validity and maturity of the obligation covered by the enforceable title (Article 804, Section 1 of the CPC). However, the enforcement authority has the duty to cancel the enforcement proceedings, where requested by the debtor, if before the date of filing the motion to initiate enforcement, the limitation period of a claim covered by the enforceable title has expired and the creditor has not proved that an event resulting in the suspension of the limitation period has occurred (Article 825, Section 1^1 of the CPC).

As of 1 January 2019, judicial enforcement officers have also been required to advise the debtors on their rights.[30] For example, pursuant to Article 763^1 of the CPC, judicial enforcement officers are required to advise the parties to and participants of the proceedings who are not represented by an attorney on the manner of and the deadline for complaining about the activities. If those persons are absent, the advice is given together with notice on the completion of the activities. Furthermore, judicial enforcement officers are required to provide the debtor during the first enforcement activity, as well as the parties and participants present during an activity performed outside the judicial enforcement officer's office, with an official form of complaint about the judicial enforcement officer's activities, unless a given activity is subject to a complaint submitted verbally (Article 767, Section 3^2 of the CPC).

Due to the information available in the media on irregularities during enforcement against movable assets, the legislator has considerably weakened the rule that existed hitherto, whereby the judicial enforcement officers had the right to attach every single thing that was actually in the debtor's possession. It was an actual presumption as a result of which the debtor or a third party were required to prove that a given thing was not the property of the debtor. Nowadays it is the judicial enforcement officer who should examine whether or not a given movable asset is the property of the debtor. In accordance with Article 845, Section 2 sentence 2 of the CPC, movable assets are not attached, unless it is evident from the facts established during the case

---

[29] P. Rylski, *Wnioski wierzyciela złożone "w celu szykany dłużnika" (art. 801 par 2 i 3 KPC)* [*Creditor's motion filed "to harass the debtor" (Article 801(2) and (3) of the CPC*] in: *Sądowe postępowanie…*, p. 126.

[30] A. Jarocha, *Obowiązek komornika sądowego w zakresie udzielania pouczeń w kontekście zmian Kodeksu postępowania cywilnego dokonanych ustawą o komornikach sądowych [Judicial enforcement officer's duty to give advice in light of amendments to the Civil Procedure Code pursuant to the Judicial Enforcement Officers Act]*, [in:] *Komornicy sądowi…*, p. 249.

that they are the property of the debtor. In practice, enforcement against movable assets is exposed to obstruction by the debtor who claims, without merit, that items in his/her possession are not his/her property.

7 Obligation of Payment of Mandatory Sum (*astreinte*) in Poland

As previously mentioned, the model of the Polish enforcement procedure was under the influence of the legal culture of Germanic countries (Germany and Austria). However, in recent years one can notice the influence of solutions applied in the Romanic systems. It is most significantly visible in the institution of the mandatory sum (penalty), which was introduced in 2012 to coerce the debtor—the solution was modelled on the French and Belgian construct of *astreinte* (Articles 1050^1–1051^1 of the CPC).[31] In the Polish legal system, that possibility was implemented to enforce non-monetary obligations in the form of activities that cannot be performed by any person other than the debtor and if the debtor fails to perform the duty to abstain from certain actions. Prior to the amendment of 2012, a fine for the State and arrest were the only coercion measures applied in the Polish legal system to enforce an activity that cannot be performed by any person other than the debtor and the performance of which depends solely on the debtor's will (Article 1050 of the CPC) and to enforce the duty to refrain from certain actions or not to disturb the actions of the creditor (Article 1051 of the CPC). Thus, the system effective in Poland was modelled on the solution adopted in Germany, Austria and, recently, also in Switzerland (the system of fines). The purpose of the coercion measures (the fine and the arrest) was to overcome the debtor's resistance and force them to take or omit a specific action. The new solution is another form of enforcing non-monetary obligations, in addition to the existing system of fines.

According to the new solution in Articles 1050^1, Section 1 and 1051^1, Section 1 of the CPC, upon the motion of the creditor, rather than threaten the debtor with the imposition of a fine, the court may, upon hearing the parties, threaten the debtor with an order to pay the creditor a specific sum of money per each day of delay in the performance of an action or for acting contrary to the duty, notwithstanding the claims the creditor might have in accordance with the general rules. When the debtor fails to take an action within the prescribed deadline or continues to violate the obligation, the court, upon the creditor's motion, will order the debtor to pay the sum of money to the creditor. A final and binding court order is an enforcement title for the creditor and there is no need to issue a writ of execution therefor. Upon

---

[31] H. Pietrzkowski, *Egzekucja prowadzona na podstawie art. 1050–1051^1 k.p.c. po nowelizacji dokonanej ustawą z 16 września 2011 r. [Enforcement pursuant to Article 1050–1051^1 of the CPC after the amendment by way of the Act of 16 September 2011]*, Polski Proces Cywilny 2012, No. 1, p. 45.

request of the creditor, the court may also increase the amount due to the creditor from the debtor.

As can be seen, the difference vis-à-vis the previous solutions lies in the fact that the fine is not ordered for the benefit of the State but rather for the benefit of the creditor. Furthermore, the amount is determined based on the length of time during which the debtor fails to fulfil the obligation or violates the obligation. The new solution was well received by the legal doctrine because it is an additional possibility of effective enforcement of non-monetary obligations. Furthermore, similar solutions were implemented to enforce the rulings of family courts concerning the removal of a minor child from parental authority and decisions concerning contacts with a child (Articles 598^{14} and 598^{15} ff of the CPC).

8 Conclusions

It is impossible to give an unequivocal evaluation of the most recent transformations in Polish procedural law. Apart from much needed and beneficial solutions, such as computerisation of enforcement proceedings or actions to counteract abuse by creditors, there have been many solutions that may give rise to concerns. The continuous efforts to reinforce solutions protecting the debtor, even at the expense of the enforcement effectiveness, is certainly problematic. It upsets the already quite fragile balance between the creditor's interest in satisfaction and the debtor's right to defence; as a consequence, the latter is favoured. Those changes are implemented by the political authorities under the influence of single media reports and they are supported by populist arguments. However, solutions that require judicial enforcement officers to be much more active in searching for the debtor's assets *ex officio* and implementation of instruments sanctioning the judicial enforcement officer's activities that are in violation of law are undoubtedly positive. The new model of enforcing non-monetary obligations in the form of a penalty for the benefit of the creditor and improvements resulting from, among other things, the implementation of an electronic auction when enforcing against movable assets is also a positive development.

References

Cichorska M (2019) Poszukiwanie majątku dłużnika przez komornika [Search of debtor's property by judicial enforcement officer]. In: Kulski R (ed) Komornicy sądowi i egzekucja sądowa w nowej rzeczywistości prawnej [Judicial enforcement officers and court enforcement proceedings in a new legal reality], Sopot, pp 279–284

Ereciński T (2005) Civil procedure. In: Frankowski T (ed) Introduction to Polish Law, Hague, pp 141–145

Kulski R (2010) Some remarks on the course od Polish electronic proceedings by writ of payment. In: Electronic and justice—present and future. Pecs 2010, p 17

Marciniak A (ed) (2016) Egzekucja sądowa w świetle przepisów z zakresu międzynarodowego postępowania cywilnego [Court enforcement proceedings in light of provisions under international civil law], pasim, Sopot
Marciniak A (2019) Sądowe postępowanie egzekucyjne w sprawach cywilnych [Court enforcement proceedings in civil cases], Warsaw, p 23
Misztal-Konecka J (2019) Postępowanie zabezpieczające i egzekucyjne w sprawach cywilnych [Interim remedy proceedings and enforcement proceedings in civil cases], Warsaw, p 201ff
Pietrzkowski H (2012) Egzekucja prowadzona na podstawie art. $1050–1051^1$ k.p.c. po nowelizacji dokonanej ustawą z 16 września 2011 r. [Enforcement pursuant to Article $1050–1051^1$ of the CPC after the amendment by way of the Act of 16 September 2011]. Polski Proces Cywilny (1):45
Rylski P (2019) Polish civil procedure: yesterday, today and tomorrow—some remarks about recent changes of procedural law in Poland. Bratislava Law Rev 2019 (1):139ff
Rylski P (2020) Covid-19 and the civil justice in Poland. Septentrio Rep (5):43–44. https://doi.org/10.7557/7.5469
Rylski P, Weitz K (2014) The impact of the Russian Civil Judicial Proceedings Act of 1864 on the Polish civil proceedings. Russian Law J 2014 (4):78
Staszewska E (2019) Quasi-pracownicze uprawnienia komornika na gruncie ustawy o komornikach sądowych [Quasi-employee rights of judicial enforcement officers under the Judicial Enforcement Officers Act]. In: Kulski R (ed) Komornicy sądowi i egzekucja sądowa w nowej rzeczywistości prawnej [Judicial enforcement officers and court enforcement proceedings in a new legal reality], Sopot, p 17ff
Weitz K (2006) Die Entwicklung des polnischen Zivilprozessrechts nach der politischen Wende im Jahre 1989. In: ZZPInt 2006, vol 11, p 89ff
Weitz K (2007) Czy nowa kodyfikacja postępowania cywilnego? [New codification of the civil procedure?]. Państwo i Prawo (3):17
Weitz K (2010) Die Bedeutung der Rezeption für die Entwicklung des polnischen Zivilprozessrechts. Ritsumeikan Law Rev. International Edition (27):141ff
Weitz K (2011) Probleme der Vollstreckung aus polnischer Sicht. In: Kengyel M, Harsági V (eds) Grenzüberschreitende Vollstreckung in der Europäischen Union, München, pp 184–185
Weitz K (2012) Reformen des Zivilprozessrechts in der Dritten Polnischen Republik. In: Sutter-Somm T, Harsági V (eds) Die Entwicklung des Zivilprozessrechts in Mitteleuropa um die Jahrtausendwende. Reform und Kodifikation—Tradition und Erneuerung, Zürich, Basel, Genf 2012, p 189ff
Zedler F (2011) Civil procedure. In: Dajczak W, Szwarc AJ, Wiliński P (eds) Handbook of Polish Law, Warsaw, pp 644–651
Zembrzuski T (2020) Zarządzenia sądu z urzędu a odpowiedzialność odszkodowawcza komornika sądowego i Skarbu Państwa [Court rulings ex officio vs liability of judicial enforcement officers and State Treasury for damages]. In: Jagieła J (ed) Sądowe postępowanie egzekucyjne [Court enforcement proceedings]. Nowe wyzwania i perspektywy [New challenges and perspectives], Warsaw, p 145ff

Piotr Rylski is a Doctor of Laws, Professor of the University at the Faculty of Law and Administration, University of Warsaw, and a member of the Supreme Court's Office of Studies and Analyses; legal adviser. The wide range of scientific interests covers the issues of civil and constitutional procedural law, as well as the practice of the distribution of justice, with particular emphasis placed on the practical aspects of applying civil procedural law and comparative procedural law. In the years 2011–2015, member of the problem team of the Polish Civil Law Codification Commission appointed for civil proceedings. Member of the Henri Capitant Association of Friends of the French Legal Culture (L' Association Henri Capitant des amis de la culture juridique française) and the International Association of Procedural Law (ORCID 0000-0002-5399-1624).

Karol Weitz (born 13 December 1974 in Rybno)—Polish lawyer, professor of legal sciences, full professor at the University of Warsaw, specialist in civil proceedings, Supreme Court judge. Curriculum vitae: In 2006, at the Faculty of Law and Administration of the University of Warsaw, on the basis of his scientific achievements and a monograph entitled National Jurisdiction in Civil Proceedings, he obtained the degree of doctor habilitated in law, specialization: civil proceedings. In 2012, the President of the Republic of Poland Bronisław Komorowski awarded him the title of professor of legal sciences. He was appointed full professor of the University of Warsaw. On the 10th of December, 2014, he became a judge of the Supreme Court (ORCID: 0000-0003-0408-5374).

Effective Enforcement of Creditor's Rights in Civil Execution Through Effective Discovery of Debtor's Assets in Taiwan

Kuan-Ling Shen

1 Development of the Taiwanese Compulsory Enforcement Act

The Taiwanese Compulsory Enforcement Act was promulgated and came into force in 1940 and was amended significantly once in 1975. Subsequently, due to the rapid growth in commerce and the change in the socioeconomic structure, the original Act became inappropriate, and it led to a comprehensive review and drafting of a brand-new Act. Finally, in 1996, the new Act was promulgated and enforced. However, economic circumstances shifted once again, causing a soar in the volume of the cases related to compulsory enforcement and delays in their settlement. As a result, the workload of enforcement courts grew heavier with time and gradually stirred discontent among the people, and thus the new Compulsory Enforcement Act was amended once more in 2000 to improve the efficiency of compulsory enforcement. Furthermore, as some provisions did not meet the constitutional requirements pertaining to enforcement, they were therefore declared unconstitutional by the Taiwanese Grand Justice. In 2010, the "Act to Implement the International Covenant on Civil and Political Rights and the International Covenant on Economic, Social, and Cultural Rights" went into force in Taiwan. To protect the basic rights of individuals, the requirements in the Compulsory Enforcement regarding arrest and taking into custody were amended and made anew in 2011 while taking into account Article 11 of the International Covenant on Civil and Political Rights (hereinafter ICCPR).

K.-L. Shen (✉)
National Taiwan University, Taipei, Taiwan
e-mail: kshen@ntu.edu.tw

M. Deguchi (ed.), *Effective Enforcement of Creditors' Rights*,
Ius Gentium: Comparative Perspectives on Law and Justice 91,
https://doi.org/10.1007/978-981-16-5609-5_20

2 Creditor's Property Rights and Debtor's Duty to Report Assets

The individual's right of claims under private law falls within the scope of property rights guaranteed under Article 15 of the Constitution. The state, in order to protect the rights of a creditor in private law, established the civil compulsory enforcement system. A creditor with an enforcement title may apply to the enforcement court to use compulsory means against the debtors' assets and satisfy the creditor's claim. Although debtors have the obligation to endure the enforcement, legislators may still balance the realization of creditors' rights in private law and the necessity to protect debtors' fundamental rights.

In order to sufficiently protect the rights and interests of creditors while enforcing private laws, Article 19 of the Compulsory Enforcement Act was amended as follows, "If the enforcement court deems a compulsory enforcement case necessary to investigate, it can order the creditor to investigate and report, or conduct investigation ex officio (Paragraph 1). The enforcement court may investigate tax or other authorities concerned, groups, or anyone else who may have knowledge of the debtor's assets or financial status. The one being investigated shall not refuse, except in the case of an individual with a reasonable ground (Paragraph 2)."

In addition, the debtor is under the obligation to inform the status of how his or her assets change during a certain period before the commencement of compulsory enforcement.

Where the discovered property of the debtor is insufficient to repay the claim for the petitioned compulsory enforcement or the debtor's property to be submitted cannot be located, the enforcement court may, upon the creditor's petition or on its own authority, determine a period and order the debtor to accurately report his or her property subject to the compulsory enforcement within one year prior to the expiration of the determined period (Article 20 Paragraph 1).

If the debtor violates the obligation of reporting and does not provide a report or provides a fraudulent report, the enforcement court may, upon the creditor's petition or on its own authority, order the debtor to furnish the security or to perform its enforcement obligations within a time limit.

If the debtor does not furnish adequate security or perform its obligations within the time limit, the enforcement court may, upon the creditor's petition or on its own authority, place the debtor into custody after interrogating the debtor and confirming that the debtor is able to report his/her property situation.

The characteristics of Taiwan's law are:

1. The debtor's property report can only be presented after the commencement of the compulsory enforcement proceedings.
2. The enforcement court may, upon the creditor's petition or on its own authority, order the debtor to report his or her property situation.
3. The elements of Property Discovery: (1) enforcement title (2) after the commencement of the enforcement proceedings (3) the property of the debtor is insufficient to repay the claim for the petitioned compulsory enforcement.

However, for the third element, the provisions do not expressly stipulate that the debtor shall be accorded an opportunity to be heard, so there are doubts about the lack of procedural protections.

4. How should the debtor do the property discovery? There is no explicit provision in our country's law to determine the period of discovery. In practice, the judge can decide whether to designate a court session or not for the debtor to report the inventory of properties.
5. Where the debtor refuses to report his/her inventory of properties and does not furnish adequate security or fulfill his/her obligations, the court may place the debtor into custody.

3 Investigating the Status Quo of Real Properties

The actual status quo of an attached real estate may influence its evaluation, the hand-over after auction-sale proceeding, and the value at which bidders are willing to purchase. Thus, in order to prevent debtors or third parties from hindering the enforcement procedure, the enforcement judge or the court clerk may unlock a closed door and enter the real estate (Article 77–1 Paragraph 1) in order to facilitate the enforcement proceeding.

Article 53 also empowers the enforcement judge and the court clerk to demand the debtor to present relevant documents. If the debtor refuses to make statements or present documents without reasonable grounds, or if he or she gives any false statement or false documentation, the enforcement court may take the debtor into custody either upon the creditor's application or ex officio; however, this can only be done after an interrogation of the debtor and with a deeming that it is apparently difficult to investigate the status quo of the real estate without taking the debtor into custody.

To investigate the situations of immovable properties or other related right and relationship, the enforcement judge or clerk may carry it out by opening the door lock to enter the immovable property, interrogating the debtor or the third party in possession of the property, and ordering them to submit the relevant documents. The enforcement judge or clerk may also investigate the police and other related authorities and groups. The respondents may not refuse. Moreover, if the third party refuses to appear, the enforcement court may impose a fine of no more than NTD 15,000 by a ruling.

4 Limitation of Debtor's Freedom

To guarantee the fulfillment of the creditor's private rights and to force the debtor to perform his or her obligations, the Act regulates that the enforcement court may issue an arrest warrant to take the debtor into custody under specific circumstances.

However, the restrictions to living quarters may restrain the debtor's freedom less heavily than an arrest warrant and can thus urge the debtor to fulfill the obligation, the provisions to restrict the debtor's living quarters was therefore added to facilitate the compulsory enforcement (Article 22 and 25).

As judicial associate officers are charged with all execution matters with the exception of arrest and taking into custody, the Compulsory Enforcement Act provides that judicial associate officers may request the enforcement court to arrest the debtor, and the court may hand over the arrested debtor to the associate judicial officer for questioning (Article 21 Paragraph 2 to Paragraph 4). After questioning, the associate judicial officers shall report to the enforcement court to order custody if necessary (Article 22 Paragraph 6).

Before issuing a custody order, the enforcement court shall order the debtors to provide securities or to perform his/her obligation within a specific period, or else they face a restriction on their residence. The measure of taking into custody shall be used as a last resort. The legal effect of violating execution orders was also amended (Article 22 Paragraph 1 to Paragraph 5).

Where the debtor is required to perform or not to perform a specific act in accordance with the enforcement court's order but fails to do so, in light of the protection of human rights, the court may place him or her into custody when the requirements of Article 21 are met. Because custody is the ultimate means of achieving compulsory execution, the court shall first impose a penalty on the debtor and determine a time limit for him or her to perform. If the debtor still refuses to carry out his or her obligation, the court may then place the debtor into custody.

Kuan-Ling Shen is Professor of Procedural Law at National Taiwan University and was also the Vice Dean of NTU Law from the year of 2017 to 2019. She earned her Ph.D. from Heidelberg University, Germany in 1999 and dedicated herself to comparative legal studies. Her research interests include civil procedure law, non-contentious law, arbitration law, family proceedings law, and bankruptcy law. She received the Senior Fulbright Research Grant to be a visiting scholar at the School of Law at the University of California, Berkeley during the 2013–2014 academic year. Professor Shen is a member of IAPL and also serves as a board member of the Research Foundation of Civil Procedure Law in Taiwan. She has published extensive articles and 6 books on Civil Procedural Law, Arbitration and Alternative Dispute Resolution.

The Problem of the Disclosure of the Debtor's Assets in Enforcement Proceedings

From a Comparative Point of View of Korean Law

Moon-hyuck Ho

1 Introduction

There is a saying that debtors are struggling enough to hang themselves in the judgment proceedings, and creditors in the execution proceedings. It is highly likely that the debtor will obstruct execution by hiding the assets subject to execution, or falsely transferring them to another person. Even if the debtor does not do this, it is very important for the creditor to identify the debtor's assets accurately. Thus, an institutional mechanism is needed to make it easier for creditors to identify the debtor's assets, prevent the debtor's obstruction of execution in advance, or impose sanctions on such obstruction to enhance the effectiveness of the execution. In Korea, there is 'assets disclosure process' and 'assets check process' as a system to identify the assets of an unfaithful debtor. Assets check process is used when the result of the assets disclosure process is insufficient. And 'the list of defaulters' was set up as a sanction against insincere debtors.

2 Assets Disclosure Process

Assets disclosure process refers to a procedure for the disclosure of assets that requires the debtor at the court's order (i) to submit a list of assets subject to execution and the disposition within a certain period of time at the request of the creditor (if the debtor fails to fulfill the obligation under the executory title for the purpose of paying money), and (ii) to take an oath of its authenticity.

M. Ho (✉)
Seoul National University School of Law, Seoul, Republic of Korea
e-mail: homoon@snu.ac.kr

M. Deguchi (ed.), *Effective Enforcement of Creditors' Rights*,
Ius Gentium: Comparative Perspectives on Law and Justice 91,
https://doi.org/10.1007/978-981-16-5609-5_21

The creditor may apply to the court for an order to disclose if the debtor fails to implement the executory title, and the court may issue the order accordingly (section 62 (1) Civil Execution Act(=CEA)). The requirements for an application for a disclosure order are as follows: ① The debtor bears the monetary debt under the executory title, ② the debtor has not performed the obligation, ③ the creditor meets the requirements for the commencement of execution, especially the creditor has been granted the executory title, and ④ the debtor's assets cannot be easily found (section 62 (2) CEA).

It is the same as the new procedure in Germany that the process of assets disclosure can be taken at the beginning of the execution process. However, what is different from Germany, which has this procedure as a bailiff's job, is that in Korea, the enforcement court is in charge of it. Germany provides access to the centralized register of disclosed assets through the central Internet portal, which Korea does not have. However, in Germany, the number of access to the information is limited to once in a two-year period according to the constitutional Principle of Proportionality.

Items to be stated include ① assets subject to execution, ② assets paid sold by the debtor within one year prior to the service of the disclosure order, ③ assets sold by the debtor to third parties other than relatives within a certain range within the one year prior to the service of the disclosure order, and ④ free disposal of the debtor's assets within two years before the service of the disclosure order (section 64 (2) CEA). The purpose of not limiting to the debtor's current assets is to make the falsely transferred assets subject to execution by returning them to the debtor.

The debtor may raise an objection to the disclosure order. If the debtor does not file an objection or the objection is rejected as being unfounded, the court designates a date for the disclosure of the assets, requires the debtor to attend and notifies the creditor of the date (section 64 (1) CEA). On the date for the disclosure of assets, the debtor must be present to submit a list of assets (section 64 CEA) and must swear an oath (section 65 CEA). Violators of disclosure obligations are subject to detention, imprisonment or fines (section 68 CEA).

There is also a difference between Germany and Korea in terms of sanctions against violators of the stated obligations. In Germany, detention is provided, and in Korea, punishment such as imprisonment and fines can be imposed as well. But the punishment in Korea is excessive and beyond the scope of the norm's purpose.

3 Assets Check Process

In the event that the debtor violates his obligation in the process of assets disclosure or that the creditor is unable to obtain satisfaction from the assets listed by the debtor, the competent court of the disclosure proceeding may, at the request of the creditor who applied for the disclosure, inquire about the assets of the debtor to the public institution, financial institution, or organization that manages the information about the individual's credit and assets (section 74 CEA).

The requirements of assets check process are as follows: ① The debtor must have been ordered to disclose the assets in the assets disclosure proceeding, and ② one of the following reasons must exist: (i) the address correction order issued by the court to the creditor due to the unserved court order to disclose the debtor's assets is not fulfilled by the creditor owing to the reason of the public service under section 194 (1) Civil Procedure Act, (ii) the assets in the list of assets submitted by the debtor alone in the process of the assets disclosure are insufficient to obtain satisfaction of the creditor's claim, or (iii) the debtor is not present at the stated date in the procedure of assets disclosure, refuses to submit the list of assets or to take an oath, or submits a false list of assets (section 74 (1) CEA).

The Korean law is different from the German law in that it includes cases where an assets disclosure order cannot be served.

Once the requirements of the assets check process are met, the court refers the check to the head of the agency or organization to identify the assets in debtor's name by the computer network (section 36 (1) of the Supreme Court Regulation). Public institutions, financial institutions, organizations, etc. that are requested to check the debtor's assets may not refuse such inquiry without justifiable reasons (section 74 (4) CEA).

According to the German law, the bailiff will inform the debtor about the information request only 4 weeks after the transmittal of the information about the account to the creditor. This regulation does not exist in Korean law.

4 List of Defaulters

The defaulter list is a system that performs indirect enforcement by listing debtors who have defaulted debts for a certain reason and allowing the general public to read them.

The reasons for the listing are as follows (section 70 (1) CEA): ① When an executory title that ordered the payment of money is finalized or the debtor fails to fulfill the obligation within six months after the executory title is prepared (except for title due to provisional execution notice), ② when the debtor is absent from the stated date or did not submit a list of assets in the process of assets disclosure, or when the debtor refuses to take an oath, or ③ when the debtor submitted false assets lists.

If the above reasons are recognized and the enforcement is not easy, the court shall judge by decision to put the debtor on the defaulter list. The term 'not easy' means not only when the debtor's assets is not easily found, but also when it is easily found, but the enforcement nevertheless takes a lot of time and money. Conversely, if the above reasons are not recognized, or even if the above reasons are recognized, but there is an obvious reason for an easy enforcement, the court shall reject the application by decision (section 71 (2) CEA).

After the court has decided to register the debtor in the list, it takes the following measures: ① Keep the list of defaulted persons in the court, ② send the copies of the register to the head of the city, district, town of the debtor's address, ③ send the copies to the heads of financial institutions and related organizations, such as the National Federation of Banks, and ④ provide the original and the copies placed in the court for viewing or copying (but not publishing the list).

The court makes a decision on the removal of the debtor's name from the list of defaulters (section 73 CEA): ① When it is proven that the debt has expired due to reimbursement or other reasons, or ② when 10 years have passed after debtor was added to the list. The court decides on the debtor's application in the case of ①, and ex officio in the case of ②. The court shall notify the head of an administrative office or organization with the copy of the list to clear the name of the debtor on the list, and the person who receives this notice shall follow the notice of the court.

5 Problem of Priority Principle

Principle of priority in execution proceedings could cause problems, according to the statement. It points out that creditors would race to start execution quickly, and in that race, information-driven creditors, such as banks, would enforce it first, so that the claims of other creditors cannot be satisfied at all. It is agreeable that there may be such problems with execution by taking priority principle. However, the reality of the Korean law, which adopted the principle of equal treatment, shows that the problem in Korea is greater. It is common for countries with a legal system that clearly distinguishes between the execution procedure as an individual execution and the insolvency procedure as a general execution to adopt the priority principle, and for countries that do not distinguish between them to adopt the principle of equal treatment. However, if the principle of equal treatment is adopted while distinguishing the two proceedings, as in Korea, the execution process can actually be an insolvency procedure because even creditors who have not obtained executory title could participate in the distribution process. These results are undesirable for both the creditor and the debtor. It is said that the priority principle creates a race for creditors, but the abolition of individual execution would cause more severe problems than that. In addition, although banks and other informative creditors are said to have an advantage due to the priority principle, they anyhow have priority rights in most obligations such as setting up collateral rights, so there will not be much difference in substance. And when multiple creditors with executory title are racing to execute each other quickly, it would be reasonable to treat it as insolvency, not individual execution.

6 International Collaboration

It is important for Asian countries to follow the example that international collaboration is well established in the process of execution among EU countries. International cooperation in execution is of great importance today, as the relationship between creditors and debtors in different countries is increasing significantly, and the need for execution of assets in foreign countries is increasing accordingly. But even though Asian countries have as much in common as European countries in terms of cultural tradition, they have not built up deep trust in the judiciary because of differences in political and economic systems. Also, there is a wide variety of the credibility of judiciary in Asian countries. Therefore, it will likely take a considerable amount of time to have the meaningful cooperation as among EU countries. This issue is in line with international collaboration to protect human rights of Asian citizens, given that smooth enforcement also contributes to the protection of fundamental rights. Only when the judicial systems of each country in Asia have a similar level of credibility will international cooperation be realizable in both areas of enforcement and human rights protection.

Moon-hyuck HO Professor Emeritus. Seoul National University School of Law. Education: Feb. 1972 College of Law, Seoul National University (Bachelor of Law), Aug. 1976 Graduate School, Seoul National University (Master of Law), Dec. 1985 Albert Ludwigs-Universtität Freiburg (Dr. Iuris). Academic Appointments: Sep. 1978—Aug. 1980 College of Law & Political Science, Yeungnam University (Fulltime Lecturer), Sep. 1980—Feb. 1986, College of Law & Political Science, Yeungnam University (Assistant Professor), Jun. 1986—Sep. 1988 College of Law, Seoul National University (Fulltime Lecturer), Oct. 1988—Sep. 1992 College of Law, SNU (Assistant Professor), Oct. 1992—Sep. 1997 College of Law, SNU (Associate Professor). Oct. 1997—Feb. 2009 College of Law, SNU (Professor) Mar. 2009—Aug. 2013 School of Law, SNU (Professor), Since Sep. 2013 Emeritus, SNU. Courses Taught: Civil Procedure; ADR; Judicial System; Law of Enforcement; Comparative Procedural Law; Academic Services: Jun. 1989—Feb. 1992 Associate Dean for Student Affairs, College of Law, SNU, Jun. 1996—Jun. 1998 Associate Dean for Academic Affairs, College of Law, SNU, Apr. 1999—Apr. 2001 Chief Editor, University Newspaper, SNU, Nov. 2005—May 2006 Vice President, University Senate, SNU, Jun. 2006—May 2008 Dean, College of Law, SNU, Jun. 2009—Mar. 2013 President, Faculty Association, SNU. Academic Associations: Since Mar. 1980 Member, Association of Civil Case Law Studies, Mar. 2006—Feb. 2008 President, Korea Civil Procedure Association, Aug. 2007—Nov. 2019 Council Member, International Association of Procedural Law, Jan. 2013—Oct. 2014 President, Organizing Committee of IAPL Annual Conference 2014 Seoul, Korea. Professional Activities: Feb. 2008—Jul. 2008 President, Korean Association of Law Schools, Feb. 2016—Jan. 2018 President, Judicial Policy Research Institute

Some Characteristics of the Recourse to Debtors' Finances and Their Other Assets in Russia

Anastasiya Chekmareva

Abstract The article covers the most urgent issues related to development and improvement of enforcement proceedings in the Russian Federation. The author provides a brief overview of the enforcement agencies system alongside with the description of the way enforcement proceedings are initiated. The research of the enforcement agencies' activities, which are aimed at the recourse to the debtors' finances has revealed complexity and inconsistencies in the procedures. Special attention is paid to the new methods of working with individuals who are in debt. These methods include urging him/her to pay the debts by limitations of some personal rights. A separate section of the article is about the problems of skip tracing both within Russian territories and abroad. The author concludes that it is necessary to widely use information technologies and create the tools for fast information exchange that might facilitate skip tracing. She also highlights the need to work out an adjustment for voluntary debt payments that could be a sign of some social consensus.

1 Introduction

Today's Russian society calls for special attention to enforcement proceedings. Enforcement proceedings in Russia are a cornerstone of the tools for human rights protection. Any civil litigation must end up with the implementation of a judicial decision. Indeed, while implementing rights, obligations, and interests guaranteed by law and confirmed by judicial decisions, true legal protection manifests itself. Shortcomings in legislation and enforcement proceedings have a negative impact on social relations. A search for non-legal ways to protect certain interests can provoke crime in various spheres of production and in society on the whole. The implementation of a judicial decision is a barometer of a socially fair solution of the conflict as well as of the rightfulness of an applied law. It also shows how effective justice

A. Chekmareva (✉)
Department of Civil Procedure, Saratov State Law Academy, 410056 Volskaya,1, Saratov, Russia
e-mail: anastasiya-chekmareva@yandex.ru

M. Deguchi (ed.), *Effective Enforcement of Creditors' Rights*,
Ius Gentium: Comparative Perspectives on Law and Justice 91,
https://doi.org/10.1007/978-981-16-5609-5_22

is.[1] In any country, enforcement proceedings play a very important role. Though the models of enforcement proceedings are different, the problems of law enforcement are very much alike. That is why comparative law studies are not only scientifically contributive but also trigger effective legal regulations and economic developments.[2]

2 Enforcement Agencies in Russia

Since 1997, the enforcement of jurisdictional acts in Russia is done by the public officials, namely by the bailiffs, working for the Federal Bailiffs Service.[3] Legitimate requirements of a bailiff must be strictly fulfilled within all the territories of the Russian Federation.

3 Agencies, Organizations, and Citizens, Fulfilling the Requirements Imposed by Court Rulings, Rulings of Other Bodies and Officials

In cases, specified by Russian federal legislation, the requirements imposed by court rulings, rulings of other bodies and officials must be fulfilled by the bodies, organizations, officials, and citizens, including the state bodies, local authorities, banks, and other credit institutions. All of them contribute to enforcement proceedings due to the obligations. Banks, for example, authorize withdrawals from accounts held by the debtor after receiving the enforcement document. Offices of the Federal Registration Service recognize rights to ownership and debar debtors from these rights according to judicial decisions. There are organizations that assess, store, and dispose the debtors' assets.

[1] Chekmareva AV (2009) Zashchita prav uchastnikov ispolnitelnogo proizvodstva (The protection of rights in enforcement proceedings). Moscow, p. 39.

[2] Yarkov V (2012) Harmonization of civil procedure law in the Eurasian Countries in the light of civil justice development in the Post-Soviet Region. In: Maleshin D (ed) Civil Procedure in Cross-Cultural Dialogue: Eurasia Context, Moscow, p. 354.

[3] The Federal Russian Law "On the Enforcement Agencies of the Russian Federation". The law with the latest revisions can be found here (in Russian): http://www.consultant.ru/document/cons_doc_LAW_15281/. Accessed 6 Jan 2020.

4 Initiation of Enforcement Proceedings

Enforcement proceedings are initiated by a bailiff on the basis of both the claimant's application and an enforcement document. The enforcement document can be a writ of execution, a court order, a notarized agreement to pay alimony, a Russian Pension Fund Act or a Russian Social Insurance Fund Act on recovering funds from the debtor, etc. The bailiff prepares an order on institution of the enforcement proceedings. The order specifies the time limits for voluntary payment of the debts (five days) and informs the debtor that if he/she does not pay the debts before the term is expired, it will be done by law, regardless of his/her will. In case of involuntary payment, the debtor must pay the enforcement fees and all the other costs.

5 The Recourse to Debtors' Finances and Their Other Assets

Under the principle of adequacy, the relief sought by the claimant must not exceed the enforcement measures, i.e. the claimant cannot take more than the debtor owes to him/her. The amount of the debt is specified in the enforcement document (plus the enforcement fees and all the other costs if the debtor has not fulfilled the requirements voluntarily). The recourse is firstly related to the debtor's finances (rubles and foreign currencies) as well as to other objects of value, including accounts and deposits in banks and other credit institutions. These banks and credit institutions are obliged to fulfill the requirements to withdraw the funds, which are referred to in the enforcement document. Omission to fulfill the requirements entails a fine for the organizations in question (50% of the sum that should have been withdrawn but not more than one million rubles). If the debtor does not have enough money, his other assets get seized.

6 Locating Debtors' Finances and Their Other Assets

When it is unknown if the debtor has enough money and other assets, the bailiff makes a request to the tax authorities, property rights registration authorities, banks, and other credit institutions. The amount of the debt is always taken into consideration. The claimant also can apply to a tax authority, asking for the necessary information. The information that might be requested is as follows:

1. The names and locations of the banks and other credit institutions where the debtor's accounts have been opened.
2. The account numbers, the amount of money, and monetary movements (rubles and foreign currencies).

3. Other objects of value, belonging to the debtor and being kept in banks and other credit institutions.

All the mentioned organizations have to provide the information within seven days after receiving a request.

The Code of the Russian Federation for Administrative Offences provides for the liability for infringement of laws on enforcement proceedings, and not only debtors can be involved. These are the cases when legitimate requirements of a bailiff have not been fulfilled or the information about a debtor's property status has proved to be false. Those who are liable are punished with a monetary penalty. The fine is 2000–2500 rubles for the ordinary citizens, 15,000–20,000 rubles for the officials, and 50,000–100,000 rubles for the legal persons.[4]

7 Skip Tracing

One of the major problems, arising while jurisdictional acts are being enforced, is the desire of the debtors to escape from the enforcement agencies and to conceal the information about their finances and property. The main part of the judicial decisions execution is skip tracing. That is what Russian enforcement agencies mostly do both in foreign countries and in the Russian Federation.

Since 2012, the Federal Bailiffs Service is exclusively in charge of skip tracing. The Service has a special skip tracing department. The process starts only in case the bailiffs' actions have not led to locating the debtor or his/her property. In 2018, skip tracing measures taken by the Federal Bailiffs Service made it possible to find 81.4 thousand debtors, including 52.9 thousand alimony debtors. Russian bailiffs also located 7.9 thousand vehicles, which belonged to debtors (405 vehicles belonged to alimony debtors).[5] It is allowed to look only for the property that belongs to the debtor. An official order is needed to start skip tracing in Russia and in foreign countries, according to the international agreements, which cover these issues.

At the international level, the steps of civil skip tracing in foreign countries are determined by the international agreements on mutual legal aid, which Russia is a party to. The process requires a complex and time-taking exchange of documents. There are still many countries that do not have legal aid agreements with Russia, and many of the existing ones were signed before the modern information technologies

---

[4] The Code of the Russian Federation for Administrative Offences (in Russian): http://www.consultant.ru/document/cons_doc_LAW_34661/1b455f796f18745c9e1380c521d5dd180ccc5b4a/, http://www.consultant.ru/document/cons_doc_LAW_34661/1b455f796f18745c9e1380c521d5dd180ccc5b4a/. Accessed 6 Jan 2020.

[5] The Summary Report on the Operational Results of the Federal Bailiffs Service in 2018 (in Russian): http://fssprus.ru/files/fssp/db/files/02019/itogovyj_doklad_za_2018_god_20193181711.pdf. Accessed 6 Jan 2020.

era.[6] In 2009, the Federal Bailiffs Service joined the International Union of Judicial Officers. We believe that it is necessary to create a centralized database, containing information about large debtors and their property. Such database could be built by accumulating the data from the International Union of Judicial Officers member states.

By the general rule, fixed in the enforcement document, a Russian bailiff should get a judgment enforced within two months. In case of skip tracing, the deadline can be extended.

A bailiff must initiate a skip tracing process in a number of cases, which are fixed by law. Skip tracing starts when it is necessary:

1. To protect the interests of the Russian Federation and the interests of its constituents if the debtor owes more than 10,000 rubles (about 130 euro).
2. To recover alimony.
3. To pay damages for injuries or compensate the death of the breadwinner.
4. To compensate harm caused by a crime.
5. To make a convicted person perform the community service.
6. To recover penalties for crimes.

When there are property claims of private creditors, skip tracing aimed at locating the debtor or his/her property can be initiated only if the debt is more than 10,000 rubles (about 130 €).

Locating a debtor or his/her property is done in the following way:

The operational information is requested from banks.
Identity and official personal documents are checked if there is a ground to believe that a person and/or his/her property is being looked for.

The officials question individuals who might have some relevant information. The supposed debtor is also questioned. It is necessary to note that by law these individuals and the supposed debtor are in no way responsible for refusal to answer the questions or for lying.

On the whole, the process includes lots of inquiries, documents examinations, and the inspection of the property in question. It is about rooms, buildings, structures, and plots of land, which may be occupied by the person sought or belong to him/her. Vehicles are also on the list.[7]

The public bailiffs who are involved in a skip tracing process can use the information received from a private detective if the creditor has employed the services of a private detective agency.

Very often the bailiffs cooperate with various public sector bodies. For example, there are co-operative activities with the General Administration for Traffic Safety.

---

[6] Dmitriev VV (2012) Ispolzovanie edinogo informatsionnogo prostranstva pri rozyske i realizatsii imushchestva dolzhnikov (The use of the shared information space while locating and disposing the debtors' assets). In: Nauchnoe mnenie (Scientific opinion), 10, p. 48.

[7] The Federal Russian Law "On Enforcement Proceedings". The law with the latest revisions can be found here (in Russian): http://www.consultant.ru/document/cons_doc_LAW_71450/. Accessed 6 Jan 2020.

Policemen from the Administration and the bailiffs can stop an offender's car and check up the information systems to know if the road traffic offender is a debtor. Besides, to get the information about a debtor's agreements for the provision of the Internet services as well as his/her cell phone numbers, and the sums paid for the services, Russian bailiffs cooperate with different commercial organizations. After submitting a request to the Internet service providers, a bailiff can find out where the debtor's computer is located. This information is used to inform the debtor about the execution proceedings against him/her and about the necessity to pay the debt. One more innovative way to collect information about a debtor and his/her property status is the use of the open-access information on social networks. The analysis of the debtors' profiles contributes to discovering both the people and the property. The search has become more efficient in many Russian regions due to the use of the registering bodies databases. The Regional Directorates for Internal Affairs in Transport cooperate with the regional departments of the Russian Federal Bailiffs Service and provide them with the information about the debtors who buy tickets.

When a debtor is found, he/she may be brought to the nearest bailiffs' office. However, in this case problems can arise. The debtor can escape once again, change his/her place of residence, move to another town, etc. It is because bailiffs do not have a right to make the debtor keep the place of residence.

8 Other Measures that Motivate Debtors to Fulfill the Requirements Specified in the Enforcement Document

There are measures, which do not mean the recourse to the debtor's assets but are aimed at urging him/her to fulfill the requirements. One of such measures is a ban to travel abroad until the debt is cancelled. Due to debts, more than seven million Russians could not leave the country in 2018.[8] That year, the measure helped to recover about 72.1 billion rubles.

Alongside with the travel ban, driving license revocation is also widely used. The debtor cannot get his/her driving license back until the debt is totally or partially cancelled. This measure is applicable in cases of alimony debts, damages for injuries, and compensations for the death of the breadwinner. On top of that, driving license revocation applies to property damage and emotional distress caused by a crime as well as to various non-property-related childcare issues and fines for violation of traffic rules.

[8] Due to debts, more than seven million Russians could not leave the country in 2018 (in Russian). https://pravo.ru/news/209465/. Accessed 6 Jan 2020.

9 Conclusion

Summing up, we would like to note the necessity to further improve the Russian legislation, covering the opportunities for effective skip tracing. First of all, it should be done with the help of the up-to-date information space. At the international level, it is necessary to work out the tools for fast information exchange. Such tools would assist skip tracing not only in Russia but in other countries. Effective skip tracing problems solving would certainly improve the effectiveness of execution proceedings, the quality of a creditor's rights protection, and credibility of justice related to the judicial decision's execution. Execution proceedings are very important in any country. However, we believe that alongside with working out and improving the enforcement tools, it is essential to build the environment for voluntary debt payment, which is rather undeveloped in modern Russia. Every year approximately 20% of debts specified in enforcement documents are paid voluntarily.

References

Chekmareva AV (2009) Zashchita prav uchastnikov ispolnitelnogo proizvodstva (The protection of rights in enforcement proceedings). Moscow, p 39

Dmitriev VV (2012) Ispolzovanie edinogo informatsionnogo prostranstva pri rozyske i realizatsii imushchestva dolzhnikov (The use of the shared information space while locating and disposing the debtors' assets). In: Nauchnoe mnenie (Scientific opinion), vol 10, p 48

Due to debts, more than seven million Russians could not leave the country in 2018 (in Russian). https://pravo.ru/news/209465/. Accessed 6 Jan 2020

The Code of the Russian Federation for Administrative Offences (in Russian). http://www.consultant.ru/document/cons_doc_LAW_34661/1b455f796f18745c9e1380c521d5dd180ccc5b4a/, http://www.consultant.ru/document/cons_doc_LAW_34661/1b455f796f18745c9e1380c521d5dd180ccc5b4a/. Accessed 6 Jan 2020

The Federal Russian Law "On Enforcement Proceedings". The law with the latest revisions can be found here (in Russian). http://www.consultant.ru/document/cons_doc_LAW_71450/. Accessed 6 Jan 2020

The summary report on the operational results of the federal bailiffs Service in 2018 (in Russian). http://fssprus.ru/files/fssp/db/files/02019/itogovyj_doklad_za_2018_god_20193181711.pdf. Accessed 6 Jan 2020

Yarkov V (2012) Harmonization of civil procedure law in the Eurasian Countries in the light of civil justice development in the Post-Soviet Region. In: Maleshin D (ed) Civil procedure in cross-cultural dialogue: Eurasia context, Moscow, p 354

Anastasiya Chekmareva Date of birth: 30.11.1978, Position: Professor, Head of the master's program «Judicial protection of civil rights and enforcement proceedings»

Academic degree: doctor of law; Education: Saratov State Academy of Law, jurisprudence department (1995–2000), qualification—lawyer, postgraduate studies (2000–2003)—Diploma in Law, doctorate (2012–2015)—Diploma Doctor of Law.

Training: The program of advanced training for teachers in the field of jurisprudence: Saratov State Academy of Law—2005, 2010, 2017. Work experience: Saratov State Academy of Law, department civil procedure (2000–present); Member of the Dissertation Council for the defense of doctoral and master's theses (2016—present).

Subject taught: "Civil Procedure", "Judicial Evidence and Proofs in Civil Procedure", "Administrative Proceedings", "Alternative Dispute Resolution", Research experience.

2003—Defense of the thesis (Candidate of Law), 2015—Defense of the thesis (Doctor of Law), Participates in international, Russian, regional conferences in Russia, Ukraine, Belarus, Greece, Germany, Japan, etc. 140 scientific and educational publications, including 4 monographs, textbooks, comments of legislation, courses, lectures, articles.

Awards: Diploma for a major contribution to the development of legal science and the improvement of the domestic legal system: the Committee of the State Duma of the Russian Federation on civil, criminal, arbitration and procedural legislation; Saratov Regional Court, etc.

Argentina: Notes on the Effective Enforcement of Judgments in Civil Cases

Eduardo Oteiza

Abstract The problem of the effectiveness of civil justice in enforcing judgments is addressed in this document in the context of Argentine procedural law. The main objective is to examine the particular aspects of the Argentine model, chiefly characterized by formalism, a fragmented approach to the proceedings and general inefficiency. In general terms, the overriding issue in Argentina is the separation between the phase of the proceedings which culminates in an agreed judgment and the phase where it is executed. The lack of a coherent model for application, which springs from the disjointed nature of the proceedings, whereby the phase leading to a judicial decision is cut off from that which should achieve that purpose, explains the bureaucratization of the latter.

1 Compliance with the Ruling and Due Process

The enforcement of a judicial decision, in terms of providing adequate legal protection, entails observing how such a safeguard can become operational. This includes determining whether it is carried out in timely fashion and achieves the results envisaged by the sentence.

Civil enforcement has traditionally been considered a second-ranking issue in Latin American procedural culture. Procedural doctrine has shown more interest in the course taken when the complaint is filed and concluding in the ruling, than what happens afterwards. The general view seems to be that the proceedings and their guarantees form a debate neatly ending with the final judgment, and that the enforcement stage is best left to the bailiffs and the means allocated by the State to bring this about. This is an error of focus. Both phases, if one arbitrarily takes this binary approach, have equal weight. They are both consequences of the same event and hence the course of action prior to the final judgment is every bit as important as the mechanisms employed to enforce it. The right to due process encompasses the

E. Oteiza (✉)
National University of La Plata, La Plata, Argentina
e-mail: eduardo.oteiza@outlook.es

M. Deguchi (ed.), *Effective Enforcement of Creditors' Rights*,
Ius Gentium: Comparative Perspectives on Law and Justice 91,
https://doi.org/10.1007/978-981-16-5609-5_23

entire debate and is only fulfilled when the restoration enshrined in the judgment is made to its satisfaction.

As pointed out by Baptista da Silva,[1] this approach is rooted in the Roman-Canon law tradition. A private judge, the *iudex* of formulary procedure, and subsequently magistrates in special proceedings, only passed declaratory judgments on the case at issue, given that the *condemnatio*, both in Roman Law and in modern judgments, is in substantive law — more than a simple statement. It was the Roman *praetor* who performed peremptory functions when issuing an interdict. Baptista da Silva's thesis contrasts *iurisdictio* with *imperium* to examine the close connection between the sentence passed and the actual protection of the right. This conceptual distinction, which still prevails at a cultural level, is one of the reasons why less attention is paid to the effectiveness of judgments, their enforcement and ensuring that the substantive protection of the right is guaranteed. The reasons for this exclusive focus on declarative aspects to the detriment of enforcement issues should thus be analysed in detail.

The enforcement of court decisions is an ongoing concern in Comparative Law. In fact, back in 1983 at the VIIth International Congress on Procedural Law held in Würzburg,[2] there was a whole section devoted entirely to enforcement.

In his report on the subject, Professor Carlos de Miguel maintained that proceedings do not conclude with the judgment, as in the event of disobedience, it is important to have the means to enforce it. Some sort of precise regulatory structure is needed to safeguard legal order and ensure the judgment is carried out in the event of possible non-compliance with the court order.

The enforcement of a judgment is aimed at restoring rights, and is thus considered part of the set of guarantees enshrined in due process. The enforcement of a sentence allows damages to be compensated in a series of ways. It is the final stage in the proceedings to achieve the effective protection of rights. Conflict, the primary issue giving rise to the creation and perfection of adversary procedural systems, does not conclude with the judgment but continues until what this orders, the *res judicata,* changes the *status quo,* the initial reason for the legal proceedings or the instance of mediation.

Article 8 of the American Convention on Human Rights (ACHR), under the heading "Right to a fair trial", requires such cases to be resolved "with due guarantees and within a reasonable time". Such a principle, repeated to a greater or lesser extent in all Hispanic American constitutions, requires the right to due process to be respected, as broadly as possible, through the stages leading up to the judgment, a judicial action ensuing from and founded in proven facts. It also covers the adoption of regulations and the ability to enforce what has been decreed. Judgment as state judicial action, with enforcement powers, may not itself be able to guarantee the protection of the

[1] O. A. Baptista da Silva, Jurisdicción y ejecución en la tradición romano-canónica, (Palestra, Lima, 2005, pp. 33).

[2] W.J. Habscheid, *Effectiveness of Judicial Protection and Constitutional Order. The Discussions of VIIth International Congress on Procedural Law*, (Würzburg, 1983—Discussionsberichte, 1985, pp. 311 ff).

rights violated. Thus, in order to ensure the sentence is effective, it is necessary to rely on proceedings to endow it with the effectiveness required, and these cannot dispense with the means required to do so, thus protecting the rights of the subject.

Argentina was convicted before the Inter-American Court of Human Rights (IACHR) for violating Art. 8 of the ACHR in the "Furlan and associates versus Argentina"[3] (2012) case. The decision passed by the IACHR allows us to understand the dysfunctional nature of the Argentine procedural model and the difficulties faced by the plaintiff in getting the State to comply with a judicial ruling issued locally. The facts of the case have to do with the ten-year period that Furlan had to wait in order to receive the verdict, a clear violation of the right to obtain a resolution within a reasonable period of time. Once the sentence was passed, the Argentine government argued that the debt had been consolidated following the country's financial crisis. Three years went by before Furlan managed to receive compensation. However, this was a mere 20% of the amount granted by the original sentence, an 80% reduction of what was initially awarded. This was raised by the IACHR in support of its decision that Argentina had violated the ACHR.

In paragraph 219 of the sentence, the IACHR expressly states that the sentence ordering Furlan to be compensated was not fulfilled, thus violating Art. 8 of the IACHR. Enforcement is an important aspect of the guarantee of due process enshrined in Art. 8 of the ACHR.

The IACHR has constitutional hierarchy in Argentina according to Art. 75, subpara. 22 of the Argentine Constitution (AC). This is why Art. 8 of the IACHR serves as a guide for judicial decisions issued within the country, proving that the right to due process protects the entire legal proceedings throughout the process until the judgment is passed and restoration measures are duly enforced.

In terms of how effective remedies can be found to rights violations, it may be maintained that the proceedings should be seen as a single process connecting the problem with its final solution. Notwithstanding the relevance of each stage in the proceedings, one should not lose sight of the fact that its ultimate purpose is to protect a right, and thus each stage should pursue this goal.

2 The General Problems of the Argentine Civil Proceedings Model

The Procedural Code adopted by the Argentine government in 1886 had its roots in the Spanish Civil Procedural Laws of the nineteenth century, characterized by a certain degree of fragmentation, written records documenting every aspect of procedural activity and an excess of formality. Today's Argentine Civil and Commercial Procedural Code (CPCCN, in Spanish), enacted in 1967 through Law 17,454, continues to respect this tradition.

3 "Furlan and family against Argentina"—Judgment of August 31, 2012. Retrieved from: https://www.corteidh.or.cr/docs/casos/articulos/seriec_246_esp.pdf.

In 2019, the Executive branch sent a draft for a new CPCCN[4] (CPCCN draft bill) to Congress, whose key feature was the proposal for ordinary proceedings to be based on hearings. The bill proposes a process including written propositions (complaint, answer and exceptions) and two videotaped hearings conducted by the judge. The preliminary hearing is an attempt to reconcile the parties and examines the admissibility of evidence according to the facts alleged by the parties. The second hearing is held to receive evidence. The draft highlights the need for collaborative work between judges, parties, lawyers, witnesses, experts and others involved in the proceedings, as well as the parties' duty to tell the truth, Law loyally and in good faith towards one another, and respectfully towards the judge. The text also envisages the digitalization of judicial proceedings, the provisional execution of sentences and small claims proceedings, among many other changes.

As for the execution of the sentence, the bill contemplates a hearing before the judge, in the presence of both debtor and creditor, to resolve the issues related to the amount to be executed and agree on the steps required to comply with the sentence. The debtor is required to submit an affidavit of the assets to be liquidated.

It should be noted at this point that Argentina is a federal country: the provinces, the Autonomous City of Buenos Aires and the Argentine Congress all have constitutional powers to adopt procedural rules. Articles 75, subsection 12 and 121 of the Constitution attribute certain powers to the Congress, including that of dictating substantive laws for the Nation, while recognizing explicitly that provincial government retain all power not delegated in the Congress. The adoption of procedural codes is one of the powers not delegated to the Argentine Congress. This is why Argentina has 25 different civil procedural codes, added to a set of laws which cover procedures in other areas (penal, labour, family, for instance), creating a patchwork of standards, some of which are similar and others markedly different. The task of providing a general overview of the medley of these regulatory systems, although not a simple one, has to some intent been simplified as many provinces simply replicated the text of the CPCCCN adopted in 1967.

In this chapter I will mainly refer to the subject of enforcing monetary settlements in individual cases, among the many and diverse ways of achieving the protection of rights, as this was the main topic of the discussions held at the Kyoto Congress. The section above was designed to explain the scope of this topic, which is far broader than the discussions held in Kyoto.

3 The Enforcement of Judgments in the CPCCN

The provisions of the CPCCN[5] dedicated to the execution of sentences establish a stage where the person convicted can file a limited number of defences. Should the party fail to provide for their defence or if it is rejected by the court upon the request

[4] See the full text at http://www.bibliotecadigital.gob.ar/items/show/2612.

[5] The enforcement of judgments is regulated by Arts. 499 to 516 of the CPCCN.

of the party in whose favour the judgment was passed, the court orders their assets to be monetized accordingly. If this entails an obligation to do something or not, in its default, the court will determine a sum of money to compensate the creditor.

The first step of the enforcement involves approving a settlement of the amount payable by the debtor, whenever this is not clearly stated in the judgment (Art. 502 of the CPCCN).

As regards the determination of the amount due, there are two issues involved: the first one has to do with the duration of the proceedings and the claim for compensatory interests on the initial monetary claim, and the second is inflation. Both factors are important to ensure that the stage to determine the amount of money payable should not take unreasonably long. The convicted person may object to the settlement amount and appeal it (Art. 503 of the CPCCN).

Once the amount payable has been decided, the judge may, upon the creditor's request, order the debtor's assets to be frozen and eventually sold (Art. 505 of the CPCCN). The notice to sell is the judge's order informing the debtor that, if the debt remains unpaid, the assets frozen will be sold in auction. Upon being notified of the sale summons, the debtor has the right to raise the following defences: (i) that the judgment to be enforced is false, (ii) that the statute of limitations on the judgment has expired, (iii) that the payment has been made, or (iv) that an agreement has been reached with the creditor to reduce or extend the terms. Evidence may be submitted regarding these four exceptions and the sentence can be appealed.

Despite its lack of detail, the description shows that the enforcement stage is regulated as a continuous process, carrying on from the stage that concluded with the judgment on the merits. However, this tends to be accompanied by a legal practice of not providing effective monitoring as to whether what is decided is carried out.

Once this stage has concluded, the assets seized are auctioned, a complex stage involving the appointment of an auctioneer to sell the assets to the highest bidder, supervised by the court. There are thirty sections of the CPCCN governing the different steps in the sale of goods (563–593), a formal process controlled by the court. Art. 593 of the CPCCN explains that the judge may fine the debtor if the sale of assets is unnecessarily delayed.

Electronic auctions have been incorporated into the Procedural Codes of the province of Mendoza (2017, Art. 278 et seq.) and the province of Chaco (2017, Art. 563 et seq.). In the provinces of Buenos Aires, Córdoba and San Luis, the Judiciary has established a procedure for electronic auctions. The draft bill of the CPCCN regulates this type of auction in Art. 548 et seq.

4 The Duty of Cooperating with the Individualization of the Debtor's Assets

The data of the assets making up the debtor's property depends on the information that the creditor is able to obtain. Third parties are only obliged to provide judges with specific information as requested, which implies previous action on the part of the creditor, who usually provides the Argentine Central Bank or other financial entities with information so that they can check whether the debtors being executed have accounts or other financial products.[6]

As regards the records for real estate or other types of property, such as motor vehicles, these institutions can only state whether a certain asset belongs to the debtor or not, as they lack the internal procedures allowing them to identify whether the presumed debtor has any property that could be foreclosed.

Moreover, there are no legal obligations in Argentine enforcement proceedings requiring the debtor to provide a detailed statement of assets in the legal action which could be used to settle the payment to the creditor.

The information on the defendant's recorded assets is included in proceedings thanks to reports or certificates provided by public records, requisitioned by the executor through a court order. Once the information has been presented by the executor, the courts order precautionary measures applicable to those assets.

When the court requires information and the respondent fails to collaborate or delays in doing so, progressive payment orders may be set (Art. 398 of the CPCCN).

Likewise, in the event that the debtor's recordable assets are not known, or if these do not cover the amount sought, it is feasible for the creditor to request and obtain a general inhibition order obliging the debtor to sell, or have their assets seized (Art. 228 et seq. CPCCN). This is rendered ineffective once the debtor is able to produce sufficient assets or security. Here again it may be seen that the task of investigating the debtor's financial situation is only incorporated into the proceedings and carried out at the creditor's exclusive request.

5 Protection of the Debtor's Information from the Creditor Concerning Certain Assets

The Argentine legal system contains general rules to protect people's data. To protect the right to control access to one's own data, the *habeas data* action was incorporated into the 1994 Constitution, in Art. 43 (3). This ensures everyone has the right to know what data is held about them, such as in public records or databases, or private ones intended to provide reports, and if the data is false or discriminatory, they can demand it be deleted, rectified, made confidential or updated. The *habeas data* action was regulated by Law 25,326 and similar laws have been adopted by the Argentine provinces.

There are also applicable laws envisaging exceptions to the seizure of certain assets for humanitarian reasons, and in order to protect the means of sustenance for a debtor's family. These include the essential items required for the minimum level of a decent standard of living and the tools used to exercise a profession or trade. The law protects a set of assets necessary for the sustenance of debtors and their families,

[6] The Central Bank provides reports about the behaviour of clients of financial entities. There are also private databases that provide information about people's assets and their commercial behaviour.

so that they can enjoy a decent standard of living, on the basis of the constitutional principle establishing the right of every person to enjoy essential goods.

Furthermore, the debtor is empowered to replace any tangible personal property seized, if this is part of a commercial or industrial enterprise or used in the debtor´s residence. Such items may be exempt from seizure if other unencumbered assets, or those already encumbered, are sufficient to cover the amount claimed (Art. 535 (3) of the CPCCN). The Argentine Civil and Commercial Code (CCCN in Spanish) lists all the items of property that cannot be seized (Art. 774).

Regarding attachments and seizures, procedural law establishes in general terms that, with the exception of the above-mentioned exclusions, a creditor can slap an attachment on any property making up the debtor's assets. However, in order to avoid the unnecessary impairment of assets, this cannot happen when attaching certain assets could cause the debtor serious harm, or if there are other items available and able to guarantee the amount claimed (Art. 535 of the CPCCN).

6 Bank Secrecy and Tax Privacy Against the Enforcement of Payment of a Debt

In Argentina, there are laws which specifically regulate and protect Bank Secrecy and Tax Privacy (or Trading Privacy). The judge only has limited powers to request this type of information.

Tax Privacy is governed by Art. 101 of Law 11,683 (as amended in 1998 and its modifications) and covers affidavits, statements and reports submitted by taxpayers, agents or even third parties to the Federal Administration of Public Income (AFIP, in Spanish). Bank Secrecy is established in Art. 39 of Law 21,526. Regulation A 6624 of the Argentine Central Bank provides that financial entities may not disclose the passive operations that they carry out, and their personnel are bound to maintain absolute confidentiality about all information. The only exception concerns reports requested by judges during legal proceedings. Moreover, Trading Privacy is established in Art. 25 of Law 26,831, which regulates the stock market.

7 Who Carries Out Enforcement Duties?

In Argentina, enforcement is driven by the party requesting satisfaction. The court may only decide on the issues brought by the parties, as it delegates the monetization of assets to an auctioneer. As with the stages leading up to the judgment, once the conflict has been resolved, there follows a sequence of events which take much longer than necessary as they are not supervised and monitored by the court. This practice has deep historical roots, is overburdened with formalities and characterised by scattered procedural acts.

The judges and officers of the court are in charge of the vast majority of enforcement proceedings. The judge appoints an auctioneer and assigns them specific tasks. However, there are certain special types of enforcement that can be partially or fully carried out in the private sector.

Law 24,441 allows for out-of-court mortgage foreclosures. Articles 52 to 67 deal with the proceedings involved, which only take place once the parties have agreed to issue the mortgage bill. After issuing an extrajudicial summons for payment of what is owed, the creditor may submit the mortgage bill to the competent judge and take temporary possession. These procedures are carried out through a notary public appointed by the creditor. Then, as provided by Art. 57 of Law 24,441, once the occupancy been verified, the creditor may on their own behalf (without judicial intervention) order the sale by public auction of the property attached to the bond by the auctioneer appointed and under normal market conditions.

Another example of the private sale of personal property (Art. 2229 of the CCCN) in Argentine law is when a pledge is executed.

8 Enforcement of a Judgment Against the State

Due to the cycle of economic crises perpetually afflicting Argentina, there are countless obstacles limiting the rights of those bringing complaints against the state. In order to enforce favourable judgments, creditors must comply with differing terms and conditions that often make these difficult to enforce.

Law 3952 on lawsuits brought against the State was enacted in 1900. Art. 7 establishes that judicial orders against the Nation should be merely declaratory in nature, as an acknowledgement of the right alleged. In the judicial precedent *"Pietranera, Josefa y otros c/Gobierno de la Nación s/desalojo"*,[7] the Argentine Supreme Court of Justice (CSJ in Spanish) found that Art. 7 of Law 3952 does not authorize the State to ignore court decisions, as that would mean placing it above the legal system, when it is precisely the State that is in charge of ensuring its observance. The CSJ further stated that once the judgment is final and the period of time for voluntary compliance has expired, the government body being sued can be requested to inform the date when it intends to comply, under penalty of this deadline being judicially set, if no response is given or the term deemed unreasonable. Once the term of the judicial order has expired without response, or if the State has failed to comply, the court has the power to enforce the judgment.

Argentina has defaulted on its foreign debt five times in its history: the first time in 1827, then during the Baring crisis, or the Panic of 1890, followed by the Latin American Debt Crisis in 1982, the 2001 Argentine economic crisis and the latest debt renegotiation rounds that began in 2019 and have not concluded. We could also add the 1989 Bonex Plan which also involved a restructuring of public liabilities.

[7] [Pietranera, Josefa and others v. the National Government in RE: eviction"] Fallos 265.291 (1966). Official Collection of Argentina's Supreme Court Decisions.

Furthermore, from 2002 to 2018, Law 25,344 was in force, entailing the declaration of the Financial Emergency of the National State and the consolidation of its debt.

It is common for the state entity required to comply with the sentence to request extensions for its enforcement, invoking its inability to comply as public interests are at stake.

If the court orders the payment of money as part of a debt consolidation regime, the creditor may only calculate this payment after the final judgment and can only sue for payment once this calculation has been approved. The creditor must thus request the Court to issue a demand for payment to the government body being sued. Should there not be any expense authorization, provision must be made to include this expense in the following year's general budget. If the budget for the financial year when payment must be made has not allocated sufficient funds, the Executive must ensure provisions are made to include it in the following year's expenditure. The payment of these obligations is made on a first-in, first-out basis (based on the notification date), until all resources assigned by the Congress have been deployed. This is why the federal government takes about three years to pay out sums arising from legal action. If, after this period has ended, the government still has not fulfilled its obligation to pay, direct enforcement procedures may be initiated.

In the "*Giovagnoli*"[8] case, the CSJ found that Article 9 of Law 24,624, which protects public sector assets from being used to cover expenditures foreseen in the budget and safeguards their availability, should be interpreted in line with the principles and guarantees enshrined in the Constitution and other legislation. It pointed out that the law should not be applied in a mechanical and generalized fashion since this would lead to the frustration of the rights of individuals in a position to execute sentences.

The court interpreted that Art. 19 was enacted to provide rational guidelines for the fulfillment of State obligations, the idea being to prevent the government from finding itself, on account of a peremptory court ruling, in a position where requirements could not be met due to insufficient funds in the budget, or where normal government operations could be impaired. This however does not mean that the State is beyond the legal system it is obliged to protect, nor that it is exempt from abiding by court judgments.

According to the CSJ, a creditor may execute a sentence requiring a sum of money to be paid, when a) despite having been served the final payment order, the Executive fails to instruct Congress to include the requisite sum in the following financial year, and ordinary sessions on the budget law which could include the need to envisage the expense, are over; or b) when the expense has been included in the general budget for the national government. The Court also held that the party requesting the application of Art. 19 of Law 24,624 must be able to show that there is no budget item to cover the monetary obligations acknowledged in court.

It should also be noted that Law 26,854 introduced a special regime for precautionary measures in those cases where the Executive intervenes. The regime envisages

[8] Fallos 322:2132 (1999).

a set of requirements and strict guidelines limiting the effectiveness of the precautionary measures that could potentially be filed against the State in order to ensure effective compliance with the sentence sought.

9 Measures to Limit Reluctance to Comply with a Decision

The rights protecting the debtor are no obstacle when it comes to taking coercive property measures, when there are elements to support this in the case.

As regards the application of penalties, Art. 37 of the CPCCN sets out that a court may issue compelling progressive payment orders to ensure that the parties abide by its rulings, in the benefit of the litigant harmed by non-compliance. The sentences will proportionally reflect the economic wealth of the debtor and may be left without effect, or be readjusted if they cease to resist and totally or partially justify their actions. Penalties may also be imposed on third parties, in the cases established by law, as may payment orders when the law so provides it. In Art. 804, the CCCN establishes that courts may issue orders, in the interests of ownership, to require compliance from those failing to comply with their legal duties according to a judgment. Compliance with court orders issued by public authorities is governed by the rules of Administrative Law.

These are provisional sanctions aimed at achieving compliance with a court order, and their severity depends on the Judge, as they are intended to discourage parties from refusing to comply with what is ordered.

There is a detailed list of procedural fines that sanction conduct contrary to procedural good faith or which obstruct the proper progress of proceedings.

The principle of the prohibition of imprisonment for debts enshrined in international law and incorporated into the Argentine Constitution is made explicit in Article 75, para. 22. Article 7.7 of the AHCR establishes that no one may be imprisoned for debts, while Article 11 of the International Covenant on Civil and Political Rights establishes that no one may be imprisoned for being unable to fulfill a contractual obligation.

10 Enforcement in Collective Redress

The reform of the Argentine Constitution in 1994 recognized the right to judicial proceedings in defense of collective interests (Art. 43). Congress has not passed any law explaining proceedings where rights may be asserted in those cases where the plaintiff represents a group of affected persons. However, the Supreme Court has issued a series of judgments establishing guidelines for litigating in defense of consumer rights, for environmental damages or problems affecting community interests.

A key precedent set by the Supreme Court on the matter is the Mendoza case,[9] decided in 2008, which concerned the damages suffered as a result of the contamination of the Matanza-Riachuelo Basin. Home to over 5 million people, the area affected is 64 km long and 35 km wide and covers an area of approximately 2,250 km^2. The Supreme Court ordered the public authorities to carry out a monitoring plan and delegated control of its execution to a judge in first instance. The ruling established general criteria which had to be met in order to restore the environment and protect people.

This is a paradigmatic case which illustrates the extent to which legal processes are bound up with the restoration of rights in complex situations. The notion of creditor is broadened as the right in question is of a social and collective nature, requiring procedural rules to include effective means for comprehensive repair beyond monetary compensations.

The Mendoza case was decided by the Supreme Court in 2008. The sentence ordered the Matanza-Riachuelo basin to be restored, improving the quality of life of the local community and preventing future damage. However, to-date, there have been no improvements, nor has there been any significant progress in the works plan, showing yet again the disconnect between the recognition of a right and its effective restoration.

11 Enforcement of Judgments of Foreign Courts

Exequatur suits may be filed by: (i) any person in favour of whom a judgment has been passed, or (ii) any injured party or one who may be stripped of a benefit as a result of the acknowledgment of a judgment or order.

Both foreign nationals legally residing in Argentina, and Argentine citizens awarded a judgment by a foreign court who wish this to be made effective in Argentina may file for this type of proceeding.

At national level, the legal regime applicable is regulated by Articles 517 to 519 of the CPCCN.

For a foreign judgment to be exequatured and enforced in Argentina, it must comply with the provisions of Art. 517 of the CPCCN. If the analysis is limited to those cases where no enforcement agreement exists between the Argentine State and the State where the foreign judgment was passed, then, for a decision to be enforced within Argentine jurisdiction, the following requirements must be met:

1. The sentence with status of *res judicata* in the State where it was granted must be issued by a competent court in compliance with the Argentine rules of international jurisdiction. It must be the result of the exercise of an action *in personam* or an action *in rem* over personal property as-and-when such property is moved to Argentina during or after the lawsuit filed abroad.

[9] Fallos 331:1622.

2. The defendant must have been personally summoned and their defence must have been guaranteed.
3. The judgment must meet all the requirements necessary to be considered as such in the place where it was passed, as well as meeting the conditions of authenticity required by Argentine law.
4. The sentence must not affect the principles of public order under Argentine law.
5. It must not be repugnant to other prior or simultaneous judgments passed by an Argentine court.

First instance courts have jurisdiction over the enforcement of a foreign judgment, depending on the matter (Art. 518 of the CPCCN). The request is to be made before such a court and should be accompanied by: (1) a certified copy of the foreign judgment (authenticated and translated into Spanish), and (2) a certified copy of the proceedings proving that the judgment is final and all other requirements have been met.

If a court orders a foreign judgment to be enforced, the proceedings involved for an Argentina court are as follows: a distinction must first be made between judgments ordering the payment of cash or a non-liquid amount, those ordering or preventing an action, and those requiring something to be handed over (Art. 518 of the CPCCN).

In the case of foreign arbitration awards, apart from the requirements listed above, Art. 519 bis of the CPCCN orders the following:

(a) It is necessary for the extension of jurisdiction in favour of a foreign arbitration tribunal to be valid, which means that only international property disputes may be handled. Thus, it does not extend to cases over which Argentine courts may have exclusive jurisdiction or when this is prohibited by law (Art. 519 bis para. 1 of the CPCCN).
(b) The issues must be admissible for arbitration under Argentine law (Art. 519 bis para. 2 of the CPCCN). The law establishes that any transactional matters may be the subject of arbitration.

Once these requirements have been met, an application must be filed for the enforcement of the foreign arbitration award before the competent court of first instance court through the afore-mentioned exequatur procedure.

In Argentina, there are various instruments of private international law that regulate international judicial cooperation for the internal execution of precautionary measures issued in foreign jurisdictions. These have been incorporated into different systems, including those in effect in the Mercosur and at inter-American level.

Overall, the requesting State may grant the precautionary measure in compliance with its own domestic legislation; however, the Court receiving the request must, in order to enforce the decision, comply with local laws for the foreign request to be viable (*lex fori*) and may refuse to enforce it if this affects international public order.

Argentina is a signatory to the Protocol on Precautionary Measures[10] enshrined in the MERCOSUR agreement, governing compliance with provisional remedies aimed at avoiding irreparable harm.

This document envisages the request for provisional remedies as part of ordinary, executory, special or extraordinary proceedings in civil, commercial, labour and criminal matters, though in this last case only when it comes to civil compensation (Art. 2).

In relation to applicable law, the Protocol points out that the admissibility of a precautionary measure is governed by the laws of the Requesting State, and decided by its courts (Art. 5). However, once granted by the Requesting State, its enforcement and any related liens should be decided by the courts from the Requested State, in accordance with its own legislation (Art. 6).

The Protocol also defines that the laws and courts of the Requested State shall govern and rule on (a) any changes deemed necessary during the proceedings to ensure full compliance or, when appropriate, reduction or substitution; (b) the penalties for malicious or excessive requests; and (c) issues connected with ownership and other rights *in rem* (Art. 7).

The court of the Requested State may refuse to uphold the precautionary measure or order it to be lifted, if it verifies its complete inadmissibility, in compliance with the terms of this Protocol (Art. 8).

As regards the party affected, the Protocol envisages that both the alleged debtor and any third parties considering themselves harmed by the measure may file against measure before the Requested judicial authorities. Notwithstanding the need to uphold the precautionary measure, and excepting matters related to ownership and other rights *in rem*, the authority will return the case to the Requesting court for a decision concerning the opposition brought according to their laws (Art. 9).

It should also be noted that, under Art. 10, compliance with a precautionary measure by the Requested judicial authority does not necessarily imply its commitment to acknowledge or enforce the foreign final judgment of the main proceedings.

Furthermore, in order to ensure adequate provisional relief in the Requested State, the Protocol empowers the court required to enforce a foreign judgment to order any precautionary measure to guarantee enforcement, in accordance with their own laws (Art. 11).

Finally, as a way of limiting the execution of a request for precautionary measures, the courts of the Requested State are authorized to refuse compliance with a letter rogatory for precautionary measures, when these are clearly contrary to public order (Art. 17).

For inter-American matters, the Inter-American Convention on Execution of Preventive Measures (CIDIP II) adopted during the Second Inter-American Specialized Conference on Private International Law (OEA) held in Montevideo (1979) was ratified by the Argentine government through Law 22,921.[11] It states that 'the terms

[10] Adopted in Ouro Preto, Brazil, on December 17, 1994.

[11] The Argentine government appointed the Ministry of Foreign Affairs, International trade and Worship as the central authority to process the measures requested within the CIDIP II framework.

"precautionary measures", "security measures" or "guarantee measures" are equivalent when referring to procedures or measures aimed at guaranteeing the results of pending or future proceedings regarding the security of persons and property. This also covers specific obligations to give, do or not do a specific thing in civil, commercial or labour matters, or in criminal cases seeking civil damages.' (Art. 1).

Precautionary measures may be granted "in accordance with the laws and by the judges of the venue where the proceedings take place. However, execution and any injunction bond or guarantee shall be determined by the judges where execution is sought, in accordance with their laws." (Art. 3). Article 12 of the CIDIP II explains that "the State of destination may decline to execute a letter concerning preventive measures that are manifestly contrary to its public policy (*ordre public*)", that is to say, when the precautionary measure requested according to the forum rule affects the fundamental principles of international public order of the Requested court. However, if this is not the case, and the measure sought abides by such principles, then its execution must proceed forthwith.

Lastly, in accordance with Art. 6 of the Convention, the execution of precautionary measures by a court of the State of destination "shall not entail any commitment to recognize and execute the foreign judgment that may have been handed down in the proceedings concerned".

12 Conclusion. Are Only the Parties Interested in Ensuring that Sentences Are Executed?

As pointed out in the introduction, the enforcement of a sentence should not be divorced from cognizance proceedings. Argentine civil process presents serious structural problems which hinder the fundamental interaction between the court and the parties. The two principal defects of this system are the lack of rules on the duty to collaborate and the lack of immediacy. These issues are exacerbated during the enforcement stage, since proceedings are tortuously slow and the procedural stage of enforcement is not supervised by the court. The problem of effectiveness should not be considered in isolation: it should be solved by adapting legislation in tandem with fostering cultural change to enable this process to be understood as essential to guaranteeing people's rights.

Reference

da Silva OAB (2005) Jurisdicción y ejecución en la tradición romano-canónica. Palestra, Lima, p. 33

Eduardo Oteiza is a full-time research professor and director of the LL Mprogram at La Plata National University (Argentina). He was a post-doc Jean Monnet Fellow at the European University Institute andvisiting fellow at the Universities of Bologna, Catania, Medellín, Yale, York,Pompeu Fabra, Genova, Turin and Lima, among others. Professor Oteiza served as President of the Ibero-American Institute of Procedural Law (2014–2018) and of the Argentine Association of ProceduralLaw (2012–2014). He is President of the International Association of Procedural Law (2019). In 2016 he received the Year Award from the Fondazione "Enrico Redenti". Heis codirector (with Michele Taruffo, Jordi Nieva Fenoll and Daniel Mitidiero) of "Process and Law", Marcial Pons Editor. He teaches and writes about legal reforms, judicial independence, procedural law principles and the dialogue between judges regarding constitutional and human rights.

Jurisdiction, Forum and Enforcement of Judgements: The Challenge of Cooperation Between Courts Before and After Brexit

(Civil Enforcement and Effective Protection of Creditor's Rights in the EU and in the UK)

Ian Forrester

1 Introduction

1. It is an honour and a great pleasure for me to be here today in this wonderful library building, established in 1905 when The Kyoto School of Law and Politics took the name of "Ritsumeikan University",[1] which has expanded 20-fold since then!

2. As the title of my lecture reveals, "Jurisdiction, forum and enforcement of judgements: the challenge of cooperation between courts before and after Brexit", I would like to explore the subject of cooperation between courts before and after Brexit. In this context, specific attention will be given to the civil enforcement and effective protection of creditor's rights in the European Union[2] and in the United Kingdom.[3]

[1] At the time, the library was 357 m^2. Now it is approximately 23.8 larger at 8530.46 m^2.

[2] Hereinafter the "EU".

[3] Hereinafter the "UK".

This paper was lectured by Prof. Dr. Ian Forrester at Ritsumeikan Kinugasa Campus Hirai Memorial Library on 17th February 2020.

Judge of the General Court of the European Union until the 31st January 2020 and Honorary Professor in Law at the University of Glasgow. Master of the Bench, Middle Temple. President of the Franco British Lawyers Society. All opinions expressed herein are personal to the author.
Immense thanks are due to Michael Clancy, OBE of the Law Society of Scotland, and M. H. Cardoso of my Cabinet.

I. Forrester (✉)
General Court of the European Union (Luxembourg), Kirchberg, Luxembourg
e-mail: ian@forrester.eu

M. Deguchi (ed.), *Effective Enforcement of Creditors' Rights*,
Ius Gentium: Comparative Perspectives on Law and Justice 91,
https://doi.org/10.1007/978-981-16-5609-5_24

3. I would like to start by sharing with you some thoughts on judicial cooperation between courts before Brexit within the framework of the European Union (Sect. 2) and subsequently on judicial cooperation after Brexit between the UK and the EU (Sect. 3).

2 Judicial Cooperation Before Brexit Within the Framework of the European Union

2.1 Judicial Cooperation in the European Union

4. As you know, the EU legal order is unique. It has its own constitutional framework, its own founding principles and a particularly sophisticated institutional structure, as well as a full set of legal rules to ensure its operation.[4]

5. In this peculiar legal order, the EU and its Member States - but also the Member States among themselves—are "linked together in a close and fruitful relationship" which involves a dialogue not only between the courts of the Member States and the Court of Justice but also among the courts of Member States.[5]

6. In order for that judicial dialogue to be fruitful, which is vital to uphold the rule of law within the EU, there must be a culture of mutual trust not only between the Court of Justice and national courts but also among national courts.[6]

7. It is because Member States trust each other in their respect for the rule of law and fundamental rights that judicial cooperation is possible.[7]

---

[4] Opinion 2/13, EU:C:2014:2454, paragraph 158.

[5] See, in this sense, the speech of Mr Koen LENAERTS, President of the Court of Justice of the European Union, *The ECJ as the Guardian of the Authority of EU Law–A Networking Exercise*, The Authority of EU Law. Do We Still Believe In It?, Congress to mark the 25th Anniversary of ERA, Trier, 19 October 2017, p. 1.

[6] See, in this sense, the speech of Mr Koen LENAERTS, President of the Court of Justice of the European Union, *Mutual Trust Between The Judiciaries of the Member States*, European Network of Councils for the Judiciary (ENCJ), General Assembly, "A Perspective on the Future of Judicial Dialogue in Europe", Warsaw, 3 June 2016, p. 3.

[7] See Koen LENAERTS, "La vie après l'avis: exploring the principle of mutual (yet not blind) trust", 2017 Common Market Law Review, p. 808–812.

2.2 *Judicial Cooperation in the Area of Freedom, Security and Justice*

8. This mutual trust—"with respect for fundamental rights and the different legal systems and traditions of the Member States"[8]—, is of essential importance in the Area of Freedom, Security and Justice, as it allows for the mutual recognition of judicial decisions in civil and criminal matters.

9. Mutual recognition implies that a court in a Member State can trust that the court in another Member State that adopted the decision provided effective judicial protection to the persons affected by the decision, including the protection of their fundamental rights.

10. According to settled case-law, both the principle of mutual trust between the Member States and the principle of mutual recognition are, in EU law, of fundamental importance given that they allow an area without internal borders to be created and maintained. More specifically, the principle of mutual trust requires, particularly with regard to the Area of Freedom, Security and Justice, each of those States, save in exceptional circumstances, to consider all the other Member States to be complying with EU law and particularly with the fundamental rights recognised by EU law.[9]

11. This requirement is illustrated by a case of the Court of Justice of the EU,[10] the Poltorak case, concerning the European Arrest Warrant. The Swedish police issued a European arrest warrant against Mr Poltorak after he was sentenced by the District Court of Gothenburg. However, the Court of Justice determined that a European arrest warrant constitutes a judicial decision that can only be issued by a judicial authority. The term "judiciary" cannot be extended to cover national police services.[11]

2.2.1 Legal Basis

12. Article 67(1) TFEU provides that "The Union shall constitute an area of freedom, security and justice with respect for fundamental rights and the different legal systems and traditions of the Member States".

---

[8] See article 67(1) of the Treaty on the Functioning of the European Union (hereinafter the "TFEU").

[9] See judgment of the Court of Justice, of 5 April 2016, Aranyosi and Căldăraru, C-404/15 and C-659/15 PPU, EU:C:2016:198, paragraph 78 and the case-law cited.

[10] Hereinafter the "CJEU".

[11] See case C-452/16 PPU, Poltorak, EU:C:2016:858, paragraph 28–35.

2.2.2 Historical Background

13. The Treaty establishing the European Economic Community provided for the establishment of a common market, characterized by the free movement of goods, services, capital and workers, and the progressive approximation of the economic policies of Member States.

14. Thus, the main objective of the integration process was to constitute an "economic Europe", but, in the fields of security, policing and justice, Member States continued to work independently.

15. Accordingly, the need arose for cooperation at European level in order to protect citizens and safeguard their freedoms.

16. The legal basis for such an area has a long and constitutionally complicated history. Several Member States were nervous of endowing the European Community[12] with competence for crime, law enforcement or the related public powers. However, it became clear to a number of officials, prosecutors, police and politicians that good cross-frontier cooperation was a necessary part of a Europe without economic frontiers. Some Member States, including the UK, favoured a cautious, non-ideological approach, rooted in intergovernmental cooperation. Accordingly, as early as 1976, the ministries of the interior established cooperative mechanisms for preventing illegal immigration and radical terrorism.[13] This regime did not create rights for individuals, nor did it imply an interpretative role for the CJEU. There was in those days no consensus to impose community norms as a sector of public law which was especially sensitive. So, pursuant to the Treaty of Maastricht, this "pillar" was governed by intergovernmental cooperation. There was a limited jurisdiction for the CJEU in that, in matters of visas, asylum and immigration, only courts of final jurisdiction could refer questions for preliminary rulings. In criminal matters the Member States individually decided if they would unilaterally accept the jurisdiction of the CJEU.

17. While this regime was a cautious reflection of the hesitations of several Member States, experience was positive. Accordingly, the Treaty of Lisbon brought these fields fully within the ambit of European Union law: competence for the Commission to propose, European Parliament as co-legislator and jurisdiction of the CJEU to interpret the texts consistently. Thus the former unilateral acceptance of jurisdiction by the CJEU, country by country has been eliminated.

18. In the framework of the Treaty, the UK, together with Ireland, have opt–outs from Title V of Part Three of the TFEU (area of freedom, security and justice) under Protocol No 21 on the position of the United Kingdom and Ireland in respect of the Area of Freedom, Security and Justice, annexed to the Treaties. The UK and Ireland have a flexible opt-out from legislation adopted in this area, which allows them to opt in or out of legislation and legislative initiatives on a case-by-case basis.

---

[12] Hereinafter the "EC".

[13] The so called "Trevi group" chose that acronym to reflect Terrorism Radicalism Extremism and Violence Internationally.

2.2.3 Objectives and Areas of Activity

19. The objectives to be pursued with the creation of the Area of Freedom, Security and Justice are to ensure the absence of internal border controls for persons; to frame a common policy on asylum, immigration and external border control, to ensure a high level of security; and to facilitate access to justice (Article 67 TFEU).

20. The Area of Freedom, Security and Justice consists of four different sectors: the area of freedom (policies relating to border controls, asylum and immigration), judicial cooperation in civil matters, judicial cooperation in criminal matters and police cooperation.

2.2.4 Main Achievements

21. Cooperation in this field is extensive and effective; not perfect, but useful. There are many references to the CJEU to determine consistently how to interpret the mass of texts on crime, security, civil justice, and ancillary matters.

22. Here is one example: a Latvian fruit picker gets involved in a brawl in Carnoustie, wounds another man seriously, and flees. Thanks to good cooperation between Scottish and Baltic authorities he is arrested in Riga. He resists deportation to face trial, claiming that his family need him in Riga and that he will not get a fair trial in Scotland. While in Riga he wears an ankle tag, is subject to a curfew, and must report to the police station daily. After 7 months he is sent to the UK and is sentenced after conviction to 3 years in prison. Can the 7 months of pre-trial light detention in Riga be credited against his UK prison sentence?.[14]

23. It should be noted that two categories of legal dispute could arise here. One would relate to what is the meaning of the underlying text. Such disputes arise routinely in examining any piece of legislation, especially one which has been drafted by diplomats who may have different views of the end to be achieved. It would be necessary to give guidance to the judiciary as to the spirit in which the texts would be interpreted. The other dispute could arise as to whether the country was violating its treaty obligations by maintaining a particular practice when applying the law. For example, is the UK entitled to deport any EU 27 person sentenced to more than 18 months in prison, regardless of the circumstances of the crime?

[14] See judgment of the Court of Justice in case C-294/16 PPU *JZ* on whether the period during which a person was subject to a curfew and electronic monitoring in the UK counts towards the custodial sentence imposed on this person in Poland.

2.3 *Judicial Cooperation in Civil Matters*

24. The EC/EU has done much to facilitate access to justice and consistency of outcome through mutual recognition, especially through consistent principles of choice of law. The first Brussels Convention of 1968 dealt with questions of proper law of the contract, forum, recognition and enforcement of judgements in civil and commercial matters. This then was superseded by the first Rome Convention on contractual obligations in 1980, then by the Brussels I Regulation, and Rome I, Rome II, Rome III and four Brussels Regulations dealing with divorce, insolvency, applicable law and a mass of other tricky, technical, important cross border problems relating to the conduct of judicial proceedings. EFTA states were brought in by Lugano I and II.

25. The UK has played an important role in the elaboration of these texts[15] and I would hope that they would not be reviled as worthlessly European. Now, interpretation of the original Brussels Convention and its successors has given rise to hundreds of references to the European Court to achieve consistency. One could imagine many questions relating to how UK judges should address a novel question relating to whether the proper law of a contract is English or Polish. It would seem highly desirable for the answer to that question to continue to be identical whether the question were asked in Inverness or in Cracow.

[15] The Brussels Convention of 27 September 1968 on jurisdiction and the enforcement of judgments in civil and commercial matters, as amended by the Accession Conventions under the successive enlargements of the European Union (hereinafter the "Brussels Convention of 1968").

The Lugano Convention of 16 September 1988 on jurisdiction and the enforcement of judgments in civil and commercial matters, which extends the application of the rules of the 1968 Brussels Convention to certain States members of the European Free Trade Association [1988] OH L319/9.

Council Regulation (EC) N° 44/2001 of 22 December 2000 on jurisdiction and the recognition and enforcement of judgments in civil and commercial matters [2001] OJ L 012 (Brussels I).

The Lugano Convention of 30 October 2007 on jurisdiction and the recognition and enforcement of judgments in civil and commercial matter [2009] OJ L147/5.

Regulation (EU) N° 1215/2012 of the European Parliament and of the Council of 12 December 2012 on jurisdiction and the recognition and enforcement of judgments in civil and commercial matters [2012] OJ L 351.

Convention of 16 September 1988 on Jurisdiction and the Enforcement of Judgments in Civil and Commercial Matters [1988] OH L319/9.

See Opinion 1/03 *Re The Lugano Convention* [2006] ECR I-1145 which confirmed the subject matter to be exclusive Community competence.

Convention of 30 October 2007 on Jurisdiction and the Recognition and Enforcement of Judgments in Civil and Commercial Matters [2009] OJ L147/5.

2.3.1 Legal Basis

26. Judicial cooperation in civil matters was not one of the objectives of the EC when the founding treaty was adopted. However, Article 220 of the Treaty establishing the European Economic Community stipulated that Member States were bound to simplify "formalities governing the reciprocal recognition and enforcement of judgments of courts or tribunals and of arbitration awards".

27. Judicial cooperation in civil matters, in the intergovernmental context of "Justice and Home Affairs", was officially included within the EU's sphere of activity by the Treaty of Maastricht (1993) as a "matter of common interest".

28. The Treaty of Amsterdam (1999) brought judicial cooperation in civil matters within the Community sphere, transferring it from the Treaty on European Union to the Treaty establishing the European Community, although it did not make it subject to the Community method.

29. The Treaty of Lisbon (2009) makes all measures in the field of judicial cooperation in civil matters subject to the ordinary legislative procedure. However, family law remains subject to a special legislative procedure: the Council acts unanimously after consulting Parliament.

30. Under the Treaty of Lisbon, "[t]he Union shall develop judicial cooperation in civil matters having cross-border implications, based on the principle of mutual recognition of judgments and of decisions in extrajudicial cases. Such cooperation may include the adoption of measures for the approximation of the laws and regulations of the Member States".[16]

2.3.2 Objectives

31. The main objectives of this judicial cooperation are legal certainty for citizens in cross-border relations governed by civil law and easy and effective access to justice in order to settle cross-border disputes, implying identification of the competent jurisdiction, clear designation of the applicable law and speedy and effective recognition and enforcement procedures.[17]

2.3.3 Main Achievements

32. The "acquis" in judicial cooperation in civil matters has grown significantly over the last two decades.

33. There are legal instruments in place, which govern jurisdiction, mutual recognition and enforcement of judgments as well as the applicable law in a broad range

---

[16] Article 81(1) TFEU.

[17] See EUROPEAN PARLIAMENT, *Judicial cooperation in civil matters*, Fact Sheets on the European Union, available at the following address: http://www.europarl.europa.eu/factsheets/en/sheet/154/judicial-cooperation-in-civil-matters.

of matters, extending from contract to successions and maintenance obligations. European legislation also provides for direct cooperation between the courts and competent authorities of Member States, for example when taking evidence abroad or in matters of child abduction. Access to justice in cross-border cases has been improved through provisions on legal aid, mediation and simplified and low-cost procedures for small and uncontested claims. In order to facilitate the application in practice, the European Judicial Network in civil and commercial matters was created.

The Brussels I Regulation

34. The main legal act in the area of determination of the competent court, recognition and enforcement of judgments and of decisions in extrajudicial cases is Brussels I Regulation.

35. The Brussels I Regulation, which entered into force on 1st March 2002,[18] replaced the previous Brussels Convention of 1968. The Brussels I Regulation was revised subsequently and a new version of the Regulation was adopted in December 2012, Regulation (EU) No 1215/2012 of the European Parliament and of the Council of 12 December 2012 on jurisdiction and the recognition and enforcement of judgments in civil and commercial matters.

36. This regulation seeks to harmonise the rules of conflict of jurisdiction within the Member States and to simplify and expedite the recognition and enforcement of decisions in civil and commercial matters.

The Jurisdictional System

37. The basic jurisdiction rule, according to Article 4 of Regulation (EU) No 1215/2012, is that, for persons domiciled in the territory of a Member State, whatever their nationality, jurisdiction is exercised by the courts of the Member State in which the defendant is domiciled.

38. Under Article 25(1), however, if the parties, regardless of their domicile, have agreed that a court or the courts of a Member State are to have jurisdiction to settle any disputes which have arisen or which may arise in connection with a particular legal relationship, that court or those courts shall have jurisdiction.[19]

---

[18] Council Regulation (EC) No 44/2001 of 22 December 2000 on jurisdiction and recognition and enforcement of judgments in civil and commercial matters.

[19] See Example 1.

Example 1

Company A from Germany has sold a truck to Company B from Belgium. Company B had submitted an offer to purchase which stated, inter alia, that the purchase was to be subject to Company B's general sales terms and conditions containing a jurisdiction clause providing that disputes would be decided by the courts of Belgium.

Company A accepted the offer in a confirmation letter.

After delivery, Company B claims that there are crucial malfunctions in the truck and has brought an action for damages for breach of contract against Company A before a Belgium court.

In the proceedings, Company A claims that this court does not have jurisdiction. It points out that a choice of forum clause contained in one party's general sales conditions is valid only if the text of the contract signed by both parties itself contains an express reference to general conditions which include a jurisdiction clause.

So the seller, Company A, prevails in the litigation, since the buyer's terms and conditions did not form part of the contract signed by both parties.

According to Article 25(1) of Regulation (EU) No 1215/2012, parties, regardless of their domicile, can agree that a court or the courts of a Member State shall have jurisdiction to settle any dispute which has arisen or may arise in connection with a particular legal relationship. Such jurisdiction is exclusive unless the parties have agreed otherwise.

The agreement conferring jurisdiction shall be either:

(a) in writing or evidenced in writing;

(b) in a form which accords with practices which the parties have established between themselves; or

(c) in international trade or commerce, in a form which accords with a usage of which the parties are or ought to have been aware and which in such trade or commerce is widely known to, and regularly observed by, parties to contracts of the type involved in the particular trade or commerce concerned.

Relevant case-law : Judgment of 8 March 2018, Saey Home & Garden, C- 64/17, EU:C:2018:173, paragraphs 23 et seq.)

Paragraph 27 : Where a jurisdiction clause is stipulated in the general conditions, such a clause is lawful where the text of the contract signed by both parties itself contains an express reference to general conditions which include a jurisdiction clause.

Paragraph 32 : Article 25(1) of Regulation No 1215/2012 must be interpreted as meaning that a jurisdiction clause set out in the general conditions of sale mentioned in invoices issued by one of the contracting parties does not satisfy the requirements of that provision.

39. Special rules are laid down regarding matters relating to insurance, consumer contracts[20] and individual contracts of employment.

40. The policy underlying these contracts is the perceived need to protect the weaker party, deemed for this purpose to be the insured, the consumer or the employee.

Example 2

Mrs A, a resident in Luxembourg, orders a book from a German bookseller and pays the price in advance. The book never arrives. She brought an action before the court of her place of residence. The bookseller claims that his general sales conditions establish the jurisdiction of the courts of Germany. However, she is of the view that the clause contained in his general sales conditions was without effect.

Under Article 18(1) of Regulation (EU) No 1215/2012, a consumer may bring proceedings against the other party to a contract either in the courts of the Member State in which that party is domiciled or in the courts for the place where the consumer is domiciled.

Article 17(1)(c) provides that this choice is open to the consumer if the contract

[20] See Example 2.

has been concluded with a person who pursues commercial or professional activities in the Member State of the consumer's domicile or, by any means, directs such activities to that Member State or to several States including that Member State, and that the contract falls within the scope of such activities.

Relevant case-law: Judgment of 25 January 2018, Schrems, C-498/16, EU:C:2018:37, paragraph 30.

Paragraph 30: Only contracts concluded outside and independently of any trade or professional activity or purpose, solely for the purpose of satisfying an individual's own needs in terms of private consumption, are covered by the special rules laid down by the regulation to protect the consumer as the party deemed to be the weaker party.

41. Article 24 of Regulation (EU) No 1215/2012 sets out the specific situations where courts of a Member State shall have exclusive jurisdiction, regardless of the domicile of the parties, when there is a presumption of a particularly close connection to the courts of a particular Member State or when there is special need for legal certainty.[21] This is the case, for example, of proceedings which have as their object rights *in rem* in immovable property or tenancies of immovable property, proceedings which have as their object the validity of entries in public registers, proceedings concerned with the registration or validity of patents or other industrial property rights or proceedings concerned with the enforcement of judgments.

Recognition and Enforcement of Decisions

42. Regulation (EU) No 1215/2012 simplified the formalities for recognition and enforcement of any judgment delivered by a court in one Member State ("the Member State of origin")[22] in another Member State ("the Member State addressed")[23] and abolished the uniform procedure for the declaration of a judgment as enforceable in another Member State, also known as *exequatur procedure.* As a result, from 10 January 2015, it is no longer necessary for a judgment creditor to apply for a declaration of enforceability, since they can apply directly to have the judgment enforced.[24]

---

[21] See, in this sense, EUROPEAN COMMISSION, *Judicial cooperation in civil matters in the European Union–A guide for legal practitioners*, Publications Office, 2015, p. 18.

[22] See Article 2(d) of Regulation (EU) No 1215/2012.

[23] See Article 2(e) of Regulation (EU) No 1215/2012.

[24] See Article 39 of Regulation (EU) No 1215/2012.

Recognition

43. According to Article 36, a judgment given in a Member State shall be recognised in the other Member States without any special procedure being required.

44. Recognition can only be refused if there is a ground for refusal of recognition as referred to in Article 45. Therefore, a judgment will not be recognised if (a) such recognition is manifestly contrary to public policy (ordre public) in the Member State addressed; (b) in case of a judgment in default of appearance, it is shown that the defendant was not served with the document which instituted the proceedings or with an equivalent document in sufficient time and in such a way as to enable him to arrange for his defence; (c) the judgment is irreconcilable with a judgment given between the same parties in the Member State addressed; (d) the judgment is irreconcilable with an earlier judgment given in another Member State or in a third State involving the same cause of action and between the same parties, or (e) it conflicts with the rules of exclusive jurisdiction or the special rules on matters relating to insurance, consumer contracts or individual contracts of emplyment.[25]

Enforcement

45. Regulation (EU) No 1215/2012 has made an important change in the procedure of rendering a judgment granted in one Member State enforceable in another.[26] The party wishing to enforce the judgment – "the judgment creditor" – shall no longer apply for a declaration of enforceability given that such a judgment will be directly enforceable in the other Member State if the court of origin issues a certificate confirming the enforceability and giving details of the judgment.[27] The certificate and a copy of the judgment are then sufficient authority for enforcement in the Member State addressed.[28]

The European Procedures in Civil and Commercial Matters—Procedures for Enforcing a Judgment

46. In the past, a creditor seeking to recover his debt in another State faced significant difficulties mainly due to the differences in national procedural law, diverging levels of efficiency of the organization of justice, additional costs triggered by cross border proceedings and linguistic barriers.

47. To address this difficulty, the EU adopted four separate Regulations, which facilitate the efficient recovery of debts in cross border civil cases. Three Regulations create uniform European procedures, which are available to litigants (the European

[25] See Article 45(1) of Regulation (EU) No 1215/2012.

[26] See EUROPEAN COMMISSION, *Judicial cooperation in civil matters in the European Union–A guide for legal practitioners*, Publications Office, 2015, p. 18.

[27] See Articles 42 and 53, as well as Annex I of Regulation (EU) No 1215/2012.

[28] See Article 37 of Regulation (EU) No 1215/2012.

Enforcement Order for uncontested claims,[29] the European Order for Payment[30] and the European Small Claims Procedure[31]). The fourth Regulation foresees the European Account Preservation Order.[32]

48. Regulation (EU) No 1215/2012 and these four Regulations enable creditors with claims for payment who secure an enforceable order in one Member State to take the order relatively simply and cheaply to another Member State for enforcement with little or no additional steps of procedure required.[33]

The European Enforcement Order for Uncontested Claims

49. In order to abolish exequatur for decisions relating to uncontested claims, the European Parliament and the Council adopted Regulation (EC) No 805/2004. The purpose of this Regulation was to create a European Enforcement Order for uncontested claims to permit, by laying down minimum standards, the free circulation of judgments, court settlements and authentic instruments throughout all Member States without any intermediate proceedings needing to be brought in the Member State of enforcement prior to recognition and enforcement.[34]

50. The European Enforcement Order is a certificate which accompanies a judgment, a court settlement or an authentic instrument and which allows this judgment, settlement or instrument to freely circulate in the European Union[35] and to be easily recognised and enforced in another Member State.[36]

51. The concept of "uncontested claims" covers all situations in which a creditor, given the verified absence of any dispute by the debtor as to the nature or extent of a pecuniary claim, has obtained either a court decision against that debtor or an enforceable document that requires the debtor's express consent, be it a court settlement or an authentic instrument.[37]

---

[29] Regulation (EC) No 805/2004 of the European Parliament and of the Council of 21 April 2004 creating a European Enforcement Order for uncontested claims.

[30] Regulation (EC) No 1896/2006 of the European Parliament and of the Council of 12 December 2006 creating a European order for payment procedure.

[31] Regulation (EC) No 861/2007 of the European Parliament and of the Council of 11 July 2007 establishing a European Small Claims Procedure.

[32] Regulation (EU) No 655/2014 of the European Parliament and of the Council of 15 May 2014 establishing a European Account Preservation Order procedure to facilitate cross-border debt recovery in civil and commercial matters.

[33] See EUROPEAN COMMISSION, *Judicial cooperation in civil matters in the European Union–A guide for legal practitioners*, Publications Office, 2015, p. 103.

[34] See Article 1 of Regulation (EC) No 805/2004.

[35] See EUROPEAN JUDICIAL NETWORK IN CIVIL AND COMMERCIAL MATTERS, *Practice Guide for the Application of the Regulation on the European Enforcement Order*, 2008, p. 7.

[36] See Example 3.

[37] Recital (5) of Regulation (EC) No 805/2004.

Example 3

Mr A has launched a pecuniary claim against Mr B by legal action in Spain, where both of them are domiciled. The court has ordered Mr B, who has not contested the claim during the legal proceedings, to pay €15 000 to Mr A. As Mr B has recently transferred all his monetary assets to a bank in Austria, Mr A asks how he can enforce the judgment in this Member State.

Under Article 5 of Regulation (EC) No 805/2004, a judgment which has been certified as a European Enforcement Order in the Member State of origin shall be recognised and enforced in the other Member States without the need for a declaration of enforceability and without any possibility of opposing its recognition.

Mr A can apply to the court of origin in Spain for certification of the judgment as a European enforcement order for uncontested claims; thus the judgment, with the certificate, would be recognised and enforceable in Austria without any further special procedure required.

52. According to the Guide *Judicial cooperation in civil matters in the European Union,* from the European Commission, this procedure provides a benefit for creditors as (a) they gain access to speedy, cheaper and efficient enforcement of judgments in uncontested claims in other Member States without the involvement of the judiciary of the Member State where enforcement is sought and (b) also dispenses generally with the need for translation since multilingual standard forms are used for certification.[38]

53. In accordance with Article 3 of the Protocol on the position of the United Kingdom and Ireland annexed to the Treaty on European Union and the Treaty establishing the European Community, the UK and Ireland have notified their wish to take part in the adoption and application of this Regulation.[39]

The European Order for Payment procedure

54. Swift and efficient recovery of outstanding debts over which no legal controversy exists is of high importance for economic operators. Late payments constitute a major reason for insolvency threatening the survival of businesses, particularly small and medium-sized enterprises, and resulting in numerous job losses.[40] So EU legislators decided to adopt Regulation (EC) No 1896/2006.

55. The purpose of this Regulation is to simplify, speed up and reduce the costs of litigation in cross-border cases concerning uncontested pecuniary claims by creating

[38] See EUROPEAN COMMISSION, *Judicial cooperation in civil matters in the European Union–A guide for legal practitioners*, Publications Office, 2015, p. 26.

[39] Recital (24) of Regulation (EC) No 805/2004.

[40] See Recital (6) of Regulation (EC) No 1896/2006.

a European order for payment procedure and to permit the free circulation of European orders for payment throughout the Member States by laying down minimum standards.[41]

56. This Regulation is applicable to civil and commercial matters in cross-border cases. It shall not extend, in particular, to revenue, customs or administrative matters or the liability of the State for acts and omissions in the exercise of State authority ("*acta iure imperii*") and it shall not apply to (a) rights in property arising out of a matrimonial relationship, wills and succession; (b) bankruptcy; (c) social security; (d) in principle, claims arising from non-contractual obligations.[42]

57. This procedure, which is purely a written procedure, does not involve a court hearing unless the defendant lodge a statement of opposition to the European order for payment.[43] Once this procedure is opposed, the proceedings shall continue before the competent courts of the Member State of origin in accordance with the rules of ordinary civil procedure.[44]

58. According to the Guide *Judicial cooperation in civil matters in the European Union,* this procedure is of particular interest to claimants which have claims which are not likely to be opposed, particularly in cases between businesses and consumers.[45]

59. The UK and Ireland, in accordance with Article 3 of the Protocol on the position of the United Kingdom and Ireland annexed to the Treaty on European Union and the Treaty establishing the European Community, have given notice of their wish to take part in the adoption and application of this Regulation.[46]

The European Small Claims Procedure

60. One of the main concerns raised against the functioning of Judicial Cooperation in Civil Matters, notably in relation to the possibility for ordinary citizens to access the courts and seek redress for claims quickly and without having to spend large sums of money on legal advice, was in the area of claims of low value.[47]

61. These claims are especially those where the time, effort and cost involved can often be grossly disproportionate to the value of the claim.[48]

62. To address this, the EU created the European procedure for small claims, established by Regulation (EC) No 861/2007, which is the third of the procedures aiming to simplify and speed up litigation concerning small claims across-borders,

---

[41] See Article 1 of Regulation (EC) No 1896/2006.

[42] See Article 2 of Regulation (EC) No 1896/2006.

[43] See Article 16 of Regulation (EC) No 1896/2006.

[44] See Article 17 of Regulation (EC) No 1896/2006.

[45] See EUROPEAN COMMISSION, *Judicial cooperation in civil matters in the European Union–A guide for legal practitioners*, Publications Office, 2015, p. 27.

[46] See Recital (31) of Regulation (EC) No 1896/2006.

[47] EUROPEAN COMMISSION, *Practice guide for the application of the European Small Claims Procedure under Regulation (EC) No 861/2007 of the European Parliament and of the Council of 11 July 2007 establishing a European Small Claims Procedure*, European Judicial Network in civil and commercial matters, 2013, p. 7.

[48] IBIDEM, p. 7.

in claims of low value and thus to reduce the costs of such litigation between the Member States.[49]

63. This procedure places emphasis on the need for relative simplicity of the proceedings, notably that the procedure should largely be written.[50]

64. This Regulation shall apply, in cross-border cases, to civil and commercial matters, where the value of a claim does not exceed 5 000 euros at the time when the claim form is received by the court or tribunal with jurisdiction, excluding any interest or expenses.[51]

65. In accordance with Article 3 of the Protocol on the position of the United Kingdom and Ireland annexed to the Treaty on European Union and to the Treaty establishing the European Community, the UK and Ireland have given notice of their wish to take part in the adoption and application of this Regulation.[52]

The European Account Preservation Order

66. A creditor who seeks to secure simultaneously bank accounts of the debtor situated in several Member States desires quick and easy access to protective measures to ensure that the debtor has not removed or dissipated his assets by the time the creditor has obtained and enforced a judgment on the merits. This is particularly important with regard to assets in bank accounts.[53]

67. Regulation (EU) No 655/2014 aims precisely at establishing a Union procedure enabling a creditor to obtain a European Account Preservation Order which prevents the subsequent enforcement of the creditor's claim from being jeopardised through the transfer or withdrawal of funds up to the amount specified in this Order which are held by the debtor or on his behalf in a bank account maintained in a Member State.[54]

68. This procedure, which can be used for pecuniary claims in civil and commercial matters[55] in cross-border cases,[56] is available to creditors as an alternative to the procedures already available under the national laws of the Member States.[57]

---

[49] See Article 1 and Recitals 1, 7 8 and 36 of Regulation (EC) No 861/2007.

[50] EUROPEAN COMMISSION, *Practice guide for the application of the European Small Claims Procedure under Regulation (EC) No 861/2007 of the European Parliament and of the Council of 11 July 2007 establishing a European Small Claims Procedure*, European Judicial Network in civil and commercial matters, 2013, p. 7.

[51] See Article 2 of Regulation (EC) No 861/2007.

[52] See Recital 37 of Regulation (EC) No 861/2007.

[53] See EUROPEAN COMMISSION, *Judicial cooperation in civil matters in the European Union–A guide for legal practitioners*, Publications Office, 2015, p. 103.

[54] See Article 1(1) of Regulation (EU) No 655/2014.

[55] See Article 2 of Regulation (EU) No 655/2014.

[56] See Article 3 of Regulation (EU) No 655/2014.

[57] See Article 1(2) of Regulation (EU) No 655/2014.

69. An important characteristic of this procedure is that it allows for a single order[58] to be made in the courts of one Member State which would be capable of 'freezing' any bank account of a debtor in any Member State.[59]

70. The Regulation binds all the EU Member States with the exception of the UK and Denmark which did not opt in.[60] Creditors domiciled in these Member States, not bound by the Regulation, cannot avail themselves of the procedure even if the competent court or the account or accounts involved are maintained in Member States which are so bound.[61]

Example 4

Creditor is domiciled in Germany which is bound by the Regulation. The creditor has a judgment from a court in this Member State for payment of 100 000 euros against a debtor who has bank accounts in three other Member States, France, Italy and Austria, all of which are bound by the Regulation.

The creditor wishes to take steps to secure each of these accounts using this order.

Under Article 6(3) of Regulation (EU) No 655/2014, where the creditor has already obtained a judgment or court settlement, jurisdiction to issue a Preservation Order for the claim specified in the judgment or court settlement shall lie with the courts of the Member State in which the judgment was issued or the court settlement was approved or concluded.

Therefore, the creditor has to lodge the application for this order to a court in Germany where the judgment was issued.

Family Maintenance Obligations

71. In order to facilitate international recovery of personal obligations between spouses and family members, the Council adopted Regulation (EC) No 4/2009 of 18 December 2008 on jurisdiction, applicable law, recognition and enforcement of decisions and cooperation in matters relating to maintenance obligations.

[58] See Example 4.

[59] See EUROPEAN COMMISSION, *Judicial cooperation in civil matters in the European Union–A guide for legal practitioners*, Publications Office, 2015, p. 29.

[60] See Recitals (50) and (51) of Regulation (EU) No 655/2014.

[61] See Article 4(6) of Regulation (EU) No 655/2014.

72. This Regulation brings together in a single instrument uniform rules on jurisdiction, applicable law, recognition and enforcement, as well as on cooperation between national authorities.

73. The central purpose of the Maintenance Regulation is to create an instrument to simplify the process by which a maintenance creditor in one Member State can apply to obtain payment of a maintenance obligation, arising from a family relationship, parentage, marriage or affinity,[62] quickly and simply from a maintenance debtor in another Member State.[63]

74. In accordance with Articles 1 and 2 of the Protocol on the position of the United Kingdom and Ireland, annexed to the Treaty on European Union and to the Treaty establishing the European Community, the UK did not take part in the adoption of this Regulation and is not bound by it or subject to its application. This was, however, without prejudice to the possibility for the UK of notifying its intention of accepting this Regulation after its adoption in accordance with Article 4 of the said Protocol.[64]

75. As the UK participated in the negotiations and opted in subsequently and is bound by the Regulation (even if it did not ratify the 2007 Hague Protocol on Applicable Law), the rules on recognition and enforcement of decisions in the Regulation apply to the UK.[65]

76. Therefore, where a decision on maintenance is given in a Member State not bound by the 2007 Hague Protocol (UK and Denmark), an enforceable decision made in these Member States can be refused recognition in the Member State where recognition is sought and requires a declaration of enforceability in the Member State addressed.[66]

3 Judicial Cooperation After Brexit Between the UK and the EU

3.1 Rendering EU Law into UK Law

77. The European Communities Act 1972 incorporated into UK law the EU treaties and the law promulgated under them and charged the UK government with enforcing this law.[67]

78. As part of the Brexit process, the Withdrawal Act ('the Act') is expected to be the mechanism to achieve national jurisdictional independence. The Act is intended

---

[62] See Article 1 of Regulation (EC) No 4/2009.

[63] See EUROPEAN COMMISSION, *Judicial cooperation in civil matters in the European Union–A guide for legal practitioners*, Publications Office, 2015, p. 63.

[64] See Recital (47) of Regulation (EC) No 4/2009.

[65] See EUROPEAN COMMISSION, *Judicial cooperation in civil matters in the European Union–A guide for legal practitioners*, Publications Office, 2015, p. 64.

[66] Ibidem, p. 68.

[67] European Communities Act 1972 (c. 68) Pt 1 ss. 2(1) & (2).

to remove EU law from its current status of primacy over the UK's domestic law and institutions.[68] The Act would thus fill the void that would otherwise be left if the UK were to renounce but not replace that vast body of law, the *acquis communautaire*, which has come into being since 1957 and into UK law progressively since 1973.[69]

79. Thus, the corpus of European law as of the date of repeal would become UK law. This 'nationalisation' will include the primary treaties, regulations, directives, and guidance offered by the Commission, and the case law of the European Courts. The total number of texts is maybe as many as 92,000 or more. The BBC has mentioned at least 80,000 distinct pieces of legal text.[70]

80. In any event, it is proposed that tens of thousands of EU texts will enter UK law via the Withdrawal Act, like a vast tangle of EU wires being plunged into a bath of electroplating to make their nationality that of the UK. They cover the environment, animal feed, quality of drinking water, data protection, seatbelt anchorage points, power consumption of vacuum cleaners, labelling for bottled water, the conditions under which a person suffering from diabetes may be issued a driver's license if they suffer hypoglycaemic episodes and many more.[71] Often the rule as originally adopted will have been changed, maybe dozens of times, to respond to technical progress. There are thousands of texts because life is complicated and highly regulated.

81. The UK will have three choices: one, set up a UK mechanism for adopting and enforcing UK standards, which will be stricter or less strict than those in the EU27; two, follow what standards are adopted by the EU27 according to procedures to be adopted case by case; or three, not regulate the topic. There may be fields where the policy of the UK would diverge from the policy of the EU: agriculture is one example; the fisheries are likely to be more difficult.

82. It may be helpful to remember the reception of Roman law in the six centuries after the death of the Emperor Justinian across what used to be the Roman Empire. Different flavours of Roman law developed, so that there was a Lex Romana Visigothorum in one territory, different in some respects to the law in what we now call Italy or Germany. Roman law was far less detailed and prescriptive. Today, EU law and national laws by contrast are very detailed and technical.

83. To reconcile the need for good regulation with the political need to escape the reach of the EU, the concept would be to bring the whole intricate mass of EU law into

[68] 'EU Withdrawal Bill: A guide to the Brexit repeal legislation', BBC [online], (13 November 2017). Available at: http://www.bbc.com/news/uk-politics-39266723 [accessed 13 March 2018].

[69] See Theresa MAY's Conservative Party conference speech on Brexit: 'Britain after Brexit: A vision of a global Britain', Politics Home [online], (2 October 2016). Available at: https://www.politicshome.com/news/uk/political-parties/conservative-party/news/79517/read-full-theresa-mays-conservative [accessed 13 March 2018]. See also HM Government, 'The United Kingdom's exit from and new partnership with the European Union', Cm 9417, (February 2017), para 2.3. Available online at: https://www.gov.uk/government/uploads/system/uploads/attachment_data/file/589191/The_United_Kingdoms_exit_from_and_partnership_with_the_EU_Web.pdf [accessed 13 March 2018].

[70] 'EU Withdrawal Bill', BBC.

[71] See e.g. Directive 2016/1106 [2016] OJ L183/59 amending Directive 2006/126/EC of the European Parliament and of the Council on driving licences. Available at: http://eur-lex.europa.eu/legal-content/GA/TXT/?uri=CELEX:32016L1106 [accessed 13 March 2018].

UK law and then, over the years, by correcting, pruning, winnowing and discarding, to arrive at a point where the UK has the legal framework that its political leaders desire. That will involve an immense amount of work by the UK's civil service, and its legislature and ministers.

3.2 *Judicial Review in the UK After a Brexit*

84. Consider the Scottish judge confronted with a textual dispute after a Brexit: What weight should be ascribed to consistency with the rules prevailing in the EU? Will such consistency be of high importance or of low importance? Will the findings of the EU Scientific Committee on Animal Nutrition be treated as authoritative or merely interesting? What technical priorities should apply in these fields? Will a high level of protection be a priority for consumers, female workers, animals, and the environment?

85. British judges could be expected to pursue consistency with the *acquis communautaire*, so as to make trade easier. Alternatively, consistency with the EU27 could be given a low priority because of the political importance of 'regaining our independence' so that judges are told to have no regard to 'European norms'. Or again, the subject could vary sector by sector: consistency with EU27 on health and safety and customs, but an 'independent' line on mutual recognition of qualifications or data protection.

86. EU law relies on principles of interpretation, some quite abstract, to achieve something like 'fairness' or 'sound government'. The high general principles of proportionality, legitimate expectations, sound administration, due process, non-discrimination, and so on, each might affect how to address a controversy. The Charter of Fundamental Rights was an attempt to codify certain basic principles of fair play into EU law. Its future after Brexit is rather entangled.

87. The Charter is not to be part of UK domestic law, but it is of course an ongoing part of EU law that Brits can refer to in UK courts when interpreting what is to be called 'retained EU law', (the directives, the regulations and other directly effective bits of EU law). So for the rules which existed prior to Brexit day, the Charter (and other general principles) can be relied on. But there will be no right of action for failure to comply with general principles of EU law. Indeed, cl. 3(2) says that after Brexit 'no court may decide that action is unlawful because it is incompatible with general principles of EU law'.

88. General doctrines and the Charter can be looked at to help interpret retained EU law, but not as means of annulling or challenging errors or excess by the administration. This is to help restore the parliamentary sovereignty that the EU had encroached upon. So old retained EU law remains supreme, yet the traditional means of challenging abuses in applying it seem to have disappeared. (There is a provision that a challenge would be valid if such challenge was provided for in 'regulations made by a Minister of the Crown'.)

89. How to reconcile parliamentary sovereignty with the need to accord to citizens the opportunity to vindicate rights created by EU law? You can see the tensions confronting the drafters. We must escape the encroachment on UK sovereignty. We cannot not regulate the areas of daily life covered by EU law today. We must shed any vague general principles of EU law which can be used abusively or excessively. But we don't want to deprive citizens of the right to challenge measures whose adoption or application was erroneous. But we don't want them to use EU law to correct errors in applying EU law. This touches upon equality of pay, the environment, health and safety, free movement, and many other aspects of daily life. It might seem that the established way to achieve judicial oversight would have been diminished.

90. I am not an expert in UK constitutional questions, and these are quite basic reactions to the extraordinary complexity of the doctrines: the ultimate shape of the Act may be different. I predict that there will be immense difficulty in deciding these questions.

91. Here are a few conclusions about how to approach these likely controversies:

- For as long as provisions of EU law are to be applied in the UK, for so long will it be necessary to think through how EU law problems will be litigated;
- It is not by 'nationalising' EU regulations that the country will free itself of EU law. Nor will disputes as to the interpretation of doubtful texts disappear;
- The current criteria for examining the legality of European law, post-Brexit, appear extremely complex;
- Political leaders will need to address the necessity of giving guidance to the judiciary about what priorities will apply in interpretation;
- The UK judge should not be blamed for a lack of patriotism if he or she chooses to follow a 'European' interpretation of the text.

92. My next point is a much less subtle one. Geographic proximity requires it. The UK has pooled its sovereignty with European partners for 47 years and has in the process opened up for its citizens and businesses a huge market by having collectively drafted rules on hundreds of matters. Withdrawing from these rules, annulling these rules, and not replacing them would trigger a number of misfortunes in matters small and large. The rules touch crucial areas of public policy which cannot be arranged informally. They depend for their effectiveness on close cooperation. But they were conceived, drafted, and governed within an EU framework.

3.3 Judicial Cooperation in Civil Matters

93. For the many UK and EU citizens, families and businesses who work, live, travel and do business abroad, the current European framework for choice of law, jurisdiction and recognition and enforcement is of paramount importance.

94. I cannot imagine not establishing a method of permitting cross-border cooperation in this field, but that will involve procedures established by EU law.

3.3.1 Legislative Background

95. The European Union (Withdrawal Agreement) Bill (WAB), which implements the Withdrawal Agreement (WA) between the UK and the EU, sets out the arrangements for the UK's withdrawal from the EU. The WAB will seek to give effect to the WA in UK law. The WA provides in Articles 126 and 127 for a transition or implementation period during which (subject to certain exceptions) EU law will continue to apply until 31 December 2020 at 11 pm.

96. The WAB clause 1 proposes to implement these provisions through amending the European Union (Withdrawal) Act 2018 by saving the effect of European Communities Act 1972 (ECA) for the transition or implementation period. In other words, the WAB will preserve the effect of the ECA during the transition or implementation period (IP) and ensure that its effect comes to an end on 31 December 2020 at 11 pm (called IP Completion day under clause 39 of the WAB).

97. Clause 26 (interpretation of retained EU law and relevant separation agreement law) provides that subject to regulations, lower courts and tribunals are not bound by any retained EU case law. Significant concerns arise from this clause because it will introduce confusion and lack of clarity about which law applies. I believe that the current situation under the European Union (Withdrawal) Act 2018, where only the Supreme Court or the High Court of Justiciary can change retained EU case law, should continue and lower courts should not be given this power.

3.3.2 The Free Trade Agreement Negotiations

98. After this point, the UK will start the negotiations with the EU on a Free Trade Agreement (FTA) and other agreements which will regulate the relationship between the UK and the EU after the end of the transition or implementation period which ends on 31 December 2020.

99. The UK government is proposing to have the agreement on the new relationship finished by the end of 2020. This means a very speedy negotiation. Also, it means that the new agreement will need to be ratified by the end of 2020. If the agreement falls fully under the EU competences and it is simply replicating existing agreements, such as CETA or EU-Japan, it may be possible for the agreement to be finalised during 2020. However, this means that it is unlikely to include any innovative elements on services or judicial cooperation as these would need to be negotiated into the agreement. Accordingly, the ambition on what can be achieved during 2020 is limited.

100. The format and speed will have an impact on the depth of the cooperation available. In particular, it will have an impact on the services provision and judicial cooperation in civil, family and criminal matters.

101. The Political Declaration (PD) that was negotiated at the same time as the WA establishes the parameters for an ambitious, broad, deep and flexible partnership across trade and economic cooperation with a comprehensive and balanced FTA at its core, including law enforcement and criminal justice, foreign policy, security and defence and wider areas of cooperation.

102. There are a number of issues raised by the WA and PD process. We will deal with these matters as follows:

(a) Relevant law applicable during the transition period under the WA;
(b) The provisions in the PD and;
(c) The negotiation positions (so far as ascertainable at the stage) of both the UK and EU.

3.3.3 The Law Applicable During the Transition Period Under the Withdrawal Agreement

Judicial Cooperation in Civil and Commercial Matters

103. Articles 66-69 of the WA confirm that the existing EU law applies until the end of the Transition Period concerning certain measures designed to facilitate judicial cooperation in civil, family and commercial matters. These concern the choice of court to be used to determine disputes, the applicable law, and the automatic recognition and enforcement of legal decisions in different Member States. They provide that the current EU civil judicial cooperation rules will continue to apply during the transition period.

104. The Justice Sub-Committee of the House of Lords EU Committee summarised the practical effect of these measures:

- In the area of family law, these measures provide certainty and protection to children and families in the often fractious and difficult environment of family disputes. Such disputes can be made additionally complicated by a cross-border element;
- In the civil field, the measures facilitate the affairs of all those engaged in the myriad cross-border links enabled by the EU's rules, from the tourist hit by a car in Warsaw, the consumer seeking redress for a defective product in Lisbon, to the employee seeking equal pay in London, and the tenant enforcing their rights in Nicosia. For businesses operating within the Single Market, from large multinational corporations to Small and Medium Enterprises, the measures offer all these people the reassurance that when problems arise legal remedies are readily available and easily enforceable across borders.

Police and Judicial Cooperation in Criminal Matters

105. Articles 62-65 of the WA confirm that the existing EU law applies until the end of the Transition Period concerning:

- Ongoing judicial cooperation proceedings in criminal matters such as mutual legal assistance, Requests, European arrest warrants where the requested person was arrested before the end of the transition period, freezing orders, confiscation orders, mutual recognition to judgments in criminal matters, new criminal proceedings, requests for information on conviction, decisions on supervision measures, European Criminal Records Information System (ECRIS), European protection orders (EPO), European Investigation Orders (EIO), joint investigation teams;

- Ongoing law enforcement cooperation proceedings, police cooperation and exchange of information;
- Schengen international police cooperation such as information, surveillance (including cross-border surveillance) covert and joint special investigation, Financial Intelligence requests asset recovery and passenger information.

3.3.4 The Provisions in the Political Declaration

Separation Issues: Civil Judicial Cooperation (CJC)

106. Under the heading Mobility and Social Security, the Parties confirm their commitment to the effective application of the existing international family law instruments to which they are parties. The Union notes the UK's intention to accede to the 2007 Hague Maintenance Convention to which it is currently bound through its Union membership (paragraph 55).

107. The Parties will explore options for judicial cooperation in matrimonial, parental responsibility and other related matters (paragraph 56).

Civil Judicial Cooperation

108. We would seek CJC at a level which would be as close to the current provisions as possible. The UK is also seeking accession to the Lugano Treaty upon which the Brussels I Regulation was based but the timeframe for this means that accession is likely to take place after the transition period ends. It is a matter of debate whether the UK should also accede to the Hague Convention on the Recognition and Enforcement of Foreign Judgments in Civil or Commercial Matters 2019 due to its comparative scope.

Law Enforcement and Judicial Cooperation in Criminal Matters

109. The future relationship will cover arrangements across three areas: data exchange; operational cooperation between law enforcement authorities and judicial cooperation in criminal matters; and anti-money laundering and counter terrorism financing.

- There will be arrangements for exchanges of Passenger Name Record (PNR) data, DNA, fingerprints and vehicle registration data (Prüm) and extradition arrangements; data-sharing arrangements for wanted and missing persons, exchange of criminal records and cooperation between the UK and Europol and Eurojust.

- The PD makes specific mention (paragraph 88) of ongoing cooperation via Europol and Eurojust. It also commits to establishing procedures for the efficient and expeditious surrender of suspected and convicted persons, as a replacement to the European Arrest Warrant. It acknowledges the need to address the potential obstacles to a third country gaining access to equivalent arrangements, namely the requirement of double criminality, and exceptions for own nationals and political offences.

4 Conclusion

110. The common market, despite its curious constitutional architecture, has delivered increased prosperity, the elimination of military rivalry and the liberation of Eastern Europe from Communism. These achievements have been based on a multitude of detailed steps reached by cooperative regulation on matters which often seem obscure, in order to expand economic opportunity, competitive choice, and to deliver prosperity to those who wanted to work in a free (or less unfree) economy.

111. I think that the EU is the only place on earth today where (almost) a continent of states have agreed to deliver to their citizens access to healthcare, equal treatment of men and women, freedom of speech, a pension, education and a minimum wage. There are assuredly imperfections and gaps and inconsistencies. The constitutional architecture of the EU is creaky. There is no government and no opposition in the European Parliament. But the achievement of delivering decent standards by exploiting the opportunities of cross-border commerce and an open labour market is real and difficult to deny. King James was not wrong to note that when merchants get rich the people prosper, and that peaceful conditions both at home and overseas are the best basis for achieving prosperity. King James would not have been enthusiastic about judicial review of executive action. Stuart history might well have been different if he had accepted that the Crown must from time to time lose in its own courts.

112. Those who celebrate the regaining of our nation's freedom and independence as a natural benefit of Brexit have presented EU law as interference with UK public policy and sovereignty. And indeed decisions of the European Court may have caused a Home Secretary much trouble over the years in the fields of deportation, health tourism, and access to other social services. My anecdotal impression is that the judges of the UK do not feel that they are subject to the yoke of Luxembourg rulings in such a manner or to such a degree as to encroach on their independence. It is true that individual decisions are criticized by academics and judges; but debate about important judgments is wholly desirable. It is not realistic to hope that the courts get it right every time, and I am sure that the courts of the EU do not achieve perfection. In order for the rule of law to be credible, the public authority must accept that it will from time to time lose in its own courts. It will be obvious to this audience that the least distinguished legal practice in a remote corner of the country

has the power to challenge a government measure in court, and win; not often, but sometimes, frequently enough to make the government hesitate before taking a potentially important step. It is of enormous importance to build into our democracy judicial review of public actions. And the European Courts have played a necessary role in that respect: their role is even more important due to the complicated structure of the European Union.

113. Two years ago, there was a birthday celebration at the Court to remember the Treaty of Rome. Some 64 delegates came from the Supreme Courts of the 27, plus Scotland, and a delegate from England. The speeches were graceful. Every language of the Union was deployed: no less than 552 interpretation combinations could have been (Lithuanian-Greek; Portuguese-Swedish) available. Brexit was barely mentioned and the working sessions touched on such matters as the anonymisation of judgments for the protection of the privacy of the individual litigant, cooperation between national courts and EU courts, and the best means of exchanging information about legal developments. There is a constant dialogue between national courts and the EU Court about many topics.

114. Then spoke the sharp clear voice of history. The President of the Supreme Court of Lithuania, Mr. Norkus, reminisced about where his country stood 60 years ago. He began by recollecting a melancholy anniversary which the Court honoured last year: the brutal suppression of the Hungarian uprising in 1956. And the less celebrated killing of Lithuanian partisans who aspired to freedom and independence.

115. He noted how in 1957:

> there were not many discussions about economy and markets in Eastern and Central Europe. Or rather, at that time many countries of this region already had a kind of single market. A market of oppression, of ideology, fake news and alternative facts, such as stating many human, political and other rights in the Constitution, but recognizing almost none of them in reality. However, there were many citizens in those countries who still had a vision. A vision which very much also drove the founding fathers of the European Union. A vision of modern democratic state, based on the rule of law, which is able to live in peace with the neighbours without building walls against them. A vision of the State protecting human rights and liberty; able to prosper by trusting, not humiliating, its citizens and neighbours. Without these citizens I doubt I would stand here today in front of you. We—Eastern and Central Europeans first of all owe very much to our citizens, less to markets.
>
> I am not sure whether we—the newcomers—share the same memories about the start of our common journey in the Union. Now we sometimes hear voices—give us our rights back. But I am not sure whether they have ever been taken away. Especially when every member can participate in creation, implementation and enforcement of them. Such judge has competence and abilities, personal strength and courage to resist choosing the easiest path and refuses to close the eyes to the law when she feels that it's threatened. Even if later such judge is downgraded to "so-called judge" and her judgment is described as ridiculous.

116. This lecture has identified a number of classes of legal problems, which will arise now after the Brexit. In some cases, the EU supplies all the regulatory principles, procedures and institutional memory. Adopting the texts into UK law will achieve the political goal of "freeing" the UK, but EU law will continue to govern until the UK has established its own procedures and principles to govern the topics of cars, medicines, air safety, environmental protection, telecommunications or pesticides.

Consistency of outcome across a continent has evident merit. Regardless of what it is said that people voted for, it will likely be necessary to accept that the EU law and courts will have a role until this country has adequate parallel arrangements for decision-making and judicial resolution of disputes. That is not because European law is interfering in the UK, but because European rule-making needs judicial oversight.

117. The wish to continue mechanisms for cooperation in the field of Justice and Home Affairs will need, presumably, to be made functional within the existing framework, which has judicial oversight.

118. In many other cases it will be necessary to decide in what spirit the UK courts should approach a textual interpretation, and what weight they should accord to judgements of the EU courts.

119. Any diplomatic agreement will be better respected if it provides a mechanism for the resolution of controversies. Two kinds of controversy can be anticipated. One is whether the existing rules were correctly applied, as in the imaginary example of the Polish child refused a grant to study in Poland. Another is whether the rules match UK obligations under the secession treaty. As to the first question, should the Scottish or UK courts apply their own interpretation to the controversy? Will consistency with EU 27 rules be a relevant consideration? Will the Court of Justice of the European Union have a role if consistency is indeed an objective? A constitutionally different question is whether the underlying rule is consistent with the UK's obligations under the secession treaty. How shall that topic be resolved and before which forum? These matters are of immense complexity, sensitivity and importance. Persons, workers, families, access to social benefits and rights to abide may well be such. Access to a profession, equivalence of qualification and related issues touching the capacity to work would be another. There is a huge difference between having a right and having a right to request in this area. In some cases, these topics may present a tension between EU law as today established and the political or administrative goals of the UK government.

(This paper was supported by a grant-in-aid from JICDF, Shihokyokai, Zengin Foundation for Studies on Economic and Finance).

Reference

Lenaerts K (2017) La vie après l'avis: exploring the principle of mutual (yet not blind) trust. Common Market Law Rev 808–812

Ian Stewart Forrester Q.C. Personal: Born Glasgow, Scotland. Son of Mr. & Mrs. A.R. Forrester. Professional: Judge; General Court of the European Union, 2015; member of the Third Chamber; Faculty of Advocates (the Scottish Bar), 1972; New York Bar, 1977 (admitted after examination, under special order of the New York Court of Appeals following challenge to the constitutional propriety of excluding non-resident aliens from bar membership); appointed Queen's Counsel, 1988; 2 Hare Court, latterly Blackstone Chambers; English Bar, 1996; Brussels Bar 1998. Co-founder of Forrester & Norall, 1981; enlarged to Forrester Norall & Sutton, 1989;

merged with White & Case, 1998. Co-founder, European Trade Law Association. Trustee, European Union Baroque Orchestra (2004); Member, Dean's Advisory Board, Tulane University Law School (2006); Honorary Professor, University of Glasgow (2010); Member, Glasgow University School of Law Advisory Committee (2010); Master of the Bench, Middle Temple (2012); Member of the Board of Trustees 2012–2015, Academy of European Law. Education: Kelvinside Academy, Glasgow, 1949–1962; University of Glasgow (1962–1967) M.A. (History and English Literature) 1965; LL.B. 1967; LLD honoris causa, 2009; Tulane University of Louisiana, New Orleans (1968–1969) M.C.L. 1969. Legal Practice: 1968–1972, experience in Scotland (with Messrs. Maclay Murray & Spens) and New York (Messrs. Davis Polk & Wardwell) on a variety of topics, ranging from the insurance aspects of the hijacking of aircraft by Palestinian guerrillas to commercial disputes and personal litigation. Devil of David Edward, then a junior advocate, 1972. Since 1972, EEC/EU practice in Brussels.

Afterword

Yasuhei Taniguchi

This book is a significant contribution to the comparative law in one of the neglected areas. Comparative studies in the procedural law had long been neglected, the main focus being the comparison of the substantive side of existing legal systems. This was unfortunate because any good rules of substantive law would be meaningless without good rules of procedural law ready to enforce them in the real world. Comparative law in the procedural law was neglected probably because procedures varied significantly country to country and were often deeply associated with the governmental and/or social systems of a particular country, which in turn made a meaningful comparison between or among different procedural systems difficult. When Prof. Mauro Cappelletti of Florence, Italy, bravely challenged in this area in the 1970s and established the International Association of Procedural Law, he organized the first international conference of the Association in Ghent, Belgium, with an enthusiastic cooperation by Professor Marcel Storme of University of Ghent. I was fortunate to be invited to serve there as the sole general reporter. Despite the unfortunate early demise of Prof. Cappelletti, the Association was successfully continued by Professor Storme. Today, the comparative civil procedure is no doubt an established discipline.

This has been a fortunate development. The comparative study of law was started and long remained in the fields of substantive law. Thanks to the establishment of the Association of Procedural Law, the comparative study of procedure has since become more accepted and widespread. But the main interest was limited to the first instance procedure up to the rendition of a final judgment. When I was involved in a project to publish a teaching material initiated by Prof. Oscar Chase of New York University Law School, I contributed a comparative overview of the systems of enforcement of money judgements. ("Proceedings for Execution of Money Claims"

Y. Taniguchi (✉)
MATSUO & KOSUGI, Tokyo, Japan
e-mail: tanigy@mknet.jp

M. Deguchi (ed.), *Effective Enforcement of Creditors' Rights*,
Ius Gentium: Comparative Perspectives on Law and Justice 91,
https://doi.org/10.1007/978-981-16-5609-5

in Chase, Hershkoff, Silberman, Taniguchi, Varano and Zuckerman, eds., Civil Litigation in Comparative Context, 2007, Thomson-West, p. 480 et seq.) My contribution consisted in two parts, namely a subsection titled "Availability of Discovery of Debtor's Assets" followed by "Treatment of Competing Creditors" because I considered these two aspects as the most important in this type of enforcement.

The first aspect, namely the availability of debtor's property subject to attachment by the creditor is the first problem faced by a creditor because the debtor anticipating an attachment by a creditor tends to hide his property from creditors, typically by transferring it to somebody else. Although such transfer may be set aside as fraudulent, that will involve a lot of trouble even if possible. In order to prevent this danger, a creditor may secure its position by resorting to the provisional attachment before obtaining an executable "title" such as a judgment, a settlement certificate, etc. A provisional attachment is frequently used to secure the priority of the attaching creditor over other creditors. If another creditor later attaches, it only secures the second priority. With good reasons, many contributions in this project are devoted to this aspect of issues. Some systems may better serve this purpose than another. Readers may reflect upon their respective systems and think about the ways for improving them.

Due to the nature of the proceedings, the usual dichotomy between Civil Law and Common Law should not be very apparent and necessary because this traditional dichotomy originates in the presence of the system of jury which has nothing to do with the enforcement. Thus the process of enforcement should be well subject to a meaningful comparative survey although possible ancillary litigation arising from an enforcement may differ between the two legal camps.Another difference may be found in the specific participants involved in the process. For example, the role and nature of the organ in charge of enforcement may differ considerably from one system to another. For example, the role and status of the enforcement officer, such as the sheriff, may largely differ.

All these differences are either just historical or result of a deliberate choice by the legislature or some agent responsible for the matter. This is an area of law where a practice rather than a rule plays a role. Readers must be reminded, therefore, of the practice behind the written rules because a practice may develop in the areas where no explicit provision of law or rules is found. Such practice may be just a matter of fact or well endorsed by the court to become a tradition. Contributions in this book, being from various parts of the world of different culture and background, will greatly serve us by shedding lights in this area of law which has been rather neglected in the comparative law.

Yasuhei Taniguchi is Professor Emeritus at Kyoto University in Japan. He obtained a law degree from Kyoto University in 1957 and was fully qualified as a jurist in 1959. His graduate degrees include LL.M., University of California at Berkeley (1963) and J.S.D., Cornell University (1964). He is internationally recognized for his expertise in comparative and transnational legal studies. He is a leading scholar in several areas of law including Civil Procedure, Alternative Dispute Resolution, Insolvency Law, and International Trade Law. He was former President of the Japanese Association of Civil Procedure. He was Vice-President of the International Association of Procedural Law. He is since 2015 Honorary Vice-President of the International Association of Procedural Law. He served as a member of the Appellate Body of the World Trade Organization, with one year as its chair(2000–2007). He served as the board member of the International Council of Commercial Arbitration (1990-2005) and as President of the Japan Association of Arbitrators (2005-2013). More recently he is serving as a member of the Ad Hoc Committee for annulment of ICSID arbitration award involving Argentina. He is Judge of the Singapore International Commercial Court and Counsel at Matsuo & Kosugi. Special Advisor of the Japan Commercial Arbitration Association and Former President, Japan Association of Arbitrators and Civil Procedure Association.

The manufacturer's authorised representative in the EU is Springer Nature Customer Service Centre GmbH, Europaplatz 3, 69115 Heidelberg, Germany. If you have any concerns regarding our products, please contact ProductSafety@springernature.com

Printed and bound by CPI Group (UK) Ltd, Croydon, CR0 4YY
30/09/2026
02225290-0011